PROPERTY MANAGEMENT

ROBERT C. KYLE

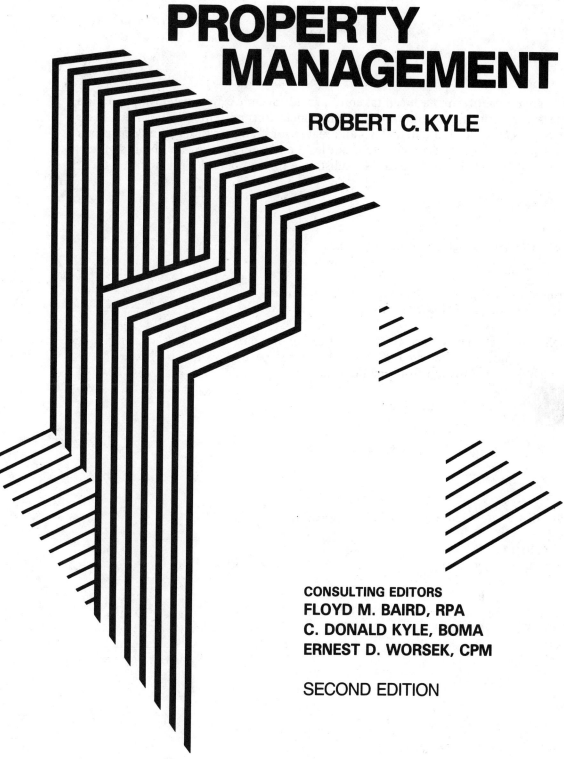

CONSULTING EDITORS
FLOYD M. BAIRD, RPA
C. DONALD KYLE, BOMA
ERNEST D. WORSEK, CPM

SECOND EDITION

REAL ESTATE EDUCATION COMPANY/CHICAGO
a Longman Group company

© 1984, 1979 by Longman Group USA Inc.

Published by Real Estate Education Company/Chicago, a division of Longman Group USA Inc.

Printed in the United States of America.

86   10   9   8   7   6   5

Library of Congress Cataloging in Publication Data

Kyle, Robert C.
    Property management.

    Includes index.
    1. Real estate management.   I. Title.
HD1394.K94   1984   333.5'068.   84-3325
ISBN 0-88462-498-6

Sponsoring editor: Bobbye Middendorf
Project editor: David Walker
Cover design: Vito M. DePinto Graphic Design

Contents

Preface

Property management is a highly specialized but rapidly growing sector of the real estate profession. If they are not property managers themselves, most real estate practitioners will work closely with property managers at some point. This book provides an overview of the field and describes the major functions of property managers, including their legal, interpersonal, maintenance, accounting, administrative, and other activities. It also details specific practices and problems in the management of various types of property: apartment buildings, cooperatives and condominiums, office buildings, retail property, industrial property, and subsidized housing. The book closes with a chapter on creative management—innovative ideas for property managers dealing with undeveloped land or existing structures. **Property Management** is intended for the real estate practitioner who wants a comprehensive introduction to the challenging field of property management and for the professional manager who wishes to gain new, practical information.

ABOUT THE AUTHOR

Robert C. Kyle (M.A., M.B.A., D.B.A.) is the principal author of this text and president of the Real Estate Education Company in Chicago, one of the nation's largest publishers of real estate textbooks. Dr. Kyle is on the board of directors of Grubb & Ellis, a full-service NYSE real estate firm with brokerage, property management and investment counseling groups to handle residential, industrial, and commercial properties. He is a member of the Realtors® National Marketing Institute, past president of the Association of Illinois Real Estate Educators and the national Real Estate Educators Association, a member of the Real Estate Advisory Committee of the University of Denver, and a former faculty member at Northwestern University. A licensed real estate broker, Dr. Kyle chaired the Educational Courses Committee of the Real Estate Securities and Syndication Institute and served on the License Law Committee and the Continuing Education Task Force of the Illinois Association of Realtors®. He helped to develop the original text of *Modern Real Estate Practice*, has been a contributor to *Real Estate Review*, and wrote a weekly real estate column in Chicago's *Daily News*. He has been active in many sectors of the industry for over 20 years.

Acknowledgments

The author is grateful for the time and resources contributed to the book by the consulting editors.

Floyd M. Baird (A.B., J.D.), the consulting editor of the second edition, is vice president and manager of Trust Real Estate for the First National Bank and Trust Company of Tulsa, Oklahoma, where he is responsible for over 750 properties of all types throughout Oklahoma and the United States. His property management career began in 1958 when he became executive vice president of a privately owned company owning multi-family, commercial, and industrial properties in several states. Included in his responsibilities were construction projects in Mexico and South America. He is presently a national director of the Building Owners and Managers Institute International and conducts seminars for the Institute on real estate law and property management. His activity in real estate education includes serving as an adjunct instructor in property management at Tulsa Junior College and the Continuing Education Center of the University of Oklahoma. He is a real estate broker and an instructor licensed by the Oklahoma Real Estate Commission, for which he has authored a number of continuing education monographs. His involvement in real estate education was recognized by the National Real Estate Educators Association in 1983 when he was named a Designated Real Estate Instructor (DREI). As a lawyer admitted in three states as well as the United States Supreme Court, Dr. Baird brings both legal and practical knowledge to the property management profession.

C. Donald Kyle began his property management career in Cleveland approximately 50 years ago. While specializing in the management of office buildings, he has also handled small and large apartment buildings, clubs, hotels, retail space, and industrial properties. During Mr. Kyle's long and active affiliation with the Building Owners and Managers Association, he was director of the Columbus Association as well as director and president of the North-Central District of BOMA, the Cleveland Association, and the Cleveland Apartment and Home Owners Association. Now retired, Mr. Kyle holds honorary life memberships in the Building Owners and Managers Association International and in the Cleveland and Columbus, Ohio Associations.

Ernest D. Worsek is president of Urban American Property Counselors, Inc., a Chicago-based firm. He is a Certified Property Manager and a member of the NATIONAL ASSOCIATION OF REALTORS®, the National Institute of Real Estate

Brokers, and the Institute of Real Estate Management. Mr. Worsek has taught classes on real estate management at the community college level and is on the national faculty of the Institute of Real Estate Management. He has written articles for the National Institute of Real Estate Brokers and the Institute of Real Estate Management.

The author would like to thank the following reviewers for their valuable contributions to the second edition of **PROPERTY MANAGEMENT**: Prof. Dudley S. Hinds, Georgia State University; Donald A. Gabriel, Ph.D., RPA, RAM, University of Baltimore; Thomas D. Pearson, North Texas State University; Henry B. Pixley, GRI, Texas Southmost College; George H. Lentz, Indiana University; Helen M. Hartmann, Portage Lakes Vo-Tech, Broker, Hartmann Realty; John Weidler, L.A. Mission College.

Thanks are also extended to David O. Diercoff, CSM, CPM, RPA; Ann M. Kennehan; and Harold Rockwood, CSM, CPM; for their contributions on the first edition.

The following have given the author permission to use the promotional materials and forms reprinted in this book:

BAIRD & WARNER, REAL ESTATE, Chicago, IL *Printing House Row* (Ch. 11) *Carriage Way Court* (Ch. 12)

BENNETT & KAHNWEILER ASSOCIATES, Rosemont, IL *Office Broker Ad* (Ch. 13)

BOISE CASCADE, Itasca, IL *Five Day Notice* (Ch. 7); *Apartment Lease* (Ch. 11)

BUILDING MANAGERS ASSOCIATION OF CHICAGO *Office Lease* (Ch. 13); *Percentage Store Lease* (Ch. 14)

CHICAGO SUN-TIMES, February 24, 1984 "A Sanctuary for Buyers Seeking Drama" (Ch. 12)

CMD MIDWEST, INC, Chicago, IL *CMD Office Park* (Ch. 13)

DAL-MAC DEVELOPMENT, Richardson, TX *Greenway I Project* (Ch. 4)

DUN & BRADSTREET, INC., New York, NY *Key to Ratings* (Ch. 6)

GRUBB & ELLIS COMMERCIAL BROKERAGE, San Francisco, CA "Shiny 40-Story Tower Proposed for Oakland" (Ch. 13); *Retail Client Requirements* (Ch. 14)

ERNEST W. HAHN, INC., shopping center developers, San Diego, CA "Set Sites on San Diego" (Ch. 14)

INSTITUTE OF REAL ESTATE MANAGEMENT, 430 N. Michigan Avenue, Chicago, IL *Office Building Inspection Report* (Ch. 2); *Management Agreement* (Ch. 3); *Apartment Interior Inspection Report* (Ch. 11); *Condominium Management Agreement* Ch. 12); *Cash Flow and Tax Benefits of Investment Property Ownership* (Ch. 17)

MORRIS & FELLOWS, INC, CONSULTANTS, Atlanta GA *Paddock Park* (Ch. 5); *Ashby's Village* (Ch. 14)

OAKLAND TRIBUNE, July 17, 1983 "Shiny 40-Story Tower Proposed for Oakland" (Ch. 13)

PENNSYLVANIA ASSOCIATION OF REALTORS, Harrisburg, PA *Rent Past Due Notice* (Ch. 7)

PROPERTY COMPANY OF AMERICA, Tulsa, OK *Maintenance Request Form* (Ch. 7)

RICHARDSON DAILY NEWS, December 18, 1983 *Greenway I Project* (Ch. 4)

SANDY TINSLEY ADVERTISING, Miami, FL *Miami Lakes Properties* (Ch. 5)

THE URBAN LAND INSTITUTE, Washington, D.C. *Percentage Lease Ranges* (Ch. 14); *ULI Report* (Ch. 17)

LAWRENCE E. WELLS, ARA *Floor Plan* (Ch. 5)

1

The Property Management Profession

The primary function of a property manager is to preserve or increase the value of an investment property while generating income for the owners. In other words, the manager attempts to generate the greatest possible net income for the owners of an investment property over the life of that property. It is a common misconception that to be effective a property manager need only collect rents, show space, and execute leases. In reality, the property manager's job is far more complex and demanding than that of a mere caretaker for another's property.

Property management, one of the fastest growing areas of specialization within the real estate industry, is emerging as a managerial science. Today, property managers must have at their fingertips the knowledge, communication skills, and technical expertise needed to be dynamic decision makers. They must also be versatile, since they may be called upon to act as market analysts, advertising executives, salespeople, accountants, diplomats, or even maintenance engineers. Interpersonal skills are needed to deal effectively with owners, prospects, tenants, employees, outside contractors, and others in the real estate business.

Titles for persons engaged in the property management profession have not become standardized. Each organization has its own system of defining job categories, with responsibilities varying according to the type and extent of properties managed. A property manager with the title of "Vice President—Director of Real Estate," for example, may perform the duties of a facility manager or an asset manager (two specialized property managers, which will be discussed in Chapter 17).

DEVELOPMENT OF THE PROPERTY MANAGEMENT PROFESSION

The demand for effective, professional property management began in the last decade of the nineteenth century and continues to increase today, because of a radical transformation in the nature of urban real estate. This reshaping of cities had its origin in three developments:

1. the creation of the steel frame building and the invention of the electric elevator
2. the construction of multifamily apartment buildings and
3. the development of regional shopping centers

The structural advantages of the steel frame building, when coupled with the perfection of the electric elevator in 1889, made possible a significant advancement in property construction—the highrise apartment and office building. Construction of all types of multifamily apartment buildings, which reached a peak in the 1920s, also contributed to the change. Finally, the evolution of the regional shopping center following World War II helped to decentralize the traditional concentration of commerce in downtown areas and started an exodus to the suburbs that is still in progress, modified in some areas by the revitalization of central cities. In recent years, the realignment and centralization of ownership of investment properties by large institutional investors and groups of investors has continued to increase the demand for professional property management.

George A. Holt, owner and manager of a 16-story Chicago skyscraper, recognized that property managers need to meet occasionally to learn and exchange information. He invited his colleagues to a dinner meeting, the outcome of which was the formation of the Chicago Building Managers Organization. The organization held its first national meeting in 1908, with 75 people in attendance. Subsequent meetings were held in Detroit in 1909, Washington, D.C., in 1910, and Cleveland in 1911, when a national Building Owners Organization was founded. By 1921, a sufficient number of groups had been formed in the larger cities of the United States to necessitate an organizational change. The Building Owners and Managers Association (BOMA) became a national federation of local and regional groups. Later, as chapters were organized in Canada, England, South Africa, Japan, and Australia, the name was changed to the Building Owners and Managers Association International. There has been a continuous association publication since 1922 and an annual *Experience Exchange Report* since 1924. Most early BOMA members were office building managers, with some participation from apartment and loft building managers. Apartment owners and managers in most of the larger cities formed their own associations during the 1930s, and a national apartment owner's association was created in the 1940s.

The depression of the 1930s had a profound influence on the evolving property management profession. The numerous failures and foreclosures of this era placed much of the nation's real estate in the hands of mortgage-lending institutions such as trust companies, insurance companies, associations, unions, and banks. For the first time, a large volume of income-producing property was owned by corporations. Many of these financial institutions formed their own property management departments. They soon learned that a landlord had to do more than select tenants and collect rents. The newly formed management departments employed contractors and builders but spent little thought and less action on the economics, advertising, and merchandising of the income property. Such considerations were relatively unexplored at the time and no facilities were available for training persons in these vital aspects of property management. As the need for more sophisticated management techniques became apparent, the profession gained stature.

In 1933 a group of property management firms created the Institute of Real Estate Management (IREM) as a subsidiary group of the NATIONAL ASSOCIATION OF REALTORS®. At its inception, the institute accepted firm memberships, but its 1938 bylaws limited membership to individuals. Currently, individuals wishing to join the institute must satisfy education and experience requirements and must pass examinations given or approved by the institute. They are then awarded the designation of Certified Property Manager (CPM) in recognition of their professional status as property managers and their affiliation with the Institute of Real Estate

Management. The institute grants qualified management firms the designation of Accredited Management Organization (AMO).

BOMA International sponsors an educational program for property owners and managers through an independent organization, the Building Owners and Managers Institute, established in 1970. Individuals who have several years of experience in the field and who successfully complete the seven courses in this program receive the professional designation of Real Property Administrator (RPA). Most RPAs are oriented toward office building management. To promote professionalism in the specialized field of retail property management, the International Council of Shopping Centers (ICSC) has also developed a series of three courses, a review, and an examination that lead to the designation of Certified Shopping Center Manager (CSM). Several organizations which offer training in apartment management will be discussed in Chapter 11. Other specialized professionals will be reviewed throughout this book.

Today, the professional property manager must have a comprehensive understanding of the economic forces at work in the real estate market. He or she must be able to evaluate the property in terms of operating income, forecast its potential for the future, and construct a management plan that reflects the owner's objectives while remaining flexible enough to be adapted to future changes in the market. A property manager must become a specialist skilled in space marketing, tenant psychology, the legal aspects of the landlord-tenant relationship, maintenance procedures, and accounting. These and related topics will be treated in detail in Chapters 2 through 10.

CLASSIFICATION OF REAL PROPERTY

Real property is defined as the earth's surface extending downward to the center of the earth and upward into space, including all things permanently attached thereto, by nature or by human hands. Manufactured attachments are referred to as *improvements.* Given this comprehensive definition, it follows that real property management can cover a wide spectrum of duties. For example, since minerals and agricultural crops are considered to be part of real estate, the management of mines and farms could be considered real property management. In these cases, though, the *process* of mining or farming is more significant than the *management* of the land itself. Activities of this nature represent specialized business enterprises and hence will not be covered in this text.

Large enterprises with extensive holdings of real estate, such as hotel and motel chains and grocery and other specialized retailers, will have a property management department staffed with experienced property managers. However, most professional property management involves structures built on real property that is not intrinsic to the operation of a business or industry. For the purposes of studying specialized property management, real estate can be divided into four major classifications: residential, commercial, industrial, and special-purpose property, each bringing into play a different combination of knowledge and skills on the part of the manager. Following is an overview of each type.

Residential Property

Residential real estate, including privately owned residences as well as government and institutional housing, satisfies the basic shelter needs of our population. It is the largest source of demand for the services of professional property managers.

Figure 1: RESIDENTIAL REAL ESTATE CATEGORIES

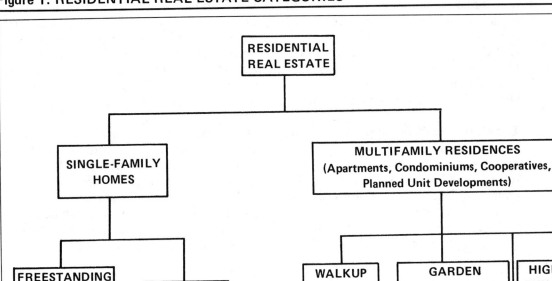

Single-Family Homes. Freestanding, single-family homes are still the most popular form of residential ownership in the United States. According to the Census Bureau, 60 percent of U.S. housing is owner-occupied. Single-family, owner-occupied homes do not require professional management. Although homes that are rented to another party are often managed directly by the owner, there is a growing trend toward professional management of such properties, particularly condominiums and vacation homes. Many large corporations hire property managers for homes vacated by employees who have been transferred.

The cost of a typical freestanding, single-family home has risen from an average of $25,000 in 1970 to over $70,000 in the 1980s. Rising construction costs and a decrease in the availability of usable land have resulted in the growing popularity of town houses, or row houses, condominiums, and cooperatives. Although each unit is a single-family residence, the individual owners of the units share certain concerns such as maintenance of the roof, common walls, grounds, and common facilities for the development as a whole. They will usually employ professional management to handle these jobs and maintain accounting records.

Multifamily Residences. Rising land and construction costs have also stimulated the growth of multifamily housing. According to the Boeckh Index of Construction Costs, the expenses of erecting a building have more than doubled since the base year of 1967, and they continue to increase steadily. The economy of design and land usage inherent in multifamily housing allows for a lower per-family cost of construction. Thus, multifamily residences are a rapidly growing segment of the national residential real estate market.

Multifamily residences can be held under various forms of ownership. Small properties of two to six units are often owner-occupied and owner-managed, whereas most large highrise apartment complexes are professionally managed for their investor-owners. Cooperative, condominium, and quadrominium apartments are larger owner-occupied buildings governed by boards of directors elected by the owners. These boards usually hire professional managers for their properties.

Structurally, multifamily residences can be classified as either garden apartments, walkup buildings, or highrise apartments. Each type is unique in its location, design, construction, services, and amenities. These distinctions will be explored in Chapters 11 and 12. Figure 1 illustrates the interrelationship of several types of residential real estate structures.

Commercial Real Estate

There are two principal categories of commercial real estate:

- office property
- retail space

Office Property. Like multifamily residences, office buildings can be either lowrise (walkup) offices, garden developments, or highrise complexes. Whether an office building is situated in a downtown commercial district or in a suburban development, its success is determined by its location relative to the prospective work force, transportation facilities, and other business services.

Office buildings can have several tenants or a single occupant, who may or may not be the owner. A number of major corporations occupy their own real estate for business purposes. Such real estate is often referred to as *institutional* property and is sometimes under the supervision of the corporation's own property management department. Some multiple-tenant office buildings accept any financially qualified business or organization, while others cater to one type of business. Medical complexes, dental complexes, and trade centers are examples of multiple-occupancy, single-use buildings. Management of office properties will be discussed at some length in Chapter 13.

Retail Property. Retail properties, the second major category of commercial real estate, include freestanding buildings, strip centers, neighborhood centers, community centers, regional shopping centers, and super regional malls. The freestanding, single-tenant building is often owner-occupied and owner-managed. Strip centers usually consist of 4 to 10 stores located on a corner of a main thoroughfare and are designed primarily for convenience shopping. Neighborhood centers are the next largest, con-

Figure 2: COMMERCIAL REAL ESTATE CATEGORIES

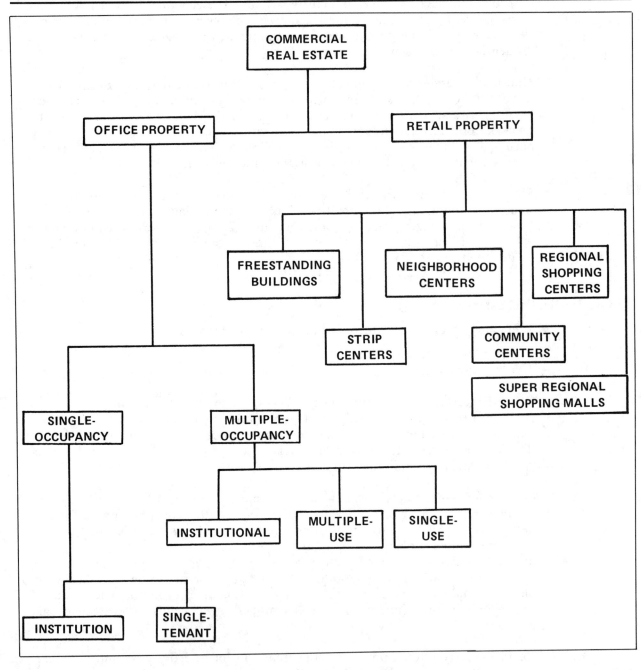

taining 15 to 20 retail outlets. Community centers may consist of 20 to 70 stores and serve an even larger area.

Regional shopping centers and super regional malls located in suburban areas are a development of the last 25 years. They have been one of the major contributing factors to the decline of the centralized urban commercial district. The size of these shopping centers and their diverse tenant mix make professional management a necessity. The success or failure of a shopping center often hinges on the property manager's ability to assess the market, to conduct sales promotion and public relations, and to act swiftly and decisively. Regional shopping center management provides one of the greatest challenges to the skills of the professional manager, as will be seen in Chapter 14. The general categories of commercial real estate are illustrated on the opposite page.

Industrial Property

The industrial process converts raw materials into finished products. It comprises all activities involved in the production, storage, and distribution of goods. Industrial property includes all land and facilities used for heavy and light manufacturing, for storage, and for the distribution of goods.

Figure 3: INDUSTRIAL REAL ESTATE CATEGORIES

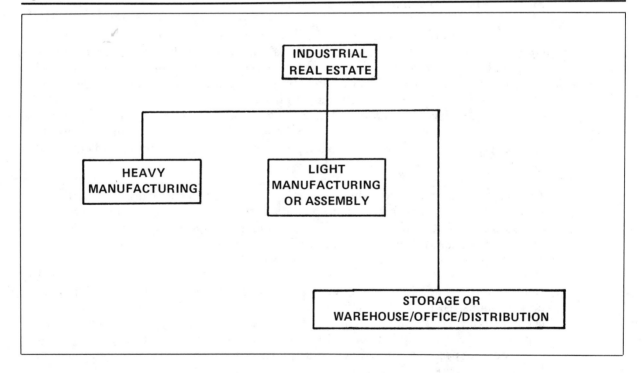

Heavy manufacturing includes industrial plants such as steel mills, automotive plants, and petroleum refineries. Access to transportation facilities and an adequate source of raw materials dictates the location of these plants. Since property for heavy industry must be designed with the specific needs of the potential user in mind, such plants are generally occupied and managed by the owner.

Light manufacturing, assembly, or warehousing, on the other hand, can usually be performed in smaller buildings that require fewer unique specifications. As a result, light industrial buildings can often be utilized by more than one type of enterprise—a fact that has stimulated some real estate speculators to build this type of facility for future lease to an industrial concern.

Industrial parks have flourished because of the migration away from the central city and the development of freeway systems to facilitate the flow of workers, materials, and finished goods. Located in suburban areas, these parks, designed for light industry, have enjoyed rapid growth over the past 20 years, while the number of urban manufacturing facilities has declined. Because of greater land availability, industrial parks in suburban areas can provide the advantages of one-story plant and warehouse design, ample parking, and extensive landscaping.

The *loft building* is an extant reminder of the former concentration of industrial activity in the central urban areas of older cities. These multistory, low-rent buildings, once used for manufacturing, are now being converted into various combinations of manufacturing, office, residential, and storage space. The thousands of square feet in loft buildings which remain to be converted and leased offer unique possibilities for the creative and ambitious property manager.

To relieve the traffic congestion of the central city, *distribution facilities,* or *warehouses,* are being built in suburban industrial parks. While the larger warehouses are usually owner-occupied, an increasing number are being built by investors for lease to various industrial users with differing space requirements. By the very nature of their use, warehouses require minimal management, and this responsibility is often shared by landlord and tenant according to the terms of the lease agreement. Like loft space, warehouses in some central city areas are currently being converted by talented property managers into shopping malls, condominium apartments, and office space.

Trends. Many business and industrial parks are no longer recognizing the traditional separation between office space and manufacturing or warehouse facilities. Many parks now offer combinations of office and industrial space, or buildings that are divided into small, different-sized units. These *incubator spaces* are designed to be adapted to the changing needs of a growing company.

Another modern development is the *miniwarehouse.* Although usually located in or near an industrial park, the miniwarehouse is not specifically designed to meet the needs of industry. Businesses rent space in miniwarehouses for storing files, extra supplies, and surplus equipment, but the primary purpose of this facility is to provide extra storage space for homeowners and apartment dwellers. On-site resident managers for miniwarehouses are becoming common.

The simplified diagram on page 7 shows the types of industrial property. Chapter 15 goes into detail concerning the management of industrial property.

Special-Purpose Property

Hotels, motels, clubs, resorts, nursing homes, mobile home parks, theaters, schools, colleges, government institutions, and churches are considered special-purpose property. Their common denominator is the fact that the activity taking place in these buildings is a special business or organizational undertaking that dictates the design and operation of the building itself. Thus, management of these properties is usually provided internally by members of the particular business or organization. These individuals must be skilled in the techniques of professional property management and knowledgeable in their specific fields of endeavor.

DUTIES OF THE PROPERTY MANAGER

Just as there are various types of real property, so also are there different classifications of property managers. A professional property manager may be an individual entrepreneur, a member of a real estate firm specializing in property management, or a member of the property management department of a large multiservice real estate company. He or she also may work within the trust department of a financial institution or within the real estate department of a large corporation or public institution. Regardless of their employment background, property managers pursue similar objectives. As the person in charge of maximizing the net income from a property, the manager may become involved in planning through budgeting and market analysis, advertising and space merchandising, screening tenants, negotiating leases, collecting rent, maintaining the interior and exterior of the premises, supervising security, obtaining insurance, paying taxes on the property, keeping accurate records, and making periodic reports to the property owner. Although management duties will vary according to the specific situation and particular property, the successful manager must be competent in all of these areas. The major functions of the property manager will be discussed individually in Chapters 2 through 10.

In addition to the tasks involved in property management per se, professional managers should take an interest in professional, social, and political organizations in their municipality. They should be active in community organizations promoting general welfare and local business opportunities and in professional and trade groups. Their long-range goals will be more easily realized if property managers take on civic responsibilities and help to implement plans for the growth and improvement of their community.

Property managers must be aware of the changing nature of professional property management, the diverse types of properties now under professional management, and the increasing variety of ownership entities employed by investors. The need for managers with sophisticated management skills and extensive technical skills increases daily with the growth in size and complexity of managed property. Continued professional training is, therefore, a must if a property manager is to grow and succeed in this profession.

SUMMARY

Around the turn of the century, the development and construction of highrise apartment and office buildings began to change the face of urban real estate. Construction of all types of multifamily apartment buildings increased rapidly. With the advent of large suburban shopping centers, the transformation of the real estate field was set in the present day mold. These three trends in urban development sparked the increased demand for trained and skilled property managers.

The first national organization for property managers, the Building Owners and Managers Association International (BOMA), was a coalition of local building owners' groups. It came into official existence in 1921 and later set up an educational institute to encourage the ongoing professional development of property managers, especially those dealing primarily with office buildings. Individuals who have completed BOMA's educational program through its institute are awarded the designation of Real Property Administrator (RPA).

In 1933 the Institute of Real Estate Management (IREM) was formed as a subsidiary body of the NATIONAL ASSOCIATION OF REALTORS®. The designation CPM (Certified Property Manager) was adopted in 1938 to denote those individuals who have successfully fulfilled all of the necessary requirements to gain admission to IREM. The International Council of Shopping Centers (ICSC) also sponsors an educational program for retail property managers that leads to the designation of Certified Shopping Center Manager (CSM).

Most property management involves property that is not intrinsic to the operation of a business or industry and thus is capable of being independently managed. For the purposes of professional property management, real estate can be divided into four major classifications: residential, commercial, industrial, and special-purpose property— each summoning a different combination of knowledge and skills from the manager.

Residential real estate is the single largest area of involvement for property managers. Whereas single-family homes are usually owner-occupied and managed, most apartment buildings (whether walkups, garden developments, or highrise) require the services of a skilled manager. The rapid rise in land and construction costs has created a demand for multifamily residences and a corresponding demand for qualified managers.

Commercial real estate consists of office buildings and retail property. Like apartments, *office buildings* can be either walkups, garden developments, or highrise complexes. A number of major corporations occupy their own real estate for business purposes. This *institutional property* may or may not be managed by the corporate owners. Most office space, however, is leased to one or more tenant businesses. Almost all multiple-tenant office buildings are professionally managed.

Retail property includes freestanding stores and restaurants, commercial strip centers, neighborhood centers, community centers, and large shopping malls. Most single-tenant buildings are owner-occupied and managed. The development of the large regional suburban shopping center over the past 25 years has provided property managers with their greatest opportunity and challenge in recent years.

The industrial process involves the conversion of raw materials into finished goods and incorporates all the activities involved in the production, storage, and distribution of these goods. Industrial property includes heavy and light manufacturing plants along with warehouses for storage and distribution of the products. Most industrial property, because of its integral relationship to the production process, requires minimal outside management. Often, the responsibility for managing industrial property is shared jointly by the owner and the tenant under the terms of the lease.

A growing number of *loft buildings* and warehouses are being converted into retail, office, and residential space. The concept of *incubator spaces* is well-established. To accommodate different types of small companies some buildings are being divided into small units of varying size, while in others office and industrial space are being combined. These incubator spaces can be adapted to the needs of a growing company.

Another modern development is the *miniwarehouse,* usually located in or near industrial parks. This facility provides the extra storage space needed by many homeowners and apartment dwellers. Businesses, too, often rent space in miniwarehouses for the storage of files, extra supplies, and equipment.

To become a successful professional today, the property manager must know the real estate market thoroughly. A property manager must be able to assess the present and future value of a property based on net operating income and to construct a management plan that will meet the owner's objectives while remaining flexible enough to respond to market fluctuations and other contingencies. The professional property manager must also become a specialist in advertising and marketing space, tenant psychology, the legal aspects of the landlord-tenant relationship, maintenance procedures, insurance, accounting, and financial reporting.

QUESTIONS: CHAPTER 1

1. The transformation of urban real estate that occurred around the end of the nine-teenth century resulted primarily from:

   I. technical advances such as the electric elevator.
   II. the increasing concentration of retail activity in downtown urban areas.

   a. I only
   b. II only
   c. both I and II
   d. neither I nor II

2. The designation of Certified Property Manager (CPM) is awarded by:

   a. NAR
   b. BOMA
   c. ICSC
   d. IREM

3. Although most freestanding, single-family homes are owner-occupied, there are often opportunities for professional management of:

   I. town homes.
   II. cooperatives.

   a. I only
   b. II only
   c. both I and II
   d. neither I nor II

4. The growth of multifamily housing has been stimulated by:

   I. the increasing price of land.
   II. declining construction costs.

   a. I only
   b. II only
   c. both I and II
   d. neither I nor II

5. Institutional property is:

   I. one type of commercial real estate.
   II. owner-occupied property.

   a. I only
   b. II only
   c. both I and II
   d. neither I nor II

6. The ability of a property manager to assess a market and implement sales promotion is most critical when dealing with:

   a. retail property
   b. industrial property
   c. office property
   d. special-purpose property

7. Modern innovations in property management include:

   I. conversion of loft buildings.
   II. incubator spaces.

      a. I only   c. both I and II
      b. II only   d. neither I nor II

8. The professional designation awarded by BOMI to individuals who successfully complete its educational program is:

      a. CPM   c. RPM
      b. RAM   d. RPA

9. Walkup buildings, garden developments, and highrise complexes are structural types that can apply to:

   I. residential property.
   II. office buildings.

      a. I only   c. both I and II
      b. II only   d. neither I nor II

10. Which of the following statements about the Building Owners and Managers Association is *incorrect?*

       a. BOMA is a national federation of local groups.
       b. BOMA distributes an annual *Experience Exchange Report.*
       c. BOMA consists largely of office building managers.
       d. BOMA is a subsidiary of the NAR.

11. Property managers concern themselves with:

    I. protecting the worth of real estate.
    II. maximizing income from real property.

       a. I only   c. both I and II
       b. II only   d. neither I nor II

12. Which of the following is a true statement?

    I. All commercial property is retail property.
    II. All retail property is commercial property.

       a. I only   c. both I and II
       b. II only   d. neither I nor II

13. List the five major types of retail property.

    a. _____   d. _____
    b. _____   e. _____
    c. _____

14. The professional designation awarded by the Institute of Shopping Center Managers is:

    a.   SCM   c.   CPM
    b.   RPA   d.   CSM

15. Special-purpose property:

    I.   is usually managed by an outside firm.
    II. includes hotels, motels, theaters, schools, and churches.

    a.   I only   c.   both I and II
    b.   II only   d.   neither I nor II

16. Which of the following titles would indicate that a person might have responsibility for property management in a company?

    I.   Facilities Manager
    II. Director of Real Estate

    a.   I only   c.   both I and II
    b.   II only   d.   neither I nor II

2
Real Estate Economics and Management Planning

The real estate market forms a major segment of the general business economy. The two are so closely allied that trends in the business economy may either stem from or result in changes in the real estate market. The condition of one directly affects the condition of the other. To assess the current and future potential of a particular property and then develop a management plan for it, the property manager must understand basic economic trends and their implications for the real estate market.

REAL ESTATE ECONOMICS

THE GENERAL BUSINESS ECONOMY

At one time, changes and trends appearing in the general economy were thought to be cyclical. More recent theory, however, suggests that such changes fall into four very different categories: seasonal, cyclical, long-term, and random. All four types of movement may occur in the economy at the same time.

Seasonal Variations

Changes that recur at regular intervals at least once a year are called *seasonal variations.* Such changes arise from both nature and custom. In the northern United States, for example, construction virtually stops during the winter months, and this seasonal change affects both the general and the real estate economy. Customs such as the nine-month school year have a seasonal effect on apartment vacancy rates in college and university towns. Moreover, retired persons fleeing cold weather swell the wintertime populations of many southern cities.

It is impossible to eliminate seasonal trends, but since these changes are predictable, property managers can be prepared to make any necessary adjustments to counter economic shifts.

Cyclical Fluctuations

Historically, economists have concentrated on *cyclical fluctuations* in the general economy. *Business cycles* are usually defined as wavelike movements of increasing and decreasing economic prosperity. A cycle consists of four phases: expansion, recession, contraction, and revival. Figure 4 shows how the phases merge.

Figure 4: THE BUSINESS CYCLE

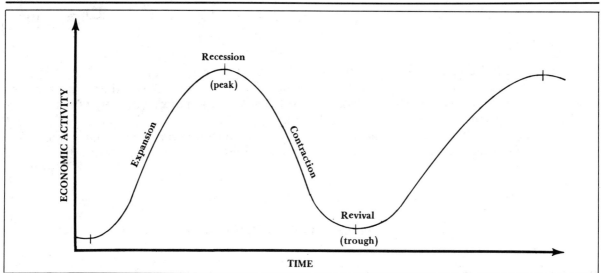

Production increases during the expansion phase. The country is working at near full-employment level, wages and consumer purchasing power are climbing to their highest point, and demand for goods is increasing. In this phase of the cycle, prices increase due to greater demand, the purchasing value of the dollar decreases, credit is eased, and more money becomes available for purchasing. At the same time, the increased profits earned by businesses attract new capital for the continued expansion of production facilities to meet product demand.

Recession is the leveling off of economic activity that occurs when supply meets and begins to surpass the demand for products and services. This is the highest point of the cycle.

Immediately after the recession phase or peak has been reached, it becomes necessary to decrease production. This downward motion is termed contraction. A decrease in production, with its concomitant layoffs, brings about a general awareness that the peak has been reached and that a period of unemployment and retrenchment is imminent. Confidence in the economy is shaken and consumers decrease spending in anticipation of lower earnings. Prices of goods are lowered in order to attract buyers, the purchasing power of the dollar rises, and credit becomes harder to obtain. This downward movement entails a cutback rather than a complete halt in business activity. Essential activities continue, since people must eat, wear clothes, and replace important appliances.

The contraction phase reaches a point where postponement of major purchases is no longer possible and excess supplies of goods have been exhausted. Consumers, lured by lower prices, venture back into the market. This begins the revival phase of the general economy. As business activity increases slightly, confidence begins to return. Slowly, production facilities gear up to meet the resurgent consumer demand, capital begins to flow back into business enterprises, and additional employees are hired. Finally, as the gradual increase in employment generates more spendable income and an increasing demand for more goods, the business cycle again enters the expansion phase.

Although business cycles technically consist of the four phases defined above, most discussions deal simply with expansion and contraction, measuring expansion from trough to peak and contraction from peak to trough. Business cycles are recurrent but not periodic; that is, they vary in duration and timing. Through empirical research, economists have observed cycles in the general economy that vary from one to twelve years in length.

Specific cycles are wavelike movements similar to business cycles. They occur in specific sectors of the general economy, such as the real estate economy, and in individual sectors of the real estate economy, such as housing starts and real estate sales. Specific cycles do not always coincide with cycles of the general business economy, but the business cycle is actually a weighted average of all specific cycles.

Regardless of the state of the national economy, certain areas will boom in recessions and stagnate in prosperous times since local demand may run counter to current broad economic trends. Areas whose economy centered on the oil industry continued to prosper long after northeastern manufacturing towns were in trouble in the early 1980s; likewise, an influx of new residents and industries into central Florida kept that area building and growing.

Long-Term Movements

Long-term movements of the general economy, usually measured over 50 years or more, reflect the overall direction the economy is taking. For example, the steady increase in goods and services produced per capita in the U.S. is a long-term movement upward. Such movements are believed to result from population growth and shifts, technological breakthroughs, the rate of savings and investment, and utilization of natural resources. Other political, bureaucratic, and contingency factors also influence a nation's growth rate.

The growth pattern in specific industries is usually quite different from the national long-term growth pattern. New industries generally consist of firms that operate and experiment on a small scale. When effective standardized methodologies are established, the industry enters a rapid growth phase. The third stage begins when the market becomes saturated and production levels off.

The real estate industry follows this pattern whenever a new land area is developed or an existing area redeveloped. Initially, few investors are willing to lend money for construction on raw land or redevelopment of slum areas. However, after a few buildings have been constructed or renovated, more investors are attracted and building activity in the area increases rapidly. When all existing land has been put to its highest and best use, construction activity virtually ceases. Thus, long-term movements in the real estate industry may be shorter than those in the general economy and occur on local levels at irregular intervals.

Random Changes

Random changes are nonperiodic fluctuations of the economy that may be caused by legislative and judicial decisions or by strikes, revolutions, wars, fires, storms, floods, and other catastrophes. These changes, impossible to predict or analyze, may affect one or more sectors of the aggregate economy. They may affect all industries in an area or one industry nationwide. Real estate activity, especially construction, is very vulnerable to labor strikes, political changes, and natural disasters. One example of a random change in regard to real estate is a national labor strike, which would halt construction activity. Another is a zoning ordinance change allowing undeveloped land to be used for industrial purposes, which would stimulate construction activity in that locality. The only way to survive random fluctuations of the economy is to be alert to them and adaptable enough to cope with events as they occur.

THE REAL ESTATE ECONOMY

As discussed earlier, the real estate economy is a large and integral part of the general business economy and as such is subject to the same four types of fluctuations. Cyclical movements (specific cycles) are the most pronounced and important trends that appear in the real estate sector. Specific cycles can be observed in all phases of real estate: land development, building, sales, finance, investment, rental, and redevelopment.

It is important to remember that cycles in the general business economy influence and are influenced by cycles in the real estate economy. For example, the availability of money in the general economy has a great impact on housing starts. By the same token, an increase in construction can significantly raise the gross national product (a good measure of general economic activity).

Most sectors of the real estate economy are subject to both long and short cycles, the former ranging from 15 to 22 years and the latter extending for about 33 months. Although the long cycles significantly affect real estate activity over a period of time, the field of property management is affected more strongly by the ramifications of short specific cycles, especially those in construction and rental activities.

The residential building cycle appears to run counter to activity in the general economy. Controlling factors in the residential building cycle are the availability of money and credit in the mortgage and construction markets. In general, when the aggregate economy is prosperous and costs are rising, investors can find more lucrative investments than banks and real estate loans. This decreases the availability of money for residential construction and causes a slump in the real estate sector at a time of economic prosperity for the rest of the country. Conversely, interest rates decline during a depression, so savings and loans attract more money with which to finance construction.

The pattern of commercial and industrial starts is very different from that of housing starts. These cycles move much more consistently with the general business economy. One explanation is that investors in large commercial and industrial construction projects command a higher, more competitive return in inflationary times than do investors in residential construction. Moreover, in times of prosperity and easy credit, commercial and industrial builders can obtain supplies and stock sufficient inventory for a construction boom. Since wages for commercial construction labor tend to be higher than wages for residential workers during commercial building booms, labor is drawn away from residential construction. During tight money markets, however, construction loans carry higher interest rates; builders of either residential or commercial property then either pass the high costs on to buyers or accept a lower profit. Either situation slows down the rate of construction and decreases builders' inventories.

All types of construction starts (residential, commercial, and industrial) lag somewhat behind the general business economy because mortgage commitments are given from 6 to 18 months in advance and because it takes considerable time to complete the actual construction. This lag time accounts for many radical swings in supply and demand. If demand slackens during the length of time involved between the planning and completion of large real estate projects, a surplus of property (notably multifamily residences and office structures) may be the result. In extreme cases, the results can be disastrous to real estate investors.

THE RENTAL MARKET

Construction cycles in residential, commercial, and industrial properties are important to the property manager because they influence supply and demand for various kinds of rental space. During upward swings of a building industry (expansion), the rental market for that type of property is generally good and vacancies are low. As the cycle peaks, the supply of occupiable space equals and exceeds the demand. At this point, rents fall and vacancy rates increase. During the contraction phase the rental market is poor, vacancy rates are high, and property owners must compete for tenants. The result is a drastic reduction in rents. As the cycle reaches the trough, the demand for space once again equals and begins to surpass the supply of available space, so rental rates as well as construction starts can also begin to increase.

A special feature of the real estate rental market is its tendency to undergo a severe and prolonged contraction phase. When the supply of a manufactured product exceeds the demand for it, the manufacturer is able to cut back on output and the merchant is able to reduce inventory in order to balance supply and demand. However, during contraction of the real estate rental market, property owners cannot reduce the amount of leasable space in their buildings. Space that was constructed to accommodate business and consumer needs at the peak of the cycle remains, vacancy rates climb, and the downward trend becomes more severe. Since a minimum rental rate must be charged to cover operating expenses on the property, rental rates generally do not drop below a certain point. Some owners will take their space off the market rather than lose money on it. A few, unable to subsidize the property, will sell at distressed prices, and mortgagees will repossess others.

Specific cycles in the residential rental market correspond roughly to cycles in multi-family residential housing starts. The rental market for commercial property lags from 6 months to a year behind residential rental market trends because commercial leases are generally longer and require more time to reflect current conditions. Since the real estate market lags behind the general economy as regards the short cycle, the general business economy can often predict trends that will eventually affect the real estate market.

Property managers who can analyze the real estate market and recognize trends will be prepared for economic fluctuations and crises. By anticipating changes in the market and adjusting rentals and other factors within their control, property managers can minimize the effect of contractions in the real estate cycle and keep their vacancy rates as low as possible. They must use their knowledge and judgment concerning market conditions when setting rental structures, allocating money for operating costs, renovating space, and making other financial plans. Knowledge of economic trends and specific cycles in the real estate sector provides a background against which to view the specific conditions and characteristics of each property. General knowledge of the market must be integrated with information about the market in the area of the property; the income, operating costs, and condition of the property; and the owner's objectives.

FORMULATING THE MANAGEMENT PLAN

In formulating the management plan, the property manager has three basic tools including:

- regional and neighborhood market analyses
- property analysis
- analysis of an owner's objectives

On consideration of these three factors, the manager should be able to draw up a management plan and budget that are feasible in terms of both present and future business and real estate economic cycles. The management plan will include market analysis, alternative analysis, proposed financing, as well as conclusions and recommendations.

Because of the time and effort involved in creating a management plan, the manager should not undertake this task unless he or she is to receive adequate compensation or has already signed a contract. However, competitive pressures may force property management firms to complete a plan on a proposed or new building in order to secure a management contract, which may affect the amount of compensation involved.

MARKET ANALYSES

When two or more persons meet for the purpose of leasing or sales, a market is created. Many commodities—office buildings, factories, warehouses, stores, and apartments, for example—are leased or sold in the real estate market. Depending on the persons or organizations involved, these transactions can occur at a national, regional, or local level. Whatever the case may be, all real property is part of the national real estate economy and is subject to the same cyclical trends. It is the responsibility of the property manager to identify major economic trends and their effect on the value of a specific property at his or her particular market level.

Regional Market Analysis

A regional market analysis is often valuable in interpreting economic trends. This report should include demographic and economic information on the regional or metropolitan area in which the subject property is located. The regional analysis typically presents population statistics and trends, a list of major employers in the area, income and employment data, a description of transportation facilities, and supply and demand trends. It should also explore the economic base of the city and prospects for the future in that locale.

Neighborhood Market Analysis

Generally, property management is carried out at the local level. In order to determine the optimum income that can be realized from a building, the property manager must first determine the economic climate of his or her neighborhood real estate market. Neighborhood analysis should begin with a tour of the area. Equipped with local maps, area zoning ordinances, applicable building codes, and statistical data on the population, the property manager should assess five major factors in the neighborhood market area.

Boundaries and Land Usage. A neighborhood is usually defined as an area within which common characteristics of population and land use prevail. There is no predetermined size for a neighborhood. In rural areas, a neighborhood may encompass 10 square miles, whereas a neighborhood in a central city might include only 5 square blocks. Before a local market analysis can be made, the property manager must ascertain the boundaries of the area. Rivers, lakes, railroad tracks, parks, or major arterial throughways may help to delineate the confines of a neighborhood. In the absence of any obvious physical boundaries, the manager must use his or her powers of observation to determine how much land is under common use and shares a similar population.

When establishing the confines of a neighborhood, the property manager should make special note of restrictions like forest preserves, recreational areas, freeways, railroad tracks, and rivers that are located in the area, for these can curtail its future growth. Any variances or restrictions in zoning should also be noted. Depending upon the type of property involved, zoning regulations may have a positive or negative effect. Commercial and industrial enterprises would be adversely affected by a zoning restriction limiting the area to multiple-family units, while a zoning ordinance favorable to industrial development would detract from the desirability of a residential neighborhood.

Transportation and Utilities. Whether the property is an apartment building, warehouse, office complex, or shopping center, transportation facilities are crucial. Close proximity to public transportation is a must for apartment dwellers in large cities, many of whom do not own cars, and for employees in office buildings, who often take public transportation to work. Access to and from major streets, traffic patterns, and the traffic count in a neighborhood are of concern to commercial ventures such as strip centers or shopping malls. Traffic counts are readily available from governmental traffic departments. Industrial enterprises must have access to transportation facilities in order to distribute their goods, so railheads, major highways, and airports are important to industrial tenants.

Residential, commercial, and industrial property users are all concerned with the availability of parking. The aggravation of overcrowded curb space in urban neighborhoods can be relieved by off-street tenant parking areas. Commercial enterprises rely heavily on adequate parking facilities for their customers, and industrial concerns require dockside space for loading as well as an area for employee parking. A shortage of parking has become a major problem in cities where there has been extensive downtown redevelopment.

The cost and quality of utility services in the neighborhood will also affect any type of real property. Residential and commercial buildings must offer certain basic amenities—electricity, gas, water, heat, and perhaps air conditioning—in order to attract individual and corporate tenants. Industrial users will be particularly concerned with heavy-duty power lines, sprinklers, separate sewage systems, and other unique utility services called for in their business.

Economy. A neighborhood that has a diversified yet well-integrated business sector is in better economic condition than an area that depends on a single major industry for its support. If that company moves, the economic framework of the area would probably collapse. The property manager can draw upon several sources of statistical information for help in assessing the economic health of a neighborhood. Brokers, appraisers, and local newspapers are fruitful sources, as is the local chamber of commerce, which should be able to supply data on the number and type of businesses in the area, the volume of their activity, and the general trend of growth in the past. Neighborhood financial institutions are another important barometer of the area economy. The volume of mortgage loans outstanding reflects the overall confidence in the real estate market. If banks will not make loans for which property in the area serves as collateral, it is a fairly safe assumption that the value of real estate in the neighborhood is declining.

The property manager must also try to assess the potential for growth within the community. Provided there are no natural or artificial boundaries or local zoning restrictions, the opportunity for growth will depend upon the amount of existing competition in the neighborhood and on the availability of loans for construction or expansion. An inverse relationship exists between mortgage interest rates and business activity: as interest rates climb, business growth drops. The manager of commercial or industrial property can secure this and other meaningful information from the local chamber of commerce and banking institutions.

Rental rates currently being charged in the neighborhood are another sound indicator of the present economic strength of the real estate market. When space is in short supply, rents are high. The consumer price index published by the Bureau of Labor Statistics displays trends in rental schedules in 20 sample cities. Housing classifieds placed in local newspapers over the past couple of years will yield information on a particular neighborhood. The best and most reliable information, of course, is obtained by the property manager through telephone calls to local businesspersons and a thorough shopping of the competition.

Supply and Demand.   The occupancy rate for a particular type of property reflects the relationship between supply and demand for that type of space at its current rental level. As occupancy and vacancy rates are continually fluctuating, so too are supply and demand.

A high occupancy rate indicates a shortage of space and the possibility of rental increases. A low rate, as evidenced by many "for rent" signs posted in the area, will result in tenant demands for lower rents, decorating or tenant alteration allowances, and other concessions on the part of the landlord, such as free rent or gifts of appliances.

The oversupply of space which results in low occupancy rates can be either technical or economic in nature. *Technical* oversupply occurs when there are more units available than potential tenants, while *economic* oversupply reflects the fact that the space available is priced beyond the purchasing power of the potential tenants.

Statistics on vacancy rates can be obtained from the U.S. Census Bureau, from current regional housing reports published by the Department of Commerce, or from local owner-manager associations. The Building Owners and Managers Association publishes local occupancy surveys that are useful to commercial property managers. Local utility companies are another fruitful source of information concerning occupancy levels. The number of inoperative meters corresponds roughly to the amount of vacant space.

To find out whether occupancy levels for a given type of property are rising or falling, and how rapidly, the property manager must survey comparable properties. The amount of similar existing space and vacancy levels in the neighborhood must be inventoried according to building type, age, size, location, features, and rental schedule. New construction must also be noted. The second step in analyzing occupancy trends is matching the local tenant population to the available space. Of interest here are the number and density of potential tenants, their ability and willingness to lease, and the stability and trend of their financial resources or income.

Information about the tenant population (whether individual, as with residential properties, or corporate, as with office space) can be obtained through government agencies, local chambers of commerce, and other outlets. The manager must then project the growth rate of the market based on past economic trends and current conditions.

Social and Cultural Aspects.   The final checkpoint in the manager's survey of a neighborhood is more relevant to residential property managers than to managers of commercial or industrial real estate. Nonetheless, any amenities that make the neighborhood attractive to potential residents will indirectly benefit business and industry by providing a local pool of potential consumers and employees. When touring the neighborhood, the manager should note the number and location of parks, playgrounds, theaters, restaurants, schools, colleges, churches, and any other social or cultural organizations that will be attractive to potential tenants.

Evaluating the Data

Once the regional and neighborhood market surveys are complete, the manager must analyze the information concerning transportation facilities, economic conditions, type and amount of similar space, rental schedules, and population composition. When reviewing this data, the manager must keep in mind the special features of his or her particular type of property and the needs of the potential tenants.

Industrial property managers should pay attention to opportunities for expansion, transportation facilities, special utility services, the availability of raw materials, and the potential work force in the area. In most locales, the chamber of commerce will have this information available. Traffic counts and patterns, the location of competitors, public transportation facilities, parking space, and the median income of the population are deciding factors for the manager of commercial property. Residential property managers will be most concerned with the size of family units, the median income level, population trends, current employment rates, and the area's social and cultural facilities.

By reconciling the data gathered from market surveys with the specific features of a particular property and the current rental rates in the area, the manager can arrive at the optimum price for a standard unit of that type within the market area. From this figure the base expected income for the property can be calculated. Regional and neighborhood analyses are only as reliable as the judgments behind them. It takes a professional property manager who is knowledgeable about real estate economic cycles to assess their impact on future trends in his or her own market area, and thus be able to take advantage of this knowledge.

PROPERTY ANALYSIS

Market analyses determine the optimum rental for standard space in the area. A *property* analysis familiarizes the manager with the nature and condition of a particular building and with its position relative to similar properties in the neighborhood. To get this information, the manager must make a thorough inspection of the subject property and use data on similar properties in the area to evaluate the subject property in terms of the comparables. Upon completion of the property analysis, the manager should know what expenditures will be needed to make the subject property competitive with the best space available in the area. He or she should also have gathered enough data to be able to estimate the average operating cost of the building.

Leases

Property analysis begins with a study of the terms of each tenant's lease. These disclose the amount and durability of rental income. The vacancy and loss rate for a property is an illuminating statistic in that it can show whether previous management was efficient or not. If leases have a low renewal rate (high tenant turnover), the quality of tenant services may be poor or the rental rate may be above the market. In any case, the leases themselves can provide insight into the management of the property, and the use of a summary spreadsheet to list and compare leases is recommended.

Quantity and Quality of Space

The appearance of the building is important. Prospective tenants will form their initial impression of the premises based on what they see as they approach the building. With this "curb appeal" in mind, the property manager's inspection should begin with the overall outward appearance of the structure, including its age and style as well as the condition of its walkways and the landscaping. If the manager's building does not present as pleasing a facade as others in the area, he or she should suggest corrective measures to improve the initial presentation of the premises.

An interior inspection should inventory the total amount of usable space or number of individual rental units in the building. The residential property manager should examine the number and size of the rooms, their layout, the amount of closet space, and the view. The ability of a space to command optimum rental for the area depends not only on the desirability of its design, but also on the quality of its fixtures. Whether the space is commercial, industrial, or residential, the condition of the hardware, plumbing, walls, and electrical fixtures should not be overlooked. Faulty appliances, worn carpeting or drapes, and dirty walls detract from the desirability of residential space. The manager should make note of any items that need replacement, repair, or painting in order to make the subject property either equivalent to the best space available in the neighborhood market, or an attractive alternative based upon special features, unique amenities, or competitive prices.

Physical Condition of the Premises

A thorough inspection of the building's exterior, common interior areas, and equipment will provide the property manager with the additional data necessary to calculate maintenance and operating costs for the upcoming year.

Exterior. An exterior inspection should alert the property manager to any major repairs that have been deferred by the previous owner or manager. The masonry, windows, eaves and trim, roof, porches, grounds, parking area, fire escapes, and any other common area must be scrutinized for defects requiring immediate attention and capital outlay.

Interior. Entranceways, halls, basement, laundry rooms, boiler rooms, and other common interior areas should be checked. Redecorating or replacement expenses should be estimated, along with expenses for personnel required to satisfy the routine housekeeping and maintenance requirements for these areas.

Equipment. The manager's tour of the building's machinery, equipment, and amenities will disclose their condition and age, need for major repairs, and the amount of personnel and supplies required to keep them operating efficiently. Included in this tour should be the heating, ventilating, and air-conditioning systems; plumbing fixtures and water heaters; machinery such as snow removers and lawn mowers; elevators; and facilities such as cafeterias, swimming pools, and tennis courts.

The physical inventory also reveals areas of deferred maintenance and curable obsolescence. It should show compliance with building, housing, and zoning codes. Portions of a comprehensive form for detailed exterior analyses of office property begin on the next page. A similar form for analyzing interior conditions is also available. The standard forms used for inspection of other types of property are quite similar and will be shown in the appropriate chapters.

Evaluation Through Comparables

The subject property can be evaluated in terms of comparable properties with respect to building size, rental rates, vacancy rates, location, construction, age, special features and amenities, condition of premises, and size of the building staff. Operating expenses for comparable properties can help the manager to develop both a rental schedule and an operating budget for the subject property's management plan. Industry standards for various types of properties are available from professional property management associations. The Building Owners and Managers Association International publishes the *Experience Exchange Report* yearly, and the Urban Land Institute periodically prepares *Dollars and Cents of Shopping Centers.*

After inspecting the property and analyzing the comparables, the manager will have a good idea of the routine operating costs over the course of the year, including salaries for the building staff; cost of utilities not charged to the tenants; contract services such as lawn maintenance, elevator maintenance, rubbish removal, and security guards; supplies and equipment; and administrative expenses for advertising and management. The manager should then be able to provide the owner with an estimate of the capital expenditures that would be required to make the building competitive with similar properties in the neighborhood, if this is consistent with the owner's goals. In any case, the manager should identify and estimate expenditures needed to yield a net return that is in accord with the owner's objectives. In preparing a budget, the manager should also set priorities for the tasks to be undertaken.

ANALYSIS OF OWNER'S OBJECTIVES

After completing market analyses and property inspections, but before drawing up the management plan, the manager must obtain and analyze the goals of the owner. (In this text "owner" denotes both an individual owner and, more commonly, an owning body, whether corporation, trust, syndicate, or other organization.) Individual, corporate, fiduciary, and government owners may vary in their intentions for the property they own.

Form 50A

THE INSTITUTE OF REAL ESTATE MANAGEMENT
of the
NATIONAL ASSOCIATION OF REALTORS®

_____ 19___

OFFICE BUILDING INSPECTION REPORT

Name of Property _____ Address _____

Type of Property _____ Office Area Rental Rate _____

No. of Stores _____ Store Area Rental Rate _____

Report Submitted By _____ Basement Area Rental Rate _____

Owner _____

EXTERIOR

Items	Character & Condition	Needs	Est. Expenses
Roofs			
1. Type			
2. Flashing			
3. Valleys			
4. Drains			
Walls - North			
5. Type			
6. Base			
7. Top			
8. Tuck pointing			
9. Stone sills			
10. Coping			
11. Parapet walls			
12. Terra cotta			
13. Metal trim			
Walls - East			
14. Type			
15. Base			
16. Top			
17. Tuck pointing			
18. Stone sills			
19. Coping			
20. Parapet walls			
21. Terra cotta			
22. Metal trim			
Walls - West			
23. Type			
24. Base			
25. Top			
26. Tuck pointing			
27. Stone sills			
28. Coping			
29. Parapet walls			
30. Terra cotta			
31. Metal trim			
Walls - South			
32. Type			
33. Base			
34. Top			
35. Tuck pointing			
36. Stone sills			
37. Coping			

GENERAL EXTERIOR

Items	Character & Condition	Needs	Est. Expenses
Walls - South (cont'd)			
38. Parapet walls			
39. Terra cotta			
40. Metal trim			
Walls - Court			
41. Type			
42. Base			
43. Top			
44. Tuck pointing			
45. Stone sills			
46. Coping			
47. Parapet walls			
48. Terra cotta			
49. Metal trim			
Chimney			
50. Type			
51. Comment			
Sidewalk Elevators			
52. Permits - expiration date			
53. Make			
54. Type			
55. Capacity			
56. Parts, oil, grease contr.			
57. Sidewalk doors			
58. Shaft			
59. Platform size			
60. Shaft gates			
61. Motors			
62. Pumps			
63. Tanks			
64. Generator			
65. Signal			
66. Safety locks			
67. Controls			
68. Pits			
69. Signs			
70. Comments			
Bldg. Entrance			
71. Doors			
72. Hinges			
73. Locks			
74. Checks			
75. Side lights			
76. Transoms			
77. Canopy			
78. Signal button			
79. Lighting			
80. Building name			
81. Street numbers			
82. Entry steps			
Exterior Fire Escapes			
83. Signs			
84. Access windows			
85. Access ladders			
86. Maintenance			
87. Ladder treads			
88. Hand rails			
Sidewalks			
89. Comments			

GENERAL EXTERIOR

Items	Character & Condition	Needs	Est. Expenses
Light Walls			
90. Skylights			
91. Roof			
92. Comments			
Fire Hazards			
93. Defective wiring			
94. Trash and rubbish			
95. Oil, gasoline or paint storage			
96. Gas leaks			
97. Self-closing doors			
98. Breeching and flues			
99. Dumbwaiter enclosures			
100. Hot-ash disposal			
101. Defective fire hose			
102. Fire extinguishers			
Windows - Office			
103. Type			
104. Frames			
105. Stops			
106. Sash			
107. Sills			
108. Lintels			
109. Anchor bolts			
110. Glass			
111. Glazing			
112. Caulking			
113. Weather strip			
114. Screens			
115. Locks			
Windows - Store			
116. Frames			
117. Transoms			
118. Sash			
119. Glass			
120. Caulking			
121. Glazing			
122. Screens			
123. Hinges			
124. Sash			
125. Locks			
Penthouse - Elevator			
126. Roof			
127. Walls			
128. Steps			
129. Doors			
130. Windows			
131. Flooring			
132. Fire protection devices			
Other Roof Structures			
Miscellaneous Extras			

Most institutional and corporate investors have well-defined goals, which are in writing as policy statements or investment guidelines and readily obtainable by the property manager. Many individual owners, however, have never developed long-range plans, and a property manager can make a real contribution by arranging a conference devoted to establishing a set of written goals. These plans may not include the continued operation of the property in its present mode since the owner or the property manager may determine that an alternate use would be more productive. Alternate uses, as well as rehabilitation, alteration, and modernization should be explored with the owner to define his or her objectives.

Individual owners are usually either private entrepreneurs seeking profit or cash flow from their investment or persons using the depreciation on their real estate investment as a tax shelter. Obviously, the profit-oriented owner who wants maximum rentals is more inclined to make capital expenditures to upgrade the property than is the person seeking a tax write-off. Owners who are looking for a positive cash flow vastly outnumber those who need a tax shelter.

Corporate owners can also be divided into two broad classes, those that own real property as an investment, such as Real Estate Investment Trusts (REITs) and syndicates, and those who own and use real property for their own benefit. Some are motivated by profit (such as Sears) while others, such as corporations formed by owners of cooperative and condominium apartments, are interested in preserving the value of their investment. Cooperative corporations and condominium associations may not be concerned with tenant-attracting amenities, but they do share with profit-oriented corporations an interest in making necessary expenditures for maintaining their property.

Fiduciary institutions become involved in real estate through the services of their trust departments, which administer properties under forms of wills, living trusts, or as executors of estates. The prime concern of the trustee is maintaining the value of the property entrusted to its care while earning a reasonable income for the trustor.

Governmental agencies such as the Department of Housing and Urban Development and the General Services Administration are also interested mainly in preserving the value of the properties they administer. Most government-subsidized buildings are low-income housing developments that do not seek a high rental income. Social service and maintenance of property value are the main objectives of most government agencies involved in real estate.

In any case, the property manager should obtain from the owner a statement of the annual real estate taxes and special assessments on the property, the cost of debt service, and the premiums for insurance policies currently in effect. These figures, along with the manager's market analyses, study of comparables, and inspection of the property, provide all the information needed to draft a management plan.

PREPARATION OF THE MANAGEMENT PLAN

The steps in the preparation of the management plan include the following procedures:

1. prepare an operating budget
2. establish optimum rents
3. determine the gross annual scheduled rental income
4. adjust to reflect anticipated market trends
5. calculate yearly operating costs
6. establish necessary reserve funds
7. predict anticipated revenue
8. review the cash flow in light of the owner's objectives
9. prepare a 5-year forecast
10. develop a comparative and expense analysis

The process involves analyzing information from regional and neighborhood surveys and a property analysis to formulate a management plan that is based on the owner's goals, as Figure 5 indicates.

Figure 5: MANAGEMENT PLAN INPUT

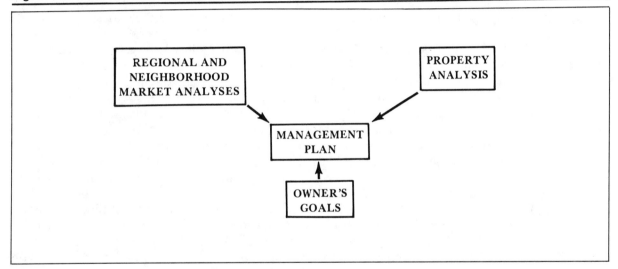

Operating Budget

The first step in preparing the management plan is to draw up a one-year projected operating budget for the property in its present condition. Regional and neighborhood surveys have familiarized the property manager with average rental and vacancy rates in the area and with the type of space most in demand. The manager's space was compared to other available local space in the property analysis. Now, the manager must evaluate the property's ability to command optimum rental rates.

Optimum Rents. The amount of rental income to be earned by each type of unit or space must be adjusted to reflect specific advantages and disadvantages of the property. If an apartment building is not convenient to public transportation routes, the optimum rental rate may have to be lowered, but if it provides tennis courts and a swimming pool, which are not standard for the area, then the optimum rental figure can be raised. The resulting figure is the base expected rental for each type of space in the building. The manager must make certain that these rates do not exceed the income capacity of the potential tenants. If they do, the rates must be readjusted to a more realistic figure.

In setting rental rates for the property, the manager could increase the rent on certain specific units based on their individual attractiveness, such as view, convenience to central facilities, etc. While this will necessitate individual unit rent administration in some cases, the increased return should more than justify the effort required.

Gross Rental Income. By multiplying the amount of space in the building by the base rental rate for that type of space, the manager will arrive at the gross annual scheduled rental income for each type of space. Apartment rentals are determined by room count, so the residential manager would multiply the number of studio, one-bedroom, and two-bedroom units times the price for each type of unit, keeping in mind the increased rental for certain units, as outlined in the preceding paragraph. Since commercial space is measured by number of square feet, the commercial property manager would multiply the square footage available on each floor of the building by the appropriate rental rate per square foot for that floor or area. The total of these estimates is the gross annual scheduled rental income for the entire property.

Market Trend Adjustment. This figure must also be adjusted to reflect anticipated market trends during the course of the year. The manager must determine the percentage of probable rent loss resulting from vacancies, tenant default on the lease, and tenant turnover. The possibility of rental increases for the leases which come up for renewal during that year must be weighed against the possibility of a reversal in the rental trend resulting in lower rents for these leases. The resulting figure is the gross adjusted rental income, sometimes termed the *gross collectable* rental income, because it represents the monies that may actually be collected after rent loss. Other sources of income from the property should be added to the rental income, as these are also part of the total income stream. Potential additional income could be earned from a parking garage, vending machines, laundry rooms, sale of utilities, and sale of tenant services. These sources of income must also be evaluated and adjusted for predicted cost, occupancy, or use changes during the budget year. The sum of the collectable rental income and the additional income constitutes the manager's estimate of gross effective revenue during the upcoming year.

Operating Costs. The next step in preparing the budget is to calculate the yearly costs of operation based on operating expenses for comparable properties and on the maintenance needs of the subject property. First, real estate taxes, salaries, utility costs, contract services, supplies, minor routine repairs and replacements, insurance, administrative costs, and management costs are included in the yearly expenses. When estimating these operating costs, the manager should consider several sources of information. Neighborhood and property analyses allow the manager to calculate average operating costs for similar properties in the area. Regional norms are available through trade associations, trade journals, local property owners groups, and professional real estate management organizations such as the Institute of Real Estate Management, the Urban Land Institute, and reports of the Building Owners and Managers Association. These figures should, of course, be modified by the manager's experience. Secondly, he or she should study the records of operating costs for the previous year, keeping in mind the prevailing rates for that year. The manager can then compare the actual costs for the previous year with figures he or she knows to be normal for the space and the neighborhood, thus identifying any excessive operating charges and expenses that can and should be reduced in the coming year. The expense section of the operating budget will reflect the manager's ability to project realistic, supportable estimates of operating expenses for that particular property. Before totaling the operating costs, the manager must determine the percent of increase that can be expected for each category during the year. The trend of the general business economy will have considerable effect on these operating costs.

Reserve Funds. There is a saying among professionals in the field of property management that "unexpected expenditures may be expected." Roof repair, boiler replacement, outside masonry repair, and expenses due to flood or electrical fire not covered by insurance are only a few of the unforeseen contingencies that can arise. Therefore any budget forecast, from an operating budget to a 5-year projection, should provide for reserve funds under the expense category. Many mortgage loans under federal government programs require that reserves for replacement expenditures be established. In large buildings, this figure is often estimated at 10 to 15 percent of the total cost of all supplies, maintenance, and repairs, but in actuality the amount of reserves necessary fluctuates greatly according to size, age, and other features of a property. Experience alone will teach the manager to calculate reserve funds realistically. They should always be an integral part of the forecast, whether they are listed separately or under the maintenance and repairs category.

Cash Flow. By subtracting the total adjusted operating expenses, plus debt service, from the anticipated revenue for the upcoming year, the manager can predict the cash flow for the property during the budget year. The cash flow figure should then be examined in terms of the owner's investment in the property. If the annual cash flow does not reflect the cost of the property and the desired return on investment, the operating budget will have to be modified. Chapter 9 explains how to calculate the return on an investment. A sample operating budget for a three-story walk-up apartment building consisting of 12 units is shown on page 34.

Five-Year Forecast

In order to present the owner with a stronger picture of the property's income potential, the manager should prepare a 5-year forecast. This is simply a long-term projection of estimated expenditures and income based on predictable changes. The stabilized budget figures in the example on the next page are arrived at by calculating and averaging all income and expenses for each of the next 5 years. Figures are rounded to the nearest $100. When preparing a long-term forecast, the manager should scrutinize all income sources and study the market trends affecting them. Before setting the median income for the forecasted period, he or she must take into consideration the current rate of rental increases in the area, the potential for growth or decline in the area, and rent increases stemming from any projected improvements to the property.

Operating expenses for the 5-year period must be realistically estimated, based on observable trends. The major influences to take into account are the rate of inflation, increases in the cost of labor and supplies, tax hikes, and raises in insurance premiums.

Figure 6: ANNUAL OPERATING BUDGET

INCOME

3 studio @ $250/mo	$ 9,000	
6 one-bedroom @ $300/mo	21,600	
3 two-bedroom @ $350/mo	12,600	
Gross scheduled rental income	$43,200	
5% vacancy and rent loss	− 2,200	
Gross collectable rental income	$41,000	
Income from other sources	+ 2,000	
Total anticipated revenue		$43,000

EXPENSE

Real estate taxes	$ 5,000	
Salaries	8,500	
Utilities	4,000	
Supplies	500	
Maintenance and repairs	1,500	
Insurance	500	
Administrative	200	
Management @ 6% gross income	2,500	
Reserves	300	
Total expense		$23,000

NET OPERATING INCOME BEFORE DEBT SERVICE		$20,000

Debt service		
$90,000 @ 10% constant	$ 9,000	

CASH FLOW		$11,000

Certain assumptions have been made in preparing the 5-year forecast shown as Figure 7. Rental increases are expected to remain at the current annual rate of 10 percent and all leases are for one-year terms. The rent loss factor also is expected to remain stable. Although fluctuation in operating expenses will vary depending on the general business economy during the next 5 years, it is assumed that they will increase at different estimated rates. The column at the far right side of the 5-year forecast shows the stabilized budget. These figures are arrived at by averaging each income or expense item over the 5-year period of the projection.

Comparative Income and Expense Analysis

The next task in formulating the management plan is to estimate the costs of improvements, alterations, or remodeling that are consistent with the owner's objectives and are needed to command optimum rentals. Any capital expenditures needed

Figure 7: FIVE-YEAR FORECAST

	Base Year	1st Year	2nd Year	3rd Year	4th Year	5th Year	Stabilized Budget
INCOME							
Rental	$41,000	$45,000	$49,500	$54,000	$59,400	$65,000	$52,300
Other	2,000	2,200	2,500	3,000	3,600	4,000	2,900
Total	$43,000	$47,200	$52,000	$57,000	$63,000	$69,000	$55,200
EXPENSES							
Real estate taxes	$ 5,000	$ 5,300	$ 5,500	$ 5,800	$ 6,000	$ 6,300	$ 5,600
Salaries	8,500	9,300	10,000	11,000	12,000	13,200	10,600
Utilities	4,000	4,400	4,800	5,200	5,700	6,100	5,000
Supplies	500	600	700	800	900	1,000	700
Maintenance and repairs	1,500	1,700	2,000	2,200	2,500	2,800	2,100
Insurance	500	600	600	700	700	800	600
Administration	200	200	200	300	300	300	300
Management @ 6% gross income	2,500	2,800	3,100	3,400	3,800	4,100	3,300
Reserves	300	300	300	300	400	400	300
Total	$23,000	$25,200	$27,200	$29,700	$32,300	$35,000	$28,500
NET OPERATING INCOME BEFORE DEBT SERVICE	$20,000	$22,000	$24,800	$27,300	$30,700	$34,000	$26,700
DEBT SERVICE	$ 9,000	$ 9,000	$ 9,000	$ 9,000	$ 9,000	$ 9,000	$ 9,000
CASH FLOW	$11,000	$13,000	$15,800	$18,300	$21,700	$25,000	$17,700

Average increase of $2,800 per year in cash flow

to remodel the space in order to make it competitive with other units in the area market, or to convert the structure to meet area demand, should also be projected. This is a very complex task, necessitating research on the costs of construction, materials, and labor involved in the proposed improvements. The manager's estimates of capital expenditures must be based on accurate information. The manager must then compute the increase in rental income that will result from these improvements. The cash flow generated after improvements should be compared with the return on investment for the property in its as-is condition. With this comparative analysis, the manager can demonstrate to the owner how long it will take to recoup the proposed capital expenditures from the future benefits to be derived from them. The comparative analysis also shows the estimated additional annual income or cash flow to be generated by the improvement.

The following analysis illustrates the increase in income that can be expected for the apartment building in the previous examples if the lobby is renovated, a laundry room installed, and a recreational area added, at a total cost of $15,000. Based on the improved appearance of the building, the added convenience of a laundry room on the premises, and the recreational amenities, all rentals can be raised $45 per month. Income from the laundry room will be $2,000 annually, offset in part by the increased cost of water. It is estimated that the water bills will increase by $500 a year. Since the gross annual income from the property will be greater, the management fee will increase proportionally. The increase in cash flow resulting from the improvements will average approximately $7,500 per year, so the initial investment of $15,000 will be returned within 2 years. After 5 years, the owner will have realized a profit of $22,500 on his or her investment in improvements. A comparative income and expense analysis showing the effect of this property improvement is illustrated in Figure 8.

Figure 8: COMPARATIVE INCOME AND EXPENSE ANALYSIS
(showing effect of capital expenditures)

	Property As Is	Property with Improvements
INCOME		
Rental	$41,000	$47,500
Other	2,000	4,000
Total	$43,000	$51,500
EXPENSES		
Real estate tax	$ 5,000	$ 5,000
Salaries	8,500	8,500
Utilities	4,000	4,500
Supplies	500	500
Maintenance and repairs	1,500	1,500
Insurance	500	500
Administration	200	200
Management @ 6% gross income	2,500	3,000
Reserves	300	300
Total	$23,000	$24,000
NET OPERATING INCOME BEFORE DEBT SERVICE	$20,000	$27,500
Debt service	$ 9,000	$ 9,000
CASH FLOW	$11,000	$18,500

Increase of $7,500 per year in cash flow. Initial investment of $15,000 to improve property will be returned within 2 years.

Different owners have different standards regarding an acceptable return on an investment. Some will not invest in an improvement which cannot be recouped in 3 years, while others may accept 7, 10, or even 15 years. Therefore, after preparing the analysis, the property manager should present the results to the owner for decision.

Presenting the Plan

After completing an operating budget, drawing up a 5-year forecast, and suggesting improvements, the manager must submit his or her proposal to the owner for review. The plan should be thoroughly and neatly prepared, for many owners will judge a property manager's ability by the appearance and accuracy of submitted documents. It is a good idea to submit this plan for review to a qualified colleague before presenting it to the owner.

Depending on the owner's objectives, he may decide to treat the manager's plan (and the property) in one of several ways. The owner may choose to authorize all suggested repairs and alterations in an effort to increase long-term income or reduce taxes. He may decide that only deferred maintenance should be performed in order to preserve the property's value without tying up additional working capital. Or the owner may feel that no changes at all should be made, preferring to get as much income as possible from the property over the short term without making any capital expenditures. This decision usually indicates that the owner lacks available resources, that a zoning change is pending, that the building has outlived its economic usefulness, or that the property will soon be used for other purposes, such as a highway or a new building. Many owners give a manager latitude to finance improvements from the proceeds of the property but are unwilling to invest any additional capital in the property. The management and improvement plan is shaped by this investment attitude and will typically be slow and evolutionary as a result.

Thus, the owner's objectives will be the deciding factor in the adoption of the management plan. If the manager cannot successfully execute a particular plan as it is outlined by the owner, the two should try to renegotiate it. One of the most challenging aspects of property management is that there is more than one answer to any given problem. When the manager and the owner are agreed upon a workable management plan for the property, it must be put into contract form so that the new management of the property can proceed.

SUMMARY

The condition of the real estate market is attuned to that of the business economy, which moves in 18- to 25-year cycles. During one full cycle, business activity progresses from a peak period in which demand exceeds supply, to a time of depressed transaction in which supply exceeds demand, and then gradually back to peak performance. One salient difference between the general business economy and the real estate market is that the economic cycle in real estate lags significantly behind the business cycle. Because of the time involved in designing, financing, constructing, and decorating a building, the real estate market's response to upward swings in the general economy is delayed.

During the downward trend in the cycle, most businesses and manufacturers can bring supply and demand back into balance by decreasing production. Because owners of real property cannot reduce the amount of leasable space in their buildings when demand falls and vacancy rates rise, the usual result is fierce competition for tenants, slashed rents, and a pronounced downward economic swing in the real estate sector.

A manager who can analyze the real estate market, recognize trends, and anticipate their effects will be able to shield the property from the impact of economic cycles. To develop an effective management plan, the property manager must conduct three specific studies, reconcile the data collected, and then formulate a proposal for the management of the property.

Regional and neighborhood analyses help the manager determine the optimum rental rate for the subject property. The *property analysis* provides information about the operating costs that can be expected for that property. Both the neighborhood analysis and the property analysis include a study of comparables that demonstrate how the subject property compares to the competition. This helps the manager to establish a rental schedule. When analyzing the *owner's goals,* the manager must consider the owner's capital resources, income needs, and profit orientation. Armed with this information the manager will be able to develop the current operating budget and 5-year forecast, which form the heart of the management plan.

The regional analysis generally includes demographic information about the area in which the subject property is located: population statistics and trends, major employers in the area, income and employment statistics, and large-scale supply and demand trends. The purpose of a neighborhood analysis is to determine the boundaries of the neighborhood and the predominant forms of land usage. The manager should also evaluate the available transportation and utility services in the area in terms of cost, convenience, and reliability. The local chamber of commerce can provide the manager with data on the number and types of businesses in the area, their volume of activity, and the general growth trend of the area, all of which are indicators of an area's economic health.

Understanding the supply and demand ratio in the neighborhood of the subject property helps the manager to predict whether demand will rise or fall and how fast the transition will occur. A study should be made of all similar existing space in the area, including building type and age, size of units, rental rates, and occupancy levels. The residential property manager can obtain employment and income statistics from the Census Bureau and other sources. These indicate the composition of the neighborhood population and serve as a basis for setting the rental schedule. An alert manager will also be aware of social and cultural organizations and facilities that might attract potential tenants.

The manager must reconcile all the pertinent data concerning the regional and neighborhood market with the specific nature of his or her property. Industrial property managers will be concerned primarily with transportation facilities for distribution of finished goods, heavy-duty or special utility services for manufacturing, a sufficient labor pool, an adequate source of raw materials, and zoning ordinances or other restrictions inhibiting growth. Managers of commercial property will pay particular attention to traffic patterns and counts, parking space, the median income of the population, and the location of competitors. The size of the average family unit, the average income level, and trends in population growth will be most significant to residential property managers. From this examination and correlation of information, the property manager can arrive at the optimum rental rates for space in that type of property in that particular neighborhood. The annual income for the property can be estimated from these figures.

The next step in developing the management plan is the property analysis. The manager must make a thorough on-site examination of the subject building, noting the number, size, and layout of the rental units. Then the manager should inspect the interior and exterior of the premises and any machinery or equipment used to operate the building. He or she should estimate the amount and cost of the staff, supplies, and additional equipment needed to perform routine maintenance, cleaning, and operating chores. Also noteworthy are any painting, major repairs, alterations, or replacements needed to make the premises competitive. Information on the cost of debt service and insurance premiums must be obtained from the owner. When the property analysis is complete, the manager will have a complete picture of the operating costs that can be expected for the subject property.

The objectives of the property owner must also be clear and set forth in writing, for they will determine what action is eventually taken on the management plan. Owners can be individuals, corporations, syndicates, financial institutions acting in the role of trustee, or government agencies. Most individual and corporate owners are profit-oriented, but some are interested in the tax shelter benefits provided by real estate depreciation allowances. Condominium owners, cooperative apartment corporations, and the government are usually concerned with maintaining the value of the property and providing decent housing for the resident-owners or tenants. Preservation of value and generation of a reasonable income stream are typical objectives of fiduciary trustees.

Keeping in mind the capital resources and income requirements of the owner (or owning body), the manager can then begin to develop the management plan. The first step is to draw up an *operating budget* for the property for the coming year, assuming that the building will remain in its present condition. This budget should be presented to the owner along with a *long-term forecast* and a *stabilized budget.* The long-term forecast predicts and averages income and expense over a suitable period, such as 5 years. When drawing up the 5-year forecast, the manager must use every available resource to anticipate future market trends in the area and to estimate increases in both operating costs and rental income. The forecast should demonstrate future cash flow benefits that the owner can derive.

When recommending any major capital expenditures for repairs, alterations, or improvements, the manager should give the owner a *comparative income and expense* and *capital expenditure analysis* showing the potential increase in income that would result from the proposed capital improvement. The comparative income and expense analysis also projects how long it will take to recoup the owner's initial capital expenditure and to begin to realize a profit on the investment in improvements.

The final decision on the management plan rests with the owner. One owner might decide to follow all the manager's recommendations for repairs or alterations in order to increase future profits; another might perform only deferred maintenance to preserve value; and still another might decide to make no repairs at all in order to avoid major capital expenditures.

If the owner challenges the plan submitted by the manager, it is up to the manager to explain the plan, negotiate with the owner, and modify the plan if necessary. When the owner and manager agree upon a workable future plan for the property, it must then be put into contract form.

QUESTIONS: CHAPTER 2

1. Cycles of the real estate market differ from those of the general business economy in that:

    I.   the general business economy is generally subject to more extreme oversupply and undersupply.
    II. trends in real estate lag significantly behind trends in the general economy.

    a. I only
    b. II only
    c. both I and II
    d. neither I nor II

2. List the five major characteristics that a property manager should assess in a neighborhood market analysis.

    a. _____   d. _____
    b. _____   e. _____
    c. _____

3. List three principal sources of information about the economy of a particular market area.

    a. _____
    b. _____
    c. _____

4. Supply and demand in a particular market area is most reliably predicted by:

    a. prevailing rental rates.
    b. occupancy rates.
    c. population statistics.
    d. new construction.

5. At the peak of the general business cycle:

    I.   supply surpasses demand.
    II. the value of the dollar is at its highest.

    a. I only
    b. II only
    c. both I and II
    d. neither I nor II

6. At the lowest point in the real estate rental market cycle:

    I.   vacancy rates are high.
    II. rents are beginning to increase.

    a. I only
    b. II only
    c. both I and II
    d. neither I nor II

7.   When more space is available than potential tenants demand, it indicates:

  a.   a demand market.
  b.   technical oversupply.
  c.   economic oversupply.
  d.   an upswing in the real estate market.

8.   When evaluating the data in a neighborhood market survey, an industrial property manager should pay special attention to:

  a.   traffic counts and patterns.
  b.   location of competitors.
  c.   median income level of population.
  d.   availability of raw materials.

9.   The purpose of a property analysis is to familiarize the manager with:

  I.   the condition of the building.
  II. the optimum rental rate.

  a.   I only   c.   both I and II
  b.   II only   d.   neither I nor II

10.   When evaluating the data in a neighborhood market survey, a residential property manager will be *most* concerned with:

  a.   opportunity for expansion.
  b.   special utility services.
  c.   traffic counts.
  d.   trends in population composition.

11.   The main objective of most investment property owners is:

  a.   positive cash flow.
  b.   tax shelter.
  c.   exchange benefits.
  d.   pride of ownership.

12.   Cooperative corporations are interested primarily in:

  I.   preserving the value of their investment.
  II. turning a profit.

  a.   I only   c.   both I and II
  b.   II only   d.   neither I nor II

13.   Preservation of the value of property is the primary interest of:

    I.   fiduciary institutions acting as trustees.
    II.   governmental agencies.

        a.   I only   c.   both I and II
        b.   II only   d.   neither I nor II

14.   Information for estimating operating expenses for a property must be obtained:

    I.   from the manager's property inspection.
    II.   from the owner.

        a.   I only   c.   both I and II
        b.   II only   d.   neither I nor II

15.   The management fee for the property indicated in the sample operating budget in Chapter 2 was charged on:

        a.   gross collectable rental income.
        b.   total adjusted anticipated revenue.
        c.   total adjusted revenue minus anticipated operating expenses.
        d.   annual cash flow.

16.   Components of the management plan that should be developed by the property manager include all but one of the following:

        a.   comparative income and expense analysis.
        b.   operating budget for one year.
        c.   5-year projection.
        d.   feasibility study.

17.   The determining factor in the acceptance or rejection of the management plan will be:

        a.   the property analysis.
        b.   the owner's objectives.
        c.   the neighborhood analysis.
        d.   the 5-year forecast.

18.   A local real estate economy may run counter to a nationwide economic trend because of:

    I.   employment levels in a large local industry.
    II.   overbuilding or shortage of a particular type of real estate, such as multifamily housing.

        a.   I only   c.   both I and II
        b.   II only   d.   neither I nor II

3
The Manager and the Owner

Once the property manager and the owner (or owning body) have agreed on principles, objectives, and a viable management plan, it is in the best interests of both parties to formalize their accord. The manager and the owner must work out the structure of their relationship, their specific responsibilities and liabilities, the scope of the manager's authority, fees, and the duration of the management agreement. In addition, the owner must turn over management records and other information to the manager to facilitate the operation of the property. The manager is expected to make every effort to open and maintain a clear line of communication with the owner.

NATURE OF THE RELATIONSHIP

Two basic relationships can exist between a property manager and the individual or corporate owner of a building: some are employer-employee arrangements, and the balance are principal-agent arrangements. Property managers in both categories are considered professionals, and their responsibilities are very similar.

Employer-Employee Relationship

The employer-employee relationship is most common to banks, colleges, large corporations, and other private institutions that require the services of a building manager for their properties. The employee-manager is directly responsible to the officers of the owner-employer corporation or institution, which may be the principal occupant of the building. Although no formalized contract is necessary in an employer-employee relationship, the issues set forth in a typical management contract between principal and agent must still be settled. The employee-manager's working relationship with the owner must be structured along the same lines as that of the property manager who operates as an agent. In lieu of a contract, the manager should obtain from the employing corporation written authorization to sign binding leases. This authorization is sometimes limited in the dollar amount or length of the lease, and many lessees, especially government agencies and corporations, request a copy of this authorization from the employee-manager.

Principal-Agent Relationship

The principal-agent relationship is created by a written contract signed by both parties, which empowers the property manager, as *agent,* to act on behalf of the owner, or *principal,* in certain situations. Specifically, the agent acts for the principal in order to bring him or her into legal relations with third parties.

Implicit in this relationship are certain legal and ethical considerations that the property manager must accord the owner. Legally, an agent has a fiduciary relationship with his or her principal. This is a confidential relationship requiring the highest degree of loyalty on the part of the agent. The property manager also has the duties of care, obedience, accounting, and notice.

Code of Ethics. The Institute of Real Estate Management has formulated its own code of ethics, based on the Code of Ethics of the NATIONAL ASSOCIATION OF REALTORS®, which outlines standards of business conduct for all Certified Property Managers. While all property managers are not CPMs, adherence to the general principles and spirit of the IREM code will help any property manager to establish and maintain a mutually satisfactory relationship with the owner of the premises and with others in the industry. Under the terms of the IREM code, the manager-agent pledges to act in the best interest of his or her principal and to handle all transactions involving the property with honesty and discretion. In essence, the property manager promises to uphold and promote the integrity of that occupation and the standards of the entire real estate profession. Many of the standards of conduct required of the agent under specific articles of the code have been incorporated in the terms of most management contracts.

State Statutes. Each state has various licensing laws and regulations governing the conduct of persons and organizations acting as real estate agents. While these laws apply mainly to sales of real estate, activities of those engaged in leasing, renting, or managing property for others are often included in the coverage of these laws. Property managers should investigate the statutes of the states where they manage property in order to be sure they are in compliance with those laws.

THE MANAGEMENT CONTRACT

Whether the property involved is a walkup apartment building, a highrise complex, an office building, or a shopping center, the responsibilities assumed by the manager are of sufficient importance to warrant a written acknowledgment of intent. A dated agreement signed by both the manager and the owner (or authorized representative of the owning body) defines the relationship between the parties, serves as a guide for the operation of the property, and provides a basis for the settlement of any future disputes.

The terms of management contracts are as varied as the types of real property and the forms of real estate ownership. Specific circumstances aside, most management contracts share certain common characteristics, or the following essential elements:

- identification of the parties and the property
- the period the contract is to run

- responsibilities of the manager
- responsibilities of the owner
- fees and leasing/sales commissions
- signatures of the parties

The standard IREM management agreement on the following pages illustrates the kinds of issues that must be resolved before the manager accepts responsibility for the property.

Identification of the Parties and the Property

Most management contracts begin with an identification of the parties to the agreement. The owner's name ought to appear on the contract exactly as it does on the title or deed to the property. If property is owned by a partnership, each partner's name should be stated in the contract and each should sign the document. When the property is owned by a corporation, the corporate name should appear on the contract, a duly authorized corporate officer should execute the agreement, and where required, the corporate seal should be affixed to the document. Corporate ownership is the most common situation the manager will encounter. When applicable, the management agency, rather than the specific individual who will be in charge of the property, should be listed on the contract. Licensing laws in many states require all listing and management contracts to be signed in the name of the broker. Laws in effect in the state where the property is located should be followed. If the manager is representing a management firm, the manager will sign as the authorized representative of the firm. Common practice is to have the manager place the firm's name alongside of his or her signature.

The street address of the property is often sufficient identification. Although a full legal description is not usually required, the property must be described fully enough so as to leave no doubt concerning its extent. With commercial property especially, it is important to supply the street address plus a careful description of the exact land area and both main and auxiliary buildings to be managed. Exclusions should also be noted. For example, if the owner of an office building that has a restaurant and bar on the first floor wants to deal directly with the restaurateur, the property description in the management contract should specifically exclude that particular area. If the property has a special name, as is frequently the case with highrise apartment complexes or shopping centers, that name should be specified in the contract.

Contract Period

In addition to identifying the owner, manager, and specific property involved, the contract must stipulate a term of service. There is no single standard term for a management contract. Its length is a function of the size of the property, the responsibilities delegated to the manager, and the future intentions of the owner or owning body.

Long-term contracts are uncommon. Owners are justifiably wary of entering into a lengthy legal agreement that allows no provision for cancellation. Owners who are thinking of selling their property in the near future would not want to hinder the

OWNER _____

and

AGENT _____

For Property located at

_____

_____

Beginning _____ 19 _____

Ending _____ 19 _____

MANAGEMENT AGREEMENT

IN CONSIDERATION of the covenants herein contained, _____
_____ (hereinafter called "OWNER), and _____
_____ (hereinafter called "AGENT"), agree as
follows:

1.   The OWNER hereby employs the AGENT exclusively to rent and manage the property
(hereinafter called the "Premises") known as _____

_____

upon the terms and conditions hereinafter set forth, for a term of _____ beginning on
the _____ day of _____, 19_____, and ending on the _____
day of _____, 19_____, and thereafter for yearly periods from
time to time, unless on or before _____ days prior to the date last above mentioned or on
or before _____ days prior to the expiration of any such renewal period, either party
hereto shall notify the other in writing that it elects to terminate this Agreement, in which case
this Agreement shall be thereby terminated on said last mentioned date. (See also Paragraph
6.3 below.)

2.   THE AGENT AGREES:

2.1   To accept the management of the Premises, to the extent, for the period, and upon
the terms herein provided and agrees to furnish the services of its organization for the rental
operation and management of the Premises.

2.2   To render a monthly statement of receipts, disbursements, and charges to the
following person(s) at the address(es) shown:

Name   Address
_____   _____

_____   _____

and to remit each month the net proceeds (provided AGENT is not required to make any
mortgage, escrow, or tax payment on the first day of the following month). AGENT will remit
the net proceeds or the balance thereof after making allowance for such payments to the
following persons, in the percentages specified, and at the addresses shown:

Name	Percentage	Address
_____	_____	_____
_____	_____	_____
_____	_____	_____

In case the disbursements and charges shall be in excess of the receipts, the OWNER agrees to pay such excess promptly, but nothing herein contained shall obligate the AGENT to advance its own funds on behalf of the OWNER.

2.3 To cause all employees of the AGENT who handle or are responsible for the safekeeping of any monies of the OWNER to be covered by a fidelity bond in an amount and with a company determined by the AGENT _____

3. THE OWNER AGREES:

To give the AGENT the following authority and powers (all or any of which may be exercised in the name of the OWNER) and agrees to assume all expenses in connection therewith:

3.1 To advertise the Premises or any part thereof; to display signs thereon and to rent the same; to cause references of prospective tenants to be investigated; to sign leases for terms not in excess of _____ years and to renew and/or cancel the existing leases and prepare and execute the new leases without additional charge to the OWNER; provided, however, that the AGENT may collect from tenants all or any of the following: a late rent administrative charge, a non-negotiable check charge, credit report fee, a subleasing administrative charge and/or broker's commission and need not account for such charges and/or commission to the OWNER; to terminate tenancies and to sign and serve such notices as are deemed needful by the AGENT; to institute and prosecute actions to oust tenants and to recover possession of the Premises; to sue for and recover rent; and, when expedient, to settle, compromise, and release such actions or suits, or reinstate such tenancies. OWNER shall reimburse AGENT for all expenses of litigation including attorneys' fees, filing fees, and court costs which AGENT does not recover from tenants. AGENT may select the attorney of its choice to handle such litigation.

3.2 To hire, discharge, and pay all engineers, janitors, and other employees; to make or cause to be made all ordinary repairs and replacements necessary to preserve the Premises in its present condition and for the operating efficiency thereof and all alterations required to comply with lease requirements, and to do decorating on the Premises; to negotiate contracts for nonrecurring items not exceeding $_____ and to enter into agreements for all necessary repairs, maintenance, minor alterations, and utility services; and to purchase supplies and pay all bills. AGENT shall secure the approval of the OWNER for any alterations of expenditures in excess of $_____ for any one item, except monthly or recurring operating charges and emergency repairs in excess of the maximum, if, in the opinion of the AGENT, such repairs are necessary to protect the property from damage or to maintain services to the tenants as called for by their tenancy.

3.3 To collect rents and/or assessments and other items due or to become due and give receipts therefor and to deposit all funds collected hereunder in the AGENT's custodial account.

3.4 To handle tenants' security deposits and to comply, on the OWNER's behalf, with applicable state or local laws concerning the AGENT's responsibility for security deposits and interest thereon, if any.

3.5 To execute and file all returns and other instruments and do and perform all acts required of the OWNER as an employer with respect to the Premises under the Federal Insurance Contributions Acts, the Federal Unemployment Tax Act, and Subtitle C of the Internal Revenue Code of 1954 with respect to wages paid by the AGENT on behalf of the OWNER and under any similar federal and state law now or hereafter in force (and in connection therewith the OWNER agrees upon request to promptly execute and deliver to the AGENT all necessary powers of attorney, notices of appointment, and the like).

3.6 The AGENT shall not be required to advance any monies for the care or management of said property, and the OWNER agrees to advance all monies necessary therefor. If the AGENT shall elect to advance any money in connection with the property, the OWNER agrees to reimburse the AGENT forthwith and hereby authorizes the AGENT to deduct such advances from any monies due the OWNER. The AGENT shall, upon instruction from the OWNER, impound reserves each month for the payment of real estate taxes, insurance, or any other special expenditure. In addition, the OWNER agrees to establish a permanent Operating Reserve Account with the AGENT in the amount of $ _____

4. THE OWNER FURTHER AGREES:

4.1 To indemnify, defend, and save the AGENT harmless from all suits in connection with the Premises and from liability for damage to property and injuries to or death of any employee or other person whomsoever, and to carry at his (its) own expense public liability, elevator liability (if elevators are part of the equipment of the Premises), and workmen's compensation insurance naming the OWNER and the AGENT and adequate to protect their interests and in form, substance, and amounts reasonably satisfactory to the AGENT, and to furnish to the AGENT certificates evidencing the existence of such insurance. Unless the OWNER shall provide such insurance and furnish such certificate within _____ days from the date of this Agreement, the AGENT may, but shall not be obligated to, place said insurance and charge the cost thereof to the account of the OWNER. All such insurance policies shall provide that the AGENT shall receive thirty (30) days' written notice prior to cancellation of the policy.

4.2 To pay all expenses incurred by the AGENT, including, but not limited to, reasonable attorneys' fees and AGENT's costs and time in connection with any claim, proceeding, or suit involving an alleged violation by the AGENT or the OWNER, or both, of any law pertaining to fair employment, fair credit reporting, environmental protection, rent control, taxes, or fair housing, including, but not limited to, any law prohibiting, or making illegal, discrimination on the basis of race, sex, creed, color, religion, national origin, or mental or physical handicap, provided, however, that the OWNER shall not be responsible to the AGENT for any such expenses in the event the AGENT is finally adjudicated to have personally, and not in a representative capacity, violated any such law. Nothing contained herein shall obligate the AGENT to employ counsel to represent the OWNER in any such proceeding or suit, and the OWNER may elect to employ counsel to represent the OWNER in any such proceeding or suit. The OWNER also agrees to pay reasonable expenses (or an apportioned amount of such expenses where other employers of AGENT also benefit from the expenditure) incurred by the AGENT in obtaining legal advice regarding compliance with any law affecting the premises or activities related thereto.

4.3 To indemnify, defend, and save the AGENT harmless from all claims, investigations, and suits, or from actions or failures to act of the OWNER, with respect to any alleged or actual violation of state or federal labor laws, it being expressly agreed and understood that as between the OWNER and the AGENT, all persons employed in connection with the Premises are employees of the OWNER, not the AGENT. However, it shall be the responsibility of the AGENT to comply with all applicable state or federal labor laws. The OWNER's obligation under this paragraph 4.3 shall include the payment of all settlements, judgments, damages, liquidated damages, penalties, forfeitures, back pay awards, court costs, litigation expense, and attorneys' fees.

4.4 To give adequate advance written notice to the AGENT if the OWNER desires that the AGENT make payment, out of the proceeds from the premises, of mortgage indebtedness, general taxes, special assessments, or fire, steam boiler, or any other insurance premiums. In no event shall the AGENT be required to advance its own money in payment of any such indebtedness, taxes, assessments, or premiums.

5. THE OWNER AGREES TO PAY THE AGENT EACH MONTH:

5.1 FOR MANAGEMENT: _____ per month or _____ percent (_____%) of the monthly gross receipts from the operation of the Premises during the period this Agreement remains in full force and effect, whichever is the greater amount. Gross receipts are all amounts received from the operation of the Premises including, but not limited to, rents, parking fees, deposits, laundry income, and fees.

5.2 APARTMENT LEASING _____

_____

_____

5.3 COMMERCIAL LEASING _____

_____

_____

5.4 MODERNIZATION (REHABILITATION/CONSTRUCTION) _____

_____

_____

5.5 FIRE RESTORATION _____

_____

_____

_____

5.6 OTHER ITEMS OF MUTUAL AGREEMENT _____

_____

_____

_____

6. IT IS MUTUALLY AGREED THAT:

6.1 The OWNER expressly withholds from the AGENT any power or authority to make any structural changes in any building or to make any other major alterations or additions in or to any such building or equipment therein, or to incur any expense chargeable to the OWNER other than expenses related to exercising the express powers above vested in the AGENT without the prior written direction of the following person:

Name   Address

_____   _____

except such emergency repairs as may be required because of danger to life or property or which are immediately necessary for the preservation and safety of the Premises or the safety of the tenants and occupants thereof or are required to avoid the suspension of any necessary service to the Premises.

6.2 The AGENT does not assume and is given no responsibility for compliance of any building on the Premises or any equipment therein with the requirements of any statute, ordinance, law, or regulation of any governmental body or of any public authority or official thereof having jurisdiction, except to notify the OWNER promptly or forward to the OWNER promptly any complaints, warnings, notices, or summonses received by it relating to such matters. The OWNER represents that to the best of his (its) knowledge the Premises and such equipment comply with all such requirements and authorizes the AGENT to disclose the ownership of the Premises to any such officials and agrees to indemnify and hold harmless the AGENT, its representatives, servants, and employees, of and from all loss, cost, expense, and liability whatsoever which may be imposed on them or any of them by reason of any present or future violation or alleged violation of such laws, ordinances, statutes, or regulations.

6.3   In the event it is alleged or charged that any building on the Premises or any equipment therein or any act or failure to act by the OWNER with respect to the Premises or the sale, rental, or other disposition thereof fails to comply with, or is in violation of, any of the requirements of any constitutional provision, statute, ordinance, law, or regulation of any governmental body or any order or ruling of any public authority or official thereof having or claiming to have jurisdiction thereover, and the AGENT, in its sole and absolute discretion, considers that the action or position of the OWNER or registered managing agent with respect thereto may result in damage or liability to the AGENT, the AGENT shall have the right to cancel this Agreement at any time by written notice to the OWNER of its election so to do, which cancellation shall be effective upon the service of such notice. Such notice may be served personally or by registered mail, on or to the person named to receive the AGENT's monthly statement at the address designated for such person as provided in Paragraph 2.2 above, and if served by mail shall be deemed to have been served when deposited in the mails. Such cancellation shall not release the indemnities of the OWNER set forth in Paragraphs 4 and 6.2 above and shall not terminate any liability or obligation of the OWNER to the AGENT for any payment, reimbursement, or other sum of money then due and payable to the AGENT hereunder.

7.   This Agreement may be cancelled by OWNER before the termination date specified in paragraph 1 on not less than ———————— days' prior written notice to the AGENT, provided that such notice is accompanied by payment to the AGENT of a cancellation fee in an amount equal to ———————————% of the management fee that would accrue over the remainder of the stated term of the Agreement. For this purpose the monthly management fee for the remainder of the stated term shall be presumed to be the same as that of the last month prior to service of the notice of cancellation.

8.   The OWNER shall pay or reimburse the AGENT for any sums of money due it under this Agreement for services for actions prior to termination, notwithstanding any termination of this Agreement. All provisions of this Agreement that require the OWNER to have insured or to defend, reimburse, or indemnify the AGENT (including, but not limited to, Paragraphs 4.1, 4.2, and 4.3) shall survive any termination and, if AGENT is or becomes involved in any proceeding or litigation by reason of having been the OWNER's AGENT, such provisions shall apply as if this Agreement were still in effect. The parties understand and agree that the AGENT may withhold funds for thirty (30) days after the end of the month in which this Agreement is terminated to pay bills previously incurred but not yet invoiced and to close accounts.

This Agreement shall be binding upon the successors and assigns of the AGENT and their heirs, administrators, executors, successors, and assigns of the OWNER.

IN WITNESS WHEREOF, the parties hereto have affixed or caused to be affixed their respective signatures this ——————— day of ————————————, 19———————

WITNESSES: OWNER:

_____   _____

_____   _____

_____   _____

                                                              AGENT:

                                                              Firm _____

_____   By _____

Submitted by

POWER OF ATTORNEY

KNOW ALL MEN BY THESE PRESENTS, THAT

_____
(Name)

_____ located at
(State whether individual, partnership, corporation, etc.)

_____ has made,
(Address)

constituted, and appointed, and, by these presents does hereby make, constitute,

and appoint, _____ , a resident of

the United States, whose address is _____ (its)

true and lawful attorney for (it) (me) in (its) (my) name, place, and stead to

execute and to file any Tax Returns due on or after _____

_____

under the provisions of the Social Security Act, now in force or future amendments thereto.

Dated at_____this_____ day of_____ , 19 _____

_____
Signature of Taxpayer

_____
Title

Executed in the presence of:

_____
Signature of Taxpayer

_____
Title

_____
Signature of Taxpayer

_____
Witness

_____
Title

_____
Witness

Acknowledged before me this _____ day of _____ , 19 _____

NOTARIAL
SEAL

_____

prospect of sale by the burden of a long-term management contract that may not be canceled.

On the other hand, the management agency that assumes responsibility for a large new property, exerting a considerable initial effort to lease the premises and set up a management system, will desire sufficient protection to compensate for its extra effort. Therefore, management agencies will usually seek a *minimum* one-year contract period. The amount of additional time requested under the terms of the contract will depend on how much initial effort is needed to take over the management of the premises and obtain a profitable lease-up rate.

For these reasons, clauses in standard management contracts leave the length of the agreement open so that a mutually satisfactory number of years can be inserted in the appropriate blank. Contracts may also contain a provision for automatic renewal on a yearly basis unless notice of termination is given within the period set forth in the contract. Both the owner and the management agent are allowed to terminate the agreement by giving the appropriate notice. Regardless of its term and other stipulations, the management agreement must contain suitable provisions for the time and method of termination.

The agreement may be terminated by the agent sooner than otherwise allowed by the contract if he or she suffers damages or liability as a result of the owner's failure to comply with the requirements of any applicable statute, law, or governmental regulation. In such cases, cancellation takes effect when the owner is served with notice of the agent's intent to terminate the agreement. Notice may be served in person or by registered mail to the address listed on the contract. Cancellation is considered to be effective when the notice is deposited in the mail. Termination by the agent due to an owner's illegal acts does not release the owner from his or her obligations under the contract terms.

Procedures for future amendments should be built into the management agreement in order to adapt the agreement to changed circumstances.

Management Responsibilities

Monthly Reports and Disbursements. A big part of the agent's job is the preparation of a monthly earnings statement itemizing income and expense for the owner's property. The management contract should specify the name and address of the person, corporation, or board of directors (in the case of a cooperative or condominium) to receive the report as well as the date on which it is to be submitted. The names, addresses, and percentage amounts for all recipients to whom the agent must dispense monthly payments are usually listed in the contract at this point.

The agent's obligations in months when disbursements exceed receipts should be clarified. Under some contracts, the manager is authorized to withhold a certain sum of money in reserve to meet expenses that may come due between the time of disbursements and the time the next monthly rental income flow begins. The amount of this reserve fund should be proportional to the size of the property.

Common practice does not dictate that the agent advance his or her own funds to cover a deficiency.

As a rule, employees of the agent who handle funds have to be covered by a surety bond, obtained at the manager's expense. Also, most contracts and many state laws require the manager to maintain a separate bank account for the owner's funds. That is, the owner's funds should never be commingled with the agent's. If the manager works for more than one owner, it is wise to use an individual account for each client. If the manager administers more than one property for the same owner, separate accounts are still an inexpensive and effective way to simplify accounting and book-keeping.

Powers for Renting, Operating, and Managing Premises. The terms of the contract should list the agent's authority for leasing, collecting rentals, terminating tenancies, returning security deposits, evicting tenants, and bringing legal action for recovery of lost rents. The most notable of these powers is the agent's authority to sign leases, for the statute of frauds in most states does not consider an oral lease agreement of more than a certain duration, usually one year, to be valid. Some owners insert a clause in the contract limiting the agent's authority to sign leases to a certain dollar amount or to a maximum period, such as five years or less in the case of many commercial properties. Agents for residential properties generally have the authority to sign standard leases for the maximum term established by the owner's policy.

Expenditures for maintenance personnel and services are an inherent feature of property management, but the amount the agent may incur without consulting the owner must be stated in the contract. Usually, a management agreement will include a clause similar to the following:

> The agent agrees to secure the approval of the owner for all expenses in excess of $_____ for any one item, except monthly recurring operating charges, and/or emergency repairs in excess of the maximum if, in the opinion of the agent, such repairs are necessary to protect the property from damage or to maintain services to the tenants as called for by their tenancy.

Some contracts also contain a clause giving the agent the power to enter into contracts not to exceed a certain amount for utility services, rubbish removal, window cleaning, or other recommended services. For the protection of the agent, clauses like this should carry a caveat binding the owner (or owning body) to responsibility for any such agreements upon termination of the contract.

Advertising is considered part of the normal operating expense of the property and, as such, is usually charged to the building and absorbed by the owner. However, an owner who does not want the agent to exceed a reasonable level of expense for the needs of the property might set a ceiling on the advertising budget. A clause similar to the limitation on operating expenditures can be used to control advertising expenses.

The terms of the management contract should also specify the agent's powers for the hiring and firing of maintenance personnel for the premises. The resolution of this question will vary from contract to contract; as a general rule, though, if the manager is to be responsible for the work done by building employees, he or she should have the power to hire and supervise them also. Employees often develop greater loyalty to the manager if they can look upon him or her as the prime authority figure. A manager who is permitted to hire the operating staff is usually expected not only to obtain liability and workmen's compensation insurance for building personnel but also to file returns and other reports required of the owner-employer by federal and state governments. The manager who hires and supervises employees must further decide whether the salaries of building employees and clerical staff will be charged to the building or to management operations. Since this can have a major impact on financial statements and returns, it too should be stated in the contract.

Owner's Responsibilities

The management agreement should spell out the owner's (or owning body's) responsibility for miscellaneous management expenses. It should contain a clear statement designating who is responsible for each item of management and maintenance expenses, including:

- payroll: maintenance, security, and supervision
- insurance: employee and fidelity premiums
- purchasing: bookkeeping and auditing
- building: office telephone
- advertising for tenants
- commissions to outside leasing agents

If this matter has not been dealt with previously, another provision in the management contract should clarify whether the manager or the owner is responsible for hiring and supervising maintenance employees. Whatever the terms of the agreement, the responsibilities of both the owner and the manager should be explicitly set forth.

Some owners reserve the right to hire, supervise, and fire employees working at the property, which is particularly true when building personnel have been employed by the owner for a long period of time. Property managers will find this a difficult arrangement, requiring very skillful management in order for the manager to be effective. If the owner reserves this right, the property manager should seek protection through a clause to the effect that building personnel are employees of the owner, not the agent. This clause should state explicitly the owner's obligation to pay all settlements, judgments, damages, penalties, back-pay awards, court costs, attorney's fees, and other costs arising from litigation of claims, investigations, or suits arising from alleged or actual violation of state or federal labor laws. The contract should also specify that the owner will carry, at his or her own expense, sufficient liability and workmen's compensation insurance. The owner (or owning body) and the manager-agent should be named as coinsureds on these policies, and the owner should provide the manager with certificates of evidence of such coverage. For the manager's protection, a stipulation should be included that the manager may purchase such insurance at the owner's expense, if certificates of coverage are not produced within a reasonable period. It is in the manager's best interests to review the terms of these policies, for the owner usually looks to the manager to work closely with the insurance agency to settle any claims that might arise.

The owner should agree in the contract to give the agent a schedule of payments that must be made for debt service, taxes, special assessments, or insurance premiums. The manager can then budget or establish reserves for these items.

Management Fees of Independent Agent Managers

Management assignments differ, as do the responsibilities of various managers. Apartment buildings do not pose the same management problems as office buildings, and inner-city property has different management needs than suburban property. Nonetheless, all contracts should specify the amount of the fee to be paid, when it is to be paid, and the manner of payment. Although there is no universal rule for establishing fees, two basic formulas will be presented in Chapter 10.

Flat Fee Versus Percentage Fee. Circumstances will dictate whether the management fee is to be paid by the flat-fee or the percentage-of-gross-income method of compensation. A flat fee often proves disadvantageous to the manager-agent, since it can be increased only by negotiation with the owner or owning body. The percentage fee, on the other hand, will increase if the manager improves the income of the building and decrease if the building revenue drops. Therefore, a minimum fee per unit or per account is sometimes established even though the management contract calls for a percentage fee.

Because low-rental units and smaller properties often require as much management time as larger, higher-income complexes, an equitable management fee may represent a higher percentage of the income on a smaller property than it would on a larger property. If the agent does not have a minimum guaranteed fee, he or she might either spend too much time on property that does not warrant such attention in terms of its return to the manager, or neglect a property that needs attention simply because it does not pay enough. A manager's legal and professional responsibility and liability as a fiduciary are the same regardless of the amount of compensation. In fact, a gratuitous agent may be held liable for negligence in failing to perform a duty. The manager should clearly define the services to be rendered in managing a property, especially when dealing with a property with a marginal financial return.

Leasing Fees. Another issue that must be addressed when setting the management fee is the possibility of a separate fee for leasing activities. A single rate of compensation usually covers all the manager's activities, but sometimes the owner will pay an extra amount for the execution of a new lease.

It is important to remember that the management agent is often not the sole leasing agent for the property, although he or she bears full responsibility for maintaining the premises. This is especially true for commercial property. Under the separate leasing fee arrangement, if another broker places a tenant in the building, the leasing fee is either split between the property manager and the leasing broker or wholly retained by the leasing broker. In some cases, the parties may agree that the owner will pay an additional amount when an outside broker or agent is involved. If the managing agent receives a single rate of compensation, and another broker places a tenant in the property, the leasing broker might receive a portion of the property manager's commission or a separate fee paid by the owner in addition to the manager's standard fee. Again, prior agreement between the parties will dictate the method of compensation.

In case the owner wants to terminate the contract prior to its scheduled cancellation date, the manager who is paid by the separate fee system should see to it that the contract contains a clause providing adequate compensation for the leases the manager has already negotiated. Under this clause, the owner will agree to pay half of the rate for the balance of the lease term negotiated by the manager. The owner is thus able to terminate the management agreement upon service of proper notice, and the agent still receives payment for negotiating leases on behalf of the owner.

TAKEOVER PROCEDURES

Once the contract between the owner (or owning body) and the management agent has been signed, the transfer of responsibilities for the property should be expedited. The owner must provide the manager or management agency with all data necessary for efficient operation of the property. A takeover checklist for residential property, including a partial list of information needed by the manager, is shown beginning on the next page.

The manager should know the owner's (or owning body's) name, address, and telephone number, social security number, and state employment number, as well as the name, address, and telephone number of the owner's attorney, accountant, insurance broker, and any other consultants for the property. If the property is new, the manager should have the name of the architect and the construction firm as well as a complete set of "as built" building plans and specifications. Data concerning financing for the property, which must be supplied by the owner, should include the name and address of any mortgagees, as well as mortgagors under any assumed mortgages on the property, and the amount and due date of loan payments. To calculate the expected income from the property, the manager must have a listing of all rental units, layout plans, the names of the present tenants, copies of all leases, a schedule of rental rates for the space, the current dates to which rents have been paid, any present delinquencies, and the sources and amounts of additional income. In many cases, the manager will have to prepare these schedules from basic documents since some owners do not keep complete and well-organized records.

Operating costs and general maintenance of the property cannot be properly regulated unless the manager is supplied with copies of current real estate tax bills, existing insurance policies, and the accounts payable ledger. The owner (or authorized representative of the owning corporation) and the manager should study the accounts payable ledger when the management agreement is executed and agree upon each party's specific liabilities for expenses. Some owners prefer to turn over all responsibility, including tax bills and mortgage payments, to the manager; others insist upon paying certain expenses themselves. Unpaid bills should be tended to, and the parties should set an exact date on which the manager will become responsible for paying expenses from his or her allotted funds. The owner should also furnish copies of all contracts for service, employment records, and federal and state employment reports. The manager must obtain the names, addresses, and telephone numbers of service contractors such as plumbers, electricians, suppliers, and on-site employees. Wages,

RESIDENTIAL PROPERTY TAKEOVER CHECKLIST

Property address: _____

Title held as follows: _____

Owner's name: _____

Address: _____ Phone: _____

Original statements and vouchers sent to: _____
_____

Additional statements to: _____

Property identification number: _____

Owner's attorney: _____

Owner's accountant: _____

Owner's insurance broker: _____

Construction firm: _____

Architect: _____

Copies of plans and specifications to: _____

Mortgagor: _____

Amount and due date of loan payments: _____

Washer and dryer service agency: _____

Percentage to building: _____

Electric account numbers: _____

Gas account numbers: _____

Water account numbers: _____

Scavenger service: _____

Exterminator service: _____

Other contractors: _____

_____

_____

CHECKLIST—Cont.

☐ Secure all employment records.

☐ Obtain copies of prior tax payments on employees.

☐ Secure current real estate tax bills.

☐ Power of attorney for taxes.

☐ Review accounts payable ledger.

Secure current list of all rents, including:

☐ Building number

☐ Apartment size

☐ Rental rates

☐ Names of present tenants

☐ Copies of all leases

☐ Special lease clauses

☐ Security deposits

☐ Vacancies

pay periods, social security number, and fringe benefits for each employee should be listed in the records turned over to the manager by the owner.

In some instances, the owner also furnishes a working capital fund to be applied to operating expenses for the property. In other cases, the working capital must be derived from current rental collections as the new manager takes over the building's assets and liabilities; this can be done by holding back the profits from the first few months' operation for contingency reserves.

After receiving the necessary information from the owner, the manager must set up accounting records and give notice of the takeover to all suppliers, service contractors, on-site employees, and tenants. The manager should personally inspect every inch of the property as part of the takeover procedure.

CONTINUING OWNER-MANAGER RELATIONS

Having assumed responsibility for the property, the manager must then maintain a mutually satisfactory relationship with the owner. The owner (or authorized representative of the owning body) should get to know the person or persons who will actually manage the property. This advice may seem superfluous, since the management agent and the owner (or owner's representative) negotiated and signed the contract. However, in many large management firms corporate officers execute the contracts and then assign separate account executives to handle the individual properties. In these cases, it is wise to introduce the owner to the specific account executive for that property. From this point on, only one member of the management firm should deal with the owner. This avoids the confusion and ill will that can arise when several people take problems and conflicting opinions to the owner. The account executive—the one who is most responsible for the property—can build a smooth and profitable working relationship between the owner and the management firm by being fully apprised of the particulars of the premises.

Monthly Reports

The principal means of regular communication between the manager and the owner or owning corporation is the monthly earnings report. This report to the owner usually includes rental receipts, miscellaneous income, gross income, an itemized list of all disbursements and operating expenses, total expenses for the month, cash on hand at the beginning of the month, amount forwarded to the principal (owner), and cash balance on hand. Monthly income and expense reports will be treated at some length in Chapter 9, which includes a sample report form. The manager should also submit a list of delinquent accounts and inform the owner of lawsuits or other events pertaining to the fiscal affairs of the property. This information can be noted either in the monthly report or in an accompanying letter.

In fact, the report should always be accompanied by a letter that demonstrates the manager's continuing personal interest in the property. In routine months, this cover letter will probably say nothing more than that operations for the period were normal. When the report deviates from the owner's expectations, the manager should explain unusual items in either the expense or income columns. If the normal income is lower than the owner anticipates, it is likely that he or she will think that the manager has failed in some way unless the manager offers a reasonable, clear, and convincing explanation of the market trends or other controlling factors. If the monthly revenue is greater than expected, the manager should tactfully explain how his or her management expertise resulted in the increase, if that is, in fact, the case.

Above all, the monthly report should be honest and intelligent, so as to assure the owner that the manager understands how all the variables interact to affect the revenue from the property.

Personal Contact

Personal contact with the owner or owner's representative can be made by a short visit or a telephone call. Letters can be used to reach an owner who is out of town and to confirm decisions already reached through personal discussions or telephone conversations.

The frequency with which the manager should contact the owner is dictated by the urgency of the circumstances and by the personal preference of the owner. Some owners hire management firms for the sole purpose of relieving themselves of all duties and decisions arising from property ownership. The monthly contact provided by the statement of earnings and supplemental information will be sufficient for them; in fact, anything beyond this might be viewed as a nuisance. Other owners only want to avoid the burden of soliciting rentals, collecting rents, handling tenant complaints, and other daily management functions. The delegation of these routine responsibilities to the manager does not mean that the owners wish to be excluded from all concerns of property ownership. In fact, owners in this category most want to take an active part in major decisions, especially those requiring a large outlay of capital, and should be consulted.

Effective communication is only one side of the business equation. The manager's ability to care for the property, coupled with the good will arising from personal contact with the owner, will build a lasting and mutually profitable business relationship between the parties. If the property manager demonstrates the skills and techniques contained in this book, the owner will be assured of the manager's competence and professionalism.

SUMMARY

When the principles, capabilities, and objectives of the manager and owner are in accord, as set forth in the management plan, the parties are ready to structure their relationship. They may enter into one of two relationships: employer-employee or principal-agent.

Banks, colleges, and large corporations that require a building manager to operate the properties under their ownership usually enter into an employer-employee arrangement with a manager. The principal-agent relationship between an independent agent property manager and an owner is created by a written contract signed by both parties. This contract confers on the manager certain powers to act as *agent* on behalf of the owner, or *principal*. Implicit in this relationship are certain legal and ethical considerations due to the owner from the manager. As agent for the owner, the manager must be loyal and pledge to act in the best interest of his or her principal and to handle all transactions in regard to the property with honesty and discretion.

Most management contracts share six basic characteristics and specify the duties and details of management operations that must be decided before responsibility for the property is transferred to the manager.

Most contracts begin with an *identification* of the property and the parties to the agreement. The owner's name should appear on the contract as it does on the title to the property. Each owner in a partnership should be listed in the contract and should sign the agreement. For corporate-owned property, the name of the corporation should appear on the contract, a duly authorized corporate officer should execute the agreement, and the corporate seal should be affixed to the document. When the property manager is an employee of a management firm, the agency name should appear on the contract with the manager signing as authorized representative. A legal description of the premises is not usually required, but an accurate identification is essential.

Most management contracts set forth a specific *term for the agreement.* The length of the contract term varies with the size of the property, the manager's responsibilities, and the future intentions of the parties. While long-term contracts are rare, the term should be of sufficient length to compensate the management agency adequately for its efforts. Management contracts usually have open-term clauses so that a mutually satisfactory number of years can be inserted in the space provided. Many contracts also include clauses providing for automatic one-year renewal, unless notice of termination is given within the stated period. Suitable provisions regarding the time and method of termination of the management agreement should be specified in the contract.

Any properly drawn contract will outline the *responsibilities of the management agency.* The primary duties of management are to provide the owner with a monthly statement of earnings and to make appropriate disbursements. The report should carry the name and address of its recipient; the due date; and the names, addresses, and percentage amounts for all recipients of monthly disbursements. The manager's obligations in months during which expenses exceed income should be spelled out. The manager's own funds are not usually used to cover shortages.

The contract must define the scope of the manager's power to rent and operate the premises. The agreement should set forth clearly the manager's authority to sign leases and to make expenditures for normal operation of the premises without consulting the owner. The manager's role and financial limit in contracting for utility services, rubbish removal, or other maintenance services should be specified. Managers who enjoy the authority to hire and fire building personnel also have the responsibility to obtain liability and workmen's compensation insurance. When the *owner* retains this authority, it is then his or her responsibility to purchase liability and workmen's compensation insurance. In any event, the owner and the management agency (or agent) should be named as coinsureds, and the manager should receive copies of all policies.

As with contract length, there is no universal formula for the computation of *management fees* for independent agent managers. Some contracts call for flat fees of a specified amount, while others provide that the manager be paid a certain percentage of the gross collectable income from the property as compensation. Although the basic flat or percentage fee usually applies to all services rendered, an additional fee is sometimes paid to the manager for his or her leasing activities. The contract should clearly state the amount of the fee, when it is to be paid, and in what manner.

The transfer of responsibilities for the property should take place as soon as possible after the contract between the owner and manager has been *signed.* To facilitate this change, the owner should give the manager the names, addresses, and telephone numbers of all persons involved in the affairs of the property, along with the owner-employer's social security number or tax I.D. number, the employee record files, and all service contracts. The manager should also have a listing of all current tenants, rent schedules, and rental units, plus copies of leases, layout plans, income records, current tax bills, insurance policies, and outstanding bills. The owner may establish a fund of working capital to cover operating costs or authorize the manager to withhold the first few months' profits for a reserve fund.

The property manager has to stay in touch with the owner and usually does so through the monthly earnings statement. This statement should always be accompanied by a cover letter explaining any unusual items in either the expense or income columns. The cover letter demonstrates the manager's personal interest in the property and knowledge of how market variables interact to affect the revenue from the property. Visits and phone calls are sometimes necessary, depending upon the urgency of the situation and the personal preference of the owner. Letters can generally be used to confirm decisions reached through telephone conversations or personal visits.

QUESTIONS: CHAPTER 3

1. A written contract is absolutely necessary to establish the following relationship(s) between owner and manager:

   I.   employee-employer.
   II. agent-principal.

       a. I only   c. both I and II
       b. II only   d. neither I nor II

2. Which of the following is *not* a common characteristic of management agreements?

       a. names of parties to the agreement
       b. provision for monthly reports
       c. specification of management fees
       d. long-term contract period

3. The management agreement should always include:

   I.   provision for termination.
   II. a legal description of the property.

       a. I only   c. both I and II
       b. II only   d. neither I nor II

4. A property manager acting as an agent:

   I.   owes care, loyalty, obedience, accounting, and notice to the principal.
   II. should maintain a separate bank account for the owner's funds.

       a. I only   c. both I and II
       b. II only   d. neither I nor II

5. A property manager's agreement provides for a leasing fee plus $13,000 per year for managerial services. This indicates:

       a. that an outside leasing agent is always used.
       b. a single rate of compensation.
       c. a flat-fee arrangement.
       d. a percentage fee situation.

6. A percentage fee is preferable to a flat fee:

   I.   just after the real estate cycle has peaked.
   II. when the agent can significantly increase the revenue of the building.

       a. I only   c. both I and II
       b. II only   d. neither I nor II

7.   As responsibility for the property is transferred to the manager, special attention must be paid to:

    a.   the accounts payable ledger.
    b.   mortgage payments.
    c.   sources of additional income besides rental.
    d.   a start-up cash fund.

8.   A monthly earnings report submitted by the manager to the owner:

    I.   is the most regular form of contact between the parties.
    II.   should always be accompanied by a personal letter.

    a.   I only   c.   both I and II
    b.   II only   d.   neither I nor II

9.   Letters from the property manager to the owner or owner's representative:

    I.   should be sent at least once a week.
    II.   can confirm decisions reached over the telephone.

    a.   I only   c.   both I and II
    b.   II only   d.   neither I nor II

10.   The monthly reports to the owner should include:

    I.   itemization of income and expense.
    II.   cash balance on hand.

    a.   I only   c.   both I and II
    b.   II only   d.   neither I nor II

11.   List the six basic characteristics of most management agreements.

    a.   _____   d.   _____
    b.   _____   e.   _____
    c.   _____   f.   _____

12.   The property manager for a new building will usually:

    I.   desire a long-term agreement.
    II.   be furnished an operating budget by the owner.

    a.   I only   c.   both I and II
    b.   II only   d.   neither I nor II

13. If a property owner violates any applicable law or regulation, the property manager:

   a. may sue for damages.
   b. should, if possible, terminate the agreement according to the provisions of the management contract.
   c. must report the owner to the Institute of Real Estate Management.
   d. may cancel the contract immediately upon serving the owner with notice of intent.

14. When disbursements exceed receipts for a certain month, the management agreement will usually provide that the manager:

   a. advance funds to cover the deficit.
   b. petition the owner to make up the deficit.
   c. stave off creditors until the next rental payments come in.
   d. pay costs from a reserve fund established previously.

15. Good management practice includes maintaining separate bank accounts:

   I. for each owner the manager is employed by.
   II. for each individual property of an owner.

   a. I only   c. both I and II
   b. II only   d. neither I nor II

16. Under what conditions would most state real estate licensing laws require a property manager to hold a license?

   I. employee of a company managing only its own property.
   II. agent of a company managing property for several owners.

   a. I only   c. both I and II
   b. II only   d. neither I nor II

4
Marketing Real Property

Developing income from a property is one of the manager's two major functions. The manager's knowledge of the form and nature of various lease agreements will be of little practical use unless potential tenants are actively being attracted to the property and the space is being skillfully shown. It is essential that the manager be adept at marketing available space.

The activities involved in a complete marketing effort can be grouped into three categories:

- advertising campaigns
- promotional efforts
- personal selling activities

Advertising refers to the media and marketing methods available to stimulate desire and action on the part of potential residents, commercial enterprises, and industrial firms. Promotional efforts are used to obtain publicity without paying direct advertising costs. Promotion includes good public relations, cooperation with outside brokers, and periodic press releases. Selling activities relate to direct personal contact with prospective tenants, from showing the property to signing the lease. Each of these activities contributes to the property manager's goal of rapid rental to a good clientele at a profitable rate.

MARKETING STRATEGY

The first step toward the manager's goals is an effective marketing campaign. As a rule, a good product backed by a well-designed advertising and promotional program will sell faster in the marketplace and for a higher price than its average competitor. In other words, well-presented quality property has a better rental rate than similar but poorly marketed space. When the real estate climate is favorable, good effectively marketed property can even be rented at a premium rate. The manager's strategy for achieving marketing goals is shaped by three major factors:

- the type of property
- supply and demand
- available financial resources

Type of Property

The kind of property to be promoted will exert the strongest influence over the design of the marketing campaign. Residential, commercial, and industrial properties have unique pools of potential tenants. New properties require a more active initial lease-up campaign than older buildings, which already have most of their space occupied and enjoy an established reputation and referral clientele. Managers leasing new properties must be able to adjust rents quickly in response to fluctuating market conditions.

The specific method of advertising used for each type of property is related to the nature and number of potential tenants whose interest must be captured. For example, industrial manufacturers who are in the market for warehouse space will probably consult an industrial broker rather than the classified section of the newspaper. They will often hunt property secretly through straw parties. A large billboard located near an industrial area and easily visible from a major thoroughfare can help to draw the attention of these potential tenants. On the other hand, a family looking for an apartment is more apt to comb the rental section of the newspaper or to canvass a neighborhood for vacancy notices. Commercial tenants often consult display advertisements in the business portion of the classified ads. A large, visible sign posted on or near an office building or in the window of a vacant store might also attract such tenants.

Supply and Demand

The supply and demand level in the area is the second determining factor in the marketing strategy. Balances of supply and demand can create two different marketing situations for a property. In an area with a low vacancy rate, or in a stable market, there will be little need for a massive marketing program to attract prospects if the units in the building are of the size most in demand in that area and the rental structure for the premises matches the consumer's purchasing power. However, a well-planned promotional effort can enhance the prestige of the building, thereby generating consumer demand for space in the premises and a higher rental schedule.

Impressive, well-designed, and often costly advertisements are needed to build a more elite image for a low-vacancy property. The desired image can be projected to potential consumers through a modulated, evenly paced advertising campaign running over an extended period.

When the vacancy rate in an area is high, property must be marketed with the intention of drawing as many potential tenants to the premises as quickly as possible. This policy may run counter to the natural instincts of some property managers to cut expenses when business is bad, but in fact the best way to avoid further losses is to advertise and promote the property more heavily. The focus, force, and frequency of the advertisements used in a high-vacancy market will differ from those implemented in a stable market. Attracting potential tenants for immediate occupancy of vacant units is a more urgent marketing concern than upgrading the image of the property. The emphasis of the advertising campaign in this situation will shift from quality to quantity, since short-term results are of greater economic import than long-range benefits.

Financial Resources

The third influence on the design of the marketing strategy is the financial status of the property. The income from the property usually has a direct effect on the total funds that can be allocated for advertising and promoting the premises. The strategies open to the manager are limited when the total advertising budget is set forth in the management contract.

A fairly clear picture of the sources of potential tenants and the demand for a particular type of space in the area should have emerged from the market and property analyses that the manager performed before submitting a management proposal. This information and the amount that has been budgeted for advertising and promotion give the manager all the data necessary to select the best techniques for reaching the largest number of prospects at the lowest possible cost.

MARKETING METHODS

The property manager can choose from a number of advertising and promotional methods and media in trying to reach a target audience. The choice for any given market situation depends partially on the type of property involved. Subsequent chapters will explain which techniques and which media are most fruitful in marketing residential, office, retail, and industrial property. The marketing techniques reviewed and illustrated in this chapter will clarify the manager's role in marketing space in general.

Signs

All residential, office, and retail properties should carry a tasteful sign affixed to the premises identifying the management firm, the type of space, and the person to call for further information. "For rent" signs stating the type of unit presently vacant and the person to contact might be posted in front of residential buildings and in vacant store windows if this is common practice in the area. Billboards are most effectively used in advertising larger industrial and commercial properties, since the industrial user often drives around the preferred area to observe buildings and call on people. Billboards are directional in nature and should carry only basic information about the property, its location, and the person to contact. Larger residential and commercial properties should have a small office on the premises where tenants and prospects can direct their inquiries. The building directory in the lobby should list this office and its room number under several headings (Building Office, Management Office, or Rental Office, for example).

Newspaper Advertising

Classified newspaper ads are listed alphabetically by subject and sometimes by area at the back or in a separate section of the paper. Classifieds, relatively inexpensive per line of copy, are the most prevalent method of advertising residential properties. This sample residential classified is brief yet informative:

```
MARINE DRIVE
Large art deco 1-bedroom.
Newly decorated, $475.
Immediate occupancy.
Call 477-9433.
```

Ad prepared by: Tinsley Advertising, 2660 Brickwell Ave., Miami, Florida.

Display ads have greater visual impact than classifieds because they are larger and more elaborate in design. Display ads for industrial or commercial property, like the one here from the *Wall Street Journal* may be placed in any section of the newspaper and often appear in the financial pages. Developers of large residential projects may promote new property complexes by inserting quarter-page or larger ads in the real estate section of major papers.

An effective advertisement has a specific potential tenant in mind. It attracts attention by stressing the benefits of the property and its services. The description of the advantages is followed by the location of the property, date of availability, times it can be seen, and names of people to contact.

Periodicals and Other Publications

Regional magazines and trade journals are reliable vehicles for advertising real estate for rent or lease. Most periodicals accept both classified and display ads. Advertising in carefully selected journals can generate a list of qualified prospects, but the manager must be sure that the property is large enough and has enough general nonregional appeal to merit this type of marketing. On a more local level, properties can be advertised in the programs distributed at sports events, plays, concerts, and other cultural events. This method can be effective for residential, commercial, and industrial spaces.

Radio

This advertising medium is quite costly. Though large, its audience is not select; many listeners are not potential buyers. Careful analysis of the cost per prospect is critical in broadcast advertising, for returns in many cases do not justify the expense. Radio is best employed on a community level for promoting large residential, commercial, and industrial developments. Local stations in major metropolitan areas can advertise available space in the surrounding suburbs.

Television

The response to television advertising has varied throughout the country, and the type of property and available budget will obviously have a great impact on any decision regarding the use of television. Because of its expense, managers should carefully research the success rate of previous television ads in their market areas. If comparable ads cannot be found to guide the manager, the initial financial obligation should be limited to a pilot program which can be used to gauge the success of further advertising.

Direct-Mail Advertising

Direct mail is favored by industrial and commercial property owners. Since it is expensive to design, write, print, and mail a brochure or flyer, this method of advertising is effective only in cases where the prospects on the mailing list are known to be qualified potential tenants for the property. Information obtained from the chamber of commerce and other local sources such as the Yellow Pages can help the manager compile a selective list of potential tenants for office, retail, or industrial space. This marketing method can be very cost-effective in terms of advertising expenditure per prospect.

The mailing list should include not only prospective tenants (such as major corporate executives in the case of commercial space), but also key brokers, either local or nationwide, depending on the appeal of the property. In either case, the manager's objective is to make knowledgeable, active brokers aware that the property exists and that he or she is willing to cooperate with them in renting or leasing the space.

Brochures. Because of the high cost of direct-mail advertising, it must be tailored to the recipients' interests and income level. Elaborate, expensive brochures unselectively mailed to a broad readership will not provide the desired result, and unsophisticated or inelegant handbills mailed to prestigious firms might actually provoke negative feedback. The advertising brochure will be more emphatic if it has a central theme than if it tries to cover every conceivable point about the property. This theme should run through the brochure's headlines, copy, and illustrations, as in the portions of the mailing shown here. The cover folder (page 75) sets the themes of quality, convenience, and market. The enclosed business park and shopping center brochures appeal to likely prospects by showing how the themes apply to their needs.

If a particular advertisement is to stand out from all others, it must have a special character and appearance. Layout should be kept simple, with lots of open space strategically arranged to guide the eye from the headline through the message to the name, address, and telephone number the reader is to contact. Short copy is best for quick and easy comprehension. Words should be used economically, and each one should expand on the basic theme.

The regional market analysis discussed in Chapter 2 will disclose vital selling points of the property. It is especially useful when designing brochures and mailing pieces to be sent to national and international tenants requiring space in several major cities. Some large management firms that cater to this type of tenant are geographically widespread; others use individual managers who travel widely. In either case, the information in the brochure and in the market analysis can motivate the prospect to investigate a particular property.

Mixed Media

An advertising campaign should not be limited to a single medium. For example, direct mail sent to a specially selected group of industries might be supplemented with a billboard placed at the side of a nearby freeway and a sign in the lobby of the property itself. Creativity is especially important. For example, an architect's model of a large development displayed in a glass case at the airport along with supporting information would attract the interest of prospective tenants relocating from other cities. Whatever the media mix, the marketing campaign will be more fruitful if it is backed up with a permanent reference such as a small sign on the premises identifying the management group or a listing in the Yellow Pages.

Broker Referral Campaign

One of the most effective ways to market residential, commercial, or industrial space is through outside brokers. A broker referral campaign can be especially beneficial when renting or leasing a new or very large development. Quite simply, the manager should send key brokers advertising pieces or a newsletter on available properties. He or she should demonstrate a willingness to cooperate with outside agents both legally and financially, by means of a split fee or other arrangement. The manager can also make brokers aware of the availability of the property in person, by means of a presentation or by sponsoring an open house to show off the features and benefits of the available space.

An outside leasing broker with a qualified prospect will often send a letter of registration stating his or her intent and the terms of the commission split before bringing

PADDOCK PARK
BUSINESS
CENTER

PADDOCK PARK
VILLAGE

Reprinted with permission. Cheri Morris is President of Morris and Fellows, Inc., an Atlanta based real estate marketing and consulting firm specializing in residential, urban mixed-use properties and corporate image programs for developers of commercial properties.

Perfectly placed on 270 green and rolling acres is the future. . . Paddock Park. It promises to be the touchstone of central Florida's growth. The benchmark by which all others are measured. The vision calls for an incomparable community of retail, office, business, commercial and residential properties blending with a synergy that ensures each component reaches its fullest potential. Precise and painstaking planning assures that each project within the master plan focuses on a true market need, adheres to the quality standards and enhances the whole that is Paddock Park.

Pleasing streetscapes present uncluttered vistas of living places and work spaces in harmony with the majestic Live Oaks, whose spreading branches dot the landscape with patches of shade. Carefully conceived development guidelines protect the integrity of the land and create tranquil yet efficient living and working environments. Homogeneous land uses and architectural styles reflect the spirit of the region and create a true sense of community.

Paddock Park is ideally situated in the city of Ocala in Marion County, Florida. . . Kingdom of the Sun. With an incredible growth rate of some eighty percent, the region leads the nation in population expansion. And Paddock Park will set the quality standards for the business and commercial boom currently underway in answer to burgeoning market demand. Ocala offers an idyllic climate; an educated and affluent population; year round recreation; excellent schools and medical facilities; and an enlightened, supportive business infrastructure. Millions of tourists each year infuse dollars into the economy and help keep the tax base low. And the region offers unmatched transportation and distribution channels from highways and railways to air and sea lanes.

A beautiful vision. An ideal marketplace. Paddock Place. . . fulfilling the promise of the future.

Paddock Park Business Center was planned for the company who wants everything. The 86,000 square foot facility in the midst of Paddock Park, central Florida's most prestigious multi-use development, offers a perfect environment for the needs of almost any growing business. The decidedly attractive building will house corporate offices, showrooms and distribution centers in an atmosphere of comfortable efficiency.

First impressions count, so the building features contemporary glass and anodized aluminum office entrances with attractive identification for each business. Space layouts are highly flexible to accommodate any combination of office, storage and service your firm may require. Easily accessible service courts with oversized delivery doors will facilitate the handling of incoming materials and outgoing products, while minimizing noise and clutter. Each space will be custom tailored to include plush carpeting, extensive use of glass, and the fine attention to detail that will make your business day pleasant and profitable.

The Ocala market area provides an incomparable setting for success. The three-county business region has a population of 233,000. Fifty thousand people live within five miles of Paddock Park, and over half of Florida's population of 10.6 million lives within one hundred twenty five miles. Ocala offers a dependable and growing work force with a spectrum of contemporary lifestyles, from young families to retirees. During the 1970's the market grew at an incredible rate of 78%, and the decade of the 80's brings a growing commercial, industrial and service base to meet the needs of a burgeoning market. Well served by all types of transportation and distribution channels, Ocala is a regional hub of healthy commercial activity. The area has an enviable quality of life, year round recreational facilities, fine residential areas, varied lifestyles, excellent schools, respected medical facilities and over two million tourists a year who help keep the tax base low.

The vicinity of Paddock Park Business Center affords a full selection of amenities and supports for the prospering business. A variety of residential housing, convenient banks, all types of shopping, the best area restaurants, and even auto service are all just seconds from your door.

As development progresses within Paddock Park, a new standard of quality will emerge for central Florida. Years of painstaking planning call for this ambitious development to feature a specialty shopping center, the largest office complex in Ocala's history, a collection of restaurants, a luxury hotel, and the market's most desirable selection of townhomes and single family living. The concept is a simple one, and it works. A benchmark community featuring the best living spaces, workable workplaces, and the highest of quality goods and services for tomorrow's lifestyle.

Move up to Paddock Park Business Center, and fulfill the promise.

PADDOCK PARK BUSINESS CENTER

This important component of the multi-purpose business, residential and retail complex sets the standard for the Paddock Park community to come. Special attention has been given to concept, planning and workmanship; right down to the smallest detail. Exceptional care has been taken with design and land planning to provide a tranquil, park-like setting. Imaginative landscaping enhances the natural roll of the terrain and creates a lush and pretty work place. Utilities are buried underground and out of sight. The buildings, designed to the highest of standards will be scrupulously maintained by an on-site management team. Protective covenants will protect your environment and investment. Paddock Park Business Center, a beautiful place to watch your business grow.

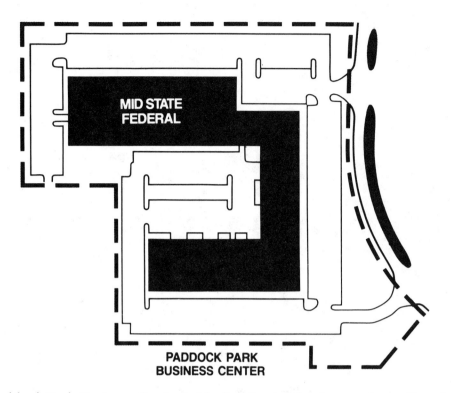

**PADDOCK PARK
BUSINESS CENTER**

Paddock Park Business Center is ideally situated for the conduct of local, regional and even national business. Marion County is not only a thriving trade area, but serves as a regional distribution center benefitting from a national transportation network of highway, rail, air and sea lanes. Interstate 75, adjacent to Paddock Park reaches the heart of America. Convenient rail lines supply bulk materials and distribute finished products. Three major airports and the seaports of Tampa and Jacksonville connect central Florida to the cities of the world.

Occupying a prime spot in Ocala's growth corridor, just three minutes from downtown, and central to the market's finest residential and commercial areas, Paddock Park Business Center is at the crossroads of success. An important location for your business.

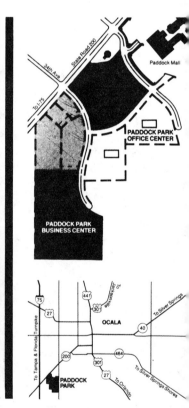

Paddock Park Village is destined to be Ocala's premier specialty shopping center. An imaginative retail concept, it combines Florida's strongest team of major stores in a delightful facility designed to create the most pleasant shopping environment possible. Twenty-five unique and attractive shops and boutiques will serve the area's affluent residents. Executive and administrative workers from the immediate vicinity's many diverse commercial locations will visit the center's stores and restaurants at lunch and after work. And the renowned central Florida tourist population will bolster the stable and growing local market.

Great care has been taken to enhance the inherent convenience of the center's location. The building configuration creates comfortable and efficient pedestrian patterns and maximum shopper exposure to store entrances. Attractive, customized storefronts reflect each shop's special appeal. The festive design personality of the center is complemented by a decorative copper canopy which communicates a contemporary quality while protecting shoppers from the elements. Thoughtful parking lot planning assures that our valued customers won't have to walk but a few steps to visit their favorite store.

The location is enviable, the development concept is strong, and the potential is unlimited.

Paddock Park Village represents an incomparable opportunity for Ocala's retailers. Containing approximately 90,000 feet of space, parking for 450 cars and a merchandise mix geared to a healthy and booming market, the center will be the retail hub of a thriving commercial and residential community. It will serve not only some of the most affluent existing residential areas of central Florida, but the thousands of people who will live and work in Paddock Park. The Village will open its doors in the fall of 1984 with an exciting cadre of retailers teamed to satisfy the expanding merchandise needs of a dynamic market.

Two heavyweight anchor stores virtually assure the success of the center. Publix Markets and Eckerd Drugs are the preeminent names in Florida retailing. They are held in the highest regard by shoppers, and have built a large and loyal customer base. The very nature of a supermarket and drug store combination creates extremely high frequency of shopper visits. Week after week, as shoppers visit these major stores, Paddock Park Village retailers will share in the success story.

It is no surprise that the Ocala and Marion County market is an incredible arena in which to do business. It is one of the fastest growing areas in the country, and its population is one of the wealthiest. Regional market population is 233,000. Within five miles of Paddock Park Village some 48,000 people reside in 18,000 households. Population is projected to increase to 55,000 by 1987, continuing the phenomenal market growth rate of 78% from 1970 to 1980. The average household income of $25,500 is well above national and state standards. Some 86% of households are families, and 95% of these families have children, characterizing an active, traditional lifestyle and a desirable "high-needs" consumer profile. Median market age is thirty-three. To these facts add the two million people who flock to the area each year. Specialty centers such as Paddock Park Village have historically had great appeal to tourists, who often schedule major shopping sprees in their vacation plans.

The center's location in the affluent and growing market segment is made even more desireable by the development activity in Paddock Park. The shopping village will be preceded by a major business center and followed by the largest office complex in Ocala's history, along with a variety of business, commercial and residential facilities within the master plan. Paddock Park Village will be the obvious retail resource for this exciting new community.

Opportunity knocks. A well-conceived shopping facility combining the convenience of an open-air neighborhood center and the merchandise selection of an upscale specialty center. A market that exhibits almost unbelievable consumer characteristics and growth patterns. An excellent location in the center of the action. Prestigious major stores. A developer with a track record of success. And a distinctive shopping setting designed to showcase your store and assist you in serving your customer. Put this unbeatable combination to work for you at Paddock Park Village, and fulfill the promise.

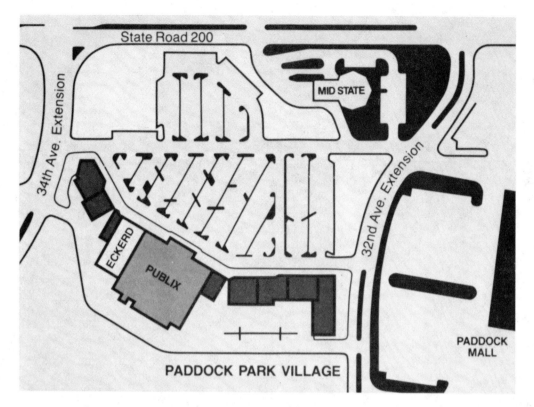

Every retailer knows that the best location for his business is where the people are. That's right where Paddock Park Village puts you. The center enjoys a highly visible location at the heavily trafficked segment of State Road 200 between 32nd and 34th Avenues, with over 20,000 cars passing daily. It is adjacent to Paddock Mall, a major regional retail magnet capable of providing millions of cross-shoppers each year. Residents within a five-minute drive of the Village have household incomes well in excess of market averages and even national norms. The huge Paddock Park office population will be able to shop or dine at the center without leaving the complex. And the interstate highway, just seconds away will deliver untold numbers of market visitors to our door.

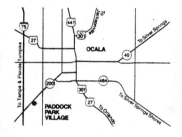

As the cornerstone of the ambitious Paddock Park center, our quality standards are impeccable. Nothing but the best will do. Every element of the development plan has been painstakingly refined. Every idea has been finely honed. And every detail has been thought out and rethought until it satisfied the toughest critic: Watkins Associated Developers, Inc., the center's creator and owner, and one of the shopping center industry's most respected real estate development and management firms.

Other Florida centers developed by Watkins include Sarasota Commons in Sarasota, Hunt Club Corners and Willa Springs in Orlando, Merritt Crossing in Merritt Island, and Sun Point in southern Hillsborough County.

Paddock Park Village

Watkins Center/Orlando
4401 Vineland Road
Suite A-2
Orlando, Florida 32811
305/843-9781

Watkins Associated Developers, Inc.
1958 Monroe Drive, N.E.
P.O. Box 1738
Atlanta, GA 30371
404/872-3841

the prospect to the manager's building. Though usually influenced by local standards, the rental commission paid to a cooperating broker ultimately depends on the owner. Some owners will pay an extra commission on rented space when an outside agent is involved, but if the management fee is high, the owner will not expect to pay leasing agent fees also. In such cases, the property manager must split the normal commission and distribute a portion of his or her fee to the cooperating broker. Another common arrangement allows the manager to pay flat finder's fees or referral fees to brokers who bring in tenants.

Cooperation between managers and brokers is now the rule, not the exception. This alliance may spark conflict, though, since an outside broker will sometimes try to keep the property manager out of negotiations with clients as much as possible. The conflict is predictable because the manager and the cooperating broker have different loyalties and because each believes that he or she can consummate the transaction more successfully than the other. It is in the best interests of both the property owner and the manager for the latter to meet and influence all prospects, despite any efforts on the broker's part to prevent this. The property owner will have to be supportive of the property manager in this effort.

The many professional organizations for real estate practitioners constitute a built-in cooperative referral network. This marketing strategy is most practical for properties with more than local appeal, since it enables the manager to reach a target group over a broad geographical area. The Society of Industrial Realtors® is one organization that can assist in leasing industrial space.

Leasing Agents

In-house leasing agents, also called real estate representatives or solicitors, are sometimes retained by property managers as an integral part of the marketing campaign. The expense of compensating traveling or local agents is usually justified only for large, relatively expensive commercial and industrial properties. Leasing agents may be paid by a flat referral fee or a split commission arrangement and may work full or part time. These representatives disseminate information about the space to be marketed and follow up leads on prospective tenants. Their success hinges on their knowledge and personal selling skills, for they contact prospects directly in an attempt to stimulate interest in the property. The manager should keep a detailed record of these prospects and their real estate needs. The advantage of in-house leasing agents over outside brokers is the additional control the property manager has over their activities. Some owners feel commission agents are expensive, but fees must be compared against total costs of continually employed in-house agents.

Referrals

Recommendations from satisfied tenants are the best and least expensive method of renting property. Tenants are most likely to give referrals on the basis of their own satisfaction with a space, but a tangible or cash incentive is sometimes offered for a referral that yields a new tenant. This method of renting space is most effective with multitenant properties, of course, but may be used for residential, commercial, and industrial space as well.

The manager should thank a tenant who supplies a lead on a prospect and should request permission to use the tenant's name when contacting the prospect. This can significantly improve the manager's chances of converting the prospect into a tenant. If the referral signs a lease, the manager should personally thank the tenant who provided the lead, preferably with a small gift. This display of appreciation will encourage more referrals. By canvassing in local buildings that are becoming empty, the manager can also establish personal contact with many prospective tenants.

Publicity and Public Relations

Potential tenants are often attracted to a manager's property because of the reputation of the management firm or the building, so it is important for a manager to maintain good relations with the real estate community, the press, and the public at large. This can be done by volunteering to address various interest groups and by sharing professional expertise.

Another way to enhance the reputation of the manager or the appeal of the property is to prepare press releases for publication. For personal publicity, a manager may write an interesting, factual article about a transaction, an idea he or she is implementing, an educational accomplishment, or a new trend in property management. To attract attention to one particular property, the news release should highlight its significant features—size, amenities, historical importance, conversion or new usage, striking architecture, and so forth. This type of article can be particularly helpful in the initial rental of large new commercial and residential developments. To attract attention to one particular property, the news release should highlight its significant features—size, amenities, historical importance, conversion or new usage, striking architecture, and so forth. This type of article can be particularly helpful in the initial rental of large new commercial and residential developments. Releases are sent to local papers and publications. Depending on the topic, real estate journals and other trade magazines might be interested in an article. Television coverage can often be arranged for new project announcements, ribbon-cuttings, and open houses. Consider also the valuable publicity generated by a news story that appears in a large metropolitan paper, as did the one on the following page.

The primary advantage of publicity over advertising is that it is virtually free. It costs the manager only the time and effort spent developing articles and press relations. News releases keep the name of a development or a management firm in front of prospective tenants and often have more credibility than paid advertising. The advantages of good publicity are so numerous that many large management companies engage independent public relations firms to work for them in this area.

Economics of Marketing

The cost of marketing property is often figured on a prospect-per-lease basis. The prospect-generating cost of various advertising media, promotional efforts, and sales activities must be calculated in order to gauge the effectiveness of a marketing campaign.

Sunday, December 18, 1983 *RICHARDSON DAILY NEWS*

Update

NTI leasing Greenway from Dal-Mac

Dal-Mac Development Corporation has leased its entire 146,704-square foot Greenway I project in Richardson to Northern Telecom Inc.

Greenway I is the first office building phase of Dal-Mac's 88-acre Greenway business park, located at the northeast corner of Campbell Road and Central Expressway.

The Integrated Office Systems (IOS) unit of Northern Telecom Inc., which has headquarters in Richardson for some 8,000 employees nationwide, will consolidate people from some of its 19 Richardson facilities into the Greenway I buildings, according to E.J. Mattiuz, group vice president, IOS.

The new facilities include a 51,920-square foot, two-story office building and a 94,784-square foot, five-story office building at Lakeside Boulevard and Lawnview Drive within the park.

Northern Telecom Inc. will occupy the two-story building in December 1983 and the five-story building during the first quarter of 1984.

The Greenway project will eventually have over one million square feet of office space. In addition, future plans call for a new Texas Commerce Bancshares bank, a 300-foot luxury class hotel, retail shops, restaurants, a health club, public gardens and jogging trail. An anticipated mass transit station for DART is also included in the master plan of Greenway.

Dal-Mac Development Corporation's Greenway I project at the northeast corner of Central Expressway and Campbell Road has been leased by Northern Telecom Inc.

Depending on market conditions and the type and size of the property, a definite standard relationship can be established between the space for rent and the number of prospects who must see it before a lease is signed. For example, a highrise apartment that rents for $600 a month might be viewed by 5 prospects before it is leased, whereas a small store in a strip shopping center might need 20 potential viewers. The cost for a $200 display ad for the highrise apartment would be a staggering $40 per prospect. Since more prospects are needed to rent the retail property, the $200 display ad would cost only $10 per prospect, a more acceptable figure.

The $10 prospect-per-lease cost figure assumes that the rental schedule for the space is accurate, the market active, and the promotion vigorous. If the market is poor, adjustments may have to be made in the marketing allowance, the rental schedule, or both. In a high-vacancy situation, for example, the manager of the highrise in the preceding example might have to run a classified advertisement for 5 days in order to get 5 prospective tenants, whereas in a good market one ad would have attracted more than enough prospects. At $25 per day for the ad, the total expenditure to lease the apartment would be $125, well above the $10-per-prospect figure.

If the highrise manager is able to run the advertisement for 5 consecutive days, the $125 expense would be justifiable in a very poor market situation, since it will result in a one-year lease worth $7,200. If the manager can advertise only on a weekly basis, the 5-week waiting period necessary to generate 5 prospects would represent, in itself, a cost of approximately $750. Adding this to the $125, we see that the new tenant would cost about $875. If the manager would be able to attract 5 prospects with one advertisement by lowering the rent to $550, the actual cost of the rent reduction over the time of the lease plus the cost of the ad would be $625 ($600 − $550 = $50 × 12 = $600 + $25 = $625), as opposed to the possible $875 cost of the 5-week advertising period. However, the manager must also consider how decreasing the rental rate for one unit will affect other, similar space in the building. A rent reduction might jeopardize the entire rental schedule of the building, so the manager must use good judgment.

SELLING ACTIVITIES

When a prospective tenant comes to the property manager's office or to the building, the first part of the marketing process, prospecting, is complete. The manager's job is to convince this consumer, who has already expressed some interest in the property, that this space is more advantageous than any other available in the area. To do so, the manager needs selling skills. These skills involve preparation, qualifying, creating interest and desire, dealing with objections, negotiating, and closing techniques. He or she must know how to show the premises and how to suggest judiciously that certain issues might be open to negotiation at the time the lease is drawn up. The manager must also be familiar with the space that is being leased in order to answer questions, overcome objections, and point out the features that are most meaningful to the prospective tenant. Lastly, the terms of the lease must be negotiated, drawn up, and executed.

Preparation

The manager should preview the space before putting it on the market to make sure that everything is clean and in good condition. This inspection will also afford the manager an opportunity to observe the unique features of the building and of the particular unit, as well as any advantages and amenities of the general area. The property manager who is working in conjunction with independent leasing agents (as is often the case with commercial and industrial properties) will want to make certain that cooperating agents who plan to show the building are well acquainted with the features and layout of the space being shown. Commissions that might have been split between the agent and the manager will be lost altogether if the agent cannot give a suitable presentation of the premises. The property must also be inspected periodically between showings by the manager and any cooperating agents.

Qualifying the Prospect

In addition to checking out the space in advance, the manager should qualify the prospect in several areas. Before making an appointment to show the space, the manager should determine the prospect's specifications and precise spatial requirements. The parties should discuss the amount of space needed (square footage or number of rooms), whether the prospect prefers a freestanding or multitenant building, the rental range desired, parking and transportation needs, the necessity for a traffic count or other demographic information, and other types of amenities the tenant will require. Many prospects do not have an accurate concept of their needs, so the manager should be honest with the client if questioning discloses that the space is not suitable. Rather than waste time showing the space, the manager should take the name and address of the prospect and check to see if there is a more suitable space available in another property managed by the same firm. If the prospect is left with a good impression of the building and the management firm, he or she may call on the manager for a future transaction.

The second area of qualification is the prospect's urgency. When is the move planned? Is relocation necessary or optional? What other factors are involved that might contribute to or detract from urgency?

Third, the manager should study the prospect's motives and how they are expressed. Residential, commercial, and industrial tenants differ in their responses. Renting an apartment to serve as a home tends to be a much more emotional decision than selecting office space, so managers of residential property must be attuned to the psychological nuances of a property's appearance. Commercial and industrial managers should be armed with facts when dealing with the more rational, dollar-oriented commercial or industrial prospects, although the intangible, prestige, can enter into their decision as well.

An additional point for the manager to consider is whether the prospect is actually the decision maker. Especially when dealing with commercial and industrial tenants, the manager must know who ultimately has the power to rent the space. The corporate representative who first contacts the manager may or may not have that authority, for leasing decisions are sometimes made by a board of directors upon recommendations. The manager should try to involve the primary decision maker in the transaction as soon as possible. This must be handled skillfully so that the immediate contact, who may have considerable influence on the decision, will not be alienated.

Creating Interest and Desire

A recital of the building's special features given in the manager's office may create interest, but it will be half-forgotten before the prospect actually sees the property. There is no effective substitute for personally escorting the prospect on a tour of the premises, and showing the premises presents a real opportunity to arouse the desire of the prospect.

The manager should follow the most advantageous route from the office to the premises, pointing out the amenities and services along the way. For example, during the drive to an industrial plant, the manager can show the prospective tenant all the transportation facilities located in the area. En route to an office complex or shopping center, the manager has an opportunity to describe the other tenants on the premises and to assure the client that there will be no close direct competition. Traffic patterns and other pertinent features of the neighborhood can be seen from the car. On the walk up to the space in question, the manager should comment on the excellent exterior condition of the building and describe the routine upkeep and operating procedures for the premises. The cleanliness of the common areas, the facilities that the building affords its tenants, and the management policy for regulating tenant behavior are important points to raise with the client.

The manager should be selective about the number of units the prospect is shown. If too much space is shown, the decision-making process will become too complicated, and doubts may arise as to why so much of the building is unoccupied. On the other hand, the manager must be able to assess the prospect's preferences and be willing to show additional space if the client is interested in a particular area or unit but is not quite convinced that it is suitable. Unimproved commercial space presents the manager with a special problem. First, the prospect has to see the clean, vacant space that is available for lease; then, if possible, he or she should be taken through comparable occupied spaces that will demonstrate the effects of tenant alterations.

While guiding the prospect through the space, the manager can subtly highlight its advantages. After demonstrating how various features of the property will work to the advantage of the prospect, the manager should allow him or her to examine the premises alone.

Dealing with Objections

Questions and objections can be fielded quickly and intelligently if the manager has previewed the space and qualified the prospect in advance. When unable to answer a question, the manager should admit it, make a note of it, and then get back to the prospect with the information as soon as possible. The admission and the actual follow-up will demonstrate honesty and professionalism. The manager might reassure the prospect that minor details such as a leaking faucet will be taken care of prior to occupancy. More substantial requests such as repainting an entire office area could be negotiated in the lease terms. Problems like these can be avoided simply by making sure that the available space is in the best possible condition before showing.

Unfortunately, many managers are oriented toward administration and the overall picture of the property rather than toward the specific needs of a prospective tenant. Although the manager's job encompasses many different functions, understanding each prospect's requirements is among the most important.

Negotiating and Closing

Negotiating and closing, which have been treated in detail in Chapter 6, are critical portions of the selling process. As an aid in the whole process, the property manager may find a Rental Center helpful.

RENTAL CENTERS

Despite the expense, a well-located, expertly staffed, and smoothly operating rental center is often the best way to market large residential and commercial complexes. The decision to use one should be based on the amount of space to be rented, the expected rent-up period, the anticipated turnover of tenants in the property, and the sophistication of both clients and competitors. Rental centers are most appropriate for larger developments, especially new or newly converted ones that must be rented initially. The higher the anticipated tenant turnover, the greater the utility of a rental center, since proper use of the center increases the ratio of new tenants to inquiries. In general, when the market is strong, there is little need for an elaborate program, but marketing methods of competitors and the expectations of the target population can induce a manager to use a sophisticated rental center.

These centers are usually located directly within the project and include a display area, furnished models of the types of space available, a closing area, and, on occasion, the manager's office. Large directional signs should be positioned on the major thoroughfares running through the area. When placed in the display area of the center, promotional aids such as brochures, site plans, floor plans, direct-mail fliers, photographs of the complex, and a scale model of the development will give the prospect an overall sense of the project and a better perspective on its buildings, interior layouts, and amenities.

Model space should be clean and attractive. Furnishings in the model units should be tailored to the taste of the target market. Traditional furniture, for example, would be more appropriate than contemporary for units that will be shown to conservative tenants. When decorating model offices, executive and clerical spaces should be highlighted, and the arrangement should emphasize the flexibility of the unit.

One idea is to set up the rental center, including model space, in one of the least attractive areas of the building or project and announce that the models themselves are available for rental. When the rental center space is leased, a less appealing area can be decorated as the rental center and subsequently rented. Managers have marketed less-than-premium space quite rapidly with this technique.

A separate closing area with small tables and chairs should be set off from the rest of the rental center to offer prospective tenants property brochures, competent service personnel, and privacy. This part of the rental center forms the backdrop against which the selling process is culminated. In the event a rental center is not established, the manager should bring the prospect back to the office to discuss the details further.

SUMMARY

The marketing goal of the property manager is rapid rental to a good clientele at a profitable rental rate. To attain this goal, the manager must be adept at advertising, promotion, and selling.

The first step is to design an effective advertising and promotional campaign. The strategy adopted will depend on three major factors—the type of property, supply and demand, and available financial resources. The *type of property* to be promoted will exert the strongest influence over the eventual design of the marketing campaign. The method used to market a specific type of property is a function of the nature and number of potential tenants whose interest must be captured.

The *supply and demand* level in the area also may determine the marketing strategy for a property. There is little need for a massive campaign to attract prospects in a stable market, but even then a promotional program can enhance the prestige of the building, thereby generating consumer demand and allowing the owner to raise the rental schedule. A high vacancy rate, on the other hand, calls for a marketing campaign that can draw as many potential tenants to the property as quickly as possible. The focus, force, and frequency of advertisements used in a high-vacancy market differ from those geared to a stable market. The emphasis shifts from quality to quantity, since short-term results are of greater economic import than long-range benefits.

The third influence on the design of the marketing strategy is the availability of *financial resources.* The income from the property usually has a direct effect on the total funds allocated for advertising.

Once the manager has selected a strategy, he or she can choose from several advertising and promotional methods that will reach a target audience. Advertising media include signs, newspaper advertisements, periodicals, radio, television, direct mail, and brochures. The decision on which method or combination of methods to use will depend primarily on the type of property to be promoted. In general, a marketing campaign should use several methods in combination, backed up with a permanent reference such as a sign on the premises or a listing in the Yellow Pages.

Broker referral campaigns allow the manager to cooperate legally and financially with other agents when leasing new or very large developments. The manager should distribute brochures and advertising pieces on available properties to key brokers. Local geographic boundaries can be transcended by employing in-house leasing agents. Their cost-effectiveness is limited for the most part to marketing larger commercial and industrial properties. Referrals from satisfied tenants are the best method of renting any property. Managers sometimes provide tenants with a cash incentive for referring prospects who then rent space.

A property manager can increase rental ratios simply through good *public relations.* Tenants may be attracted by the reputation of the manager or the property itself. Time invested in establishing a good public image as a real estate professional will bring significant economic returns. Press releases sent to local newspapers and journals are another efficient means of gaining publicity for specific properties. An important benefit of publicity is that, unlike advertising, it is virtually free. With a small expenditure of time and effort, the manager can attract both public attention and prospective tenants.

The cost of marketing property is often figured on a prospect-per-lease basis. Subject to market conditions and the specifications of the property, a definite standard relationship can be determined between the space for rent and the number of potential prospects required before one unit is actually leased. To judge the effectiveness of a marketing campaign, the management firm must keep accurate records of the number of prospects produced by the advertising and promotional efforts employed and then calculate the prospect-generating cost of each.

The manager can convince the prospect that the space in question is more advantageous than any other available space by skillfully showing the premises, by highlighting important features and benefits, and by knowing which issues might be open to negotiation. Before space is put on the market, it is imperative that the manager preview it to make sure that everything is in good condition and that the premises are clean. This inspection will also afford the manager an opportunity to note the unique features of the building and of a particular space. Managers working in conjunction with leasing agents should make certain that any agent wishing to bring a prospect to the building is well acquainted with the space.

The manager must also *qualify* the prospect in several areas. Before showing the space, the manager should discuss the prospect's spatial requirements and other specifications. If the property in question is not suitable, the manager should check the files for available space in another property managed by the same firm, or at least take the prospect's name and address in case a suitable property becomes available. Nothing can be gained from wasting a client's time. It is far better to make a good impression and lay the groundwork for future business contact. The prospect should also be qualified for urgency—the strength and immediacy of the need for suitable space. Commercial and industrial property managers especially need to determine whether the person they are dealing with has the authority to sign a lease and make decisions.

There is no substitute for personally guiding the prospect through the premises, for only in this way can the manager select the most advantageous approach route and emphasize the benefits of the area, the building, and the space. The manager's selling skills come to the fore as he or she guides the prospect through the unit, highlighting its advantages and discussing important features of the space. If the client shows displeasure over minor details, the manager might reassure him or her that minor problems will be corrected before occupancy and that larger problems may be negotiated when the lease is drawn up.

Rental centers are a very effective method of showing all types of property to the best advantage, but they can be prohibitively expensive. The manager should consider the size of the development, the number of apartments to be rented initially, the expected tenant turnover, and other factors when deciding whether or not to establish a rental center. Rental centers usually include a display area containing promotional aids such as brochures, site plans, floor plans, photographs, and a scale model of the development. The center should also include model units and a separate closing area where prospects can consult quietly with the manager and complete the lease application.

QUESTIONS: CHAPTER 4

1. List the three major categories of marketing activities a property manager must be adept at.

   a. _____
   b. _____
   c. _____

2. List the three factors that must be considered when designing the marketing strategy for a particular property.

   a. _____
   b. _____
   c. _____

3. The most popular medium for advertising residential properties is:

   a. billboards.   c. display ads.
   b. classified ads.   d. direct mail.

4. Display ads in newspapers and periodicals are often employed in marketing:

   I. commercial properties.
   II. industrial properties.

   a. I only   c. both I and II
   b. II only   d. neither I nor II

5. When developing advertising brochures, the property manager should observe all but one of the following rules:

   a. Include comprehensive property information.
   b. Keep the layout simple.
   c. Work around a central theme.
   d. Gear costs to target prospects.

6. List three ways a property manager can disseminate information about a property he or she is marketing to facilitate a broker referral campaign.

   a. _____
   b. _____
   c. _____

7. List two advantages publicity (press releases) has over advertising.

   a. _____
   b. _____

8. A property manager is trying to market 4,000 square feet of retail space at $7 per square foot in an unfavorable market. One alternative is to run a $250 per day display ad in the local paper for a full 7-day week, which will probably attract about 15 prospects and rent the space at the desired rate. The other alternative is to lower the rent to $6.50 per square foot, at which rate the manager has a qualified prospect who will rent the space immediately for a 5-year term. Which of the following is *not* true?

    a. The manager should consider lowering the rent and accepting the immediate tenant.
    b. The loss of one week's rental on the property is about $538.
    c. The cost of the ad will be $1,750.
    d. The cost of the rent reduction over the term of the lease is $2,000.

9. What two activities should the manager perform as preparation to showing a property to a prospective tenant?

    a. _____
    b. _____

10. List the three areas in which a prospect should be qualified by the manager.

    a. _____
    b. _____
    c. _____

11. List four factors to consider when deciding whether or not to establish a rental center for a particular property:

    a. _____   c. _____
    b. _____   d. _____

12. The three basic components of a rental center are:

    a. _____
    b. _____
    c. _____

13. A campaign to increase the prestige of a property should logically be undertaken:

    a. when supply is high.
    b. if vacancy rates are increasing.
    c. in a stable market.
    d. when consumer pressure is great.

14. The initial rent-up of a large commercial development could be effectively accomplished by which of the following market methods:

   I.   broker referral campaign.
   II. leasing agents.

     a.   I only   c.   both I and II
     b.   II only   d.   neither I nor II

15. A $250-per-month apartment requires 7 prospects before it is leased during active market conditions. If a $30 classified ad must be run for 2 days to attract this number of prospective tenants, the prospect-per-lease cost figure for this marketing effort would be:

     a. $3.57   c. $4.17
     b. $8.57   d. $5.00

16. What are the disadvantages of using television in marketing real property?

     a.   _____

     b.   _____

5
Leases

As explained in Chapter 3, the management contract formalizes the relationship between owner and manager and specifies the rights and duties of each party. The property manager usually takes responsibility for leasing the premises, although the role will vary according to the terms of the contract. One manager might be the sole leasing agent for the building, while another might share this duty with independent leasing brokers. A few property managers perform only maintenance duties.

Even those managers who have no active role in leasing are consulted when drawing up the terms of the lease. Their knowledge of the costs and requirements for operating and maintaining the premises will have a direct impact on the lease terms. Although the attorneys for the parties to the lease are responsible for its legal and technical details, property managers must be familiar enough with leasehold estates and basic lease clauses to recommend the most suitable lease for a particular situation. Owners are best served by managers who can cooperate knowledgeably with attorneys and leasing brokers.

Historically, leases have been drafted by attorneys hired to represent property owners and managers, so it is not surprising that most contracts and leases have favored the lessor. The character of the typical lease form is changing, though, thanks to recent legislation and judicial interpretation favoring the tenant.

LEASEHOLD ESTATES

A leasehold estate arises when an owner, or a property manager acting as his or her agent, grants a tenant the right to occupy the owner's property for a specified period of time in exchange for some form of consideration. In some states, this leasehold interest is considered to be the *personal* property of the tenant and may be sold, traded, or assigned. In other states, it is held to be *real* property. As such, the leasehold interest can still be sold, traded, or assigned, but *not* without a deed. In some parts of the country, a leasehold interest can be pledged as collateral to secure a mortgage loan. A leasehold mortgage secured by a tenant may jeopardize the owner's financial position and property rights, so the manager must know the law governing his or her state. The lease should stipulate that the tenant cannot sell, assign, or pledge the leasehold interest without prior written approval of the property owner.

Estate for Years

An estate for years is the leasehold estate that most property managers use when renting residential, commercial, and industrial space. A lease creating an estate for years grants the tenant possession of the property for a *specified period* of time under the terms of the lease agreement, whether it be for a month, a year, or a decade. This lease is sometimes called a "lease for a stated period." When the designated term of the lease expires, the estate for years terminates without notice. The tenant must then surrender possession of the property to the owner. An estate for years does not terminate upon the death of either the landlord or the tenant. All rights and obligations pass with the estate of the deceased party.

Estate From Period to Period

An estate from period to period is a leasehold estate granted by owner to tenant whereby the premises are leased for a term that is automatically renewable for an indefinite number of successive similar terms. The most common example of such an interest is an estate from year to year, although month-to-month and week-to-week estates also exist. To terminate an estate from period to period, one of the parties must give proper notice. The form of notice required and the time at which it must be given are usually determined by state statutes. The latter may vary from a minimum of one month to a maximum of six months prior to termination. This type of estate is not terminated by the death of the owner or the tenant.

An estate from period to period may be created either by agreement or, more commonly, by operation of law. Express agreement is made when the owner actually leases his or her property to a tenant "to hold from year to year." Operation of law takes effect when a tenant has possession of the property and pays rent under an invalid lease or a lease that does not specify the duration of the tenancy. The frequency of rent payments in this case will determine the period of the estate. If rent is payable monthly, the tenancy is from month to month. A more prevalent situation in which an estate from period to period is created by operation of law arises when a tenant holding an estate for years remains in possession of the premises after expiration of the lease. The owner may elect to let this holdover tenant stay on without drawing up a new lease agreement. Acceptance of rental payments by the owner or property manager is considered legal proof of the owner's acquiescence to the holdover tenancy. Laws in most states consider a holdover tenant's leasehold interest to be of the same duration as that specified in the original lease agreement, up to a maximum term of one year. The leasehold interest of a holdover tenant can be limited by inserting an appropriate clause in the original lease agreement, and it is often in the property manager's best interests to do so.

Tenancy at Will

Tenancy at will gives a tenant the right of possession with the consent of the landlord for an *indefinite period* of time. This type of estate, like the estate from period to period, may be created either by express agreement between owner and tenant or, more commonly, by operation of law. It exists only as long as both parties wish the estate to continue. In the past, an estate at will could be terminated without notice, but most states now require the party who wishes to terminate the tenancy at will to give some advance written notice. Property managers should consult their state statutes for the rights and obligations involved in tenancy at will. Unlike an estate for years or an estate from period to period, an estate at will is terminated by the death of either party.

Tenancy at Sufferance

Tenancy at sufferance occurs when a tenant obtains possession of the premises legally but then remains on the property after the expiration of his or her leasehold interest *without* the consent of the owner. This tenant has no right to possession.

An example of an estate at sufferance is the tenant who fails to surrender possession of the premises on the date specified in the lease agreement. The owner, or the property manager as the owner's agent, has two options when dealing with a tenant at sufferance. He or she may either evict the tenant without notice or acquiesce to the tenancy. The owner's acceptance of rent payments constitutes acquiescence and creates an estate at will or an estate from period to period. This is a complex issue, and the property manager can sidestep costly legal entanglements by having written leases with all tenants which conform to local laws and statutes. Special lease provisions can sometimes alter or clarify the rights and obligations of the parties.

TYPES OF LEASES

The three basic lease forms that the property manager will be expected to administer are the gross lease, the net lease, and the percentage lease. The three types are differentiated by the manner in which rental compensation is computed and paid.

Gross Lease

The tenant pays a fixed rental and the owner pays all other expenses for the property under a gross lease. Utility charges can be negotiated between the parties. The most common form of gross lease is the apartment lease, illustrated in Chapter 11.

Net Lease

Theoretically, there are three variations of the net lease. Net, net-net, and triple net leases usually run for a longer term, sometimes for periods of 50 years or more. Under the terms of a strictly *net lease,* in addition to the stated rent, the tenant is obligated to pay utilities, real estate taxes, and other special assessments levied against the property. The *net-net lease* generally requires the tenant to pay all items included under the net lease terms plus the insurance premiums agreed upon in the contract. Agreed-upon items of repair and maintenance are added to the net-net payments to derive the tenant's total payment obligations under a *net-net-net,* or *triple net lease.* In practice, there is a great deal of overlap in the common usage of these terms. Because the difference between net and triple net leases is a matter of degree—how many extra expenses the tenant is required to pay—the property manager should be explicit about the types of expenses the tenant will assume under a net lease and should call for a precise definition of net, net-net, or triple net lease whenever these terms arise. A net lease is shown in Chapter 15. As property usage becomes more specialized, triple net leases are being more widely used, especially for industrial property. They are also used by national franchising chains in leasing their retail outlets. The owner of a tract of land frequently leases the property to a tenant who then constructs a plant or store on the site. The period covered by any such net lease must be long enough to make the tenant's building investment worthwhile. This type of lease is also called a ground lease, or land lease.

Percentage Lease

The percentage lease, computed on a monthly basis, is most often used for retail property. It usually provides for the payment of a fixed rental fee plus a percentage of the tenant's gross income in excess of a predetermined minimum amount. A percentage lease could require that the tenant make minimum monthly payments of $1,200 plus an additional amount equivalent to 4 percent of gross sales in excess of $30,000. Under the terms of this lease, a tenant with a monthly gross income of $60,000 would pay $2,400 rent for that month: $60,000 − $30,000 × .04 = $1,200 + $1,200 (base rate) = $2,400. The percentage rate charged will vary greatly depending upon the nature and location of the property, the type of business occupying it, and the general economic climate. Percentage leases also may be based on a straight percentage of the tenant's gross sales, with no minimum.

To ensure that the landlord receives the anticipated rental rate for the space, percentage leases often contain a *recapture clause,* which sets a minimum amount of rent that must be generated by the percentage of gross sales. If the percentage actually generated by the tenant's business is below the minimum rental amount specified in the recapture clause, he or she may be permitted to pay an extra rental fee so that the lease will not be canceled. This provision makes the recapture clause more equitable to the tenant.

Statistics showing typical percentages currently being charged to the various types of businesses in a particular area can be obtained from the Institute of Real Estate Management, the Building Owners and Managers Association International, and trade periodicals such as the *Journal of Property Management.* Chapter 14 contains a sample percentage lease, as well as a detailed discussion and a table showing some typical percentage rates for various types of businesses.

ESSENTIAL PROVISIONS OF A VALID LEASE

Since a lease is a contract, the general requirements for a valid lease are similar to those for a legally enforceable contract: both parties to the lease must have the *legal capacity* to enter into the agreement and must reach a *mutual accord.* As with any contract, the *objectives* of the lease must be legal in nature. The document must be dated and must provide for valid *consideration* to be paid. The basic elements of a lease include the following:

- complete and legal name of both parties
- description of property
- term of lease
- consideration or amount of rent
- use of premises
- rights and obligations of both parties

Statute of Frauds

Written, oral, and implied leases are all covered by the statute of frauds of the state where the property is located. This statute requires that any lease not fully performed within one year of its execution be in writing in order to be legally enforceable. Although an oral lease agreement for less than one year is usually enforceable if the facts of the situation can be established to the satisfaction of the court, it is wise for the property manager to protect the interests of the owner by executing all leases in writing.

Signatures

A lease is both a contract and a conveyance of an interest in real estate. It must contain the names of both lessor and lessee, and it must be signed by the property owner or a legally empowered representative of the owner. As pointed out in Chapter 3, the power to execute leases can be delegated to the property manager under the terms of the management agreement.

If the tenant and all other involved parties have not signed the lease, the property manager will have problems enforcing the lease terms. Practically speaking, the manager should make sure that the tenant does not take possession of the premises until after the lease is signed. If the tenant is an organization or corporation, the lease must be signed by an authorized officer of the corporation and affixed with the corporate seal when this is required by state law. The requirement for additional signatures from witnesses and an acknowledgment seal from a notary public varies from state to state, but witnesses and notaries are not generally required for leases of less than one year. All leases must be delivered and accepted to be valid.

Description of the Premises

If the property to be rented includes land, which might be the case when leasing industrial or commercial space, the lease agreement should include a legal description of the property. A lease for a portion of space in a particular building, such as an office or apartment, must accurately describe the bounds of the space itself. It is imperative that a ground lease contain an accurate legal description of the land.

The apartment number and the street address of the building are usually sufficient identification in an apartment lease. For commercial space, a floor plan showing the area to be leased should be appended to the lease. An example of a floor plan showing the premises leased in a shopping center appears on the next page.

Figure 9: LEASE FLOOR PLAN ATTACHMENT

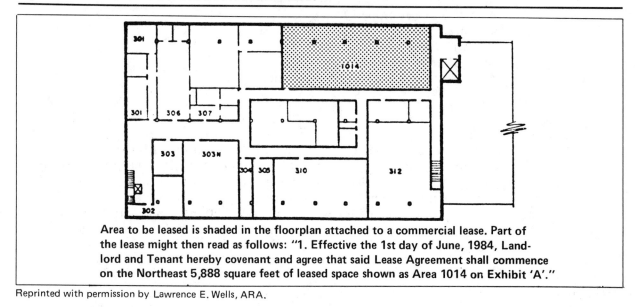

Area to be leased is shaded in the floorplan attached to a commercial lease. Part of the lease might then read as follows: "1. Effective the 1st day of June, 1984, Landlord and Tenant hereby covenant and agree that said Lease Agreement shall commence on the Northeast 5,888 square feet of leased space shown as Area 1014 on Exhibit 'A'."

Reprinted with permission by Lawrence E. Wells, ARA.

It is a good idea to include both a description of the real estate or space and a statement of the tenant's right to use common elements such as stairways, elevators, halls, driveways, and alleys. An itemized list of furnishings or personal property and a description of their condition should be attached to the lease if these are involved in the rental. Any supplemental space covered by the lease—a garage, storage area, or patio—also must be identified.

The lease should describe in detail any alterations that will be completed by the landlord for the benefit of the tenant, a common concern with commercial and industrial properties. It should specify what improvements are to be made, how the expenses are to be divided, and who will arrange for the work. An office lease may stipulate that the landlord furnish interior partitions, doors, venetian blinds, telephone jacks, outlets, and electric switches in the area to be rented; or it may detail the amount of painting and decorating as well as the type of floor covering, heating, ventilating, and air conditioning to be supplied. Blueprints, carpet samples, and pictures of fixtures usually accompany these specifications. Since this information makes the lease bulky and complex to renew, some managers describe all such tenant alterations in a separate contract that is contingent upon the signing of the lease. This is legally valid and simplifies the lease by allowing the one-time alteration specifications to be agreed upon independently.

Term of the Lease

The lease should bear its beginning and termination dates as well as a statement of the total period it covers. This can be done in a clause that reads, "for a term of 30 years beginning June 1, 1984 and ending May 31, 2014."

Many leases contain an option to renew, a covenant giving the tenant the right to extend the lease for an additional period of time on specified terms. To take advantage of this option, the tenant merely gives sufficient notice of intent. The option clause states the date by which the tenant must give notice, the form of notice, how and to whom it must be delivered, term of renewal, and rate of compensation. It could read as follows:

> At the expiration of the term specified in Section _____, Article _____, said term shall be extended, at the option of the tenant, for an additional subsequent period of _____ years on the same terms, covenants and conditions herein set forth, except as to renewals and except that the net yearly rental for this renewal term shall be $_____, payable in advance in equal monthly installments commencing on the first day of the first calendar month of said renewal term. Tenant shall give landlord notice in writing of his or her desire to extend the original lease term six months prior to the expiration of such term.

Since options to renew favor the tenant, an owner often will insist on higher rental rates if the option is exercised. A lease containing an automatic extension clause will be renewed indefinitely until one of the parties gives proper notice that he or she wishes to terminate at the end of the term. Leases for indefinite periods are usually not valid unless the language of the contract and the circumstances involved clearly indicate that the parties intended to create such an agreement. The maximum term for any lease must conform to the statutes of the state in which the leased property is located.

Some leases include a clause allowing tenants to cancel the agreement before the expiration of the term if they pay a penalty. Other leases, especially those for industrial land on which tenants have constructed a plant, give them the option to purchase the property upon termination of the lease agreement.

Possession of the Premises

Landlords in most states are contractually obligated to give the tenant *actual occupancy* of the premises described in the lease. If the premises are still occupied by a holdover tenant on the date of the new lease, the property owner, or an agent of the owner, must take action to recover possession and bear the cost of this action. In other states, landlords need only convey to the tenant the *right of possession.* It is the tenant's obligation to bring any court action necessary to secure actual possession.

Valuable Consideration

All lease contracts must be supported by some type of valid and valuable consideration given by the tenant to the landlord for the right to occupy the leased premises. Quarterly or monthly payment of rent is most common but is not essential, as long as some form of consideration is discussed in the lease and granted at the time the agreement is signed. Whether the lease is gross, net, or percentage, the amount and time of payment of rent must be clearly stated. When rent is expressed or quoted on a square foot basis, it is assumed the figure is "per square foot per year."

After the method and original amount of compensation have been stipulated in the lease, certain clauses may be added to allow for rental rate adjustments. This is an important consideration because most courts will not enforce an increase or reduction in the original amount of rent unless such changes are authorized in the contract. It is advisable to anticipate increased operating costs under a long-term lease and to allow for adjustment of the rental rate when drafting the agreement.

Rental rates may be increased by several methods. One is the *step-up clause,* found in both gross and net leases. Leases with step-up clauses are called *graduated leases.* They provide for specific increases at specific times. A long-term lease for a luxury highrise apartment, for example, might require monthly payments of $400 for the first 2 years, $500 during the third year, and $600 for the last 2 years. Step-up clauses are often used with commercial space in order to help a new business or professional get started. The following is a typical step-up clause.

> The LESSEE hereby covenants and agrees to pay to the LESSOR as rent for said premises during said term, the sum of THIRTY-SIX THOUSAND AND 00/100 Dollars ($ 36,000.00) per term   payable at the office of LESSOR or of LESSOR's agent, in monthly   installments, each in advance upon the first day of every calendar month during said term, payable as follows at the office of the Lessor or the Lessor's agent: FOUR HUNDRED AND 00/100 DOLLARS ($400.00) per month for the first six (6) months; SIX HUNDRED AND 00/100 DOLLARS ($600.00) per month for the next forty-two (42) months; SEVEN HUNDRED AND 00/100 DOLLARS ($700.00) per month for the last twelve (12) months.

By its very nature, the percentage lease provides for a rise in the rental rate as the tenant's gross or net income increases. Because the income from professional offices, service firms, financial institutions, brokerage houses, and similar businesses cannot be reasonably and effectively adapted to the percentage lease pattern of rental payments, an increase or decrease in their rent is often tied to a selected index of economic conditions. For this reason, leases containing *escalation clauses* are called *index leases.* The index used in establishing the escalation clause must be reliable and published on a regular and continuing basis by an independent and reputable agency. It should bear a close relationship to the nature of the tenant's business. The most frequently used indices are the consumer price index (cost-of-living index) and the wholesale price index. The sample escalation clause below bases its terms on the consumer price index.

Figure 10: ESCALATION CLAUSE

> Commencing May 29, 1984, the Lessee shall pay rent as follows:
>
> A. Forty-eight Thousand Dollars ($48,000.00) per annum in equal monthly installments of Four Thousand Dollars ($4,000.00) per month, due on the first day of each month, subject to adjustments provided for in Subdivision "B" of this paragraph.
>
> B. Tenant agrees that in the event the **1967 Consumer Price Index (Series A) for Urban Wage Earners and Clerical Workers (1967=100),** for all items for U.S. City Average, issued by the Bureau of Labor Statistics of the United States Department

of Labor (hereinafter called "Price Index") or successor or substitute index appropriately adjusted, reflects an increase in the cost of living over and above such cost reflected by the Price Index for the calendar month of May 1984, the rent payable under Subdivision "A" shall be adjusted as follows:

(i) On June 1, 1987, and every third year thereafter during the term of this lease on June 1st of each such third year, the monthly rent provided for in Subdivision "A" (hereinafter "Base Rent") shall be increased by an amount equivalent to the percentage of the increase, if any, of the Price Index for the calendar month of the March preceding the applicable June 1st (hereinafter "Current Index") over the Price Index of May 1984, which is 120.8 (hereinafter "Base Index"), subject to the limitation hereinbelow set forth.

To illustrate the intent of the parties hereto as to the computation of the aforementioned adjustment, if any:

Assume the Current Index to be	157.04
Subtract the Base Index	120.8
Increase	36.24

The increase of 36.24 in the said Consumer Price Index would represent 30% of the Base Index and the Base Rent for the ensuing three year period would, therefore, be increased by the application of that percentage which is equal to $14,400.00, making the total annual yearly rent for said three year period $62,400.00.

(ii) In no event shall the "Base Rent" be reduced if the "Current Index" hereafter drops below the "Base Index."

(iii) In the event the said Consumer Price Index shall hereafter be converted to a different standard reference base or otherwise revised, the determination of the Base Index and the Current Index shall be made with the use of such conversion factor, formula, or table for converting index figures as may be published by the Bureau of Labor Statistics or, if said Bureau shall not publish the same, then with the use of such conversion factor, formula or table as may be published by Commerce Clearing House, Inc. or any other nationally recognized publisher of similar statistical information. In the event the Consumer Price Index shall cease to be published, then, for the purposes of this Section, there shall be substituted for such Consumer Price Index such other index as Landlord and Tenant shall agree upon and there shall be substituted for the Base Index such figure as the Landlord and Tenant shall agree would have been derived under the substitute index for the month of May 1984 and, if they are unable to agree on one or more of said matters within ninety (90) days after the Consumer Price Index ceases to be published, such matter or matters as to which they are not in agreement shall be determined by arbitration in accordance with the then applicable rules of the American Arbitration Association.

The frequency and amount of the adjustments is a matter for negotiation between the parties to the lease agreement. A lease might require a minimum rent of $600 plus a one percent increase for every point the consumer price index rises during the course of the year. If the index rises six points during the first year of the lease, the rental level for the next year will be $636 ($600 × .01 = $6 × 6 = $36 + $600 = $636).

An escalation clause can be tied to outside factors other than economic indices. Union pay scales, taxes, utility rates, and overall operating costs for the premises are common controlling factors. When operating costs are used as the basis for an escalation clause, the lease should cite specific costs that will be used. Ceilings are sometimes imposed when escalation clauses permit rent increases based on the average increase of the other rental rates in the building.

An increasing number of leases today contain a provision for *tax participation.* These clauses require the tenant to pay, in addition to his or monthly rental, a pro rata share of any increase in taxes or assessments in excess of those rates for an established base year. Given the present economic climate, such tax participation provisions afford valuable protection for the owner's investment.

ADDITIONAL COMMON LEASE PROVISIONS

The lease provisions treated in the ensuing discussion cover the major points that must be resolved in order to create an effective, mutually beneficial contract. The specific manner in which each of these issues is handled varies widely from lease to lease in response to the divergent needs of the parties and differing state statutes. Property managers should determine their latitude in regulating the use of the premises, subletting privileges, and related matters. The best leases are those that leave no issue open to dispute or interpretation at a later date.

Use of the Premises

The property owner may restrict the use of the leased premises by including a special provision in the agreement. *Restrictive clauses* are prevalent in office and industrial leases which might, for example, restrict the tenant to using the premises "for the purpose of carrying on a general insurance agency only, and for no other purpose." Residential leases, too, can limit the number of persons to reside in the apartment. The wording of such clauses must be clear and unambiguous, for the courts will resolve any doubt as to the meaning of a restrictive clause in favor of the party who is restricted by it. In the absence of written restrictions, the tenant may use the premises for any lawful purpose.

Most leases for multiple-occupancy buildings have an auxiliary section entitled "Building Rules." These rules are usually made part of the lease agreement by reference and provide a more detailed treatment of day to day matters, such as the tenants' use of common areas, parking spaces, and hours of building operations. They are designed to protect the condition, reputation, and safety of the property and to promote compatibility among the occupants. Building rules apply to all tenants of the same type. They cannot be arbitrarily or selectively enforced, although rules for upper-floor residential tenants can differ from those for ground-floor, commercial stores. The property owner reserves the right to add to or change these rules in a reasonable manner during the term of the lease, after giving proper notice.

Most lease forms also include a clause providing for equitable cancellation of the agreement in the event that the tenant is denied use of the property because it has been either appropriated or condemned by a government agency.

Assignment and Subletting Provisions

Provided that the terms of the lease do not prohibit such activity, a tenant has the right to assign or sublet his or her interest in the property. Assignment of a lease transfers all of the tenant's remaining right in the property to a third party, whereas subletting transfers only part of the tenant's interest. Most leases prohibit the tenant from assigning or subletting the rented space without the owner's prior written approval. This ensures that the owner has stable and financially secure tenants on the property.

Fire and Casualty Damage

State statutes and lease provisions for fire loss, damage, and property restoration vary widely. When drafting a lease, the manager should keep in mind the types and amounts of insurance to be carried on the property, who will pay the premium, and who will receive the proceeds if there is a loss.

Leases for agricultural land or for land upon which the tenant has constructed a building usually remain in force even when the buildings on the property are damaged or destroyed. By the same token, a tenant who is the sole occupant of the building is said to be leasing the underlying land as well. Under most state laws, this tenant's rental obligation continues even if the premises are damaged or destroyed.

When a multiple-tenant property is damaged or destroyed to such an extent that enjoyment of the premises is impaired, the tenant may vacate immediately and notify the landlord in writing of the intent to terminate the lease as of the date he or she surrenders possession. The landlord also may be given the option to repair the damage and make a rent allowance to the tenant for a certain period. If portions of the premises are still habitable, the tenant can vacate the unusable area and reduce his or her rent proportionately. If the destruction can be tied to negligence on the part of the owner, some state statutes even allow the tenant to recover damages.

For the owner's protection, the manager should be certain the lease includes a clause stating that damage caused by a tenant will be repaired without a rent abatement and that the owner may take legal action against a tenant. Most leases permit the owner to terminate the tenancy if fire completely destroys the property's usefulness.

Tenant's Obligations

Tenants are required by law to comply with local building and housing code provisions regarding health and safety. They should be required in the lease to take good care of the rented space, repair any damage they directly or indirectly cause, and comply with all applicable rules and laws. The terms of the lease should demand that tenants use all plumbing fixtures, elevators, and other facilities in a reasonable manner. They should be prohibited from willfully destroying or damaging the premises, or allowing others to do so, and from disturbing the quiet enjoyment of other tenants. Tenants should not be allowed to make alterations without advance written consent from the landlord, who must be informed of such alterations and protected from all liabilities arising from them.

Most tenant improvements to the property are classified as fixtures and become part of the real estate. However, a commercial or industrial tenant may be given the right to install trade or chattel fixtures for business use. These are the personal property of the tenant and may be removed before or upon expiration of the lease agreement, provided that the building is restored to the condition it was in at the time the tenant took possession.

The wording of the clause that allows the tenant to remove trade fixtures is crucial. Some lease forms stipulate that the property must be restored to the condition it was in as of "the tenant's taking of possession," whereas others require restoration only to the condition that prevailed "as of the beginning of the lease." This minor difference in phraseology can have a major impact on the owner, as it did in the case of the long-term tenant who installed fixtures during the first lease and later removed them under the terms of the third lease, which required restoration only to the beginning of the lease. The tenant was obligated to restore only those alterations made under the third lease. Alterations made under the first lease were not covered by the terms of the last lease, so the owner had to bear the expenses for restoration.

The lease should also list the amount and kind of security deposit due from the tenant as well as the conditions under which it will be refunded. A security deposit may be cash, negotiable securities, or a surety bond. In some areas and under certain conditions, interest must be paid on cash security deposits. If any part of the security deposit is retained by the owner or manager, it must be demonstrably proportionate to damages suffered. The property manager must be aware of state and local regulations regarding security deposits.

It is also in the best interests of the owner to include a clause that obligates the tenant to remove personal property from the premises and to clean the rented area at the termination of the lease. Any property left behind is considered abandoned and may be removed from the premises at the tenant's expense. The procedure for handling abandoned personal property in residential tenancies is often governed by specific state statutes.

Landlord's Obligations

Disclosure and Billing. On or before the commencement of a tenancy, the landlord should disclose in writing the name and address of the property manager and of the person who is authorized to receive legal notice on behalf of the owner. The lease should provide that rent bills and other notices can be sent to the tenant by registered mail, left at the premises, or delivered personally, as long as they are submitted at the appropriate times.

Quiet Enjoyment. The owner or property manager grants the tenant a covenant for quiet enjoyment as one of the major benefits in the lease. This right to use also implies a right to possession. Since the tenant is thereby given the exclusive use and possession of the space, the terms of the lease must limit the cases in which the owner or manager is allowed on the premises. Most leases allow the owner to enter in emergencies, for necessary repairs, and to show the space to prospective tenants for a given period near the end of the lease. Managers who deal with commercial and industrial property should reserve the right to enter and inspect the premises at will. This is the only way to ensure that lease provisions are not being violated, that the space is being used properly, and that no unauthorized building or alteration is under way. An astute property manager can predict a tenant company's expansion or impending failure from periodic inspections.

Maintaining the Premises. The landlord is under no obligation to make repairs unless required to by the lease or by statute. Nonetheless, most residential and commercial leases, and even some industrial leases, make the owner responsible for all repairs necessary to keep the premises fit for use. The owner, or the owner's agent, must comply with local building and housing codes by maintaining in good operating condition all elevators and other facilities as well as electrical, heating, and plumbing systems. Through the property manager, the owner tends to the upkeep of common areas, trash removal, window cleaning, and other services promised in the lease terms. Running water, a reasonable amount of hot water, and heat during the required season are usually supplied by the landlord unless the tenant has exclusive control over these installations or unless the building is not required by law to be equipped for these purposes.

Under some leases the landlord must furnish utilities, while in others, such as the triple net lease, the tenant has to pay for any or all utility services. If submetering is legal, the landlord may buy utilities such as electricity at a lower rate and resell them to the tenants at the prevailing rate. This is common practice with office and retail space. In any case, the lease should outline the landlord's and tenant's responsibilities for providing services and maintaining the property.

The manager should try to draft a lease that relieves the landlord of responsibility for maintaining the premises and supplying service if compliance is prevented by conditions beyond his or her control. The lease should further state that if the property is sold, the obligations of the owner cease as of the date of sale, with the exception of the responsibility to return or transfer security deposits to the new owner.

Tenant's Remedies for Noncompliance

Noncompliance With Rental Agreement. If the property owner or manager fails to perform his or her duties, the tenant may sue for damages or terminate the lease by giving the landlord the specified notice for breach of contract. Many leases stop termination proceedings if the owner or property manager begins a good faith effort to remedy the breach by the deadline stated in the termination notice.

If corrective action is not taken within the specified time, the tenant can sue for damages, obtain a court injunction directing the landlord to remedy the breach, or terminate the tenancy. If the landlord's noncompliance is willful, the tenant may also recover reasonable attorney's fees. Again, the procedures and outcome in any situation are ultimately determined by state statutes and the wording of the particular lease agreement in effect.

Failure to Deliver Premises. Some states require the owner to convey only the right of possession of the leased premises to the tenant. In others, the owner must grant actual occupancy. If the right to possession or actual possession is not conveyed, the tenant does not have to pay rent. He or she can terminate the rental agreement or sue for specific performance and thereby obtain possession, reasonable damages, and attorney's fees. It is not uncommon for a property manager to be unable to deliver possession because the previous tenant has not vacated the premises or because repairs and alterations have not been completed. The manager should protect the owner's interests by making sure that leases contain a covenant postponing the beginning of the term if necessary, waiving rental payments until the tenant is given substantial possession, and requiring the tenant to take the space even if there is some delay. A covenant like this might stipulate that:

> If tenant is not given substantial possession of the premises at the beginning of the term of the lease, this shall not be a basis for damages, nor shall it affect the validity and other terms of the lease, except that the lessor shall waive rentals until lessor can give substantial possession of the premises.

Failure to Supply Essential Services. *Constructive eviction* occurs when the tenant must actually abandon the premises due to the landlord's negligence in supplying essential services. Examples of constructive eviction include failure to supply heat or water, failure to repair untenantable premises, or other major material default that renders the premises unusable by the tenant. Constructive eviction is recognized by most state courts as the basis for termination of the lease, an action to recover possession, or a suit for damages. For the owner's protection, the lease should require the tenant to give notice of any failure and allow the landlord time to remedy the situation before the tenant claims constructive eviction.

Partial eviction occurs when a tenant has not physically moved out, but is unable to use part or all of the premises for the purposes intended in the lease due to failure on the part of the landlord. In cases of partial eviction, state statutes sometimes allow the tenant to give written notice of the breach of contract to the landlord. After allowing time to correct the breach, the tenant can take appropriate measures to obtain the services needed and then deduct the cost from the rental payments. In other cases, the tenant may simply be allowed to withhold rent until the breach of contract is corrected.

Landlord's Remedies for Noncompliance

Noncompliance With Rental Agreement. In the past, most leases included a judgment clause wherein the tenant agreed to forego certain rights, to authorize any person to confess judgment in court against him or her on a claim arising from the lease, and to pay the owner's attorney's fees. Although current protenant attitudes and legislation have rendered such provisions unpopular and, in some areas, illegal, the landlord should still be provided with certain remedies in case the tenant fails to meet the terms of the lease. According to most leases, the landlord may deliver written notice to the tenant within a specified period, stating the nature of the contract breach and calling for a good faith effort on the tenant's part to repair the breach within a reasonable time in order to prevent termination of the lease.

The lease should further state that if the tenant's noncompliance can be remedied by the repair or replacement of damaged items, and the tenant does not make such repairs within a reasonable time after notice is given, the owner or owner's agent may enter the premises and have the necessary work performed. Then, an itemized bill for the actual and reasonable cost of the work may be presented to the tenant as due with the next rental payment. The lease should also provide that if the landlord chooses to terminate the lease, the bill comes due immediately upon presentation.

Dispossess proceedings can be brought against a tenant for several reasons: nonpayment of rent, illegal possession of the premises after termination of the lease, unlawful use of the premises, nonpayment of charges attributed to the tenant under the terms of the lease, and certain other breaches of the lease contract. When a tenant has failed to perform in one of these areas, the landlord may file a court suit for recovery of the premises after giving the tenant sufficient notice. This proceeding is commonly known as a suit for eviction, a suit for possession, or a forcible entry and detainer suit. If the court issues a judgment decree for possession in favor of the owner, the tenant must peaceably leave or the landlord can have the decree enforced by an officer of the court, who will then forcibly remove the tenant and the tenant's belongings. This process is known as *actual eviction.*

Default. Because statutes regarding a tenant's default under the terms of a lease vary from state to state, the lease should include a clause to the effect that if the tenant defaults on rent payments, the owner or manager can terminate the tenancy.

Bankruptcy. Because of recent changes in federal bankruptcy laws and court decisions interpreting them, property managers should review bankruptcy default clauses in leases with an attorney. Advice should be sought to determine proper procedures to follow if a tenant declares bankruptcy.

Uniform Residential Landlord and Tenant Act. Many common lease provisions reflect the protenant attitude that has prevailed in recent years. The Uniform Residential Landlord and Tenant Act, drafted in 1972 by the National Conference of Commissioners on Uniform State Laws, was designed to standardize and regulate the relationship between property owners and their tenants. Variations of the Uniform Act have been incorporated into the statutes of several states, so property managers should study modifications found in local laws.

One of the more notable provisions of the Uniform Residential Landlord and Tenant Act is that, unless otherwise specified, a tenant is considered to have an estate from period to period. A tenant who pays weekly rent holds tenancy from week to week, while all others hold an estate from month to month. If the landlord or tenant signs and delivers a written lease, and if either party pays or accepts rent, the lease is considered to be binding even without the other party's signature because of the payment or acceptance. The Act also establishes standard lease termination procedures.

Under the Act, leases may not contain a judgment clause, a clause in which the tenant waives any rights or remedies, or any clause contravening the Act. Although the rental agreement may limit the landlord's liability for fire, theft, and damage in common areas, the Act is clearly protenant in establishing the landlord's responsibility for keeping the premises fit for habitation. Equally representative of the protenant awareness that characterizes the Act is a provision prohibiting a landlord from increasing the rent or decreasing services to a tenant who complains to the landlord or to a government agency, or of one who joins a tenants' union.

If a legal dispute arises between landlord and tenant, the court may refuse to enforce all or part of a lease which it finds to be grossly unfair. The Act further stipulates that landlord and tenant should make a joint inventory detailing the condition of the premises and all rented furnishings and appliances within 5 days after the tenant takes possession. Both parties should sign and retain a copy of this inventory.

Specific guidelines are established regarding security deposits, which have been one of the largest single sources of disagreement between landlords and tenants. Security deposits are generally limited to one month's rent for unfurnished apartments and to one and one-half month's rent on furnished units. At the end of the tenancy, the landlord may deduct any unpaid rent or damages from the security deposit, but he or she must submit an itemized list of damages and return the balance of the deposit to the tenant promptly; otherwise, the tenant can take action to recover the deposit plus damages and attorney's fees. Finally, the Act prohibits the tenant from deducting all or part of the deposit from the last month's rent.

The Act authorizes the landlord to establish building rules concerning use and occupancy, as long as they are reasonable and equitably enforced. These rules must be in writing, and the tenant must agree to them. The landlord is given the right to enter rental units, after giving reasonable notice, to inspect, make repairs or improvements, supply services, or show the unit. Only in extreme emergencies may the landlord enter without prior permission from the tenant.

The Uniform Residential Landlord and Tenant Act establishes certain standard remedies for noncompliance with the rental agreement. The tenant must comply with applicable laws and ordinances, use facilities and fixtures in a reasonable manner, avoid damage or destruction of the premises, and preserve other tenants' quiet enjoyment. If the tenant breaches the lease, the landlord may give legal notice and force compliance. If the tenant does not respond within a specified time, the landlord may terminate the lease and claim possession, rent owing, damages, and attorney's fees. A tenant who abandons a unit remains liable for the rent unless the unit is rerented or the landlord releases the tenant from the obligation. The landlord is required to make a reasonable effort to rerent the unit in cases of abandonment.

A tenant's remedies for the landlord's noncompliance with the lease are also set forth in the Act. If the landlord does not begin a good faith effort to remedy the fault, the tenant may terminate the lease after giving notice. The tenant is entitled to his deposit plus any prepaid rent, and may also sue for damages and attorney's fees. Should the landlord fail to deliver possession or illegally exclude the tenant from the premises, the tenant may give legal notice and obtain the essential services himself, sue for damages, or vacate the premises. If a unit is rendered uninhabitable by fire or other casualty, the tenant may give notice and terminate the lease immediately. If damage is partial, the tenant may reduce his rent proportionately.

SOURCES OF LEASES

Standard lease forms are usually available through stationery stores and local real estate boards and organizations. These may be combined with riders and addenda to cover almost any leasing situation. Many of the larger management firms and property owners have developed standard leases that may be modified to cover most eventualities. Larger buildings, particularly commercial ones, may also utilize their own lease forms.

One of the advantages of employing a standard form is that the property manager can become thoroughly familiar with its provisions and legal ramifications. This benefits a manager who administers a single large property or several smaller properties. When employing standard leases, however, the manager must respect the opinion of the tenant's attorney and the special position of each prospective tenant.

The disadvantages of using standard leases are that they require considerable revision and may be out of date. Also, standard leases utilized by national chains are sometimes not subject to negotiation.

Unless the manager is a lawyer, he or she should not write lease clauses or any form of legal statement that may bind ownership. The manager's or the owner's attorney should advise the parties about leases and riders.

SUMMARY

The property manager's role in obtaining tenants for the premises will vary according to the terms of the contract with the owner. The manager may be the sole leasing agent for the premises, share this responsibility with other leasing brokers, or be concerned strictly with operating the building. Whatever the case, the property manager's knowledge of the costs and requirements for operating and maintaining the premises will be invaluable when leasing space.

An owner who leases property to a tenant grants the tenant the right to occupy the premises for a specified period of time in exchange for some form of compensation and subject to certain responsibilities and restrictions. The tenant's right to occupy the property during the term of the lease agreement is called a *leasehold estate,* or interest, in the property. There are four major kinds of leasehold estates.

If the beginning and end of the lease term are clearly identified in the agreement, the leasehold interest is an *estate for years.* An *estate from period to period* occurs if the tenant leases the premises on a weekly, monthly, or yearly basis for an indefinite period of time. When the owner allows a tenant holding an estate for years to remain after the expiration of the lease without drawing up a new lease, the holdover tenant has tenancy from period to period for a duration equal to that of the original lease agreement, but not to exceed one year. A leasehold estate that gives the tenant the right to possession of the property with the consent of the owner for an indefinite period of time is called *tenancy at will. Tenancy at sufferance* occurs when a tenant obtains possession of the premises legally but then retains possession after the expiration of the leasehold interest and without the owner's consent.

The method by which the tenant pays valid consideration determines the type of lease contract. The three basic lease forms are the gross lease, usually used with residential space; the net lease, common to industrial space; and the percentage lease, for most commercial space.

A *gross lease* makes the tenant responsible for a fixed rental and the owner responsible for expenses arising from the property. Under the terms of a *net lease,* the tenant pays some or all of the expenses usually allotted to an owner, such as taxes, insurance, utilities, and maintenance. A *percentage lease* usually calls for payment of a percentage of the tenant's gross income as rent.

The general requirements for a valid lease are similar to those for any legally binding contract. All parties to the lease must have the *legal capacity* to enter into the agreement and must be in *mutual accord.* The document itself must have *legal objectives* and provide for valid *consideration* to be paid. Leases for longer than one year must be in writing in order to be enforceable under the statute of frauds.

Since a lease is both a contract and a conveyance of an interest in real estate, it must contain the names and signatures of both the tenant and the property owner (or a legally designated agent of the owner). Leases for corporate tenants must be signed by an authorized officer of the firm and generally affixed with the corporate seal. In some states, the signatures of the parties must be acknowledged by a notary public, or witnessed. The lease must also be delivered and accepted.

A description of the premises is essential to the lease agreement. If the property to be rented includes land, the legal description should be included. In an apartment lease, the apartment number and street address usually suffice. When renting a portion of space, the bounds of the space must be accurately described. A floor plan showing the dimensions of the space is sometimes attached to commercial leases. The lease should state the tenant's right to use common areas, itemize any personal property to be rented, and describe supplemental space such as storage areas.

The length of time a lease is to run should be specified in the agreement. Leases may contain an option to renew, an automatic extension clause, or a clause allowing the tenant to terminate the agreement prematurely upon payment of a penalty.

Like all contracts, leases must be supported by some form of valuable consideration, usually in the form of rent. The amount and time of payment must be clearly stated. The basic method of compensation determines the type of lease—gross, net, or percentage. After this basic issue has been resolved in the lease, certain clauses may be added to provide for rental rate adjustments over the term of the lease. A *step-up clause* provides for rental rate increments of a definite amount at specified times, whereas an *escalation clause* adjusts the rent based on outside economic factors such as the consumer price index, property taxes, or the overall cost of operating the premises.

Several additional provisions are commonly included in residential, commercial, and industrial leases. Most leases include a provision outlining rules for occupancy and restrictions on the use of the premises. The owner usually retains the right to refuse any intended assignment or subletting of the leased premises by the tenant The rights of owner and tenant in the case of fire loss and damage should also be included in the lease.

Obligations of both owner and tenant must be clearly stipulated within the terms of the lease. Each party must be granted some means of legal redress of grievance if the other does not comply with the contract terms.

The Uniform Residential Landlord and Tenant Act is a model law that reflects the protenant attitude prevailing in recent years and attempts to provide some uniformity and regulation of the landlord and tenant relationship. The Act applies in the absence of a written lease, and clauses in written leases which contain terms in violation of the Act are unenforceable. The law addresses several valid issues that should be considered in residential leases, even in areas where the Act is not enforceable.

A management firm can develop its own standard lease forms that can be modified to cover most leasing situations, or it may obtain them through local real estate boards and organizations. One of the advantages of utilizing a standard lease form is that the manager can become thoroughly familiar with its provisions and practical effects. Any standard lease will probably have to be tailored to a certain extent to fit each specific situation, and legal counsel should always be consulted when doing so.

The property manager must scrutinize each lease carefully to ensure that it is the most beneficial contract possible for the owner while still being fair to the tenant. An equitable lease will set the tone for future owner-tenant relations.

QUESTIONS: CHAPTER 5

1. List the four major types of leasehold estates.

    a. _____   c. _____
    b. _____   d. _____

2. Leasehold estates that continue for an indefinite period of time include:

    I.   estate for years.
    II. tenancy at will.

    a. I only   c. both I and II
    b. II only   d. neither I nor II

3. Leasehold estates that continue for a specified period of time include:

    I.   estate from period to period.
    II. tenancy at sufferance.

    a. I only   c. both I and II
    b. II only   d. neither I nor II

4. List the four general requirements for a valid lease that are necessary to any enforceable contract.

    a. _____   c. _____
    b. _____   d. _____

5. Gross leases are most often used with:

    a. apartments.   c. office space.
    b. retail space.   d. industrial property.

6. Net leases are commonly used with:

    a. apartments.   c. office space.
    b. retail space.   d. industrial property.

7. Percentage leases are most often used with:

    a. apartments.   c. office space.
    b. retail space.   d. industrial property.

8. A property manager leases office space with dimensions of 30 feet by 40 feet for $7.25 per square foot. The rent per month is:

    a. $1,200   c. $8,700
    b. $507.50   d. $725

9. The manager in the preceding question is paid a commission of 7 percent of the first year's rent, or:

   a. $609   c. $7,308
   b. $1,008   d. $507.50

10. An individual property of 6,000 square feet is rented at $2,000 per month. The rate of rent per square foot is:

    a. $40   c. $4
    b. $33   d. $3

11. A retail establishment has a completely percentage lease at a rate of 2.5 percent of gross monthly sales. First quarter sales were: January, $5,270; February, $4,500; March, $6,320. The total rent the tenant paid for the first 3 months was:

    a. $270.50   c. $244.25
    b. $289.75   d. $402.25

12. To be valid, a lease must be:

    I. delivered.
    II. acknowledged.

    a. I only   c. both I and II
    b. II only   d. neither I nor II

13. When describing the premises to be rented in an apartment lease, the contract should include:

    a. the street address of the building.
    b. the legal description of the property.
    c. the dimensions of the space.
    d. the floor plan of the building.

14. A tenant's option to renew in a lease:

    I. favors the landlord.
    II. is also called an automatic extension clause.

    a. I only   c. both I and II
    b. II only   d. neither I nor II

15. A lease clause which provides for increases of a definite amount at specific times over the term of the lease is:

    a. step-up clause.   c. index clause.
    b. escalation clause.   d. percentage clause.

16.   An escalation clause:

   I.   creates an index lease.
   II.   often relates to taxes.

         a.   I only   c.   both I and II
         b.   II only   d.   neither I nor II

17.   Name two disadvantages of "form" or "standard" leases from the viewpoint of a landlord.

         a.   _____

         b.   _____

6
Negotiating Lease Terms and Signing the Agreement

All the activities involved in marketing rental space are directed toward a single goal—the signing of a lease agreement between the owner or manager and the tenant. No single part of this process is more integral to its overall success than that performed by the manager after the prospect has responded favorably to the premises. Before deciding whether or not to lease, the prospect will try to determine whether the space is the best available at the price and whether to act immediately. The manager's objective is to influence the prospect to respond positively to both questions.

There are several closing techniques that the manager can use to guide the prospect to a successful close. In one approach, often termed the *question close,* the manager asks direct questions aimed at eliciting an affirmative decision, such as, "Which space do you prefer?" Another method closes with a *summary* of the benefits of the space, emphasizing the fact that the space satisfies the tenant's needs. The manager may need to summarize the benefits repeatedly throughout the showing and closing in order to reassure an indecisive prospect that the space is ideal. These basic closing techniques can be used singly or in combination, as the situation demands. If a proposed commercial lease is completely filled out in advance of the first interview with the prospect, this could provide a basis for discussion and give the leasing agent a sense of confidence in answering questions.

When prospecting for tenants, a property manager must *qualify tenants* by investigating their financial standing and other appropriate factors. The business practices and reputation of commercial tenants must be checked, and the rental history of residential tenants must be examined.

When the prospect *does* decide to act, the final step of the marketing program can be completed; that is, the terms of the lease agreement can be discussed and agreed upon and the contract drawn up. Depending upon the extent to which the prospect has been qualified before being shown the property, he or she will probably be qualified further and asked to fill out an application for a lease. At this point, the prospective tenant should also review the lease agreement (with an attorney if necessary), sign the lease, and initial any negotiated changes or addenda. In most cases, the manager will then verify and evaluate the application and sign the negotiated lease agreement. If he or she has not been authorized to do so under the terms of the management contract, or if the owner wishes to be consulted, then the manager must relinquish this responsibility to the owner. Once the manager or the owner signs the lease, the agreement is consummated and the marketing goal has been achieved.

NEGOTIATING THE TERMS

The negotiating process begins when a prospect expresses definite interest in the space being marketed. Negotiation itself consists of bringing the prospective tenant to an agreement on lease terms that will be satisfactory to the owner. The goal is a signed lease beneficial to both tenant and owner. Since lease negotiations usually involve several steps amounting to a series of compromises on terms, the property manager must monitor the process continually. If the manager loses control, the transaction probably will never be completed. Professionalism is the key to control of the negotiating process. It reassures both owner and tenant that the manager will effect a mutually satisfactory lease agreement.

The property manager is paid to avert personality conflicts that can prolong or even ruin a transaction. In most cases, the owner and the prospect should be kept apart, at least until negotiations have been concluded and the lease is ready to be signed. Often, successful leasing agents develop a negotiating strategy that requires the owner to remain outside of the immediate negotiations. The leasing agent works directly with the prospect and "recommends" action to the owner. This allows more response time to analyze prospect requests and negotiate favorable compromises on major points. Many times the leasing agent can avoid a concession by simply stating, "Oh, the owner will never approve of that!"

An outside leasing agent is often involved in leasing retail and industrial property. This third-party interest will complicate the negotiation process unless the property manager coordinates his or her efforts with those of the outside agent. They should decide beforehand, for example, who will deal with the prospect. The manager usually assumes this responsibility in order to expedite direct negotiations with the prospect without affronting the cooperating broker. It is worthwhile to cultivate the loyalty of the prospect, especially in a tenant's market, for the cooperating broker has no special allegiance to the manager, the owner, or the space in question.

The attorneys of both the owner and prospect should whenever possible be excluded from the negotiating process. When attorneys, especially lessees' attorneys, become involved in transactions too early, they can retard progress or even kill the possibility of a successful conclusion. The property manager's task is to control negotiations and strike an agreement between the parties. The attorneys' task is to formalize the agreement by translating it into legal terms after it has been established. Property managers should, however, evaluate each situation, because many lessees hire attorneys to monitor each step in the negotiating process and will not act without their guidance.

Concessions

Almost every item of the leasing contract is open to discussion. Depending upon the relative strength of the manager's and the prospect's positions, any number of concessions might be made to induce the prospect to sign a lease agreement. Three factors can help a manager decide how far to go in granting concessions to attract tenants: the owner's financial and strategic position (his or her long-range goals and urgency to lease), the competition in the area market, and the urgency of the prospect's need to move. A worthwhile concession alleviates a basic problem or specific financial pressure felt by the prospect. Nothing is gained by giving away something of little or no value to the recipient, regardless of its importance to the owner. Thus, the importance of qualifying the client and knowing his or her needs is evident. On the other hand, every concession means money and affects the total economic value of the lease to the owner. Keeping in mind the owner's position, the manager must not negotiate for more than the owner can afford to deliver.

Rent Schedules and Rebates. Residential rental rates usually reflect the differing demand for particular areas of a building. A basic graduated rental structure facilitates a balanced rental of all space. For example, the manager of a walkup building might be able to charge $375 per month for the first-floor apartments but only $335 for similar third-floor units, which are less convenient in a walkup. Similarly, the manager of a luxury highrise should charge premium rates for corner units that command a view and lower rates for apartments located in the center of the building. Graduated rental structures founded on a base standard rental rate are also used for office space, where the base standard rental is assessed on a per-square-foot basis. Standard rental rates in a highrise office building usually ascend with each floor. Space on the quieter 35th floor might rent for $23.80 per square foot, whereas similar units on the less desirable 14th floor would go for $21.20. Corner office space might cost an additional $2.00 per square foot above the base rent for any floor. The rental rate per square foot for retail and industrial sites is likewise a function of the location of the space.

The owner's costs for preparing and altering the space to suit a new commercial or industrial user must be figured into the rental rate. These costs may even include interest on the money borrowed for tenant alterations. Also, the rental schedule should be such that the expense to the property owner is completely amortized over the term of the lease, but no longer. Alteration costs for new tenants will be explained more fully later in this chapter.

One of the most important and complex issues to be broached when negotiating lease terms is, obviously, the rental rate. Although deviations from the basic graduated rental schedule are undesirable from both a manager's and an owner's standpoint, they may become a necessity in a competitive market. In every situation, however, the manager must analyze the advantages and disadvantages of making a significant concession on rent. An informed decision will take into account the worth of the space to be rented and the cost of a lower rental rate over the term of the lease. In a very poor market, it is sometimes best to leave space vacant for a period of time and rent it at a higher rate later. Accepting a tenant at a low rental rate that fails to cover operating expenses, or under a long-term lease that provides little or no profit, is more disadvantageous to the owner than vacancy.

Temporary free rent is the major concession granted to balance the needs of the tenant and the prevailing market conditions. For example, if vacancy rates are high, the manager might offer the prospect two months' free rent as an inducement to sign the lease. The manager tries, however, to remain within the basic rental schedule even when offering one-time rebates or other short-term concessions. The overall losses incurred by lowering the rent over the term of the lease will usually exceed the cost of temporary free rent. In addition, they will lower the value of the property.

All negotiations regarding rent reductions and rebates should be made on an individual basis. Not all tenants want, nor do all deserve, the same rent concessions. Unfortunately, compromises with one tenant often necessitate compromises with the others as well. Rumors spread quickly throughout multitenant buildings, creating ill will and an array of management problems. Failure to enforce the basic rental schedule, the manager soon learns, can result in a general downgrading of the rental structure and significant income loss. A general rule to follow for industrial and commercial lease concessions is that the larger the tenant and the longer the lease, the more acceptable the rent concessions.

Length of Lease Period. Unless the lease has an escalation clause covering cost increases, it is not common practice to grant residential leases of more than one year's duration. Nonetheless, the manager of a newly renovated building in a newly upgraded area might be willing to give 2- or 3-year leases to financially responsible tenants whose presence over a period of time will strengthen the reputation of the building and the neighborhood.

Office and retail leases generally have a longer minimum length of from 5 to 10 years, whereas industrial leases often run for periods of 10 to 25 years or more. Commercial property managers try to negotiate a lease term that is long enough to recover any expenditures made to alter the space for a particular tenant. A long-term commercial lease with an escalator clause is definitely to the owner's advantage, but a manager may not want to grant a long-term percentage lease unless the prospect is a major corporation of proven reputation. Chapter 15 describes the unique situations in industrial leasing.

As explained in Chapter 5, options to renew a lease for an additional term are sometimes granted as a concession to the tenant. Tenants whose presence lends prestige or draws traffic to a commercial or industrial development can usually get renewal options. Other tenants may be granted such options as a trade-off for a higher rental rate or other point of negotiation. During periods of high vacancy, tenants can sometimes insist on a cancellation option in the lease agreement. This clause provides that the tenant may cancel the lease at the end of a predetermined term. Another option available during depressed market conditions allows the tenant to reduce the total amount of rented space at the expiration of a set period. This option may or may not be accompanied by a penalty to the tenant. A contract with either of these options should also require the tenant to pay all or part of any remaining unamortized costs for alterations done for that tenant.

Tenant Alterations. New tenants will have widely divergent requests for alterations or improvements before they move in. Residential tenant demands are usually restricted to decorating expenses such as painting, drapery cleaning, and new carpeting; in fact, many new residential complexes allow incoming tenants to select the decor of their unit prior to occupancy as part of the promotional package for the development. The decision to redecorate an older building is usually tied to the market situation and the urgency of either the landlord's or tenant's situation. An apartment will usually be painted before a tenant moves in, but if the vacancy rate in the area is low, or if the tenant is anxious to occupy the unit, the landlord might agree to furnish the supplies provided that the tenant does the work. Decorating projects for residential property are often undertaken on the strength of an informal verbal agreement between the property manager and the new tenant.

Space for commercial and industrial firms usually has to be highly customized in order to meet the needs of the business activities. The nature and cost of these alterations and the parties responsible for their payment are incorporated into the terms of the lease agreement. Most commercial and industrial buildings will have an established *building standard*—a specified number of outlets, light fixtures, windows, etc.—that are provided in the rental space at the owner's expense. Any equipment or facilities beyond the building standard, such as additional stairways, partitions, doors, truck docks, or sprinkler systems, must then be paid for by the tenant. There is a definite correlation between the nature of the tenant's business and the amount of tenant alterations and amenities required over and above the building standard. Insurance firms usually accept the standard equipment and facilities, but law firms require much more than the building standard because of their emphasis on private offices and attractive decor. Medical offices have particularly expensive requirements.

Tenant alteration costs are a major point of negotiation when dealing with commercial and industrial tenants. When granting concessions on this matter, the manager must consider not only the type of alteration required, but also its total expense to the owner. Negotiation usually involves trade-offs for certain items. The manager should determine a cost ceiling for tenant alteration charges and allow the tenant to specify the particular amenities desired. In this situation, the prospect should be ignorant of what the landlord is willing to spend, perceiving only that he or she is willing to fill certain specified needs.

If a tenant wishes a more luxurious or expensively finished space than the owner can provide, a tenant can be given a straight dollars-per-square-foot allowance. The property manager must determine exactly what the tenant plans to do and make certain that the tenant can and will complete the space accordingly. Tenant improvements should become an asset to the property, and no liens should arise as a result of a tenant's work in the building.

The current trend is for commercial and industrial space to be rented with very few amenities (a minimal building standard). Retail and industrial space especially is often leased as a bare building shell with central heating, ventilating, and air-conditioning systems. The tenant then pays for wall finishing, partitions, and other construction and decorating costs. This is a popular arrangement because the tenant gets a better tax break for financing the alterations than the landlord would. To attract firms to their property, some large commercial and industrial buildings offer a plan for financing tenant alteration costs. The total cost of the improvements, plus interest at a reasonable rate, is amortized over the entire lease term. Package plans for financing the cost of furnishing and equipping the space over the lease period are also offered in some instances.

When an owner pays for tenant alterations, he or she is, in essence, merely financing the costs, which will ultimately be charged back to the tenant in the form of rent.

The manager must outline building standards for the prospect and explain that alterations beyond these standards will either be paid outright by the tenant or reflected in the rental rate. Periodic decorating or upgrading of the space can be incorporated into the lease terms when the market is poor or the tenant desirable. For example, a prestigious blue-chip corporation leasing space in a new office complex might be entitled to have the space repaired every 3 years and recarpeted every 6 years.

Expansion Options. Expansion options usually guarantee that a tenant may lease additional adjacent space in a property after a certain period of time. They are not common in residential leases but are worthwhile concessions to growing commercial and industrial firms. A tenant should be allowed to exercise an expansion option only after a specified term, so that the space can be leased to another tenant in the interim. Obviously, the more fully tenanted a commercial or industrial property is, the less need there is for an expansion clause, since most of the space will already be leased or under option to other tenants.

Noncompeting Tenant Restrictions. Such clauses grant a tenant an exclusive right to operate without competition in the property. Most often found in commercial (especially retail) leases, the clause also may be relevant to service businesses such as barber shops. In general, if a noncompeting tenant restriction can benefit the prospect without damaging the owner's interests, or if the prospect is willing to pay a premium rental rate for it, the concession should be made. It should not be granted if it would exclude prospective tenants who might otherwise be valued occupants of the building. Managers of large shopping malls should avoid granting exclusive rights at all costs, since there are many similar shops in large retail centers and the total effect is to stimulate business and encourage competition.

Defraying Moving Expenses. Lessening the burden of moving costs, either directly or indirectly, is another way to make a lease attractive to a prospective tenant. A prospect may like the space but feel disinclined to move because of an unexpired existing lease. In some situations, it might be economically feasible for the manager to assume a tenant's unexpired lease. This is simply a transaction between the tenant and the property owner (or manager as an agent) whereby the latter agrees to take over the payments on the tenant's current lease, contingent upon the tenant renting space in the manager's building. The viability of lease assumption will depend upon the terms of the present lease, the period remaining, the possibility of subletting, and the amount or value of space the prospect will be leasing in the manager's building. The tenant must, of course, have the right to assign or sublet the space. Other factors to consider in deciding whether or not to assume the lease are the existence of a cancellation penalty, an escalation clause, or any other provision affecting the cost of the lease to be assumed.

Most residential leases are for terms of one year, so it is usually easier for the manager to pay the cancellation charge on the tenant's former space than to sublet the space for the short time left. Lease assumption and subletting, then, are most often used for long-term commercial and industrial rental agreements. In these cases, the manager must make certain that sufficient time remains under the present lease to make it possible to sublet the premises; otherwise, the risk of lease assumption will offset any advantage gained by securing a new tenant. The manager should also consider the amount of space the tenant will occupy, the rental rate for the space, and the overall worth of the new lease over its term. Unless these factors more than compensate the manager for the effort and possible loss incurred in lease assumption, the concession should not be made. As a general rule, a tenant whose lease has been bought or assumed should not expect to be given a rental rebate as well. A more indirect way to ease moving costs is to offer stationery and sign allowances to commercial and industrial tenants. An otherwise hesitant prospect might be convinced to make the move if letterhead stationery and advertising signs reflecting the firm's new address are supplied free of charge.

QUALIFYING THE TENANT

A prospective tenant's real estate needs, financial capability, and long-range business objectives are usually at least partially qualified before he or she applies for a lease. The lease application itself is a very good source for this information. In any event, the manager should always deal with the person who has authority to enter into contractual agreements on behalf of a company or organization.

Lease Applications

Every prospect, whether residential, industrial, or commercial, should be required to fill out an application for a lease. The range of information requested on the application may vary, depending upon the type of tenant involved and the demands of the owner. The manager must look closely at the prospect's identity, rental history, and financial status.

Figure 11 is a form typical of the kind furnished for residential applicants. It asks for the prospective tenant's present address and phone number, social security number, employment history, and banking references. Information on the spouse's employment record is also requested, as is the name and address of the applicant's present landlord.

The questions in the commercial lease application on page 128 are indicative of the type of information requested from office, retail, and industrial tenants. The business location, the organizational structure, and banking references must be listed. Office, retail, and industrial lease applications emphasize the profit and loss record of the company over the past several years. Because of the greater net worth of such leases, it is important that commercial and industrial tenants be financially sound. The economic growth pattern of the tenant is of special significance when leasing retail space in a shopping center, where each business depends upon the strength and success of its neighbors to generate the customer traffic needed to make a profit.

Evaluation of Data

Identity. The personal satisfaction of each tenant is dependent to some degree on the congeniality of the group as a whole. The nature of the prospect's family or business will have a direct bearing on his or her compatibility with other tenants of the property. A pawnbroker would be out of place in a building occupied predominantly by distinguished attorneys, as would a family with three children in a building

Figure 11: APPLICATION FOR LEASE, RESIDENTIAL

Date _____

Address _____ Unit No. _____ ID No. _____

Monthly Rental $ _____   Damage Deposit $ _____   Security Deposit $ _____

Lease Term: Start _____ End _____

Parking Rental $ _____ Space No. _____

Other Charges _____

Remarks _____

Applicant _____

Applicant _____

Name and Relationship of Others Who Will Occupy Unit _____
_____

Personal Reference _____ Relationship _____

    Address _____ Phone _____

Present Address _____ Rent $ _____

How Long There _____

Reason for Moving _____ Pets _____

Landlord's Name _____ Phone _____

    Address _____ _____

Previous Address _____ Years _____

Previous Landlord _____ Phone _____

Applicant's Employer _____ Years _____

    Address _____ Phone _____

    Position _____ Supervisor _____

Spouse's Employer _____ Years _____

    Address _____ Phone _____

    Position _____ Supervisor _____

Annual Income _____ Applicant _____ $ _____

    Spouse _____ $ _____

    Other _____ $ _____

    Total Income . . . . $ _____

(continued)

LEASE APPLICATION—Cont.

Bank:

Checking _____ Acct. No. _____

Savings _____ Acct. No. _____

Credit References:

Name _____ Acct. No. _____ Mo. Payment $_____

Name _____ Acct. No. _____ Mo. Payment $_____

Name _____ Acct. No. _____ Mo. Payment $_____

Have you ever had any judgments, liens, or bankruptcy?

If yes, explain _____

Source of Referral: Newspaper Ad ☐   Sign ☐   Other ☐

Directory Listing to Read:

I (we) hereby make an application for lease for the above described premises and services, on the terms above specified, and deposit herewith the sums of $ _____ as an earnest money deposit and $10.00 to cover the cost of a credit report. The earnest money deposit is to be refunded unless this application is accepted within a reasonable time from the date hereof. **It is understood that the credit report fee is not refundable.** As an inducement to the owner of the property and to to accept this application, I (we) warrant that all statements above set forth are true. I (we) further agree to abide by the rules, regulations, and obligations which are included or attached to the lease.

The undersigned applicant(s) hereby authorize(s) _____ and any consumer or credit reporting agency or bureau employed by it to investigate our (my) character, general reputation, mode of living, credit and financial responsibility and the statements made with this Application, and to inquire of and check with the persons and references named therein, and also authorize(s) such credit or consumer reporting agency or bureau to make a consumer or credit report in connection therewith.

If you accept this application and deliver a lease to me (us) for execution on the above terms in the form prepared by you, I (we) shall within seven days thereafter execute and deliver the same to you and deposit with you simultaneously a sum equal to one month's rent together with the security deposit for the faithful performance by me (us) of all the terms, conditions, and covenants by said lease, less the earnest money deposit you shall then apply to the security deposit. If I (we) fail or refuse to execute and deliver the said lease to you within the seven-day period, the earnest money deposit made herewith is to be retained by you as liquidated damages, and there shall be no further liability on the part of the owner, or the undersigned in respect to said proposed lease or this application.

This application shall not be binding upon the owner until accepted in writing. The delivery of a lease to the undersigned for signature shall not be construed as an acceptance of this application nor shall such lease be binding upon the owner until it has been executed on the owner's behalf and delivered to the undersigned.

Applicant's Signature _____ Date _____

Date _____

Earnest Money Deposit _____ First Month's Rent _____

Credit Report Fee _____ Security Deposit _____

Other Deposits _____

Application Taken By _____ Total Due _____

APPLICATION APPROVED: _____ DATE: _____

Figure 12: APPLICATION FOR LEASE, COMMERCIAL

Date _____

Application is hereby made for lease of the following described premises:

Location _____ Square footage: _____

Use _____

By _____

Incorporation, State of _____

From _____ to _____

At a monthly rental of _____

Number of years in business: _____

Present locations: 1. _____

2. _____

3. _____

4. _____

Present landlords: 1. _____

2. _____

3. _____

4. _____

First bank reference: _____

Officer with whom business is done: _____

Second bank reference: _____

Officer with whom business is done: _____

Business references: 1. _____

2. _____

3. _____

4. _____

Personal references: 1. _____

2. _____

Applicant's name _____

Business address _____

Business telephone _____

Residence address

Residence telephone _____

Signature: _____

tenanted by young singles. Special attention must be paid to the nature of a prospective tenant's business when leasing commercial space, since existing tenants may have leases containing noncompeting tenant restrictions. Tenant mix is especially important in retail properties.

When assessing the compatibility of prospective tenants, the manager must be careful not to violate the Civil Rights Act of 1968, also known as the Fair Housing Act, which makes it illegal to refuse a prospective tenant on the basis of race, religion, or country of origin. Fair housing posters must be displayed on certain premises. The property manager has to be familiar with the terms of the Fair Housing Act in order to fulfill his or her obligations as stated therein. In addition, the Civil Rights Act of 1866, as affirmed by the U.S. Supreme Court in the case of Jones vs. Mayer in 1968, prohibits racial discrimination in the sale or leasing of any type of property, real or personal.

Rental History. The stability of the tenant's rental history will also influence the manager's or owner's final decision. A property manager is likely to consider a family or a company that changes locations frequently a poor rental risk. With commercial or industrial space, which must be heavily modified to meet the tenant's specifications prior to occupancy, it is especially important that the prospect have a stable past record. The future expansion of the prospective tenant should also be considered. It may not be wise for the manager to act favorably on an application from a firm or family that is in a growth stage, for space that is adequate now may not be in several years. The tenant's growth pattern will necessitate a temporary occupancy. The property manager will have to evaluate such situations carefully and consider all circumstances.

Financial Status. It is always in the owner's best interests to verify the references given on the application. Brief phone calls to banking and employment references listed on the application are often sufficient when residential tenants appear to qualify in all other ways and when the amount of money and lease term are not too great. Property managers wanting to make a more in-depth analysis of a prospective tenant can submit a formal request for a credit report to a local company offering this service. The credit bureau will then send the manager a report on the financial reliability of the prospect. This statement is a codified itemization of the status of the prospect's past and current accounts, usually identified by industry (bank, department stores, and so on). The quantity and dates of all payments are listed on the report along with an indication of their regularity. All outstanding balances are reflected. The last column reveals by code the prospective tenant's usual method of payment. The letter indicates the type of account (open, revolving, installment) and the number refers to the payment pattern. A rating of 1 is the highest, given for payments made as agreed; bad debts that must be turned over to a collection agency receive a rating of 9.

Financial status of commercial or industrial tenants can be ascertained by consulting a Dun & Bradstreet reference book or report. Dun & Bradstreet is an international credit reporting agency that many large management firms subscribe to. Figure 13 shows a summary of the company's rating system. The reference book provides information on the nature and age of each listed firm, along with a composite credit rating and estimated financial strength. The coded rating, ranging from a high of 5A=1 down

Figure 13: DUN & BRADSTREET RATING SYSTEM

Key to Ratings

ESTIMATED FINANCIAL STRENGTH		COMPOSITE CREDIT APPRAISAL			
		HIGH	GOOD	FAIR	LIMITED
5A	$50,000,000 and over	1	2	3	4
4A	$10,000,000 to 49,999,999	1	2	3	4
3A	1,000,000 to 9,999,999	1	2	3	4
2A	750,000 to 999,999	1	2	3	4
1A	500,000 to 749,999	1	2	3	4
BA	300,000 to 499,999	1	2	3	4
BB	200,000 to 299,999	1	2	3	4
CB	125,000 to 199,999	1	2	3	4
CC	75,000 to 124,999	1	2	3	4
DC	50,000 to 74,999	1	2	3	4
DD	35,000 to 49,999	1	2	3	4
EE	20,000 to 34,999	1	2	3	4
FF	10,000 to 19,999	1	2	3	4
GG	5,000 to 9,999	1	2	3	4
HH	Up to 4,999	1	2	3	4

GENERAL CLASSIFICATION

ESTIMATED FINANCIAL STRENGTH		COMPOSITE CREDIT APPRAISAL		
		GOOD	FAIR	LIMITED
1R	$125,000 and over	2	3	4
2R	$50,000 to $124,999	2	3	4

EXPLANATION

When the designation "1R" or "2R" appears, followed by a 2, 3 or 4, it is an indication that the Estimated Financial Strength, while not definitely classified, is presumed to be in the range of the ($) figures in the corresponding bracket, and while the Composite Credit Appraisal cannot be judged precisely, it is believed to fall in the general category indicated

ABSENCE OF RATING (- -) THE BLANK SYMBOL

A blank symbol--should not be interpreted as indicating that credit should be denied. It simply means that the information available to Dun & Bradstreet does not permit us to classify the company within our rating key and that further inquiry should be made before reaching a credit decision.

EMPLOYEE RANGE DESIGNATIONS IN REPORTS ON NAMES NOT LISTED IN THE REFERENCE BOOK

Certain businesses do not lend themselves to a Dun & Bradstreet rating and are not listed in the Reference Book. Information on these names, however, continues to be stored and updated in the D&B Business Information File. Reports are available on such businesses and instead of a rating they carry and Employee Range Designation(ER) which is indicative of size in terms of number of employees. No other significance should be attached.

Dun & Bradstreet Credit Services
a company of The Dun & Bradstreet Corporation

1984

KEY TO THE D&B PAYDEX (PAYMENT INDEX)

PAYDEX	PAYMENT
100	ANTICIPATE
90	DISCOUNT
80	PROMPT
70	SLOW TO 15 days
50	SLOW TO 30 days
40	SLOW TO 60 days
30	SLOW TO 90 days
20	SLOW TO 120 days
UN	UNAVAILABLE

KEY TO EMPLOYEE RANGE DESIGNATIONS

ER1	1000 or more	Employees
ER2	500-999	Employees
ER3	100-499	Employees
ER4	50-99	Employees
ER5	20-49	Employees
ER6	10-19	Employees
ER7	5-9	Employees
ER8	1-4	Employees
ERN		Not Available

99 Church Street
New York, N.Y. 10007

18B-7 (831130)

to HH=4, indicates the payment pattern of the business. Dun & Bradstreet reports are more detailed analyses of a single company. They are supplied to Dun & Bradstreet subscribers upon request and payment of a service fee. The reports list the assets, liabilities, and officers of all public (and some private) companies.

When a Dun & Bradstreet report is unavailable or inadequate, a credit report can be obtained from a national credit reporting service. The local chamber of commerce or better business bureau should also have information relevant to the prospect's financial standing and reputation in the community. A follow-up check of the major suppliers for the prospect's business should reveal other facts concerning the company's payment record.

The corporate structure of a prospective commercial or industrial tenant is also important when considering its financial capability. The manager must first determine if the firm is independent, part of a franchise, or a wholly owned subsidiary. In some cases, a prospect may give information about the owning corporation when in fact this corporation will not guarantee the lease or be responsible for losses. Commercial and industrial property managers can avoid this pitfall by finding out if any financial responsibility exists between the franchisee and franchisor, or parent and subsidiary companies.

The rationale behind validating any prospect's financial references is simple. Research indicates that slow or erratic payers generally retain this pattern when making mortgage or rental payments, while prompt and steady payers are consistent in meeting their obligations. A prospective tenant with a history of erratic and delinquent payments should be turned down. If there are only one or two lapses in an otherwise satisfactory record, though, the prospect should be invited to explain these discrepancies before a final decision is made.

SIGNING THE AGREEMENT

After the application has been filled out, verified, and evaluated, and the tenant is found to meet the manager's standards, then the economic viability of the negotiated lease terms must be considered. If the total value of the lease agreement justifies the cost of the concessions, the owner (or the manager as an agent of the owner) will sign the contract and return a copy to the tenant.

Usually a security deposit of at least one month's rent, in addition to the first month's rent, must be paid when the lease is signed. Residential property managers often require deposits to ensure against damage by pets or children. A security deposit is not required for commercial or industrial tenants if the company's net worth is at least two or three times the value of the lease over its entire term. The manager must make sure that the new tenant is given a receipt for all advance charges, security deposits, and additional fees, indicating the purpose for which these payments are made.

Landlord-tenant misunderstandings can be avoided by establishing clear guidelines at the outset. The manager also should give the new tenant a copy of the building regulations and explain them fully. Questions concerning the obligations and rights of the parties under terms of the lease should be settled before occupancy. When at last the lease has been signed, monies received, receipts given, and obligations outlined, the merchandising goal has been attained—the space is leased. From this point forward, responsibility for the success of the landlord-tenant relationship during the lease period will fall largely upon the property manager.

SUMMARY

After merchandising the property, the next step in leasing space is to convince the prospect that the available space is the most suitable at that price. The manager can choose from several closing techniques to convince the prospect to take immediate action.

Negotiation consists of bringing the prospect to an agreement on satisfactory terms for the lease. The manager must maintain control over the process by acting in a professional manner, establishing a direct relationship with all prospects (even when an outside broker is involved), and preventing undue complications stemming from premature involvement of either party's attorney. Almost every item in the lease agreement is a potential point of negotiation. Depending upon the relative strength of the manager's and prospect's positions, certain concessions might be made to induce the prospect to sign. Knowledge of the owner's financial and strategic position, the area market, and the prospect's motivation will show the manager how many and what kind of concessions should be made to attract tenants.

Concessions on rent are the most powerful and potentially detrimental leasing inducements available to the manager. They should be used only in an extremely competitive market. The manager's objective is to adhere to the basic rental schedule for the property while granting temporary free rent to tenants if necessary. Free rent for a short period will usually cost the landlord much less than lowering the rent even a small amount over the term of the lease. Rental rebates are commonly given on a per-month basis and should be negotiated on an individual level. As a general rule, the larger the tenant and the longer the lease, the greater the justification for a rent concession.

Other lease terms often subject to negotiation are the length of the lease period, renewal options, cancellation options, the amount and type of tenant alterations to be undertaken by the owner, expansion options, noncompeting tenant restrictions, and the defraying of some moving costs. The owner may agree to assume the unexpired lease on the prospect's current quarters, depending upon the terms of the existing lease, the period remaining under the lease, the rentability of the space, and the value of the new lease to be executed.

The real estate needs, financial capability, and suitability of prospective tenants must be qualified before the negotiated lease is accepted by the owner or manager. When dealing with corporations, the manager must ascertain whether the person he or she is dealing with has the authority to sign the lease. The most important source of information used in qualifying a prospect is the lease application, although most prospects will have been at least partially qualified before they apply for the lease.

When reviewing a lease application, the manager should first consider the prospect's *identity*. The satisfaction of each individual tenant is dependent to some degree on the congeniality of the tenant group; thus, the prospect's family or business will have a direct bearing on his or her compatibility with the other tenants of the property.

The *stability* of the tenant's rental history must also be taken into account. The manager might question the financial solvency of a family or firm that changes location frequently.

As a minimum precaution, the employment and banking references listed on the rental application should be *verified* by phone. If a more thorough check appears to be in order, a formal request for a credit report can be submitted to one of the many companies offering this service. When running a complete credit check, the critical item to examine is the prospect's method of payment. Research indicates that slow or erratic payers generally retain this pattern in their rental payments, while prompt and steady payers are consistent in meeting their obligations.

Once the tenant has been found acceptable, the economic viability of the negotiated lease terms must be considered. If the total value of the lease agreement justifies the concessions given, the owner, or the manager as the owner's agent, should sign the contract and return a copy to the tenant. At this time the manager should collect the advance deposits and explain the lease terms and building regulations.

QUESTIONS: CHAPTER 6

1. The manager can facilitate lease negotiations by:

    I.   encouraging the prospect and owner to get together and discuss important points.
    II. preventing both parties' attorneys from entering into the negotiating process prematurely.

    a. I only   c. both I and II
    b. II only   d. neither I nor II

2. List three factors that help a manager determine whether or not to grant concessions to a tenant.

    a. _____
    b. _____
    c. _____

3. Graduated rental structures are *not:*

    a. founded on a base standard rental rate.
    b. used for both residential and commercial property.
    c. assessed on a per-square-foot basis for office space.
    d. a concession to the tenant.

4. An office building has a base standard rental rate of $7.60 per square foot for the second floor, and this base rate increases $0.05 per square foot on each higher floor. The rental rate for corner office space is $0.25 per square foot over and above the rate for any floor. How much annual rent must a firm pay for 4,000 square feet on the 14th floor if 500 square feet of the area is corner space?

    a. $32,925   c. $32,800
    b. $28,700   d. $35,425

5. When forced to make rental rate concessions during poor market conditions, the manager tries to:

    I.   lower the basic rental schedule by a very small amount.
    II. grant a temporary rental concession such as a few months' free rent.

    a. I only   c. both I and II
    b. II only   d. neither I nor II

6. A long-term lease is generally to the owner's advantage when:

    I.   negotiating a commercial lease with an escalator clause.
    II. the owner has made significant alterations in the space to suit the tenant.

    a. I only   c. both I and II
    b. II only   d. neither I nor II

7. Options to renew:

    a. can compensate for lower rent payments.
    b. favor the owner.
    c. are often granted to tenants who lend prestige to a building.
    d. are never used with industrial property.

8. Select the *incorrect* response. Concessions on tenant alteration costs:

    a. include the owner's financing of improvements made by the tenant.
    b. should be negotiated on a strict dollar basis with the prospective tenant.
    c. are a major negotiating point with commercial and industrial tenants.
    d. involve equipment, facilities, and amenities beyond the building standard.

9. Expansion options:

    I.   are advantageous to the owner.
    II. are not common with fully tenanted, established properties.

    a. I only   c. both I and II
    b. II only   d. neither I nor II

10. List two methods of defraying moving expenses in order to induce a tenant to lease.

    a. _____
    b. _____

11. The three basic areas in which a prospective tenant is qualified in the application to lease are:

    a. _____
    b. _____
    c. _____

12. When renting residential property:

    I.   a manager should obtain individual credit reports.
    II. a manager cannot, under the fair housing laws, refuse a prospect unless that person has an unsatisfactory credit report.

    a. I only   c. both I and II
    b. II only   d. neither I nor II

13. List four sources of financial information about commercial and industrial tenants.

    a. _____
    b. _____
    c. _____
    d. _____

14. Security deposits:

   I.   are usually at least one month's rent for residential units.
   II. are often not required of large, financially sound corporate tenants.

   a.   I only   c.   both I and II
   b.   II only   d.   neither I nor II

15. When renting or leasing space, good closing techniques include:

   I.   summarizing the benefits of the space and explaining how they satisfy the prospect's needs.
   II. direct questioning to elicit a positive or negative response, such as, "Are you interested in renting this space?"

   a.   I only   c.   both I and II
   b.   II only   d.   neither I nor II

16. What should a property manager determine when a tenant wants to make leasehold improvements at the tenant's expense?

   a.   _____
   b.   _____
   c.   _____

7
Tenant Relations After Leasing

The ultimate success of a property manager will depend greatly on his or her ability to maintain good relations with tenants. Dissatisfied tenants eventually vacate the property, and a high tenant turnover means greater expense for the owner in terms of advertising, redecorating, and unearned rents. The increased attention being given to landlord-tenant relationships by legal and judicial systems has added to the significance of this issue.

An effective property manager will establish a good communication system with tenants, use intangible as well as tangible benefits to keep tenants satisfied, ensure that maintenance and service requests are attended to promptly, and enforce all lease terms and building rules. The property manager must be able to handle recalcitrant residents who do not pay their rent on time or who break building regulations and breed dissatisfaction among the other tenants. Close record keeping will show whether rent is being remitted promptly and in the proper amount. Records of all lease renewal dates should be kept so that the manager can anticipate expiration and retain good tenants who might otherwise move when their leases are up.

If a manager is ineffective for long, the owner's profits will disappear as tenants move out, expenses increase, and unpaid past-due notices pile up. A good manager is tactful and decisive and will act to the benefit of both owner and occupants.

ESTABLISHING A SOUND LANDLORD-TENANT RELATIONSHIP

At the beginning of the tenancy, the manager should inspect the premises with the tenant to determine if promised repairs or alterations have been made, or are in progress. If they have been completed, a written concurrence should be signed by the tenant. In a residential tenancy, inspection of the premises with the tenant is a must. The left column of the residential checklist on page 151 is designed for this initial inspection. This document, signed by the tenant, must be kept by the property manager with the lease records until termination by the tenant, at which time the right-hand column is completed.

Once a mutually satisfactory lease has been signed and the tenant has moved in, the manager's skill in human relations will keep the tenant. Tenants are more likely to renew their leases and remain on the premises if they feel that they are receiving the attention they deserve. The foundation for sound tenant relations is a good reputation for the maintenance and management of the property.

The common theory of constant conflict between landlord and tenant need not be true. In general, owners want a fair return on their investment in the property, based on current market conditions. Tenants, on the other hand, want the best value for their rental dollar and all the services promised to them during lease negotiations. These interests are not mutually exclusive. Though the manager's first responsibility is to the owner, the successful property manager will encourage both parties to work together. Good tenants are an asset. They remain in residence, thereby saving the owner costs of maintenance and tenant turnover. These economic facts can be used to convince the owner that it is more economically advantageous to provide good service to tenants than to concentrate on short-term financial rewards.

Servicing Leases

The first prerequisite for a sound manager-tenant relationship is reciprocal communication. The manager demonstrates good will and availability by staying in touch with tenants, either by telephone or in person. A newly appointed manager must make a special effort to meet each tenant personally as soon as possible. Tenants' comments on the amenities, services, maintenance, and general management of the building should be actively solicited. Some managers do this very amicably by means of an annual or quarterly meeting, or by a written questionnaire. Other managers have strong feelings against holding tenants' meetings, particularly in residential projects, preferring to keep in contact with tenants on an individual basis. One manager, upon taking over a complaint-ridden complex, turned it around in a remarkably short time simply by appearing at poolside every Saturday morning with doughnuts and coffee to solicit tenants' comments. Monthly newsletters or notices are an innovative way of educating occupants about current market conditions, improvements being made to the property, building activities, and other events, such as the appointment or promotion of management personnel.

At the outset of each tenancy, the manager should establish a basic understanding with the tenant on all matters relating to the lease terms. A tenant brochure that outlines all policies and procedures should be given to each new tenant. Managers must not become closely associated with tenants on a social basis since such relationships can cause embarrassment and problems in dealing with other tenants.

The procedures for rent collection should be reviewed by the property manager in detail in a tenant conference when the lease is signed, and tenants should be impressed with the importance of paying rent on the date due. Two schools of thought exist, concerning the imposition of late charges upon tenants delinquent in paying their rent. Some managers reject late charges, preferring to emphasize prompt payment and strict collection procedures; others maintain that late charges are necessary to affirm rigid collection standards. The paying habits of the tenants are a direct reflection of the manager's attention to and enforcement of firm collection policies. A manager taking over an existing complex or center must establish a consistent policy immediately upon taking charge.

The tenant should also be apprised of the penalties for failure to comply with building regulations. The legal aspects of building regulations were discussed in Chapter 5; Figure 14 is an example of typical rules for residential property.

The astute property manager, whether residential, industrial, or commercial, will also cultivate pride and a sense of community among the tenancy. Living and conducting business in the building can be made as pleasant as possible by offering both tangible and intangible benefits. Extra features such as conference rooms, employee lunchrooms, child-care facilities, game rooms, swimming pools, and tennis courts can enhance the appeal of larger office and residential complexes. These amenities are useful in marketing the space and in cultivating a stable tenancy. However, the manager's personal efforts will do more than the amenities themselves to establish friendliness and loyalty among the tenant population. He or she should publicize building activities to encourage tenant identification with the building as a whole. Thoughtful gestures such as providing free coffee in the office cafeteria or decorating a Christmas tree for the lobby every year can enhance the image of the property in the minds of tenants and the public. The manager must keep in mind the importance of prestige and make every effort to create an aura of desirability around the property. A little extra effort and creativity on the part of the manager can go a long way toward developing tenant pride and interest in the building. A satisfied, stable tenant population solidifies the earning capacity of the property and improves the stability of the income, thus fulfilling the manager's primary obligation to the owner.

Maintenance is the single most important factor over which the property manager has control. Chapter 8 is devoted to the various types of maintenance and to the implementation of management programs. A prerequisite for enlightened property maintenance is a system for channeling tenants' service requests to the appropriate parties. A copy of the form used by Lincoln Property Company is shown as Figure 15. The manager must first make certain that the tenant understands the building's maintenance procedures and the proper division of this responsibility between tenant and owner. The tenant should be told what areas are covered under the terms of the lease agreement and also how and to whom to make service requests. While residential leases are generally uniform, rarely will two commercial or industrial leases have the same maintenance provisions. Therefore, a nonresidential property manager must usually consult a commercial lease to verify whether the requested action is the responsibility of the tenant or of the owner. If the tenant is responsible, the tenant must be advised; otherwise, the manager should promptly service the request.

The success of tenant relations also depends to a great extent on the speed of the landlord's response to the tenant's needs. When any service request is made, the tenant should be told immediately when it will be taken care of. If the request is denied, the manager should be honest with the tenant and explain why. The best way to alienate a tenant is to allow him or her to expect something and then to procrastinate and evade the issue if delivery becomes impossible. Excessive service demands from some tenants are a common management problem. The manager should listen courteously to requests and then explain to the tenant that peripheral services will necessitate a rent increase to cover the extra expenditures requested. Because the price of labor is currently rising faster than that of any other commodity, service is becoming more and more prohibitively expensive; hence, increased service demands

Figure 14: RULES AND REGULATIONS FOR RESIDENTS

GENERAL

1. The resident is responsible for the proper conduct of family members and guests and for seeing that they understand and observe all rules and regulations.

2. While the buildings are well-constructed, they are not 100% soundproof. Reasonable consideration of one's neighbors is therefore important.

    a. No resident shall play, or allow to be played, any TV, radio, hi-fi, organ, piano or other musical instrument at a sound level that may annoy or disturb occupants of other units. Particular care must be exercised in this respect between the hours of 10:00 P.M. and 9:00 A.M.

    b. No resident shall make or permit any disturbing noises in the building or adjacent grounds by himself, his family or visitors, nor permit anything by such persons that will interfere with the rights, comforts or convenience of other residents.

    c. Hallways, laundry rooms and storage areas are not play areas for children and should not be used as such. They should be used only for the purpose for which they were originally intended.

3. The installation of aerials or antennas of any kind is not permitted outside of apartments or townhouses.

4. Common areas of buildings such as stairs, stairwells, halls, lobbies, etc., are to be used only for the purpose intended. No articles belonging to owners should be kept in such areas. Boots and rubbers should not be left in corridors nor should doormats be placed outside the front doors.

5. To prevent water damage to their own or adjoining apartments, residents should close all windows tightly when leaving the apartment and building. When the resident is absent from the unit during the heating season, the thermostat shall be placed at a minimum 62-degree setting to avoid freezing pipes and resulting damage.

6. Residents shall not store anything in their apartment or storage room that can create a fire hazard.

7. Soliciting of any type will not be permitted in the buildings at any time, except by individual appointment with a resident.

PATIOS AND BALCONIES

1. Mops, cloths, rugs, brooms, vacuum cleaner bags, etc., must not be dusted nor shaken from apartment windows, halls or stairwells.

2. Residents shall not sweep or throw, or permit anyone to sweep or throw from apartments or balconies, any dirt, dust, cigarettes, cigars, ashes, water, paper or other material.

VEHICLES

1. No vehicle belonging to a resident or a member of the resident's family, guest or employee shall be parked in such a manner as to impede passage in the street or to prevent ready access through the adjoining alley.

2. Cars, trucks, and motorcycles are not to be driven on the lawns or in any area other than parking areas, streets or driveways.

RULES AND REGULATIONS—Cont.

STORAGE ROOM

1. Each apartment has a numbered storage locker. If your storage locker has a lock on it or contents in it, call the office and the contents shall be removed.

2. All contents must be placed inside the locker. Anything left outside the lockers shall be removed.

3. Flammable liquids or gas-powered engines and empty boxes are not allowed in the storage areas by Fire Code.

4. It is recommended that all items be stored on wooden pallets or bricks in case of water leakage.

5. Valuable items should not be kept in the storage locker. Lockers are in a low-traffic area of the building and hence are more easily accessible to burglars. Report any suspicious person around the area to the police.

LAUNDRY FACILITIES

1. In consideration for other residents, common laundry facilities should be utilized only between the hours of 8:00 A.M. and 10:00 P.M.

2. Equipment failure or malfunction should be reported to the number posted on the machine so that prompt repairs may be made.

WINDOWS

All windows should be draped with curtains or drapes. Blankets and sheets are not suitable unless converted to drapes or curtains, not simply tucked or hung over drapery rods.

MISCELLANEOUS

Please note that although the fireplaces in many of the apartments were once functioning, they are no longer usable. Fires of any kind present extreme hazards to all residents due to the dangers of smoke and carbon-monoxide poisoning. For this reason, the fireplaces are decorative and **NONFUNCTIONING**. Do not attempt to burn in them. The chimneys have been sealed to prevent heat loss and to help us reduce our heating costs.

Figure 15: MAINTENANCE REQUEST FORM

LINCOLN PROPERTY COMPANY **Maintenance Request**		No. 34456

APT. #

NAME

TELEPHONE NO.

DEAD BOLT INFO.	RECEIVED	COMPLETED

UNABLE TO ENTER

WORK REQUESTED:

PARTS TO BE ORDERED:

DATE ORDERED:

DELIVERY SCHEDULED:

REMARKS:

UNABLE TO COMPLETE BECAUSE:

SPECIAL LOCK

PET

FILTER CHANGE

APARTMENT CONDITION

GOOD

POOR

ASSIGNED TO   COMPLETED BY   TAKEN BY

ORIGINAL

Reprinted with permission of Property Company of America.

that call for additional personnel must ultimately result in disproportionately higher rents. If tenants realize this, they will be more amenable to a compromise.

No matter how responsive management might be to tenant demands, good relations with tenants can be swiftly destroyed if tenants are made to feel that their requests are an annoyance. Maintenance personnel, the superintendent, and the staff of the management office should handle tenant requests in a pleasant manner. Likewise, service personnel should be taught to speak courteously, especially on the telephone, where they are judged only by sound. On-site maintenance people should be neatly groomed; in fact, service uniforms are a good idea if they prove to be economically feasible. The property manager must set a good example in this regard.

LEASE RENEWALS

Unless the lease agreement includes an automatic renewal clause, it will expire on the date specified in the contract. A tenant whose lease is expiring usually has no overwhelming need or desire to move to new quarters. Whether or not the tenant stays depends upon the tenant-manager relationship and the terms of the new lease.

Market conditions at the time of expiration will exert a strong influence over the concessions or terms granted under the new lease. In general, bargaining will center around three factors—the length of the new lease term; the extent of repairs, alterations, or redecorating to be done; and the amount of rent to be paid.

The actual negotiation of lease renewals follows the same basic pattern as that discussed in the preceding chapter on securing the initial rental agreement. If the general economic trend is inflationary, the manager should probably push for an increased rental rate and a short lease term or for an escalation clause. During a deflationary trend the manager should favor a longer lease term in order to secure the current higher rental rate for as long as possible. The tenant will usually expect to receive other concessions in return for signing a longer lease at a fixed rent rate during a time of falling prices.

In a lease renewal situation, the manager must weigh one additional factor that was not present during the initial negotiations. A stable tenant with a record of timely rental payments is a proven quantity and an asset to the owner. Furthermore, the present tenant will probably make fewer demands for redecorating or other alterations than would a new occupant.

The extent of repairs, alterations, or redecorating to be done will be influenced by market conditions, particularly by the competition in the market, and the manager will have to be up to date on concessions being offered by competitors. If an alteration desired by a tenant will become a permanent improvement to the property, the manager may be able to charge it to a previously allocated fund which could allow some flexibility in the rental rate.

Naturally enough, the most important issue in lease renewals is the rental rate. Rental increases necessitated by rising operating costs are the most frequent cause for contract changes. With commercial property especially, the rent paid over the initial lease term may have included the cost of extensive preparation and tenant alterations. Since this work has been paid for by the time the lease is renewed, the rental rate may then revert back to the base rent, plus any increases deemed necessary by management. According to surveys made by the Building Owners and Managers Association and the Institute of Real Estate Management, operating costs (excluding taxes and insurance) consume more than 43 percent of an office property's gross income and approximately 41 percent of an apartment building's income. Wages and taxes are currently increasing at a faster rate than rents in most areas.

The manager can avoid the irritation, inconvenience, and legal complications of a holdover tenancy by communicating with the tenant some time before expiration of the lease. Residential tenants can be approached about 90 days before lease expiration, but commercial and industrial tenants should be contacted from 6 months to a year before the expiration date. The time interval generally depends on the tenant, the property, and the specific lease.

RENTAL INCREASES

Both the tenant and the manager dislike rental increases. The former does not want to pay more, and the latter fears that a high vacancy rate will discredit him or her as a manager. Actually, a 100-percent occupancy level may indicate that the rental schedule for the building is too low in comparison to the area market and that it is time for an increase. The tenant and the manager must accept the economic realities involved in making real estate investments show a profit. Cutting expenses by eliminating certain services or maintenance activities (such as exterior upkeep) is a self-defeating proposition. Tenants may not complain about these cuts as volubly as they would about a leaking faucet that was not repaired, but a cutback in exterior maintenance expenditures will detract from the general appearance of the property. Over a period of years, high-grade tenants will be replaced by lower-quality occupants, and the property will become even less desirable. The only effective method of strengthening a property's earning power is to raise rents while striving for better operating efficiency.

The threat of organized tenant protest against rent increases is greatly overstated. Although the manager might receive an initial flurry of termination notices, the number of tenants who actually move after they have had a chance to shop the market will be considerably less. Even if a few of the tenants do vacate, the higher rental schedule for the property will tend to absorb the brief vacancy loss until the units can be rented at the new rate. In fact, despite the loss of some tenants and a temporary increase in the vacancy rate, total income for the month immediately after the increase may sometimes exceed that for the previous month. This holds true only if the rental increase is justified in terms of the property and the area market.

For example, when the average rent for a 50-unit apartment building with full occupancy was increased from $350 to $385, 20 percent of the tenants threatened to move at first. However, by the time the increase went into effect only three tenants had gone, for an overall occupancy level of 94 percent. Before the rent increase, the 50 units earned $17,500 per month. After the raise, even with a 6-percent vacancy factor, the 47 occupied units brought in $18,095—a monthly increase of $595 over the previous month at full occupancy.

Once the manager understands the logic behind a rental raise, he or she can apprise tenants of the need for the increase and maintain good tenant relations while renewing leases. A line graph illustrating the steady increase in operating costs for the building could be included along with the notice of the rent change. Notices citing the specific rising operating costs that necessitated the rent hike could be put in the tenants' mailboxes or posted in common areas. When tenants understand the reason behind a rental increase, their attitudes toward lease renewal will change drastically. When rents are increased, the manager should make sure that building maintenance and services either improve or remain at the same level. Often a simple cosmetic improvement will satisfy the tenants of the owner's good intentions. Regardless of the justification, the combination of increased rent and a decline in service will usually provoke tenant resistance and dissatisfaction. Implementing a quickly completed improvement will help to make a favorable impression on tenants at this critical time, and allow the manager to postpone a more complicated project without losing tenant goodwill.

RENT COLLECTION

Although the manager should provide prompt, efficient service to the tenants in order to establish a solid management-tenant relationship that will encourage lease renewals and maintain a low turnover rate, the tenant should never be accommodated at the expense of the owner. The manager must first serve the interests of his or her principal by setting up a viable system for collecting rent and dealing with uncooperative tenants. Whether the leased space is an office, store, warehouse, or apartment, it is standard practice for rentals to be paid in advance. For convenience, accuracy, and speed in rent collection and record keeping, most monthly rentals are made payable on the first of the month. The promptness with which tenants pay their rent is directly related to the efficiency of the manager's collection policy. Tenants will lose respect for the authority of a manager who is apathetic about rent collection.

There are several approaches the manager may take to elicit prompt payments from tenants, but the most basic is a *clear-cut understanding* between the manager and the tenant. The requirements for prompt payment of rent and the provisions for default should be reviewed when the tenant signs the lease. The manager should explain in a firm but friendly manner that after a specified time, the tenant will be treated as delinquent and that appropriate legal action will be taken if necessary. The manager must not bluff: he or she should follow an established procedure which is rigidly adhered to without exception.

Whether or not tenants receive a rent bill for each payment period is a matter of building policy. Itemized, individual rent statements are a must for buildings whose tenants use variant services. For example, an office building manager might need to issue separate bills reflecting each occupant's share of the operating expenses based on that tenant's utility consumption during the billing period. Commercial tenants may also be billed separately for electricity, light bulbs, special janitorial services, special carpentry or plumbing jobs, and late charges. Machine- or computer-operated accounting systems can print rent bills and receipts simultaneously, but these expensive systems are normally restricted to larger properties and management firms.

Delinquency and Eviction Suit

Although the tenant has been apprised of the fact that immediate action will be taken in the case of delinquency, it is good public relations for the manager to allow a reasonable period of time between the due date and the announcement of action for recovery. This should be a fixed, predetermined period, and in most cases, this interval should not exceed 5 days. During this grace period, the tenant should be sent a reminder notice that states the penalty and warns that further action will be taken if payment is not received immediately. A sample past-due notice used in Pennsylvania is shown here. Any form adopted must conform to the laws of the state where the property is located.

In lieu of a reminder letter, the manager can personally advise a delinquent tenant of the overdue obligation by phone, thereby establishing two-way communication with the delinquent tenant. If the reminder elicits no response from the tenanat, the manager

---

RENT PAST DUE NOTICE _____ 19___

RE: _____

Our records indicate that as of this date, the rent payment for the above property has not been received in our office. If you have paid the rent since this mailing, please disregard this notice.

If the rent has not been paid as of this date, we wish to remind you that all rents are due and payable on the _____ day of each month. After 5:00 PM on the fifth day after due date, all rents will be subject to a _____ late charge. Payments not made by 5:00 PM on the 10th day after due date will be referred to constable for collection. This is established company policy and is not directed to any one individual.

⌐   ⌐ Thank you,

L   ⌐ By _____
Please notify us of any discrepancy or uncertainty.

---

can then initiate a suit for eviction to regain possession of the premises, for a vacancy is better than an occupied space earning no rent. To bring an eviction suit, the manager must fill out an eviction form in triplicate. A sample form used in Illinois is shown as Figure 16. One copy is to be served to the tenant, another is given to the manager's attorney to be filed in court at a later date, and the third is retained by the manager. Care must be taken when completing this form, as improperly drawn notices are frequently thrown out of court. An attorney familiar with the requirements of the jurisdiction where the property is located should draft this form.

Precise eviction procedures are regulated by state statute. In some states, the manager must wait only 3 days after giving the eviction form to the tenant before allowing the attorney to file the notice in court; in other states, this period may be as long as 10 days.

Other Reasons for Eviction

In addition to nonpayment of rent, other permissible grounds for eviction of a tenant include certain breaches in the terms of the lease agreement as discussed in Chapter 5. If no written lease is in effect, grounds for eviction would usually include noncompliance with building rules, misrepresentation or fraud, violation of the law, excessive occupants on the premises, excessive use of utilities, abuse of fixtures, and any miscellaneous activities that disrupt the other tenants' right to quiet enjoyment of the premises.

Legal eviction procedures for any of these causes are the same as those for nonpayment of rent, as determined by state law. Before legal action can be taken, the tenant must always be given notice of breach or improper conduct and an opportunity to rectify the situation. Only if the tenant fails to make a good faith effort to correct the situation can the manager initiate dispossess proceedings and a judgment decree for damages.

Figure 16: FIVE-DAY NOTICE

To_____

      You are hereby notified that there is now due the undersigned landlord the sum of_____

_____Dollars and_____Cents,

being rent for the premises situated in the_____, County of_____

and State of Illinois, described as follows, to wit: _____

_____

_____

together with all buildings, sheds, closets, out-buildings, garages and barns used in connection with said premises.

      And you are further notified that payment of said sum so due has been and is hereby demanded of you, and that unless payment thereof is made on or before the expiration of five days after service of this

notice your lease of said premises will be terminated_____

_____ is hereby authorized to receive said rent

so due, for the undersigned.

      Dated this_____day of_____, 19____

                                                          _____
                                                               Landlord

            By_____
                                                            Agent or Attorney

STATE OF ILLINOIS   } SS.   AFFIDAVIT OF SERVICE—When served by a person not an officer.
COUNTY OF_____ }

_____, being duly sworn, on oath deposes and

says that on the_____day of_____, 19____ he served the within notice

on the tenant named therein, as follows:*

    (1) by delivering a copy thereof to the within named tenant,_____.

    (2) by delivering a copy thereof to_____,
a person above the age of ten years, residing on or in charge of the within described premises.

    (3) by sending a copy thereof to said tenant by ** {certified / registered} mail, with request for return of receipt from the addressee.

    (4) by posting a copy thereof on the main door of the within described premises, no one being in actual possession thereof.

    Subscribed and sworn to before me this

_____day of_____, 19____ }
                                 *Strike out all paragraphs not applicable.
_____ }   **Strike out word not applicable.
      Notary Public

George E. Cole ® Legal Forms, reprinted with permission
of Boise Cascade Corporation. This form applicable only in
Illinois. No representations are made as to its legal sufficiency
or accuracy due to the possibility it has become outdated as
a result of changes in the law.

TERMINATING THE TENANCY

Notice of intent to vacate must be given within a specified period, which should be included in the terms of most lease agreements. If a good tenant decides to move, the manager should contact him or her immediately to find out whether the decision was prompted by any oversight on the part of management. If so, the manager should ascertain if the situation can still be corrected, thereby retaining a valuable tenant. Even if the tenant's decision is irreversible, the manager should note the reasons behind it and file them for future reference. An exit interview between manager and tenant should be made in person if possible and should be a routine procedure; Figure 17 is a sample form for this type of interview. A compilation of the responses of all tenants who have moved recently should give the manager some insight into possible improvements that could be made in the management of commercial, residential, or industrial properties.

Similarly, the manager can refuse to renew a lease by giving the tenant appropriate notice of termination. This procedure can be used in lieu of the more expensive and time-consuming court eviction suit, provided that the tenant's conduct is not too destructive and the remaining lease term is short. In order to stay on firm legal footing, the manager who does not renew a lease should have demonstrable proof of just cause for the refusal.

Inspection of the Premises

Whenever a lease is terminated by either party, the manager should inspect the space with the tenant before the tenant leaves to determine the repainting and refurbishing that will be needed before the space can be rented again. A second inspection should be conducted directly after the tenant has removed his or her personal property. Further maintenance needs will become apparent on this tour of the unit and any deductions to be made from the security or cleaning deposits can be calculated at this time. To facilitate this procedure, the manager might carry along a checklist, such as the one in Figure 18, to make note of the condition of each room or area, repairs needed, and when they can be scheduled. Similar forms should be used for commercial space.

Sometimes tenants are poorly informed as to the notice required, the cleaning they are expected to do, and other details of vacating their space. Misunderstandings can be avoided by a letter from the manager outlining the procedures tenants should follow when moving out. When a security deposit is refunded to a tenant, it should be accompanied by another letter explaining any deductions from the deposit funds.

SECURITY DEPOSITS

Prompted by the Uniform Residential Landlord and Tenant Act, many states have passed security deposit statutes, which are becoming more detailed and stringent, and the manager must be aware of them to develop an equitable and legal policy. In some states, landlords are required to keep security deposits in a federally insured financial institution based in the state where the property is located. Some states

Figure 17: TENANT EXIT INTERVIEW

Date: _____   Property: _____

Name: _____

Length of Tenancy: _____   Type of Space: _____

Reason for Moving: _____

_____

_____

_____

_____

_____

Comments/Suggestions: _____

_____

_____

_____

_____

_____

_____

_____

Completed By: _____

_____

_____

_____

_____

require that interest be paid on such deposits. Generally, the amount of the deposit is not set by law.

The laws provide a detailed procedure for the return of a security deposit. Generally, the tenant must make a written demand for the return of the deposit within a certain period after termination of the tenancy. If no demand is made, often the deposit will revert to the landlord.

If the landlord proposes to apply any part of the deposit to sums due from the tenant because of noncompliance with the rental agreement, the landlord must itemize the deductions in a written statement which must be furnished to the tenant. Failure to follow this procedure can result in severe criminal and civil penalties. Acceptable grounds for retaining part or all of the security deposit typically include damages to the premises; unauthorized, nonstandard, or irreversible decorating; excessive cleaning expenses; and unauthorized alterations. Charges made against the security deposit must be documented to establish the case against the tenant, and an inspection checklist is the best means of verification. It is also critical to return the deposit or balance thereof promptly. Again, property managers need to follow local law strictly.

In the past, residential tenants sometimes used security deposits as the last month's rent, but current legislation in some states forbids this practice. If it is not prohibited, the manager should discourage it.

Security deposit legislation also covers the handling of security deposits upon change of ownership of dwelling units. Under the law, the person holding a security deposit must either return the deposit to the tenant or transfer it to the new owner while giving notice to the tenant.

When a property manager is required by law to be licensed as a real estate broker, trust account laws and regulations governing brokers also apply to funds held by a property manager on behalf of tenants.

SUMMARY

The effective property manager will establish personal but not unduly familiar relations with the tenant population, enforce all lease terms and building rules, and be able to handle residents who do not pay their rent on time. If a manager is ineffectual, the net operating income from the property will decline.

The foundation for sound tenant relations is a good reputation for the management of the property. Tenants tend to renew their leases if they are getting the services and benefits they contracted for. Lease renewals eliminate the costs of high tenant turnover, and satisfied, long-term tenants take personal interest in the upkeep of the property, thereby cutting the owner's maintenance costs.

The manager is responsible for maintaining communication and mutual understanding between landlord and tenant. New occupants should be familiarized with rent payment and collection policies and building regulations. The manager should make every effort to instill in them a feeling of involvement and pride in the property.

Figure 18: RESIDENTIAL CHECKLIST

Property: _____

Apartment: _____ Date: _____

Tenant: _____

Tenant should complete this checklist on taking possession of the apartment. Please note existence and condition of each item and sign at bottom.

Keys _____	Keys _____
General cleanliness _____	General cleanliness _____
Kitchen tile _____	Kitchen tile _____
Stove _____	Stove _____
Refrigerator _____	Refrigerator _____
Ice trays _____	Ice trays _____
Countertop _____	Countertop _____
Sink _____	Sink _____
Cabinets _____	Cabinets _____
Dishwasher _____	Dishwasher _____
Disposal _____	Disposal _____
Tub _____	Tub _____
Basin _____	Basin _____
Commode _____	Commode _____
Medicine cabinet _____	Medicine cabinet _____
Bathroom tile _____	Bathroom tile _____
Light fixtures _____	Light fixtures _____
Wallpaper _____	Wallpaper _____
Paint _____	Paint _____
Windows _____	Windows _____
Screens _____	Screens _____
Floors _____	Floors _____
Fireplace _____	Fireplace _____
Air conditioning _____	Air conditioning _____
Thermostat _____	Thermostat _____
Other _____	Other _____

The right column heading: Manager should complete this checklist when tenant vacates premises.

Tenant _____   Manager _____

Manager _____   Date _____

Date _____

Another major factor that determines tenant satisfaction is the actual maintenance of the property. The manager should make certain that the tenant knows the correct procedure for making service requests and what services can be reasonably expected. When service requests are made, the tenant should be told immediately either when the job will be done or why it cannot be performed. All maintenance and management office personnel should be pleasant and accommodating in their dealings with tenants.

The manager can take advantage of the fact that a tenant whose lease is expiring may have no specific need to move. Whether or not a tenant decides to renew a lease usually depends on the nature of the tenant-manager relationship and the terms of the new lease. Bargaining will center around the amount of rent, the extent of alterations or redecorating, and the length of the new lease term. Rising operating costs are the usual cause of rent increases. The manager must look at both the present market conditions and the value of a stable tenant when deciding whether or not to accept new lease terms.

Besides providing prompt, efficient service that will establish a management-tenant relationship conducive to lease renewals, the manager must also protect the owner's interests by setting up an effective system for collecting rent and coping with uncooperative tenants. At the time the tenant signs the lease, the lease terms should be reviewed with the tenant, and he or she should be told about the penalties for failure to pay rent promptly and for noncompliance with other lease terms. The owner has the right to bring a court suit for eviction and a judgment for damages against any delinquent or disruptive tenant. Before initiating legal action, however, he or she must give the tenant sufficient legal notice and time to remedy the situation.

Under most lease agreements, tenants must give notice of intent to terminate within a specified period. The manager should question a valued tenant to determine if the decision to move is based on any management oversight that can still be corrected. Even if the tenant's decision is final, the manager should note the reasons for the move. A compilation of the responses to all tenants who have moved recently should give the manager some insight into possible improvements that might be made in the management of the property. Security deposits must be administered according to local law.

QUESTIONS: CHAPTER 7

1. As the costs of operating a property rise, the manager should:

    I.   cut expenses by eliminating certain service and maintenance activities.
    II. raise the rental schedule.

    a.   I only   c.   both I and II
    b.   II only   d.   neither I nor II

2. List three ways a property manager can maintain good communications with the tenant population.

    a.   _____
    b.   _____
    c.   _____

3. Even if there are no compliance problems, tenants should always be informed about:

    I.   the manager's rent collection policy.
    II. building rules.

    a.   I only   c.   both I and II
    b.   II only   d.   neither I nor II

4. An office building of 200,000 square feet has an average rental rate of $8.50 per square foot and an overall occupancy level of 97 percent. The manager determines from market and property analyses that if the rental rate is raised by $0.20 per square foot, the occupancy level will drop by 2 percent. If the rental rate is raised by $0.40 per square foot, the occupancy level will drop by 6 percent. Conversely, if the rental rate is *decreased* by $0.30 per square foot, the occupancy level will increase to 100 percent. The optimum average rental rate for this office space would be:

    a. $8.50   c. $8.70
    b. $8.90   d. $8.20

5. An apartment building of 75 units, each leased at $310 per month, enjoyed full occupancy. The property manager then instituted a 10-percent rental increase, and five tenants moved out, leaving an occupancy level of 93 percent. The month after the change, the gross rental income:

    a.   decreased by $1,550.   c.   was $23,250.
    b.   increased by $620.   d.   was $21,622.

6. When negotiating lease renewals, bargaining typically centers around these three factors:

    a.   _____
    b.   _____
    c.   _____

7. When renewing a gross lease during a sharply inflationary trend, the property manager should attempt to negotiate:

   I.   an increased rental rate.
   II. a long-term lease.

   a. I only   c. both I and II
   b. II only   d. neither I nor II

8. A tenant's promptness in paying rent depends on:

   I.   an understanding of the tenant's obligations and the consequences of failure to meet them.
   II. the consistency of the manager's collection policy.

   a. I only   c. both I and II
   b. II only   d. neither I nor II

9. To bring an eviction suit, the manager must complete an eviction form in triplicate. List the parties who should have copies of this form.

   a. _____
   b. _____
   c. _____

10. Grounds for termination of a lease and eviction of the tenant usually include:

   I.   violation of building rules.
   II. material breach of the lease.

   a. I only   c. both I and II
   b. II only   d. neither I nor II

11. When negotiating lease renewals, the manager should consider:

   I.   the stability of the present tenant as an asset.
   II. the current market conditions.

   a. I only   c. both I and II
   b. II only   d. neither I nor II

12. List two forms that are essential to an effective rent collection system.

   a. _____
   b. _____

13. Before a landlord takes legal action against a defaulting tenant, the tenant must be given:

   I.   30 days' notice.
   II. an opportunity to rectify the breach.

   a. I only   c. both I and II
   b. II only   d. neither I nor II

14. Enlightened property managers realize that:

   I.   the interests of the owner and tenants are mutually exclusive.
   II. a stable tenancy is an asset.

   a. I only   c. both I and II
   b. II only   d. neither I nor II

15. In general, building rules and regulations serve to protect:

   I.   the owner's investment.
   II. the quiet enjoyment of all tenants.

   a. I only   c. both I and II
   b. II only   d. neither I nor II

16. In general, the management and control of tenant security deposits is:

   I.   at the discretion and control of the landlord.
   II. governed by local laws, such as landlord/tenant legislation.

   a. I only   c. both I and II
   b. II only   d. neither I nor II

Maintaining the Premises

Maintenance is a continuous process of balancing service and costs in an attempt to please the tenancy and preserve the physical condition of the property while holding a ceiling on operating expenses and improving the owner's margin of profit. Efficient property maintenance demands accurate assessment of the needs of the building and the number and types of personnel that will meet these needs. Staffing and scheduling requirements will vary with the type, size, and regional location of the property, so owner and manager usually agree in advance on maintenance objectives for the property. In some cases, the most viable plan might be to operate with a low rental schedule and minimal expenditures for services and maintenance. Another property might be more lucrative when kept in top condition and operated with all possible tenant services because it can then command premium rental rates. Specific maintenance requirements of each major classification of property will be explored in Chapters 11 through 15. This chapter outlines the basic procedures for a sound maintenance program.

BASIC MAINTENANCE PROCEDURES

The successful property manager must be able to function effectively at four different levels of maintenance operations:

- preventative maintenance
- corrective maintenance
- routine maintenance
- new construction

Preventative maintenance is aimed at preserving the physical integrity of the premises and eliminating corrective maintenance costs. Regular maintenance activities and routine inspections of the building and its equipment will disclose structural and mechanical problems before major repairs become necessary.

Corrective maintenance involves the actual repairs that keep the building's equipment, utilities, and amenities functioning as contracted for by the tenants. Repairing a boiler, fixing a leaky faucet, and replacing a broken air-conditioning unit are acts of corrective maintenance.

Routine housekeeping chores are the third and most recurring type of maintenance activity. Common areas and grounds must be cleaned and patrolled daily. Some chores such as vacuuming elevators in office buildings must be done more than once a day, while others—cleaning gutters and windows, for instance—are performed less frequently. Routine maintenance is a major operating expense, consuming as much as 18 percent of the budget for commercial properties. Cleaning and housekeeping should be carefully scheduled and controlled, since costs can easily become excessive.

New construction may be considered a category of maintenance because it includes tenant alterations undertaken at the beginning of a tenancy, alterations requested by the tenant during the lease term, and cosmetic changes designed to increase the marketability of the property. Cosmetic changes include the construction of game rooms, conference rooms, swimming pools, and other major additions intended to make the property more competitive.

THE PROPERTY MANAGER AND THE RESIDENT MANAGER

Most properties of 16 units or more have a manager on the premises at all times. These resident managers (often called *superintendents*) coordinate and execute all maintenance operations for the building. Although a resident manager's responsibilities will increase with the size of the building, this individual always reports directly to the property manager. With this system, a single property manager can stay abreast of the maintenance needs of several large buildings without becoming bogged down in the daily operating routine of each. In addition to reviewing the reports submitted by resident managers, the property manager should visit each building regularly to gather information on necessary maintenance and repairs. Periodic inspections will show the property manager where operating costs can be cut, help him or her enforce the tenants' leases, and give evidence of the resident manager's effectiveness.

As the property management field grows more sophisticated and building equipment becomes more complicated, managers who perform all four maintenance functions have become the exception rather than the rule. Today, it is usually sufficient for a property manager and a resident manager to be aware of the maintenance needs of the property and to know where to turn for help with specific maintenance problems. A property manager need not be a combination decorator, painter, roofer, and plumber, but he or she should understand the rudiments of all mechanical and electrical systems well enough to make intelligent decisions about their care and operation. The manager must also be conversant with the economics, staffing, and scheduling involved in the smooth performance of maintenance tasks. The people who execute the work will be employees of the building or outside personnel engaged on a contract basis.

ON-SITE MAINTENANCE STAFF

The manager's hiring policy for on-site maintenance personnel will usually be based on the cost differential between maintaining a permanent building staff and contracting for the needed services. The amount of construction activity stemming from tenant alteration should determine the hiring policy. When substantial tenant alteration is a regularly recurring event, as it often is in industrial and commercial space, a permanent staff of professional carpenters, electricians, and plasterers might prove cheaper and more efficient than using outside contractors on a steady basis. On the other hand, if a building's leasing policy is such that units are seldom restructured for tenants, then a full-time crew of experienced construction personnel would not be justified. It makes sense to hire outside contractors for major construction jobs and for smaller buildings that cannot bear the expense of a permanent staff.

Minimum personnel requirements should be studied carefully in order to make certain that the full-time staff is large enough to meet the routine maintenance chores of the building. Just as overstaffing can be expensive, so, too, can understaffing. Poor building maintenance will downgrade the premises, and when displeased tenants vacate, rental income drops.

Local union membership policies will also affect the composition of a building's maintenance staff. Semiskilled janitors, skilled general maintenance engineers, electricians, and other artisans are represented by different unions, and union rules generally prohibit the hiring of nonunion workers. Therefore, when hiring a permanent building staff, the manager must consider the possible expense and inconvenience that might arise from mixing union and nonunion workers, or even members of competitive unions.

The hiring and firing of employees should be under the control of the property manager or the owner's agent, and not left to the discretion of the resident manager or superintendent. When screening employees, though, the property manager might welcome the resident manager's opinion of their integrity, industry, and skills. Each applicant for a maintenance position should complete an employment application similar to Figure 19. Although past employment references are important when evaluating an applicant, the manager's hiring decision should not be influenced unduly by them, for personality conflicts sometimes result in an unfavorable report from a former employer, regardless of the capabilities of the employee. The appearance, demeanor, motivation, experience, education, reliability, and performance capabilities of the prospective employee should be the overriding factors.

To avoid future misunderstandings, each newly hired employee should be taken to the premises and shown the specific responsibilities of the job. Simple job descriptions listing the employee's various responsibilities can be helpful during the orientation period.

The manager will want to stress that since each employee represents the owner to the tenant, members of the building staff must be pleasant, businesslike, and neat. Many knowledgeable managers provide service uniforms for maintenance personnel to enhance the prestige of the building and to strengthen employer-employee identification among the maintenance team.

CONTRACT SERVICES

Services performed by outside persons on a *regular basis* for a specified fee are known as contract services. For the protection of both the manager and the owner, service

Figure 19: EMPLOYMENT APPLICATION

PERSONAL INFORMATION	Social Security Number_____

Name   Age   Sex

Present Address   City   State

Permanent Address   City   State

Phone

Date of Birth

Can you legally work in U.S.?

If related to anyone in our employ,
state name and department.

Referred by

EMPLOYMENT DESIRED

Position   Date You Can Start   Salary Desired

Are you employed now?   If so, may we inquire of your present employer?

Have you ever applied to this company before?   If so, when?

EDUCATION	Name and Location of School	Years Attended	Date Graduated	Subjects Studied
Grammar School				
High School				
College				
Trade, Business or Correspondence School				

Subjects of Special Study or Research

EMPLOYMENT HISTORY	Name and Address of Employer	Salary	Position	Reason for Leaving
From				
To				
From				
To				
From				
To				
From				
To				

REFERENCES: Name three people not related to you whom you have known at least one year.

	Name	Address	Business	Years Acquainted
1				
2				
3				

PHYSICAL RECORD

Were you ever injured?   Details

Have you any hearing defects?   Vision?   Speech?

In case of emergency notify

Phone

I AUTHORIZE INVESTIGATION OF ALL STATEMENTS CONTAINED IN THIS APPLICATION. I UNDERSTAND THAT MISREPRESENTATION OR OMISSION OF FACTS CALLED FOR IS CAUSE FOR DISMISSAL. FURTHER, I UNDERSTAND AND AGREE THAT MY EMPLOYMENT IS FOR NO DEFINITE PERIOD AND MAY, REGARDLESS OF THE DATE OF PAYMENT OF MY WAGES AND SALARY, BE TERMINATED AT ANY TIME WITHOUT ANY PREVIOUS NOTICE.

Date   Signature

DO NOT WRITE BELOW THIS LINE

Interviewed By   Date

REMARKS:_____

Neatness		Character	
Personality		Ability	

Hired   Position   Salary

Approved: 1.   2.   3.

EMPLOYMENT MANAGER   DEPT. HEAD   GENERAL MANAGER

contracts should always be in writing and contain a termination provision. The latter stipulation becomes important if service is not satisfactory or if the property is sold or destroyed. When a substantial amount of labor or material is involved, an escalation clause might be incorporated into the contract as protection against inflation.

Before entering into any service contract, the manager should solicit competitive bids on the job from several local agents. He or she can then compare the cost of contracting out with the expense of using on-site personnel. The terms of the management agreement often set a ceiling on the service contracts the manager can execute without approval from the owner. Window cleaning, refuse and snow removal, pest control, and security are services that usually can be performed more efficiently and cheaply by outside contractors. A contracting firm's references and work history should be checked out before it is employed. The manager will also want to know whether its employees are bonded and whether the firm has the necessary licenses or permits.

CONTRACTING FOR NEW CONSTRUCTION

As mentioned earlier, new construction is sometimes required to protect the worth of the property, improve its net income, increase its marketability, or meet the specifications of its tenants. Minor remodeling, cosmetic changes, and tenant alterations are part of the normal maintenance expenses for the property. The basic construction of a new building, especially a commercial one, often includes only the shell and the heating, ventilating, and air-conditioning systems. When space is rented, significant tenant alteration is needed, both up to and beyond the building standard. Typically, the owner pays for improvements up to the building standard. The tenant pays for more extensive alteration and renovation, but such work is often arranged and handled by management as a convenience.

The first decision the manager faces when contracting for construction is whether to let the job to a *prime contractor,* who will sublet the work to the various skilled trades and supervise the project, or whether to act as his or her own prime contractor and let the work directly to the necessary architects, engineers, carpenters, plumbers, and suppliers. Most large alteration and construction jobs are let to a prime contractor, but a manager who performs this function can save money—if he or she has the time, skill, and construction knowledge to supervise and settle differences between the various trades. Moreover, with a prime contractor only one set of plans and specifications is needed, whereas a manager acting as the prime contractor must develop and supply separate plans and specifications for each class of work, while scheduling and coordinating each job.

After deciding whether to hire a general contractor or to contract with the various skilled trades separately, the manager must determine how to obtain the actual contracts. There are two types of contracts for construction—*competitive bids* and *negotiated contracts.* The former are far more prevalent, although there is a trend toward negotiated contracts. Competitive bids may be obtained from general contractors or directly from representatives of skilled trades and suppliers.

Managers who let many large construction projects often opt for the other alternative, negotiated contracts. The manager will first choose one general contractor or one reputable contractor in each field. They will submit a joint proposal estimating the cost of the project. Even if a single general contractor is involved, the estimate should be the end result of collaboration between the plumbing contractor, electrician, hardware supplier, and other tradespeople. The manager and the owner can either accept this single bid and sign a contract or reject it and take further bids. Often, because the contractors in a negotiated bid situation know that they have the manager's commitment to use their services if the price is acceptable, they will do their best to shave costs. Thus, property manager, owner, and contractor all may benefit from negotiated contracts.

Although most construction contracts are negotiated on a *flat-fee basis,* a trusted contractor might ask to be paid on a *cost-plus basis.* In this case, the contractor will furnish a preliminary estimate on the proposed job and will be paid the actual cost of the work plus a percentage for profit, usually around 15 percent. This method of payment is advisable only when dealing with established contractors.

Because of the amount of money they involve, contracts for alterations, remodeling, and other construction should be scrutinized by the manager. The agreement should specify exactly when the contractors will be paid. It is customary to pay about 40 percent of the costs when the job is half-done, but at least 10 percent should be held back for a month after the work is completed in case additional service is necessary. The contract should include a penalty for late completion of the work, and the manager must remember that there is no substitute for personal inspection of the work in progress. On certain projects, the manager may want to engage an architect or engineer to review the contracts and inspect the work as it progresses.

Many owners insist upon a performance bond when letting construction contracts. A performance bond is an insurance policy which guarantees that the work will be completed despite any financial or other problems the contractor may experience. Should the contractor fail to complete the work, the bonding company will arrange for others to finish the job.

The nature and size of the project, as well as the reputation, experience, and financial standing of the contractor help the owner determine whether to demand a performance bond. Small contractors may be unable to secure performance bonds because of small financial resources, in which case the owner or property manager will have to make a business judgment on whether to proceed without a bond.

PREVENTATIVE MAINTENANCE AND MAINTENANCE INSPECTIONS

Preventative maintenance has become a highly developed set of procedures over the past few years. At its best, it involves carefully scheduled maintenance activities and prepared inspection forms that list the important characteristics of the property's physical elements and systems. The purpose of preventative maintenance is twofold— to cut down on repair and replacement costs and to avoid interruptions in service to the tenants. Preventative maintenance programs should be implemented in both small and large properties and may range from the efforts of a part-time maintenance worker to a sophisticated computerized program headed by a full-time employee.

Designing the Program

There are five basic steps in designing a preventative maintenance program to fit the needs of a particular building:

1. take an inventory of equipment and building
2. determine necessary tasks
3. calculate the cost
4. schedule the tasks
5. keep records

Selection of proper building products is critical when space is remodeled or new space is constructed. A property manager should keep up to date on new products through subscriptions to trade magazines or a service which publishes information, such as *Sweet's Catalogue* or *Hutton's Building Products Catalogue.* The Construction Specifications Institute also has published a standard filing system for building products, which is followed by most manufacturers and used by architects and contractors.

First, make a complete inventory of all equipment. Each item should be listed and described, including its manufacturer, operating procedures, location in the building, date and place of purchase, and existing warranties. The inventory should indicate where to obtain parts and service and when each item needs to be lubricated, cleaned, or overhauled. Physical elements such as walls and supports should be listed by location and described. A complete set of such records will ensure systematic preventative maintenance, relieve the tenant of interruptions in building service, and save the owner money. The manager can then decide what equipment and physical structures should be included in the preventative maintenance program.

Second, the manager and the maintenance superintendent must decide what type of inspections and preventative maintenance tasks should be performed, and how frequently. Structural items such as walls and roofs should be scheduled for inspection, painting, and patching. Equipment such as elevators, air conditioning, heating plants, pumps, and motors also should be inspected and serviced regularly. Spare parts should be kept on hand to replace broken or worn machine parts. Figures 20 and 21 are typical forms used for preventative maintenance of certain elements of the heating and cooling system in a large regional shopping center. The exterior and interior of the building should be checked periodically. Some areas need to be checked daily, while others can be examined less frequently. The resident manager or superintendent should submit daily and weekly inspection reports to the property manager.

Next, the manager must calculate how much time, labor, and money the preventative maintenance program will require. The final figures must be realistic in terms of both the budget and the amount of work involved.

In a fourth step, the manager will schedule the necessary preventative maintenance tasks. Since these tasks vary in frequency—some performed weekly, some bimonthly,

Figure 20: CHILLER WINTER INSPECTION

Ref. File		Sheet
No. _____		_____ of _____

Unit No. _____   Year _____   Division _____

MAINTENANCE CODE	CONDITION CODE
TOP — test operation (observe, correct calibration, adjust as required)	G — good (minor deterioration)
VIS — visual inspection	F — fair (moderate deterioration)
LUB — lubricate (change oil)	P — poor (replace this inspection)
CLN — clean as required	
REP — replace	

ITEM	MAINT. CODE	COND. CODE	SET POINT	DATE	ENGINEER INITIAL
condenser	VIS-CLN				
evaporator	VIS-CLN				
lube oil cooler	VIS-CLN				
control ampl. tubes	REP				
refr. filter/dryers	REP				
oil reservoir	LUB				
purge oper. contr.	VIS-TOP				
purge hi-limit contr.	VIS-TOP				
purge oil reservoir	LUB				
lube oil filter	REP				
cond. corrosion plugs	VIS				

Remarks: _____

_____

_____

_____

_____

Figure 21: MOTOR STARTER INSPECTION

Ref. No.		Sheet
_____		_____of _____

Equipment No. _____ Year _____ Division _____

MAINTENANCE CODE

BO — blow out dust and dirt	DR — dress/polish
CB — check for binding and rubbing	MEG — megger motor
	TOP— test operate and calibrate
CCP— check contact points for corrosion and pitting	TT — tighten terminals
CFR — check fuse rating	VI — visually inspect
CI — take contact impressions	VS — verify size of overload
CLN — clean	
CT — check tension	
CW — check for wear	

CONDITION CODE

G — good (minor deterioration
F — fair (medium deterioration)
P — poor (usable, replace next inspection)
N — new (replace this inspection)

ASSEMBLY	MAINT. CODE	COND. CODE	REMARKS
main contacts	CLN-CW-CT-DR-CI-CCP		
holding coil	CLN-MEG-TT		
contactor armature	CLN-CB		
shunts	CLN-VI-TT		
arc chutes	CLN-VI		
blowout coils	BO-CLN-VI-TT		
secondary contacts	CLN-VI-DR-TT-CCP		
thermal overloads	BO-VI-VS-CB-CCP-TT		
control switch	CLN-VI-TT		
control fuses	VI-TT-CFR		
float switch	CLN-VI-TT-TOP		
alternator	CLN-VI-TT-TOP		
secondary circ.	TT-VI		
press switch	CLN-VI-TT-TOP		
temp. control switch	CLN-VI-TT-TOP		
limit switches	CLN-VI-TT-TOP		
selector switches	CLN-VI-TT		
disconnect switch	VI-TT		
motor	MEG-TT		

MOTOR   MEG   OHM   Reading _____ Line Voltage _____

O/L Heater Size No. _____ AMPS _____Fuse Type _____VOLTS _____ AMPS _____

Date _____ Man Hours _____ Engineer _____ Review _____

others seasonally—a full-year schedule should be worked out, along with a system for issuing work orders and checking the completion of this work.

Lastly, the manager must follow through on the program by keeping records on the results of preventative maintenance inspections and tasks for each piece of equipment. These records will eventually show whether certain checks and activities can be performed less frequently, thereby saving labor and money, or whether certain items should be inspected more often. They also verify that maintenance personnel are actually performing these tasks and demonstrate the cost-effectiveness of the preventative maintenance program.

A well-designed and implemented preventative maintenance program may not show significant results or savings for 6 months to a year, but it will ultimately pay off in terms of increased efficiency and economy of operations.

Routine Inspections

From a practical viewpoint, the manager's first responsibility is to be aware of the overall condition and operations of each property under his or her care. The manager's effectiveness as a maintenance administrator will depend upon the thoroughness of the routine inspections and on the manager's ability to pinpoint and correct laxness in the maintenance team. In addition to reviewing the preventative maintenance reports, the property manager should conduct his or her own spot checks and a tour of the premises, preferably once every month or 6 weeks. These inspection trips allow for a more extensive check of the systems, equipment, and condition of the building. Seasonal checks of the building's weatherproofing are also the usual responsibility of the property manager.

The most important feature of a maintenance check is that it be a routine procedure. Many potentially serious problems can be averted by regular inspections. The inspections will be more comprehensive if the manager brings along checklists of the building features to be examined. These should include the names of the maintenance personnel employed by the building and the tasks for which they are responsible. The manager can then rate the performance of building employees while touring the physical premises. Sample inspection forms for the different types of property are provided in the appropriate chapters.

In general, the manager should inspect all interior and exterior features of each property for which he or she is responsible. The exterior check includes comments on the condition of the grounds, walls, entrance steps, doorways, mailboxes, fire escapes, windows, eaves, and roof. Maintenance needs and their approximate cost should be entered on the checklist to help the manager set up a performance schedule and operating budget. While it is not wise to become enmeshed in trivial daily maintenance problems, the property manager must be aware of all major concerns around the premises since he or she is ultimately accountable for all maintenance expenditures. The inspection checklist can help the manager explain to the owner any expenditures made for maintenance service and repairs.

When examining the interior of any property, the manager should observe the condition of the entranceway, stairwells, corridors, elevators, light fixtures, lobby and other common areas, heating and ventilating plant, hot water heater, plumbing system, and sewage disposal unit. Needed repairs and their anticipated cost should be noted on the checklist. Doors, locks, transoms, ceilings, baseboards, windows, light fixtures and switches, electrical outlets, floors, plumbing, and any permanent fixtures also should be inspected when checking recently vacated space.

The property manager should tell all tenants to report problems and maintenance needs immediately to the management or building office. Tenants should be personally thanked by the manager for passing on information about needed repairs in their rented space or public areas, even if the manager was already aware of the condition. Building employees should be alert to maintenance needs of the property and know how to report such problems.

SETTING UP A COST-EFFICIENT MAINTENANCE PROGRAM

A program to reduce maintenance costs is not easily engineered, implemented, or maintained. It requires the cooperation of all persons involved in the management of the property—from the resident manager or superintendent through the maintenance crew. On the average, maintenance costs consume about 20 percent of the gross rental income for apartment buildings and over 26 percent of the gross operating income for office properties. Since the beginning of the inflationary spiral in the early 1970s, expenditures for supplies, wages, contracted services, alterations, repairs, and other maintenance costs have risen steadily. There is a definite need for both long-range and short-range planning techniques to control rising maintenance costs.

Long-Term Plans

The first step in long-term cost-control planning is to identify opportunities to save on operational expenses. The property manager should study the functional alternatives for the property's major mechanical and electrical systems and examine ways to save on maintenance, labor, and wages. For example, it might be cheaper to hire a handyman instead of a janitor. Although the salary for the former is higher, the extra expense is justified because the versatility of the handyman saves the wages that would otherwise be paid to contract personnel for repairs and other jobs.

Fuel consumption costs, a large part of most properties' operating expenses, vary widely. The cost of running a heating plant and maintaining its equipment should be monitored over a period of time, for expensive fuels are sometimes cheaper and more efficient in the long run. Representatives of utility companies can provide helpful information on types of service and ways of decreasing utility costs.

Short-Term Plans

Redecorating, landscaping, and supply stocks offer short-range opportunities to exercise cost control. Careful planning in these areas will result in a small but immediate reduction in expenses. Bulk purchasing of supplies, also known as volume buying, is one of the most effective cost-control tools available to the manager. In some cases, it has increased the margin of profit on a property by as much as 3.5 percent. No savings will result from bulk purchasing if funds are wasted on unneeded items or on a large supply of a product that deteriorates rapidly. An accurate inventory system will enable the manager to identify items that are used infrequently or that have a short shelf life. These supplies can then be purchased as needed. In order to buy in large lots, the manager must have storage space for at least a 6-month supply of goods.

Security measures must be instituted to protect valuable stock from theft. One system to deter theft is to purchase liquid supplies in drums and issue only the amounts needed for a pending job. The cost of frequent inventories, supervision of issue, and other security measures necessary with large stocks have to be measured against the higher cost of smaller purchases. One company solved the problem of expensive central control by maintaining small stocks of frequently used items at the offices of resident managers.

Control Plans

Control techniques will ensure an ongoing, cost-efficient maintenance program. When analyzing long- and short-term cost-reduction goals, the manager may set up new operating procedures or revise present ones. Cost-reduction opportunities should be identified and ranked according to their ability to generate savings. Procedures for initiating work orders, timekeeping, control of materials, work scheduling, and control reporting can then be reassessed in light of new data gathered during the cost-reduction analyses.

In larger properties especially, the key to a successful maintenance program is separation of the administrative and performance functions. The specific work executed by on-site or contracted maintenance personnel must be determined and planned by a maintenance administration staff. This administrative arm, which may consist of only the property manager and the resident manager or of several highly trained employees, also should be responsible for budgeting, material control, and management reports.

Detailed plans are the foundation of effective maintenance supervision. Programmed plans of action outlining the specifics of each job should be designed for all repair, housekeeping, and construction tasks to be performed by maintenance personnel. The degree of detail included in the advance planning program will vary from building to building, but the more control the administrative arm exerts, the more effective and cost-efficient the actual maintenance program will be.

Even the simplest maintenance plan should touch on seven basic points. The *scope* and *location* of the job should be accurately described. The instruction to "replace the grounding wire for the TV antenna in 3C" is much more explicit than "fix the TV antenna on the third floor." The maintenance crew sent out to perform the job will be able to determine in advance where they will be working and what tools they will need for the job.

Job priorities are determined and assigned by the administration staff. The sequence in which the work for the day, week, or month is to be performed should be specified. Immediate problems such as a broken water pipe or window will take precedence over routine service checks and minor difficulties such as a leaking faucet.

The maintenance plan should also specify the best *method* of accomplishing each job. From this information, the administrative staff can determine the *materials* needed to complete the task and can have the appropriate supplies on hand. Employees will also recognize in advance the special tools, equipment, and safety requirements for a particular job.

In order to schedule maintenance crew time efficiently, the administrative staff should study all foreseeable jobs and project the *number of personnel* required and the *hours of work* that will be needed as far ahead as possible. The scope of the job, naturally, will dictate how detailed the data have to be. Appropriate and realistic allocations of time and personnel should result in effective job performance at a reasonable cost, thereby avoiding tenant unrest due to inadequate service. A well-planned maintenance program also protects the profit position of the owner by holding tenant turnover to a minimum and maintaining the physical integrity of the property. By skillfully assessing and balancing service needs and maintenance costs, the manager works for the mutual benefit of all parties concerned.

ENERGY MANAGEMENT

With energy costs increasing at a rapid pace, a property manager can demonstrate his or her professional ability and achieve dramatic savings through effective energy management.

Some energy saving measures are relatively easy, such as reducing the size and number of electric lights or installing storm windows; others involve extensive programs of replacing or upgrading heating and air conditioning equipment (called retrofitting) often controlled and monitored by a computer.

All energy management experts agree that the greatest savings can be achieved by simple measures which either cost little or nothing. These include reducing temperature settings, turning off lights and equipment when not in use, keeping the equipment properly maintained, caulking, and weather stripping. Before redesigning or adding new controls to existing equipment, present heating and air conditioning equipment should be placed in top operating condition and kept in that condition by proper preventative maintenance.

Whether conservation measures involve simple manual methods or complicated computerized controls, the basic steps in instituting an energy management plan or system are the same and involve the following:

1. Convert consumption costs into British Thermal Units (BTUs). This permits comparison of actual past and future consumption, without the distortion caused by fluctuating energy rates.

2. Document how and where energy is being used. The number of BTUs consumed in lighting, heating, refrigeration, etc., should be calculated separately.
3. Select areas where savings appear possible.
4. List various methods of effecting savings and determine the cost of each.
5. Analyze each method to determine cost effectiveness, using the payback method and life cycle costing.
6. Select the method to be used.
7. Prepare a plan for implementation, including sequence and timing.
8. Execute the plan.

An energy management system must involve all the personnel in a company or an organization to be wholly successful, and the property manager must involve tenants in conserving energy. In large installations, conservation is accomplished through the use of automatic controls which are preset and cannot be altered except by management.

The ultimate in energy management is to take heat producing articles in a building, such as electric lights, motors, copy machines, etc. and channel this wasted heat into areas where it can be utilized. Some managers have eliminated heating plants in their premises entirely by the use of this type of heat recovery system.

LIFE CYCLE COSTING

Computing the payback period for a remodeling project is explained in Chapter 2, and equipment is evaluated in the same manner. However, the cost of the equipment over its entire useful life or life cycle costing must also be considered. Life cycle costing simply means that both the *initial* and the *operating* costs of equipment over its expected life must be measured to compare the total cost of one type of equipment with that of another. Often, a higher-priced "energy efficient" appliance may be the least expensive product because of its lower operating costs. An investment tax credit, discussed in Chapter 9, which varies according to the type of personal property, must also be considered in life cycle costing.

SUMMARY

To handle the property's maintenance demands, the manager has to know the needs of the building and the number and type of personnel required to perform the maintenance functions. Staff and scheduling requirements vary with the type, size, and regional location of a property, but several underlying principles of maintenance are universally applicable.

There are four different types of maintenance operations. *Preventative maintenance* attempts to preserve the physical integrity of the premises by routine scheduled inspections of the interior and exterior of the building and all equipment. *Corrective maintenance* involves the actual repairs necessary to keep all structures, amenities, and utilities functional for the tenants. *Routine housekeeping,* including cleaning, is the most recurring maintenance task. *New construction* includes remodeling, additions, and structural alterations made to satisfy tenants' specifications or to improve the marketability of the property.

Most properties of 16 units or more have a resident manager or superintendent on the premises to coordinate and execute all maintenance operations for the building. Resident managers for several buildings may report to one property manager who, as representative of the owners, serves as the final authority. The property manager should be familiar with the details of maintenance work and should know experienced people to handle these jobs.

Although the property manager usually retains control over the hiring and firing of employees and contractors, input from the resident manager or superintendent can be enlightening. The craftspeople who ultimately do the job may either be employees of the building or outside personnel engaged on a contract basis. The hiring policy for on-site maintenance staff will depend on the cost differential between maintaining a permanent building staff and contracting for the needed services. The circumstances of a particular property will dictate which alternative is more efficient and economical.

Services performed by outside persons on a regular basis for a specific fee are known as *contract services.* Before signing any written service contract, the manager should solicit competitive bids from several local agents, check their references and reputations, and make a cost comparison. Window cleaning, refuse and snow removal, pest control, and security protection are services that can often be performed more cheaply by outside contractors. When contracting for new construction, the manager must first decide whether to let to a prime contractor, who will sublet the work to laborers and suppliers, or whether to let the work directly to the skilled trades and suppliers and supervise the construction him- or herself. Because of the additional time, knowledge, and experience necessary to coordinate construction work, most managers leave the task to a prime contractor.

The two methods of obtaining contracts for construction are the *competitive bid* and the *negotiated contract.* Competitive bids for construction are handled in much the same way as competitive bids for regular contract services. The negotiated contract process begins when the manager selects one general contractor or one representative firm for each type of service or supply—carpentry, electrical work, plumbing, plastering, or hardware. He or she then asks these contractors to collaborate and submit a joint bid approximating the total cost of the proposed work. The manager or owner always retains the right to reject the proposal if it is economically infeasible.

Preventative maintenance is a relatively new focus of professional property management. Scheduled maintenance activities are monitored on prepared inspection forms listing all the important physical elements of a property. The major benefits of a preventative maintenance program are decreased repair and replacement costs and improved service to tenants. The basic steps in designing a preventative maintenance program are as follows: (1) inventory all equipment and physical elements; (2) decide on the nature and frequency of inspections and preventative maintenance tasks; (3) calculate the time, labor, and money that will be involved; (4) schedule the preventative maintenance tasks; and (5) keep records of the implementation of the program. The property manager should review preventative maintenance reports and oversee the program. He or she should also conduct spot checks and comprehensive periodic inspections of the property.

Maintenance costs can account for 20 to 26 percent of a property's annual gross income, including supplies, wages, contracted services, repairs, alterations, and other expenses. Due to the steady inflationary trend of our economy, there is a definite need for both long-range and short-term cost-control plans. For effective long-term planning, the manager should investigate opportunities to save on operational expenses for the major mechanical and electrical systems of the property and should examine possible cutbacks in maintenance wages or labor. Short-term opportunities to exercise cost control can be found in such areas of maintenance as tenant alterations and redecorating, landscaping, and volume buying of supplies.

To ensure an ongoing, cost-efficient maintenance program, the manager needs a system for initiating work orders, timekeeping, material control, work scheduling, and reporting. These tasks are the responsibility of the property manager or the maintenance administration staff in larger operations. The repairs, housekeeping, and construction work to be performed by the maintenance crew can be scheduled by either the administrative staff or the property manager. Advance-action programs should include all the details of any job to be completed: scope, location, priority, method, materials, number of personnel, and hours of work. The greater the control exerted by the administrative arm, the more effective and cost-efficient the maintenance program will be.

Energy management measures, which reduce operating expenses, must involve all the personnel in an organization. Some inexpensive energy saving steps can be taken by simple conservation, while others require large expenditures for retrofitting and computerizing heating and air-conditioning systems. Developing an energy management system involves: (1) converting consumption costs into BTUs, (2) documenting where and how energy is used, (3) selecting areas of possible savings, (4) listing and comparing methods of savings, (5) determining an energy management method, and (6) preparing and executing the plan. Some buildings have been heated entirely from recovered heat from lights and machinery.

Life cycle costing is a method of measuring and comparing not only the initial cost of similar pieces of equipment, but also the operating costs over its useful life to determine the cost effectiveness of one particular brand of equipment over another.

QUESTIONS: CHAPTER 8

1. List the four major types of maintenance activities.

   a. _____   c. _____
   b. _____   d. _____

2. The property manager should make periodic inspections of all property to determine:

   I. maintenance needs.
   II. the effectiveness of the resident manager.

   a. I only   c. both I and II
   b. II only   d. neither I nor II

3. Before entering into a contract for services such as window washing:

   I. competitive bids should be solicited.
   II. the manager should consider using on-site personnel.

   a. I only   c. both I and II
   b. II only   d. neither I nor II

4. Replacing the damaged sprinkler system in an industrial property is an example of:

   a. preventative maintenance.   c. cosmetic alteration.
   b. corrective maintenance.   d. functional obsolescence.

5. The factor to weigh most heavily in deciding whether to hire on-site maintenance personnel or contract out for certain services is:

   a. the amount of construction required.
   b. union activity.
   c. required staff.
   d. the relative cost of each.

6. List two ways of obtaining a contract for new construction.

   a. _____
   b. _____

7. A contract for construction work typically states that:

   I. front money will be provided to contractors before the work is started.
   II. a percentage of the fee will be held back until all work has been completed and approved.

   a. I only   c. both I and II
   b. II only   d. neither I nor II

8. A property manager's preventative maintenance program would *not* include:

    a. regular inspection and servicing of equipment.
    b. rating of building personnel.
    c. routine inspection of the building's interior and exterior.
    d. cosmetic alterations.

9. Maintenance costs for a property:

    I.   are a negligible portion of the total operating budget.
    II. have risen steadily over the past few years.

    a. I only   c. both I and II
    b. II only   d. neither I nor II

10. The most popular and immediate method of shaving a property's operating expenses is:

    _____

11. Effective maintenance planning depends on detailed descriptions for each task to be performed by maintenance personnel. List the seven basic points that should be covered when planning each maintenance activity.

    a. _____   e. _____
    b. _____   f. _____
    c. _____   g. _____
    d. _____

12. List the two major benefits of an effective preventative maintenance program.

    a. _____
    b. _____

13. While investigating alternatives for heating a small shopping mall, a property manager determines that the current heating plant consumes 165 gallons of fuel costing $0.40 per gallon each month. By switching to a better grade of fuel costing $0.45 per gallon, the manager could increase the plant's efficiency and decrease the amount of fuel used by 10 percent. Maintenance of the heating system, including cleaning, currently costs about $50 per month. Increasing maintenance activities by 10 percent would result in a 12-percent savings of fuel. In order to cut operating costs, the manager should:

    a. buy the cheaper fuel and increase maintenance activities.
    b. buy the more expensive fuel and increase maintenance activities.
    c. buy the cheaper fuel and limit maintenance costs to $50 per month.
    d. buy the more expensive fuel and limit maintenance costs to $50 per month.

14. The maintenance program for each specific property must be based on:

    I.   the owner's objectives.
    II. the size of the building.

      a.   I only   c.   both I and II
      b.   II only   d.   neither I nor II

15. The addition of a sauna room to the common area of a multitenant development would be an example of:

      a.   corrective maintenance.   c.   contract service.
      b.   tenant alterations.   d.   new construction.

16. Energy management experts agree that:

    I.   the greatest savings can be achieved by simple measures which are generally inexpensive.
    II. present heating and air conditioning equipment must be placed and maintained in top operating condition.

      a.   I only   c.   both I and II
      b.   II only   d.   neither I nor II

17. Life cycle costing:

    I.   compares the initial cost of similar pieces of equipment.
    II. considers operating costs over the useful life of equipment.

      a.   I only   c.   both I and II
      b.   II only   d.   neither I nor II

9
Operating Reports and Property

Records are kept and information is compiled to help the manager or the owner decide upon a course of action for the property. The manager's performance reports on the property's operations gauge the profitability of the owner's investment. They give the owner a clear picture of how the property was managed during the past year, what should be done differently, what can be expected for the upcoming year, whether the property is worth keeping, and how successful the manager has been. The law requires that certain tax-related forms and reports be prepared and filed with state and government departments. Operating license fees, inspection fees, and other fees also must be paid.

As we have seen in the preceding chapters, the property manager is an advertising and leasing agent, custodian, and contract businessperson. As such, the manager handles his or her own office records as well as the principal's funds and important documents. Insurance against loss during the routine performance of the manager's duties is valuable protection for both parties and should be purchased by the manager as a good business investment. Although the manager has no insurable interest in the property itself, he or she should be named as a coinsured on all liability insurance policies that the owner holds on the premises. The usual form of a manager's general liability insurance policy does not cover accidents arising because of the management of properties.

OPERATING REPORTS

Income and Expense Report

The most important operating record is the manager's monthly report on income and expenses. The quarterly, semiannual, or annual profit and loss statement for the property will later be compiled from these monthly reports, which break down the different categories of income and expense and detail all delinquencies. The report is usually accompanied by a note from the manager explaining any abnormal items.

Income. The income portion of the monthly report includes gross rentals billed as well as all revenues from security deposits, back-rent payments, vending contracts, utilities, storage charges, and sale of extra services to tenants. Then, any losses incurred from evictions and from uncollected or delinquent rentals are deducted from the total gross revenue. The resulting figure is the gross collectable income.

As a control measure, some owners require a property manager to indicate separate categories on a monthly report which show the cost of building space not producing income, such as:

1. vacant rental units;
2. supportive space (for example, the manager's office or residence and maintenance or storage areas); and
3. vacant space under major repair

Regardless of the categories desired in the report, all the rental space in a project should be considered when computing the gross possible income. The rental value of each space not producing income is deducted from the gross possible income to equal the gross billable rental income, or:

total rentable space − all space not rented = gross billable rental income

Expense.   *Operating expenses* fall into four general categories: wages paid to building personnel, general operating expenses (such as utilities), maintenance expenses, and administrative costs. *Fixed expenses* do not fluctuate with rental income and can be either *regularly recurring costs* or *periodic costs.* Regularly recurring costs arise each month. Employee wages, basic operating costs, and maintenance expenditures fall into this category of expense. Periodic costs such as property taxes and insurance premiums recur at longer intervals.

Management charges and wages for specialized maintenance services such as roof repair, utility charges, refunds, and capital expenditures are *variable expenses.* These increase or decrease with the rental income and occupancy level. Variable expenses can be either *recurring* or *nonrecurring.* Decorating costs, minor repairs or replacements, and replenishment of supplies will predictably occur at varying intervals during the year. Variable operating expenses—capital improvements, alterations, additions, or repair of fire damage—may or may not occur in any given year.

When both fixed and variable expenses are deducted from gross collectible income, the resulting figure is the month's net operating income before debt service. Net operating income minus mortgage payments (another fixed expense) and deposits to reserve accounts equals the cash flow, or net receipts remitted to the owner for that month. The monthly income and expense report could be expressed in the following formula:

gross rental income billed + income from other sources − losses incurred =
total collectable income

total collectable income − operating expenses = net operating income
before debt service

net operating income before debt service − mortgage payments = cash flow
(net amount remitted to owner)

Figure 22 is a sample form for a monthly income and expense report.

Accounting for Funds. In the preparation of the monthly income and expense report, the manager must set up his or her own personal method of accounting for funds received and disbursed. Laws in some states prescribe rules for handling trust and operating accounts of licensed brokers. Rent bills and receipts can provide an adequate record of income, but an accounts receivable ledger is preferable because all cash receipts can be posted to the appropriate ledger card. The manager should never rely on memory to verify expenses. Written orders should be issued for all purchases, and purchase orders should be matched to incoming invoices before payment is made. If this system is too sophisticated for the manager's accounting needs or capabilities, the voucher portion of the checks written during the month can provide a record of expenditures.

Profit and Loss Statement

The manager must prepare a profit and loss statement quarterly, semiannually, or yearly. Monthly income and expense reports provide the raw data for these statements. Most such statements list gross receipts rather than itemized sources of income, and the total of all operating expenses instead of individual expenditures.

The entire amount paid for debt service should not be considered an expense on the profit and loss statement as it is on the monthly reports. Only the interest portion of each mortgage payment should be deducted. The balance of each mortgage payment is actually applied toward retiring the total debt, thereby increasing the owner's equity in the property and accruing to his or her benefit. After the total mortgage payment has been deducted from the gross receipts, the mortgage loan principal must be added back in to obtain the net profit on the profit and loss statement. The general formula for preparing a profit and loss statement for any type of property is:

$$\text{gross receipts} - \text{operating expenses} - \text{total mortgage}$$
$$\text{payment} + \text{mortgage loan principal} = \text{net profit}$$

A sample profit and loss statement might look like this:

PROFIT AND LOSS STATEMENT

Period: January 1, 1984 to December 31, 1984

Receipts	$158,594.52
Operating Expenses	– 54,434.48
Operating Income	$104,160.04
Total Mortgage Payment	– 44,723.18
Mortgage Loan Principal Add-Back	+ 4,259.26
Net Profit	$ 63,696.12

Figure 22: INCOME AND EXPENSE REPORT

PROPERTY: Period covered: _____
                                                              Date

INCOME
Rental (minus rent loss)   _____
Service and Repairs charged to tenants   _____
Miscellaneous   _____
Vending Machines   _____
Total Income   _____

EXPENSE
Routine Operation and
    Maintenance Expenses
        cleaning   _____
        HVAC   _____
        elevator   _____
        general   _____
        administrative   _____
        electricity   _____
        fuel   _____
        water   _____
        telephone   _____
Total Operating Expense   _____

Alterations, Decorating, Repairs
        alterations—tenants' premises   _____
        decorating—tenants' premises   _____
        repairs—tenants' premises   _____
Total Alterations and Decorating   _____

Fixed Charges
        insurance   _____
        taxes   _____
Total Fixed Charges   _____

Total Expense   _____

NET OPERATING INCOME
  BEFORE DEBT SERVICE   _____
Debt Service   _____

Reserves   _____

CASH FLOW TO OWNER   _____

The Operating Budget

After developing the profit and loss statement for a specific period, the manager should compare the actual results with the original operating budget drawn up either at the beginning of that period or at the time that the manager assumed responsibility for the property. A sample operating budget was illustrated in Chapter 2.

The budget gives the owner an idea of the cash yield to expect from the property during a fixed period, traditionally a year. The budget serves the manager as a guide for future operation of the property and as a measure of past performance. If the projected budget for a period does not agree with the actual monthly income and expense reports and the profit and loss statement for the same period, appropriate adjustments should be made in subsequent operating budgets or in operating procedures. In fact, many managers divide their annual operating budget into 3-month segments so that they can compare the budget with actual income and expense on a quarterly basis. This helps to pinpoint expense items that are out of line before a whole year has passed.

A sound general rule for the manager to follow when preparing a budget forecast is to be conservative. It is preferable to base estimates on present rental rates rather than anticipated increases in revenue. Then, if the profit and loss statement at the end of the period shows a greater revenue than originally indicated on the budget projection, the manager will be able to point out what he or she has contributed to the increase.

While it is necessary to set high standards to make progress, the manager should resist any tendency on the part of the owner to order unreasonably high figures as goals to be achieved by leasing agents or site managers. Since unreachable goals are self-defeating, the morale of the organization will suffer, and competent personnel will quietly seek other employment. Wise managers should set *realistic* goals which cause the company to grow and prosper.

A decrease in the expected revenue requires an explanation which the manager should be prepared to make in order to show the actual cause. The budget forecast should make allowances for vacancies and delinquent payments during the period to be covered. The income and expense reports for the preceding months will tell the manager how much of an allowance to grant. The relationship between rentals billed and monies collected can be used to project an actual occupancy ratio for the property.

For example, a residential building having four 5-room apartments, each of which rents for $300 per month, billed $14,400 in rents during the last fiscal year (4 × $300 = $1,200 × 12 = $14,400), but actual rental collections amounted to only $13,680. Based on these figures, the occupancy rate for the building can be calculated at 95 percent ($13,680 ÷ $14,400 = .95). In this case, when preparing the budget for the upcoming term, the manager should deduct 5 percent from gross rent receipts to be billed in order to allow for vacancies or loss of rent. This method of computing an occupancy level can also be used for commercial and industrial properties that charge on a per-square-foot basis. For instance, an office building has 2,000 square feet of rentable space. The gross rent billed is $1.00 per square foot per month, or

$24,000 for the entire building over a one-year period ($1.00 × 12 = $12.00 × 2,000 = $24,000). Rental collections for the past year came to $18,000, so from these figures the occupancy rate for this building can be projected to be about 75 percent ($18,000 ÷ $24,000 = .75).

When forecasting expenses for the new budget term, the manager should examine all discrepancies between anticipated costs, as projected in the budget for the preceding year, and actual expenses incurred, as shown on the income and expense reports from the same period. Substantial differences indicate either problem areas for management or items for which the projected estimates were unrealistic. After determining the reason for the difference in costs, the manager should then adjust either the operating policy or the forecast for the new budget period.

An accumulation of budgets over an extended period of time provides a valuable synopsis of recent trends and alerts the manager to areas of unfavorable progress. The owner also uses the budgets to judge the manager's skill in recognizing financial and market patterns and in coping with problem areas.

Because of the large sums of money involved, the books and records of the management firm should be audited at least annually. Not only is this a proof of good faith, but many lenders and other parties require an audit before they will execute mortgages and other legal documents pertaining to properties under outside management.

RECORDS FOR TAX PURPOSES

U.S. income tax laws have been changed by Congress with increasing frequency during the past several years. The Internal Revenue Service has issued a stream of regulations governing their application, and the federal courts continue to decide cases which change the administration of particular portions of these laws and regulations. For these reasons, the information given here must necessarily be of a general nature. Property managers should obtain the latest IRS Circulars and consult with competent tax counsel before filing tax returns of any type.

Employee Reports

Property owners who pay people to work for them may be considered employers for federal and state income tax purposes and may be required to file certain reports with the appropriate government agencies. Most states have precise specifications as to the minimum number of persons on the job, total amount of wages paid, and working conditions that must exist before an owner is classified as an employer.

The difference between an employee and an independent contractor is also significant in terms of federal and state taxes. Workers are deemed to be employees if the person for whom they work has the right to direct and control when, where, and how the work is done and to define the desired end result of the work. Independent contractors control when, where, and how they perform their own jobs and are hired to produce an end result. An agreement between owner and independent contractor must include a clause providing for the right of termination by either party upon notice to the other. This is just one of the many fine distinctions that must be considered when contracting for work and when deciding if a worker is to be considered an employee or a special contractor for tax purposes. Managers must not attempt to disguise employees as independent contractors when a bona-fide independent contractor relationship does not actually exist since the penalties from tax and liability standpoints can be severe.

If the workers at a building are employees under the law, the owner must obtain an employer identification number from the Internal Revenue Service. All employees must have a social security number and fill out Form W-4: Employee's Withholding Allowance Certificate, stating the number of tax exemptions that they intend to claim on their tax reports. The government charges the employer with the responsibility for obtaining these W-4 certificates and for complying with other important regulations concerning employees. The owner usually delegates to the property manager the job of complying with federal and state requirements for employers, including supplying the appropriate forms and making all necessary payments.

Income Tax Withholding. In addition to providing all employees with W-4 forms, an employer must file the Employer's Quarterly Tax Return Form 941 for all income taxes withheld from employee wages. When filing the 941 form for the final quarter of the year, the employer must also transmit Forms W-2 and W-3:

- Form W-2 is the Wage and Tax Statement for each employee, showing the total wages paid and amounts withheld during the year.
- Form W-3 is the Transmittal of Wage and Tax Statement. W-2 forms for all employees must be attached to the W-3 form, and the amount shown on the W-3 must equal the total of all the W-2 slips.

Property managers should follow the latest filing guidelines, published in Circular E, *Employer's Tax Guide,* by the Internal Revenue Service.

In order to fulfill state income tax obligations, the employer must also register with the state in which he or she operates. These obligations and the specific forms used vary from state to state, but the W-2, W-3, and W-4 forms are generally used to document both state and federal income tax withholding liabilities.

Free Rent. When computing income for federal tax purposes, managers must indicate wages paid in any form other than money at their fair market value. Included in this category are automobiles furnished to employees and quarters provided for on-site managers. A qualified accountant or attorney must determine the proper treatment of any item of compensation given to an employee in lieu of salary. Different treatment and amounts are applicable depending upon the item and circumstances in each case. Under current regulations, the fair market value of living quarters, furnished to a manager at the place of employment, is not taxable to the employee, if the employee is required to reside on the premises as a condition of employment.

Insurance. The Federal Insurance Contributions Act (FICA) provides for social security retirement fund taxation to be paid by employers of one or more persons. The rate of tax is set by Congress and shared by the employer and employee. The employer must withhold the proper amount from employees' paychecks and submit the total contribution from both parties to the federal government. The frequency of payment varies with the amount of the contribution; again, check the latest regulations available from local social security offices. When computing the FICA payment due, compensation other than wages (including a free apartment) must be shown as income at fair market value.

In addition to social security, both disability insurance and workmen's compensation insurance must be carried on all employees. Some states obtain these through a government agency, while others use private insurance companies.

Unemployment Taxes. A Federal Unemployment Tax Act (FUTA) return must be filed by every employer of one or more persons who work for some portion of a day for 20 weeks during the year or earn at least $1,500 during the year. The total tax levied will vary according to the amount of state unemployment tax paid by the employer for each employee. A credit against FUTA payments is given for any state unemployment taxes paid. Because the laws governing state unemployment taxes vary, the property manager must pay special attention to the applicable laws in his or her area.

Cash Flow Statement for Tax Purposes

Whether the owner's federal and state income tax returns are to be prepared by an accountant, the property manager, or the owner, it is often the manager's responsibility to compute the tax liability for the property's revenue by drawing up a cash flow statement for the fiscal year. The cash flow statement adjusts the total net income from the property to allow for depreciation of the premises during the year.

Depreciation. Depreciation generally is divided into three major categories: physical deterioration, functional obsolescence, and economic obsolescence. For tax purposes, only depreciation from physical deterioration is deductible from the property's income.

Formerly, there were three standard methods for computing the rate of physical deterioration—the straight-line method, the declining balance method, and the sum-of-the-years'-digits method. These three methods still apply to property acquired prior to 1981. The straight-line method of computing depreciation assumes that the deterioration proceeds at a stable rate over the useful life of the building. The yearly percentage of the building's cost which is lost through depreciation (depreciation rate) is found by dividing 100 percent by the years of useful life of the building. For example, if a property can be expected to be used for 50 years with normal maintenance, the straight-line depreciation rate is 2 percent (1.00 ÷ 50 – .02). The annual depreciation rate is multiplied by the building cost to obtain the dollar amount of depreciation per year. This figure can be multiplied by the age of the building to find the total dollar amount of accrued depreciation. If the property in the previous example is worth $60,000 and is currently 3 years old, the dollar amount of depreciation would be $1,200 per year (.02 × $60,000). The property would have depreciated by $3,600 ($1,200 × 3) and would currently be worth $56,400 ($60,000 – $3,600).

The declining balance method and the sum-of-the-years'-digits method are both forms of *accelerated* depreciation. They are based on the premise that property depreciates more rapidly in its early years; hence, larger deductions are made in the first year of the property's economic life, with decreasing deductions throughout the later years. The most common method of computing accelerated depreciation is the declining balance method, which adjusts the straight-line rate according to a percentage factor depending on the type of property. For example, the 200-percent declining balance method doubles the straight-line rate. If the straight-line depreciation rate is 2 percent, the percentage multiplier used in the 200-percent declining balance method would be 4 percent. For a building costing $50,000:

$50,000 × .04 = $2,000 depreciation after 1 year
$50,000 − $2,000 = $48,000 undepreciated balance after 1 year
$48,000 × .04 = $1,920 depreciation after 2 years
$48,000 − $1,920 = $46,080 undepreciated balance after 2 years

Other common declining adjustment rates are 150 percent and 125 percent of the straight-line depreciation rate.

The sum-of-the-years'-digits method of computing physical deterioration is demonstrated by the following formula:

$$\frac{\text{remaining years of economic life}}{\text{sum of the years' digits}} \times \text{remaining value} = \text{depreciation}$$

The denominator of the depreciation formula is the sum of all the years in the remaining economic life of the property. The specific method used for computing the allowable depreciation deduction will be determined by the type of property and by IRS regulations. Once the depreciation of a property has been calculated by a certain method, another method cannot be employed without authorization from the IRS.

Accelerated Cost Recovery System (ACRS). Congress established the Accelerated Cost Recovery System (called "acres" from its acronym, ACRS) for property placed in service in 1981 and subsequent years. ACRS prescribes methods of recovery of expenditures through a depreciation allowance which varies according to the type of property being depreciated. Depreciation is calculated over 3, 5, 10, or 15 years, depending upon the type of property. Tables, published by the IRS, set forth the ACRS percentages by property type and for the period the property is held. The tables for real estate are applied on a monthly basis in the first year the property is placed in service and allow a 15-year recovery. Percentages for real estate except low-income housing and percentages applicable only to low-income housing are shown in two separate tables.

Investment Tax Credit. Federal income tax credits are allowed for certain depreciable property investments, and regulations vary for energy, antipollution, employee stock ownership plans, and other categories of property investments. If an Investment Tax Credit is claimed and the property is sold or disposed of before a certain period of time, the Investment Tax Credit must be repaid to the Internal Revenue Service.

Tax credits are also available for "qualified rehabilitated buildings," generally more than 30 years old, and for the restoration of "certified historic structures." Unlike depreciation, a tax credit is not an expense item for calculating taxable income, but rather a direct offset against tax liability.

After-Tax Cash Flow. Once the appropriate rate of depreciation has been determined and the allowable deduction computed, the depreciation allowance is subtracted from the total net income from the property for the year. The resulting figure represents the owner's tax liability on the profit from the property during that year. The actual tax due is taxable income times the appropriate percentage rate determined by the owner's tax bracket. Taxable income minus tax due, minus the principal add-back, plus depreciation equals the after-tax cash return on the property.

Figure 23: AFTER-TAX CASH FLOW STATEMENT

Gross Annual Income	$100,000
Operating Costs	– 60,000
Annual Income Before Debt Service	40,000
Mortgage Payments	– 30,000
Cash Flow After Debt Service	10,000
Mortgage Principal Add-Back	+ 20,000
Net Income Before Depreciation	30,000
Depreciation Allowance ($600,000 × .01/yr × 1 yr)	– 12,000
Taxable Income	18,000
Tax Due ($18,000 × .50)	– 9,000
Net Income Return After Taxes	9,000
Deduct Principal Add-Back	– 20,000
Cash Flow Before Depreciation Add-Back	($ 11,000)
Depreciation Add-Back	+ 12,000
After-tax Cash Flow	$ 1,000

For example, an apartment building valued at $600,000 when new has a gross annual income of $100,000 and average annual operating expenses of $60,000. Mortgage payments amount to $30,000 annually, and $20,000 of this amount is payment on the principal balance. The property has a straight-line depreciation rate of 2 percent and is a year old. If the owner is in a 50-percent tax bracket, the cash flow would be calculated as shown in Figure 23.

When a property's depreciation allowance exceeds its net income, the tax liability is a negative amount, also known as a *tax loss.* This loss can be used to shelter other taxable income of the owner and, in effect, increase the overall cash flow from the property. In such cases, the cash flow statement would be computed as shown in the example worked out in Figure 24. Note that two computations are necessary. First, the amount of the tax loss must be determined. Second, the total dollars resulting from sheltering income from the building must be added to the dollars saved by sheltering income from another source and then subtracted from the mortgage principal add-back. The other income sheltered by loss is computed by multiplying the total tax loss from the property by the percentage tax rate that the owner must pay on his or her personal income.

The mortgage amortization ($5,000 principal add-back payment in Figure 24) represents a buildup of the owner's equity if the property does not decrease in market value. This increase in equity is not translated into a positive cash flow until the property is either sold or refinanced.

Figure 24: AFTER-TAX CASH FLOW STATEMENT (sheltering other income)

Computation of Tax Loss:

Gross Annual Income	$80,000
Operating Costs	– 60,000
Annual Income Before Debt Service	20,000
Mortgage Payments	– 19,000
Cash Flow After Debt Service	1,000
Mortgage Principal Add-Back	+ 5,000
Taxable Income Before Depreciation	6,000
Depreciation Allowance ($250,000 × .04/yr)	– 10,000
Tax Loss (Must be a negative figure)	(–4,000)

Computation of Cash Flow:

Tax Loss	(4,000)
Other Income Sheltered by Loss ($4,000 × .50)	+ 2,000
Taxable Income Before Depreciation	+ 6,000
Mortgage Principal Add-Back	– 5,000
After-Tax Cash Flow	($ 1,000)

The after-tax cash flow statement in Figure 24 illustrates the benefits of a tax shelter investment property. A building worth $250,000 (not including land) when new has a gross annual income of $80,000 and expenses of $60,000. Mortgage payments for the year include $14,000 interest and $5,000 principal. The property has a straight-line depreciation rate of 4 percent. The owner is in a 50-percent tax bracket.

DETERMINING PROFITABILITY

The manager's monthly income and expense reports, profit and loss statements, and cash flow analysis help the owner to decide whether the manager is competent and whether the property itself is profitable enough to keep.

Break-Even Analysis

The primary method of calculating the profitability of a building is to determine its *break-even point:* the percentage of occupancy at which gross income is equal to fixed costs including mortgage payments plus all variable costs incurred in developing that income. The owner can derive fixed and variable costs for the year by totaling the appropriate amounts on the monthly income and expense reports for the property. Variable costs are usually expressed as a ratio to total rents—that is, as a percentage of total rental income. A property with an annual income of $140,000 from rents collected and variable costs of $28,000 for the year would have a 20-percent variable costs ratio (VCR = $28,000 ÷ $140,000 = .20).

The formula for calculating a property's break-even point is:

$$BE = \frac{FC}{100\% - VCR}$$

$$BE = \text{break-even point}$$
$$FC = \text{fixed costs including mortgage payments}$$
$$VCR = \text{variable costs ratio}$$

A break-even point can also be expressed as the percent of occupancy necessary to show a profit and can be computed as follows:

$$\frac{\text{Total Expense plus Debt Service}}{\text{Potential Gross Income}} = \text{Percent of Occupancy}$$

Caution must be used in employing this formula since "Total Expense" can only be estimated. The percent of occupancy will have an effect on variable expenses— the higher the occupancy, the greater the variable costs.

If a property has fixed costs of $100,000 and a VCR of 20 percent, the break-even point would be $125,000 ($100,000 ÷ .80). If the property contains 30,000 square feet of space, which rents at a fair market value of $5 per square foot per year, approximately 83 percent of this space would have to be rented before the property would begin to show a profit ($125,000 ÷ $150,000 = 83.3%). A comparison of this rent-up figure with the occupancy level predicted in the forecasted budget will tell the owner at a glance whether the property can operate at a financially feasible level.

An examination of occupancy levels of similar properties in the area will reveal the comparative position of the owner's property within the present market. If the break-even point of a property requires an occupancy rate in excess of the market average, the owner might ask the manager for an analysis and explanation of the fixed costs and variable cost ratio for the year. On the other hand, if the break-even point for the property is in line with that of similar buildings in the area, but the occupancy rate during the past year was below standard, the owner should investigate the manager's maintenance and tenant relations policies.

Capitalization Rate

The *capitalization rate* is another index of the profit on a particular property. The general formula for calculating the capitalization rate is as follows:

$$R = I \div V \times 100\%$$

R = capitalization rate
I = net operating income
    before debt service
V = value of property

The capitalization rate of a property is usually expressed as a percentage, and the larger the rate the more profitable the investment in the property. For example, if an office property is appraised at $60,000 and its annual net income is $7,200, the capitalization rate would be 12 percent. This rate may then be compared with the capitalization rate of similar properties to evaluate the quality of the investment in the subject property.

Return on Investment

Another measure of profitability is the ratio of money invested in a property (equity) to the property's net income after taxes, as shown in the after-tax cash flow line on the cash flow report. This ratio can be converted into a percentage return on investment and measured against the owner's desired yield. In formula form, the return on the owner's investment can be derived as follows:

$$ROI = BLR \div E \times 100\%$$

ROI = return on investment
E = equity
BLR = after-tax cash flow

For a property with a $15,000 after-tax cash flow in which the owner has an equity investment of $100,000, the rate of return is 15 percent ($15,000 ÷ $100,000 × 100 = 15%).

When an owner's cash investment is analyzed in this manner, it is often called a "cash on cash" return. In the foregoing example, a $100,000 initial cash investment yields a cash on cash return of 15 percent ($15,000 ÷ $100,000 × 100 = 15%). The term *cash on cash* may be quoted on either a before- or after-tax basis.

As a general rule of thumb, the rate of return should be equal to or above the rate of interest the owner could obtain with a savings account or a time note. If it is not, the owner is not receiving maximum return on his or her investment and should take steps to adjust operating costs, financing arrangements, depreciation rate, or taxes in order to increase the yield. The manager can keep the local property taxes and special assessments on a property at a reasonable level by contesting its assessed valuation on behalf of the owner. If there is no way to improve the return on investment, perhaps the owner should consider selling the building in favor of a more profitable investment.

Internal Rate of Return

The internal rate of return, or discounted cash flow, is determined by a complicated mathematical calculation which will produce a discounted rate of return on an initial investment. The calculation is used to standardize the rate of return of investments of all types by use of a single common measurement, but it does not measure the variation in risks between investments. The internal rate of return is calculated from the cash flows which result from the initial investment and must be estimated for several years in advance, which is a hazardous undertaking. The goal in calculating an internal rate of return is to determine the *rate of discount* at which the present worth of future cash flow from the project (the discounted value) equals the initial investment. Since it is difficult for many investors to understand, its use is not advised by managers of property.

RISK MANAGEMENT AND INSURANCE

One of the most critical areas of responsibility for a property manager, because of the possible dollar losses, is the field of insurance. The property manager should have a working knowledge of casualty, liability, and special lines of insurance and an understanding of the whole field, its theories, principles, and practices. Insurance has expanded from its beginning several centuries ago as a pooling of risks by merchants to its present day sophistication in which the insurance professional is now called a "risk manager."

The Risk Management Theory

In a risk management approach, the first question asked is, "What will happen if something goes wrong?" In answering this question, the perils of any risk are evaluated in terms of options. In dealing with a possible loss, a property manager may take the option to:

- AVOID IT
- RETAIN IT
- CONTROL IT
- TRANSFER IT.

Avoid It. To avoid a loss, a manager would simply not engage in an activity which is risky, or own a piece of equipment which would create a loss situation. For instance, if a property has a swimming pool, diving board accidents can be avoided by eliminating the diving board. This has been done almost universally in public accommodations. To illustrate further, swimming pool liability can be avoided by not installing a swimming pool. Accidents and injury can also be avoided if a manager does not purchase maintenance equipment which could be dangerous in the hands of untrained personnel. For instance, it is safer to buy fireplace wood than to take a chainsaw to the forest to cut it.

Retain It. The second option is to retain some of the loss; in other words, the owner of the property shares a portion of the loss. A common example is the deductible clause in an automobile insurance policy in which the first $50 or $100 of collision damage must be paid by the owner.

The ultimate in retaining loss is to self-insure completely. The property manager who does not insure the plate glass in his building or complex, but bears the occasional expense of replacing a window, is opting for self-insurance. Another means of retaining loss is to insure property or a piece of equipment for less than its value. This "80% coinsurance clause" which every property manager should understand is explained in detail on page 193.

Control It. A risk can be controlled in many ways. Risk of financial loss is controlled by limiting the amount of cash kept in the office while risk of loss to property is reduced by the installation of sprinklers in buildings, automatic fire doors, fire-resistant fabrics, etc. Signs or physical barriers can protect people from risks caused by hazardous obstacles or situations.

Transfer It. By taking out an insurance policy, a risk can be transferred.

The Property Manager as a Risk Manager

The first step for the property manager to take in managing risks is to make a survey of the physical plant, operating equipment, and jobs being performed by various personnel, particularly in maintenance areas. Hazards and dangerous equipment or operations should be eliminated or examined in terms of the other three options.

Risks which might cause losses which can comfortably be retained, should be retained. For instance, the collision deductible on automobiles used by property management could be $250 instead of $100. The option of control calls for a thorough inspection of all areas to eliminate hazards. Often, a safety engineer is available free of charge through insurance agents, or the fire department may offer fire prevention inspections.

After the manager has avoided, retained, and controlled risks, those risks of losses which would result in a serious financial loss are candidates for transfer by means of insurance. Generally, insurance falls into three categories which cover the basic risks including:

1. Loss caused to other persons. This is the broad area of liability insurance.
2. Loss of user value. An example is business interruption insurance against loss of rents in the event a managed property burns to the ground.
3. Loss of property. The destruction of a retail store building by a tornado would fall into this category.

Two questions must be asked in determining whether there is a need for insurance:

- What is the loss exposure, or what can happen to cause loss of this particular property, or create liability?
- What is the loss potential, or in the event of a single loss, how much would be lost?

If the potential loss is greater than the owner of the property can or is willing to bear, appropriate insurance coverage must be purchased. This requires knowledge of the various types of policies and exactly what each policy covers or insures against.

TYPES OF INSURANCE

The basic purpose of insurance is to reduce the loss caused by unforeseen misfortunes. Both property owner and manager are exposed to the risk of loss and need the protection offered by various types of insurance.

Owner's Policies

A property owner will want to obtain the best insurance coverage against as many risks as possible at the most reasonable rate. Since different localities and operating conditions demand variant forms of coverage, the owner often relies on the experience and judgment of the property manager in securing adequate protection for a property. In fact, many property managers are also insurance brokers. As a representative of the policy buyer, the insurance broker must determine the risks involved, shop the market for the best and most economical coverage, and then purchase the required policies on behalf of the owner. The most common categories of insurance coverage are the standard fire insurance policy; extended coverage and collateral fire lines; machinery and equipment insurance; consequential loss, use, and occupancy coverage; and general liability and workmen's compensation insurance.

Standard Fire Insurance. Several standard forms for fire insurance policies are currently in use, all of which are intended to simplify the adjustment procedure in case of loss. In general, there is a standard policy designed especially for each type of property: apartments, office buildings, warehouses, row houses, and fireproof structures. This type of fire insurance policy contains two parts—an agreement and contract section and a listing of stipulations and conditions.

The agreement section describes the property insured, the amount of the premium paid, the period of coverage, and any endorsements altering or extending the contract. It also states that the company insures the person named in the policy against all direct loss or damage to the specified premises not in excess of a net dollar amount. The second part of most standard fire insurance contracts contains a provision voiding the policy if the insured conceals or misrepresents any material facts concerning the property when applying for insurance. Fires caused by certain specified perils are also usually excluded from coverage under the standard form. Typical exclusions are fire loss due to enemy invasion, insurrection, civil war, or neglect on the part of the insured. Many standard fire policies carry a clause suspending or restricting insurance if the chance of fire is increased in any manner within the control of the owner.

Other clauses in the standard insurance policy will specify the procedure to be followed in the event of loss. The pro rata amount of liability, the rights and interests of the mortgage holder and coinsureds, the insurance company's options for repair or replacement of the property, and the time within which a settlement will be made in case of loss are usually outlined in the standard forms.

The annual premium for a basic insurance policy is computed by multiplying the amount of the policy by a rate that represents the risk of physical loss. It is imperative that a property be adequately insured, particularly as labor and construction costs rise. The owner should obtain a current estimate of the value of the building when buying standard fire insurance. The policy should exceed a certain percentage of the insurable value, due to coinsurance. The manager should also make sure that the owner carries adequate coverage and that it is increased annually to cover the increased value of the improvements.

80% Coinsurance. The coinsurance provisions of an insurance policy are probably the least understood aspect of purchasing insurance. In buying coinsurance, the manager/owner is promising the insurer that: 1) the property will be insured to its full value, or to a prescribed percentage of value, and 2) the insured will maintain insurance coverage on that property at that percentage level.

In return for that promise, the insurer will charge a lower rate, but the responsibility for maintaining the required amount of insurance is upon the manager/owner. In inflationary times, this can be a problem, and every property manager should periodically review the limits of his/her policies, property by property.

In underwriting practice, an insurance company will charge about the same amount for 50% "straight coverage" as it would for coverage under the 80% coinsurance method. The premium for $50,000 of insurance on a building without coinsurance is about equal to the premium for $80,000 of insurance on a $100,000 building using a coinsurance clause. In a typical situation, the actual cash value of a property is $100,000, and under the 80% coinsurance clause this property should be insured for $80,000. If there is a loss of $40,000, the insurer will pay the entire loss, but if there is a loss of $100,000, the insurer will pay $80,000.

If the value of the building, through inflation or otherwise, has increased to $200,000 while the insurance policy has not been increased, there is a partial loss of $40,000. The recovery of proceeds of insurance will be determined according to the following formula:

$$\frac{\text{amount of insurance}}{\substack{\text{80\% of what it should} \\ \text{have been insured for}}} \quad \times \quad \text{partial loss}$$

$$\frac{\$80,000}{\$160,000} \quad \times \quad \$40,000$$

or expressed as a fraction: ½ × $40,000 = payment for loss. In this case, the insurer will pay only $20,000 of the partial loss.

In the event of a total loss of the $200,000 building, the insurer will pay the full amount of the policy, $80,000. The owner, who has failed to keep the property insured to 80% of the value, must stand a loss of $120,000.

Extended Coverage and Collateral Fire Lines. An extended coverage endorsement can be appended to the standard form to compensate for the various exclusions under the standard fire policy. Damages from windstorm, hail, explosion, riot, civil strife, aircraft, and smoke are common additions under extended coverage plans.

Equipment and Machinery Insurance. Insurance policies may also be purchased on machinery such as boilers, turbines, power plants, and heating plants. Direct-loss equipment insurance covers damage to the insured equipment and its surroundings, damage to the property of others, employee liability, and public liability. Plate glass insurance and boiler insurance may be purchased separately. The latter is especially important in older properties. Any vehicles such as trucks, forklifts, or cars used in the operation of a property also must be insured.

Consequential Loss, Use, and Occupancy. In addition to insurance against direct property loss, protection also can be purchased against loss of revenue due to property damage. Business interruption insurance might include rental value insurance, use and occupancy protection, profits and commissions coverage, and protection against miscellaneous risks such as rain damage. Rental value insurance guarantees rental income in case the premises become uninhabitable. It is a wise investment for properties that have a small profit margin and a heavy debt load with no reserves.

General Liability and Workmen's Compensation. Liability insurance, including workmen's compensation coverage, involves the legal responsibility of the property owner for damage to the person or property of others. Under the law of negligence, the property owner has a duty to act in a manner and to maintain the property in a condition such that others will not be injured on the premises. Failure to act in a responsible manner can result in a fine, imprisonment, or a judgment decree for damages, depending upon the severity of the owner's neglect. Thus, liability insurance is valuable protection. General liability insurance usually consists only of a bodily injury and a property damage policy, but a personal injury endorsement may be added to protect against the possibility of false arrest, libel, or slander on the part of the insured.

Insurance for the Manager

The manager, as both a custodian and a contracting businessperson, may hire employees or contractors; handle client funds, documents and records; and maintain an office and files. Common sense dictates that the manager should protect him- or herself with insurance. Floater and office contents insurance is necessary to protect equipment and supplies in the management or building office. The manager should also carry errors and omissions insurance for at least 10 percent of the total annual collections to protect against possible mistakes or oversights in accounting. Because the management firm and its employees must handle large amounts of money, bond insurance is also necessary. Bond coverage includes fidelity bonds on employees of the firm and the firm itself, for the protection of the owner. The manager should require service contractors to post surety bonds covering successful completion of their contracts. Loss of valuable records, theft, holdup, messenger robbery, general liability, workmen's compensation, and extended coverage on standard fire insurance should also be considered for the protection of the manager in the exercise of his or her duties.

In addition to carrying his or her own insurance coverage, the property manager, as part of the management contract terms, should ask to be named as coinsured in the owner's liability insurance policies. As a rule, no additional premium is charged for this protection.

SUMMARY

The manager's performance reports on the property's operations enable the owner to measure the profitability of the property and the performance of the manager. The manager also usually prepares and files all federal and state reports for tax purposes and secures adequate insurance coverage for the premises.

The most functional reports the manager prepares and presents to the owner are the monthly *income and expense reports,* which serve as the foundation for later, more comprehensive reports. Monthly income includes all rents actually collected plus any additional revenue from the property. Fixed and variable expenses are deducted from this amount. *Fixed expenses* are operating costs—security expenses, for example—that remain the same regardless of the rental income. Expenditures such as water consumption, which increase or decrease with the occupancy level, are termed *variable costs.* Collectable income less operating costs leaves the month's net operating income before debt service. The net operating income minus the mortgage payment for the month equals the cash flow, the amount remitted to the owner along with the monthly income and expense report.

These monthly reports supply the information needed to draw up a quarterly, semi-annual, or annual *profit and loss statement.* The total amount of a mortgage payment cannot be considered an expense on the statement because the portion of the payment that goes to reduce the principal debt accrues to the owner's benefit. Only the interest on the mortgage may be deducted as an expense. Therefore, the total of all mortgage payments must be subtracted from the net income, but then the principal amount paid on the mortgage must be added back in. The resulting figure is the net income from the property for a specified period.

An analysis of recent monthly income and expense reports should help the manager draw up a *budget forecast* for the year to come. At the end of the budget period, the forecasted figures can be compared to actual results.

Any property owner who is considered an employer for federal and state income tax purposes must file various reports with the appropriate government agencies. Specific rules as to working conditions, total amount of wages paid, and minimum number of persons necessary to classify the owner as an employer vary from state to state. If the workers at a building are termed employees under the law, the owner must obtain an employer identification number from the Internal Revenue Service. All employees must have a social security number and fill out a W-4 form (Employee's Withholding Allowance Certificate). The employer is charged by the government with the responsibility for obtaining and filing various state and federal income tax forms and returns, computing and paying social security taxes, filing state and federal unemployment tax returns, and complying with a number of other regulations concerning employees. The job of interpreting and fulfilling all the various federal and state requirements, including supplying the appropriate forms and making the necessary payments, is often delegated to the property manager.

The manager can compute the owner's tax liability on the revenue from the property by drawing up a *cash flow statement* for the fiscal year. This statement adjusts the total net income from the property, as shown on the profit and loss statement, to allow the appropriate deduction for depreciation of the premises during the year. The income left after deducting the tax on the property from the adjusted income is the *after-tax cash flow* and represents the owner's profits from the property in that year. By analyzing the after-tax cash flow with respect to comparable properties in the area and the desired yield from his or her investment, the owner can determine whether the manager is performing well and whether the property itself is profitable enough to keep. Other measures of a property's profitability include the *break-even* analysis, *capitalization rate* calculation, and *return-on-investment* computation.

One of the major concerns of a property owner is obtaining insurance coverage against as many risks as possible at the most reasonable rate. Some property managers are also insurance brokers; those who are not may be called upon to advise property owners on insurance matters. As risk managers for the owner, property managers examine potential risks to see which should be *avoided, retained, controlled,* and *transferred* through the purchase of insurance.

As representatives of policy buyers, they shop the market for the most comprehensive and economical coverage. The most common types of insurance needed by property owners are the standard fire insurance policy; extended coverage and collateral fire lines; equipment and machinery insurance; consequential loss, use, and occupancy coverage; and general liability and workmen's compensation coverage.

The manager is both an agent and a contracting businessperson, in which capacities he or she engages employees and contractors; handles client funds, documents, and records; and maintains his or her own office and files. Extended fire coverage is a must for the manager's offices, as is floater insurance on office contents, errors and omissions insurance, bond coverage, valuable records replacement and theft insurance, general liability policies, and workmen's compensation. The manager should also be named as coinsured on all of the owner's liability insurance policies.

QUESTIONS: CHAPTER 9

1. Building employee wages are an example of a:

   a. regularly recurring cost.
   b. periodic cost.
   c. recurring variable expense.
   d. nonrecurring variable expense.

2. The addition of an employee cafeteria to an office building is an example of a:

   a. regularly recurring cost.
   b. periodic cost.
   c. recurring variable expense.
   d. nonrecurring variable expense.

3. What is the general formula used to obtain a figure for net operating income before debt service in the monthly income and expense report?

   _____

4. The general formula for preparing a profit and loss statement is:

   _____

5. The principal amount applied to reduce the mortgage on an income property is deducted when computing:

   I. monthly income and expense reports.
   II. profit and loss statements.

   a. I only
   b. II only
   c. both I and II
   d. neither I nor II

6. When completing a budget forecast, the property manager should:

   I. study past budgets and income and expense reports.
   II. be optimistic about future rental income.

   a. I only
   b. II only
   c. both I and II
   d. neither I nor II

7. A commercial property containing 35,000 square feet is rented at $6 per square foot. However, actual rental collections over the past year amounted to only $168,000. What occupancy rate should be used in the budget forecast for the next year?

   a. 79 percent
   b. 48 percent
   c. 80 percent
   d. 72 percent

8. The government requires certain reports to be filed on workers who are considered employees under the law. List four forms that must be completed for tax purposes.

   a. _____   c. _____
   b. _____   d. _____

9.   An office building worth $100,000 has a useful life of 75 years. Using the straight-line method of computing depreciation, what would this property be worth at the end of 4 years? Calculate to 5 decimals.

     a. $53,330   c. $96,667
     b. $94,667   d. $98,667

10. Using the 150-percent declining balance method of computing depreciation, what would the property in the previous example be worth at the end of 2 years? Calculate to 5 decimals.

     a. $97,351   c. $97,022
     b. $94,090   d. $96,040

11. List two methods of computing *accelerated* depreciation.

     a. _____

     b. _____

12. An apartment building has fixed costs of $75,000 per year and a variable cost ratio of 25 percent. What is the break-even point for the property expressed in dollars per year?

     a. $100,000   c. $68,750
     b. $75,000   d. $300,000

13. If an owner has an equity investment of $50,000 in a property that provides an annual after-tax cash flow of $12,000, what is the percentage rate of return on investment for the property?

     a.   12 percent   c.   24 percent
     b.   4 percent   d.   30 percent

14. List four common types of insurance coverage that should be carried by a property owner.

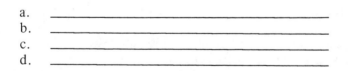

     a. _____

     b. _____

     c. _____

     d. _____

15. Computation of internal rate of return:

   I.   attempts to standardize the rate of return of investments of various types by use of a single common measurement.

  II. requires estimation of cash flows for several years in advance.

     a. I only   c. both I and II
     b. II only   d. neither I nor II

16.   Risk management theory has the following options for dealing with a possible loss.

     a.   _____

     b.   _____

     c.   _____

     d.   _____

17.   Insurance covers three basic risks:

     a.   _____

     b.   _____

     c.   _____

18.   In tax matters, a property manager:

    I.   can rely on experience and past procedures.

    II.   must constantly be alert for changes in tax laws and regulations.

     a.   I only   c.   both I and II

     b.   II only   d.   neither I nor II

10

Administrative Management Office

The bulk of the real estate management profession is made up of three major groups. Most property managers are employed directly by owners of individual buildings. Although these *individual managers* may retain the right to act as agents for other owners as well, their activities are most often restricted to serving their employers exclusively. Individual managers may operate as employees or as independent contractors, in which case an agent-principal relationship is created. In other cases, property managers are employed by a *management firm* that oversees many buildings on behalf of numerous individual or corporate owners. Property managers in the third category work for a *real estate agency management division.* Full-service real estate agencies offer their clients property management services in addition to leasing, insurance brokerage, sales, counseling, appraisal, financing, and mortgage banking. Management firms and management divisions both have an agent-principal relationship with the property owner, and the individuals who manage the properties are employees of the management organization.

Office space is needed to conduct daily business and to store records, reports, and other documents for the property. The location, organization, equipment, and staff of the management command post will vary with the scope of the operation. Private managers, for instance, and management firms or departments that are in the early stages of development are likely to have only a property manager and a secretary-bookkeeper on their staff.

ESTABLISHING THE MANAGEMENT OFFICE

Location and Layout

When most of the management operations are conducted at the building itself, the most logical site for the manager's office is on the premises. Even when a manager has a home office elsewhere, a small office to be used for specific functions is often set up in the property.

The office should be conveniently located, but it should not occupy space that has a specialized high rental value, such as the ground floor of an office building. Small independent real estate agencies are usually located as close as possible to customer traffic. In a lower-rent building located on a side street near a neighborhood shopping center, the agency management office will probably be found at ground level. Management firms and large real estate agencies in metropolitan areas often have a main office in prestigious high-rise quarters in the center of the business district. As business expands, they then establish smaller ground-level offices in outlying neighborhoods or in managed properties.

Wherever the office is located, it should accommodate the basic functions of property management. Prospective clients and service personnel will look for a reception area. Space also should be allotted for comfortable private interviews with clients, potential employers, and businesspeople. Existing tenants need an accessible and private place to pay their rent, make service requests, or negotiate lease renewals. Although the management office need not have the latest in decor, furnishings should be affordable, attractive, tasteful, uniform in style, and well arranged. A chaotic office atmosphere says a lot about the manager's approach to his or her work.

Office space is necessary for the personnel and paperwork involved in administrative functions such as timekeeping, payroll, purchasing, billing, accounts receivable, bookkeeping, collections, and preparation of government reports. The management office also has to have an area large enough for the accounting personnel, equipment, and files required to prepare and store income and expense records for the properties.

Files

A good filing system is at the core of an efficient management office. A sensible filing system is one that provides for the easy collection, retention, and retrieval of records. Data should be sorted and segregated into separate files for easy access. It should also be reviewed periodically to eliminate outdated information that is merely taking up space. Office records can be divided into five general categories for filing purposes.

The *lease files* should contain current lease instruments as well as credit and reference data on the tenants. Leases usually are filed first by building and then by unit number. A lease expiration list or tickler file of lease expiration dates should be kept with this file so that the manager can see at a glance which leases are coming up for renewal. Expired leases should be removed to a separate system and filed alphabetically by tenant name.

A *general correspondence* file contains all communications with tenants. Correspondence is usually filed according to building, with each building then subdivided alphabetically according to tenant name. This type of file should be updated on a yearly basis and old records discarded after 3 years.

When placing service contracts and contracting for new construction, the manager usually solicits bids from two or more contractors. These *work estimates* should be filed according to the property involved, because even if the job is not placed with a particular bidder at the time of the solicitation, these bids can provide important comparison data when considering future projects. New files should be set up yearly, as cost estimates do not remain relevant for very long.

Check registers, canceled checks, receipts, and disbursement records are usually retained for a 10-year period in a *financial file* organized by building. The file also organizes budgets, monthly income and expense reports, yearly profit and loss statements, and other financial records for each building and its employees. These basic documents should be retained for the duration of the management operation. Large organizations may microfilm these records to save space.

A *permanent file* holds the management contract, mortgage and title information, labor contracts, a legal description of the property, and similar documents. Insurance policies on the property may be kept in this file, but it is preferable to have them in a separate folder with the coverage terms, policy limits, and expiration date clearly visible on the outside for quick reference. Insurance policies should be reviewed at least every 6 months to determine whether or not the coverage is still adequate. A separate tickler list of policy expiration dates should be posted in the permanent file so that new entries can be made immediately and expiration dates monitored regularly.

Equipment

If less than 400 units are under the management of one person, it is usually possible for that manager to run the office literally "by hand" with the help of a secretary-clerk. Once the scope of the manager's activity passes this mark, however, some machine assistance will be needed to keep up with the work load. The amount of automated help needed depends again on the size of the operation and the type of properties involved. Office equipment such as typewriters, dictating equipment, calculators, specialized accounting equipment (including computers), and duplicating machines are fundamental once the business begins to grow. Machine capabilities in these areas, especially the critical bookkeeping function, can always be expanded with future growth.

Even with the aid of specialized accounting equipment or computers, the receiving, posting, and banking of rental payments is a complex procedure. It can be made much more efficient with electronic data-processing equipment, but in general the purchase of a computer cannot be justified until monthly business exceeds a certain volume, which will vary according to the type of property and its geographic spread. Where volume is not sufficient for a computer to be a cost-effective capital expenditure, contract bookkeeping is available from firms that specialize in selling time-shared data-processing services. Banks also have entered this field.

Electronic data processing is being widely used for property management income and expense accounting. More than half of all property management firms currently use some form of data processing, and the number is constantly increasing. The greatest advantage appears to be in the collection of rents and the accrual of information regarding expenses to date by category. When calculating the cost of computerized accounting as opposed to staff accounting, the management operation must consider the price of machines, the salaries for their operators, and the rental on the space needed for these machines. Savings tend to be greater for larger companies, usually because they can get quantity discount rates for processing.

Just as accounts receivable and payable can be processed more efficiently with the aid of machines, so too can the monthly rental billings. This process is so unchanging that a simple machine like an addressograph can facilitate the task and save both labor and money. Addressographs and word processing equipment can do double-duty by running off envelopes and correspondence on a regular basis for firms, such as suppliers or utility companies. Advertising mailing lists also can be set up on these machines. For large-volume operations, rent bills can be prepared by computer. The machine will issue a punched card, part of which is returned with the rent payment to facilitate data processing.

Postage scales are a must for any efficient mailing operation. Incorrectly stamped mail is a waste of money, if not an annoyance. Mailings that reach clients with postage due cast a bad light on the manager's capabilities. Motor-driven mailing machines which automatically seal and stamp the envelope with the correct postage are available for more sophisticated operations such as direct-mail advertising campaigns.

COMPUTERS IN PROPERTY MANAGEMENT

The spread of the use of computers into smaller businesses, farms, and homes is a phenomenon of the 1980s. The field of real estate has been radically affected by this innovation, first in the analysis and investment area, then in the listing and sales industry, and now in the property management field. Property managers must be familiar with computers and their capabilities both in financial data processing and word processing.

There are three categories of computers, based on size, function, and method of operation: mainframe, mini, and micro. Mainframes, which are the largest, fastest, and most expensive computers with the highest memory capacity, can be centralized or part of a network. Real estate computer networks have been established to allow salespeople to access listings in various parts of the country. Minicomputers, or medium sized, and microcomputers, the smallest and least expensive, have more limited capabilities.

Two terms, which should be learned in becoming acquainted with computers, are *hardware* and *software*. Hardware includes those physical parts of the computer that can be seen and touched, such as the keyboard, printer, and display screen or terminal. All programmed instructions used to run the computer are referred to as software, and include user programs stored on disks, cassettes, and tapes, as well as programs, written by computer manufacturers to control the input/output devices.

Microcomputers

The microcomputer is the most adaptable computer available to property management operations, because of its size, convenience of use, and cost. Typical microcomputer equipment consists of the following four main elements:

- processor and keyboard
- visual display terminal (CRT)
- disk drive
- printer.

The processor performs several mathematical and logical functions and can access data from a disk or cassette. This data can be viewed on the CRT (which looks like a television screen) and altered, updated, or deleted. Then, with a few keystrokes, standard forms can be filled in, filed, and printed on an attached printer. The processor also connects the CPU or processor with peripheral devices through the use of interface cards.

Software is the key to any successful microcomputer operation, and a vast amount is already available to perform financial analysis, planning, electronic filing, graphic design, word processing, and many other specific business applications. In evaluating software programs, a manager should preview the program to determine how user friendly or how easy it is to use. Most computer stores have demo copies, and salespeople can also make recommendations.

Microcomputer Functions

One microcomputer system with proper general utility software can function as an electronic:

- financial spreadsheet
- filing system
- typewriter
- drawing board.

Electronic spreadsheet programs permit manual bookkeeping calculations to be performed automatically, and a change in one spreadsheet or ledger item will change all the related numbers. The spreadsheet function can be used in financial planning and for calculations that need to be retained and used again, such as monthly budgets and cash flow studies.

The electronic filing feature of the microcomputer permits retrieval of data in a manner and file structure prescribed by the user. Instead of maintaining two separate files for tenant information and lease data, all of this information can be stored on a single disk. Bookkeeping data, kept on a disk, can be sorted and "filed" according to check numbers, account numbers, vendors' names, or any other classifications established by the user.

The word processing programs for microcomputers can be used to compose almost any type of letter, report, or statistical table. It is easy to change, insert, or delete letters, words, lines, paragraphs, or even pages of typewritten material. Besides features, such as automatic margins and page lengths, microcomputers can merge mailing lists and form letters and allow users merely to fill in the blanks on forms, such as leases, which were typed onto disks. The printing unit must have a high-quality printing capability, and the microcomputer must contain the basic elements of a good word processing machine, including automatic paper insert, left and right justification, automatic centering, carriage return, pagination, deletion and insertion, and indentation.

The electronic drawing board program produces graphics in the form of line, bar, or pie charts for presentations and reports, such as those covering vacancies or square foot sales in shopping centers. The microcomputer automatically plots the data (which will require either a plotter or dot matrix space printer) and provides flexible formats and labels.

Software currently on the market combines the foregoing functions in an "all-in-one" software package. However, separate programs are also available for the spreadsheet, data management, word processing, and graphics functions.

Purchasing a Computer

Before purchasing any computer, the prospective buyer should have a specific purpose in mind, and personnel must make a commitment to learn and use the equipment. Most microcomputers are sold with tutorial textbooks, which are not complex, but it requires practice and time to develop speed and accuracy.

Microcomputers can be counter-productive. Since there is a definite tendency to overuse or to misuse them, the manager must know when the micro should be used and when a calculator or a simple sixteen column accounting paper will suffice. Also, the tendency to play games on the computer needs to be controlled.

It is not possible to take an inexpensive cassette recorder, combine it with a small computer keyboard and a ten-year-old color TV with the thought that one will then have a good computer business system. Minimum business system hardware will consist of the following:

- computer (processor) with at least 64K of memory
- black and white or green phosphorus monitor
- two disk drives
- back-up diskettes
- dot matrix printer.

There are several hundred microcomputers available on the market, and a property manager must determine the manufacturer/dealer support, hardware/software features, and price which will suit his or her needs. In analyzing support from the manufacturer or dealer, the potential buyer should evaluate whether the company or the dealer will be able to service the equipment and whether the software features will remain the same for the next few years. How much and what type of software is available is another consideration.

While programs can be conceived and developed by users, there are already programs on the market which should be analyzed before resorting to building from the bottom up. The minimum software required includes an electronic spreadsheet and a data management program. Since the deluge of new products and innovations is constant, the property manager must seriously evaluate the cost of these items. In addition to the foregoing programs, word processing would add considerably to the total cost.

However, various hardware and software should be evaluated in light of property management requirements. Price should be the last consideration, since prices are generally competitive and are constantly being lowered. A manager should not purchase equipment on the basis of price alone at the sacrifice of a needed or useful feature.

STAFFING THE MANAGEMENT OFFICE

No matter how plush the office space or how modern the equipment, the management operation will not succeed if office personnel are not efficient and loyal. The most basic qualification for an employee in the field of property management is versatility, for few management organizations are large enough to support a staff of specialists. As noted earlier, the property manager and a secretary-bookkeeper may be the only staff running the business in its early stages. Conversely, large, established management firms or departments often employ several people in each of the positions described here.

Property Management Executive

The ultimate success or failure of management operations depends upon the talents of the chief property manager, or property management executive. The manager must be knowledgeable and experienced, as he or she will be controlling both the strategic and operational aspects of property management. In the growth stage of a business, the property management executive will be concerned with *strategic* issues such as financial planning, market analysis, soliciting new business, personnel training, and long-range goals. He or she will also have to manage the *operational* activities, which include rentals, collections, property inspection, supervision of maintenance, and procurement of supplies and labor.

The responsibilities of the manager during the growth years can also be classified as executive or administrative. *Executive functions* include preparing budgets; developing an advertising program; leasing; inspecting properties; communicating with tenants; contacting owners; contracting for services; hiring, training, and supervising both office and on-site employees; directing major repairs; and supervising all administrative functions. As part of his or her *administrative functions,* the property management executive oversees collections, disbursements, payroll preparation, and recording; submits monthly operating reports; and keeps records in all areas.

Obviously, some of the tasks listed above are best performed by on-site managers, property supervisors, or skilled clerical personnel. As soon as the organization is large enough to make it economically feasible, the management executive should hire and train subordinates to assist with the work. Eventually, he or she may have property supervisors in the field, resident managers, a maintenance and janitorial crew, a comptroller, at least one cashier-bookkeeper, secretaries, and service request clerks. A staff this size will allow the executive to devote full attention to setting the general policy for the organization, developing new business, supervising operational costs and activities, and building employee morale and motivation.

The scope of the organization's activities and the personality of the executive property manager are the major determinants of the management office's staffing plan. Although some basic job categories can be identified, management offices will not necessarily fill each of these positions, due to telescoping of functions. Figure 25 illustrates the staff of a typical, fairly large management firm or department. A very large firm may add another level or two in the supervisory hierarchy, while a smaller firm may function as a one- or two-person operation.

Figure 25: MANAGEMENT ORGANIZATION

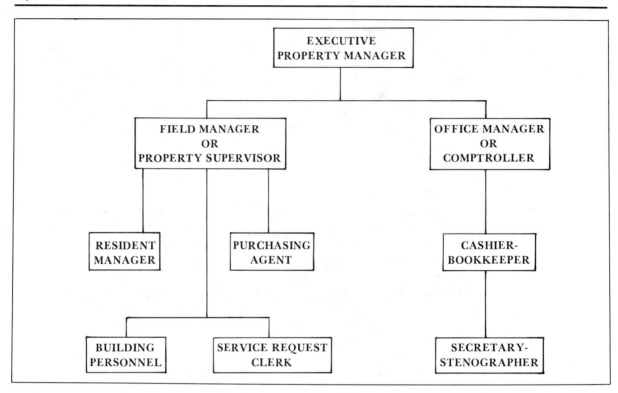

Field Manager (Property Supervisor)

The property supervisor takes care of the general administration and daily operation of the property. The demands on the property supervisor's time will vary with the condition of the premises, number of major problems, type of ownership, distance from the management office, and number of other properties to be supervised. Taking these variables into account, one person can efficiently manage anywhere from 5 to 20 buildings which should, if possible, be concentrated in one neighborhood. The supervisor reports directly to the property management executive. Part of the supervisor's responsibility is to establish a personal but businesslike relationship with the tenants and the owner. As the person in charge of lease renewals, he or she should reply courteously to tenant calls and take steps to collect delinquent rents or initiate legal proceedings. Besides seeing that all units are well maintained, competitively priced, and actively shown (if they are vacant), the property supervisor regularly inspects the premises and the activities of employees. Hiring policy and salary levels for the resident manager and other building employees are set by the property supervisor so that the payroll will reflect the actual requirements of the premises.

The property supervisor usually has the added responsibility of comparing bids and obtaining outside contract services for corrective maintenance, housekeeping, and new construction. He or she monitors building and office employees, makes maintenance decisions, and approves purchase orders for supplies and services. When maintenance jobs are completed, the supervisor inspects the work and the materials.

On-Site Manager and Building Personnel

Many states demand that residential properties above a specified size employ a given number of resident personnel. Under normal conditions, an on-site manager can handle up to 150 or 200 units without an assistant. The number of assistants (janitors, engineers, etc.) hired depends on the amount of space and the number of buildings to be managed.

The on-site manager is a key figure on the management team. Candidates for this position must be carefully selected and qualified. Various professional property management associations offer educational programs for on-site managers, which are detailed in later chapters. These programs can benefit both the individual and the management organization as a whole.

The on-site manager is sometimes given the authority to hire custodians, handymen, and other maintenance workers, but the property supervisor will want to retain the right to hire the chief custodian and approve all other help engaged by the on-site manager. The size of the area one custodian can service depends upon the nature of the services, the number of partitioned areas, and the type of tenancy. At average estimates, one person can service 15,000 square feet of open space as opposed to 6,000 square feet of partitioned area. One handyman usually services approximately 100 tenants. As explained in Chapter 8, only very large buildings can economically justify the hiring of in-house craftspeople to do tenant alteration work. Plumbers, carpenters, and electricians can be hired on a contract basis for jobs that are beyond the capacity of the on-site maintenance staff in a smaller building.

Purchasing Agent

The responsibility of the purchasing agent is to oversee all purchases made by or through the management organization. Only very large organizations can justify a full-time position for this function. With the help of on-site personnel, the purchasing agent will judge the basic value of new appliances, supplies, services, equipment, and materials. By considering factors such as quality, cost, and efficiency, the agent should be able to formulate a general purchasing policy for supplies, maintenance service requests, and equipment requisitions. Good judgment is critical when an agent is trying to shave expenses through volume buying. In smaller management offices, the property supervisor or an accountant usually performs the job of the purchasing agent by compiling a list of preferred suppliers, contractors, products, and equipment.

Office Manager (Comptroller)

Cost accounting is imperative for a profitable property management operation, but unless the bookkeeper's tabulated data are analyzed in terms of possible operational adjustments, the bookkeeping records are not being used to their best advantage. The comptroller (or office manager) must interpret the income and expense reports, make major decisions regarding new procedures, and submit profit and loss statements to the owner. A single comptroller is usually responsible for all of the properties managed by the firm. Because this is a crucial function, the executive property manager in a smaller operation will usually assume responsibility for it.

Cashier-Bookkeeper

Bookkeepers spend most of their time preparing rental bills, receiving and recording rent payments, keeping an account of monthly income and expenses for each property, and handling accounts payable and receivable. They also handle the payroll and maintain operating cost records for the management firm's operating costs. Depending upon the owner's demand for detail and the type of accounting system in use (manual, machine, or computer), a single bookkeeper can usually handle about eight to ten properties. The number increases in a large management firm because the assumption of more properties justifies a more sophisticated accounting system, which requires less time and labor per property.

Regardless of the competence of the bookkeeping staff, it is wise for a management office to have an outside accounting firm audit its books semiannually or annually, as recommended in Chapter 9. This is especially true when rental rates are tied to an index such as operating costs.

Clerical Personnel

The size of the clerical staff will be determined by the total number of property management executives, supervisors, and comptrollers. Clerical personnel can be divided into two major groups. *Secretary-stenographers* are responsible for answering telephones, maintaining contact between the field managers and the central office, and handling the general correspondence of the management organization. Establishing a word processing center is the most cost-efficient method of accomplishing these tasks, although some firms assign one secretary to each property supervisor, one to the comptroller, and one to the management executive. General reception for the main office can be performed by these employees or by a special receptionist. *Service request clerks* should be on hand to accept phone calls from tenants. This will ease the burden on the secretarial staff and provide a team of persons ready to respond promptly and patiently to tenant requests. These clerks can also act as liaison agents between the main office and the building, notifying the custodian of a service request, writing the purchase order for items needed by the on-site staff, having it approved by upper management, and then routing the requisitioned material to the appropriate building once it arrives. Besides fulfilling the functions mentioned above, service request clerks enhance good tenant relations by keeping the tenants apprised of the disposition of their requests. In smaller operations, the secretarial staff of the management office must act as service request clerks.

Branch Offices

As the management organization grows, branch offices may be opened in outlying areas to handle newly acquired business more efficiently. Traditionally, each outlying office was run by a property manager and a salesperson in charge of new accounts, assisted by a receptionist, bookkeeper, secretary, and at least two accounting clerks—one for accounts receivable and another for accounts payable. However, this staffing pattern quickly reaches a point of diminishing returns for the management organization. The buildings serviced by branch offices are usually smaller than those managed by the downtown office. Smaller properties often do not generate enough revenue to justify the existence of a separate branch to service them, much less the expansion of the branch staff that inevitably results from acquisition of additional neighborhood buildings to manage. The alternative is for the management organization to centralize all of the functions of its branches in one main office. With this approach, though, the organization runs the risk of losing walk-in business. Property managers take the chance of becoming too far removed from their responsibility, thereby losing the owner's confidence.

To avoid the problems of complete centralization, management functions that are integrally related to the neighborhood can be performed at branch offices, leaving the main office to take care of more standardized activities. Centralized accounting systems require only a property manager, a secretary-receptionist, and a salesperson who solicits local accounts at each branch. This arrangement can reduce the staffing needs of a branch office by 40 percent or more, with a concomitant increase in the overall efficiency and profit margin of the management company. Accuracy and uniformity of reports and records is a by-product of centralization, but perhaps the greatest benefit is that new properties can be acquired and managed with no additions to the branch office, and with minimum additions at the main office.

DETERMINING MANAGEMENT EXPENSES

Before any management fees can be set, the management executive must first know how much it costs the organization to provide its management services. A budget that includes the direct and indirect costs of operation will show the total cost of doing business.

Direct Costs

Direct costs are easy to ascertain. In fact, all costs incurred by an individual manager or management firm can be considered direct costs. If management operations are a division of a real estate agency, however, direct costs would include all expenses incurred during the performance of the management business which are not charged to or shared by another department of the parent company. General office expenses included in direct costs are the payroll for the management staff; depreciation on office furniture and equipment; equipment maintenance or rental; insurance premiums; legal, auditing, and other professional fees; stationery and postage; utilities; taxes; office supplies; and office rent. Business promotion and automobile expenses are also considered to be direct costs.

Indirect Costs

Indirect expenses are incurred when a management department shares facilities and expenses with other divisions of the parent company or real estate agency. Although they may amount to 25 percent or more of the total cost of operating, they are less visible than direct costs and therefore are often ignored when drawing up a management department's budget. A proportionate share of occupancy costs, general office overhead, and accounting overhead should be assigned to the management department as its indirect costs.

Indirect *occupancy cost* can be calculated by multiplying the ratio of space occupied by the management division per total space times the overall company expenditure for rent, utilities, depreciation, and maintenance. *General office overhead* includes items that cannot be charged specifically to any particular division, such as corporate salaries, wages for general company personnel, corporate advertising costs, stationery, office supplies, and legal fees. These general office overhead costs can be allocated by several methods. The easiest way to determine the share accrued by the management division is to compute the ratio of revenue from management services to total company income, and to multiply this percentage figure by the total office overhead. *General accounting costs* also must be distributed among the various divisions of the parent company. These costs include the payroll for the general accounting staff and management, computer time, and certain supplies. After the total dollar amount has been calculated, it must be allocated equitably according to the total hours of accounting staff or computer time used by each division, the number of accounting transactions made on behalf of each division, and the number of personnel in each department who are on the general payroll.

COMPUTING THE MANAGEMENT FEE

As mentioned earlier, most management fees are related to the property's gross collectable income. Fees may range from as little as 2 percent to as much as 20 percent of the gross collectable income from a property, depending on the management risk, the size of the building, and the profit margin. Because of the numerous variables involved, there is no universally valid formula for the computation of management fees. The problems of managing an apartment building are quite different from those involved in managing industrial property. The size of the building, its condition, its location, and other factors also have an effect on the profitability rate for the management of the property. In general, however, there are two ways of computing management fees. One method bases the fee on the per-unit cost of management, which is derived from the operating budget for the management organization. A second method employs a standardized management pricing worksheet.

Per-Unit Cost Method

The first step in arriving at the per-unit cost is to total the direct and indirect costs of management operations over one year. The number of units the firm is capable of managing when working at full capacity must then be determined. It is important to use the number of units the firm is *capable* of managing as opposed to the number of units the firm is *actually* managing currently, or the per-unit cost will be unrealistically and uncompetitively high. To compute the per-unit management cost, divide the total management costs by the number of units the firm is capable of managing and add a percentage amount for profit. Although each management firm decides upon its own profit margin, the typical range is from 10 percent to 20 percent. For example, a management firm with total operating expenses of $100,000 and the capability to handle 1,000 units will have a yearly per-unit cost of $100. Adding 20 percent for profit, the per-unit cost is $120. This figure represents the minimum *per-unit* fee that must be obtained regardless of the type or number of buildings or units being managed.

Adjustments to Per-Unit Fee. As pointed out, numerous variables are involved in managing property, and no standard method of setting a fee can possibly make allowance for every contingency. Therefore, the per-unit rate often has to be adjusted to reflect the economics of a particular situation. For example, one large building with 500 units is cheaper to manage than five separate properties of 100 units each. The travel time involved in field supervision of separate buildings is much greater, as is the total number of personnel and separate operational systems that must be inspected. The per-unit fee for a small 100-unit property should be raised to compensate for the inefficiency of decentralization. The per-unit rate should also be increased for buildings with internal problems, a significant amount of deferred maintenance, or a pressing need for new construction or repairs. An owner who wants to be informed of every detail of operation (and this category often includes government agencies) will take more management time and should be charged accordingly. Properties located in depressed areas tend to be more time consuming for the manager because of vandalism and related social ills. Any factor that adds to the time spent in caring for the premises should be reflected in the per-unit rate.

Percentage Rate. The next step in setting an appropriate management fee is to use the per-unit fee, the total number of units in the building, and the gross income of the property to calculate the *percentage rate.* First, multiply the adjusted per-unit fee by the total number of units to obtain the dollar amount that must be recovered if the management contract is to be profitable. Next, determine the gross collectable income for the property by subtracting a realistic vacancy and loss rate from the annual gross income. Finally, divide the dollar amount of the management fee by the gross collectable income. The resulting figure, when expressed as a percentage, is the base property management fee. Expressed as an equation, this calculation reads:

$$\frac{\text{adjusted per-unit fee} \times \text{total number of units}}{\text{annual gross income} - \text{vacancy and loss rate}} = \frac{\text{dollar amount of fee}}{\text{gross collectable income}} \times 100\% = \text{percentage management fee}$$

For instance, a 20-unit building has a gross income of $36,500 per year. Using the per-unit cost of $120 calculated in the previous example, the amount to be recovered for this property is $2,400 ($120 × 20 = $2,400). Assuming a 5-percent vacancy rate, the gross collectable income for the property would be $34,675 ($36,500 × .05 - $1,825; $36,500 – $1,825 = $34,675), so the percentage rate would be about 7 percent ($2,400 ÷ $34,675 = .069). The management fee for this property would be quoted at 7 percent of gross income.

Both owners and managers generally prefer a percentage fee to a flat rate because it gives the manager an inducement to increase the income of the property. The percentage rate gives the manager an incentive to raise rents, cut operating costs, and maximize the owner's profits. Because a flat fee is constant and can be increased only through negotiation with the owner, it may encourage a certain laxness in administrative and executive functions (especially rental) on the part of management. A manager may be justified in charging a flat fee for properties with much deferred maintenance, excessively high tenant turnover, or an undesirable tenant population that will have to be evicted. In such cases, the manager might want to consider a flat-fee agreement, at least initially, to compensate for extra work and lower profit.

As mentioned in Chapter 4, some management contracts provide for a management fee plus a separate fee for obtaining new rentals. This practice is prevalent when dealing with retail space. The disadvantage of this compensation arrangement is that it may encourage the manager to allow or create a greater tenant turnover than is warranted. Many managers prefer to build the compensation for their leasing activities into the basic management fee by raising it slightly.

Management Pricing Worksheet

This method of computing the management fee relies on the same principles as the per-unit cost method, but the approach is completely different, as shown by Figure 26, a sample worksheet. Begin with the first section (the list of services provided by the property supervisor) and record how many inspections, visits, meetings, and the like will be necessary for the particular property on a monthly basis. These figures, when multiplied by the number of hours each activity will consume, amount to the total number of hours the property supervisor must devote to the property per month. The time spent traveling to the site and preparing and checking reports also must be added. Then the figures in the "Total Hours" column should be multiplied by the cost of the property supervisor's time. In the example in Figure 26, the cost is $20 per hour. The total cost for each category is recorded in the far right-hand column. The total of these dollar amounts, plus travel expense, is the estimated total cost of the property supervisor's services.

Section II itemizes the executive property manager's activities with regard to the property. Total hours spent and total cost are calculated in the same manner as above, although the executive manager usually charges a higher fee per hour. On the sample management pricing worksheet, the fee is $100 per hour.

Section III allows the management firm to determine the total number of hours that will be spent monthly in credit and collections, accounts payable and receivable, payroll, preparation of financial statements, and related matters. The total number of hours spent in these activities should then be multiplied by the *average* hourly wage of accounting and clerical personnel ($10 an hour in the example) to calculate the total direct cost of these services. Item IV is a subtotal of all direct management costs.

Section V deals with overhead and profit. The management firm should know by experience what percentage of its income goes toward general overhead (office rental, utilities, phones, supplies) and marketing. The firm must also select an acceptable profit margin, usually from 10 percent to 20 percent. The next step is to multiply the percentage rates for overhead, marketing, and profit by the subtotal of costs in Item IV. These dollar amounts should be recorded in the far right-hand column in Section V.

The total of items IV and V is actually the monthly management fee, but it is expressed as a flat rate. If a percentage rate is desired, the dollar amount of the monthly fee must be divided by the average monthly gross collectable income. The quotient is the estimated percentage management fee. The example in Figure 26 shows a gross monthly income of $89,600. $5,390 divided by $89,600 is approximately 6 percent.

Figure 26: MANAGEMENT PRICING

Property _____

No. of units ___300___ Residents ___1200___ Offices _____ Stores _____ Boat slips _____

Age and present condition of property and improvements _____
_____15 years old; good condition_____

Miles from office _____20_____ Number of employees _____4_____

Gross common area charge _____

Management/Leasing _____ Leasing _____

	No. Per Month	Hours Each	Total Hours	Cost
I. PROPERTY SUPERVISOR'S SERVICES				
Inspections	1	6	6	$ 120
Site visits	1	4	4	80
Capital improvement supervision	—	—	—	—
Owner/Investor/Association meetings	1	2	2	40
Travel time: $_20_ per hr. x _4_ hrs.			4	80
Office hours per month			10	200
Travel expense: _100 mi._ x _25_ ¢ per mi.				25
Total				545
II. PROPERTY MANAGEMENT EXECUTIVE'S SERVICES				
Owner/Investor/Association meetings	1	2	2	$ 200
Site visits	—	—	—	—
Surveys and consultations	1	2	2	200
Inspections	1	4	4	400
Statement review	1	4	4	400
Budget preparation	—	—	—	—
Travel time: $_50_ per hr. x _3_ hrs.			3	150
Travel expense: _75_ mi. x _15_ ¢ per mi.				12
Total				1,362
III. ACCOUNTING & CLERICAL SERVICES				
Receipts accounted for: days per mo.	4	8	32	
Disbursements: invoices, payments	4	8	32	
Monthly billing	1	10	10	
Payroll: checks issued	2	8	16	
Owner/Assoc. statement preparation	4	4	16	
Resident statement and preparation	50	1	50	
Statement duplication	10	2	20	
Owner consultation	—	—	—	
Total				$2,210
IV. SUBTOTAL BEFORE OVERHEAD AND PROFIT				$4,117

V. OVERHEAD AND PROFIT	Percent of Total			
General overhead	10%			$ 411
Marketing	1%			$ 41
Profit and contingencies	20%			$ 821

VI. TOTAL MONTHLY FEE $5,390

$ _____ Fee ÷ Units = $ _____ each

$ ___5,390___ Fee ÷ Gross = _____6_____ %

Compiled by _____ Approved _____

When setting management fees, the pertinent variables must be evaluated and assigned an order of importance. If the estimated percentage rate is too high, it will not be competitive with the market rate and business will be lost. On the other hand, cutting back on necessary management services and staff in order to lower management operational expense, or accepting management contracts that will not cover costs, will only deteriorate the management organization's reputation, impair its financial structure, and hurt its business. A sound policy is to review all management contracts annually and raise fees on properties that are causing problems or consuming an inordinate amount of time without generating sufficient monetary compensation.

SUMMARY

The bulk of the real estate management profession is composed of three major groups: individual managers, who are directly employed by owners of individual buildings; management firms, which employ many property managers to oversee the numerous buildings under their care; and managers who work for real estate agencies that offer a variety of services, including a property management division. Managers may be either employees or contractors (agents) of the owner. Those who work for management firms and real estate agencies are employees of the organization, which in turn is the agent of the owner or principal.

The management office, where daily business is conducted, should reflect the scope and nature of management operations. Offices may be located at the buildings themselves, in a central downtown metropolitan area, or in outlying areas. In any case, the office area and its furnishings have to accommodate the basic functions of property management and create a good impression of the organization. There should be enough space for the firm's records and accounting system and for the reception of tradespeople and tenants.

The selection of office equipment is governed by the size of the management operation. While smaller operations may be run "by hand" by the manager and a secretary-clerk, larger operations will require machine assistance. Specialized accounting machines may be adequate for modest operations, but larger firms may benefit from contracting electronic data-processing services or purchasing data-processing equipment.

Property managers must be familiar with computers and their capabilities. *Hardware* refers to physical parts of the computer, while *software* encompasses all programmed instructions used by the computer.

The microcomputer is the computer most adaptable to property management operations. Software is the key to any successful microcomputer operation. A vast amount of software is already available to the property manager to perform financial analysis, planning, electronic filing, graphic design, word processing, and many specific business applications. One microcomputer system with proper general utility software can function as an electronic *spreadsheet* for financial analysis, *file* for data management, *word processor* for typing, or *drawing board* for graphics.

Before purchasing any computer, the prospective buyer should have a specific purpose in mind, and personnel must make a commitment to learn and use the equipment. Programs already on the market should be researched before resorting to building from the bottom up. In selecting a particular microcomputer, manufacturer/dealer support, hardware/software features, and price must be investigated. Price should be the least important consideration, since prices are generally competitive and are constantly being lowered.

Within the management office, the *property management executive* shoulders most of the responsibility for the success or failure of the organization. At the outset of a business, he or she will perform both strategic and operational management tasks and will have to coordinate a variety of executive and administrative responsibilities. As the organization grows, the management executive can hire and delegate work to staff people.

The *field manager,* or *property supervisor,* administers the properties. He or she must respond to tenant calls; collect delinquent rents; regularly inspect the premises; and supervise resident managers, building personnel, and contract service or maintenance personnel.

In larger management operations, the *purchasing agent* controls all purchases made by or through the management organization. This individual also inspects the quality of supplies and equipment delivered.

The accounting and bookkeeping staff handles the management firm's financial operations. The *comptroller,* or *office manager,* oversees the accounting department, interprets the income and expense reports on properties, initiates new procedures, and provides the owner with profit and loss statements. There is usually at least one *cashier-bookkeeper* who receives rents, handles credit and collections, records accounts payable, completes the monthly income and expense statements on properties, and provides the owner with profit and loss statements.

Clerical personnel can be divided into two major groups: *secretary-stenographers,* who handle general correspondence and maintain contact between the field managers and the central office; and *service request clerks,* who take telephone requests for service from the tenants.

As the management operation grows, branch offices may be opened in outlying areas. Because these offices usually service smaller properties than those managed by the downtown office, and hence bring in smaller fees, accounting functions should be centralized to cut down on the branch staff and ensure the financial feasibility of the branch office's operation.

There are two general methods of setting management fees. Both are based on the organization's cost of doing business, including direct and indirect costs of operation. Most management fees are a percentage of the property's gross collectable income, but since numerous variables affect the profit potential for the management of the property, there is no absolute formula for the computation of management fees.

The first method of determining a management fee is known as the per-unit method. To begin, the per-unit cost of management must be derived from the operating budget for the management operation. The per-unit cost is calculated by dividing the total of direct and indirect costs by the number of units the firm is capable of managing when working at full capacity. A percentage amount is added to this figure for profit, resulting in the minimum per-unit fee. The per-unit fee often must be adjusted to reflect certain variables. Any factor that causes the manager to spend more time than normal in caring for the premises should increase the per-unit rate for that property.

After determining the adjusted per-unit rate, the manager must compute the annual gross collectable income for the property by subtracting an allowance for vacancies and other rent loss from the total annual income. Then, the actual percentage management fee can be calculated by the following formula:

$$\frac{(\text{adjusted per-unit fee}) \times (\text{total number of units})}{\text{gross collectable income}} \times 100\% = \text{percentage management fee}$$

The second method of computing a management fee uses a management pricing worksheet. The worksheet consists of an itemized list of all management activities, the time they consume per month, and the direct cost of having the appropriate person perform them. The total of these direct costs, plus general overhead and a margin for profit, is the dollar amount that should be charged to the owner for management services. To obtain a percentage fee, the total monthly fee is simply divided by the gross collectable income from the property during an average month.

Percentage fees are generally preferred to flat rates because they give the manager an incentive to increase the income from the property. The most important fact to remember in setting management fees is that all pertinent variables must be evaluated and ranked to maintain comfortable profit margins and competitive rates.

QUESTIONS: CHAPTER 10

1. List the five general categories of management office records.

    a. _____   d. _____
    b. _____   e. _____
    c. _____

2. When computing a management fee using the pricing worksheet, a manager determined that the total direct cost for all management activities for that property would be $2,500 per month. If the gross collectable income from the property is $50,000 per month and the manager needs an additional 30 percent of the direct costs to cover overhead and profit, what percentage fee should be charged?

    a. 5 percent   c. 13 percent
    b. 6.5 percent   d. 8 percent

3. An executive property manager's responsibilities can generally be classified as either executive or administrative. *Executive* functions would include:

    I.   contracting for services.
    II. preparation of yearly budgets.

    a. I only   c. both I and II
    b. II only   d. neither I nor II

4. Name the three categories of computers:

    a. _____
    b. _____
    c. _____

5. The location of a property management office is governed by:

    I.   convenience to clients and tenants.
    II. rental value of the space used for the management office.

    a. I only   c. both I and II
    b. II only   d. neither I nor II

6. Financial files on subject properties of a property management firm should be:

    a. updated annually.
    b. updated every 3 years.
    c. retained indefinitely.
    d. kept at the site of the property itself for easy reference.

7. The permanent property file should include:

   I.   the management contract.
   II. the yearly budgets.

   a. I only   c. both I and II
   b. II only   d. neither I nor II

8. The field manager or property supervisor is usually responsible for:

   I.   evicting tenants if necessary.
   II. periodically inspecting the interior and exterior condition of properties.

   a. I only   c. both I and II
   b. II only   d. neither I nor II

9. If management operations are too limited to justify hiring a comptroller, the comptroller's tasks should be assumed by the:

   a. purchasing agent.   c. bookkeeper.
   b. resident manager.   d. executive property manager.

10. List the two major categories of clerical personnel necessary in a large, fully staffed management firm.

    a. _____
    b. _____

11. Management firms with several branch offices usually centralize some management functions and leave others to the branch offices. Operations that lend themselves to centralization include:

    I.   rental billing and receipts accounting.
    II. purchasing of supplies.

    a. I only   c. both I and II
    b. II only   d. neither I nor II

12. List three types of indirect costs that should be considered when drawing up the budget for the property management department of a real estate agency or other organization.

    a. _____
    b. _____
    c. _____

13. A small management operation has direct costs of $35,000 and indirect costs of $20,000 annually. It can handle about 750 units and wishes to make a 20 percent profit. What is the minimum per-unit fee that should be charged?

    a. $73   c. $47
    b. $88   d. $164

14. List four factors that would increase the per-unit fee charged by a property manager.

    a. _____

    b. _____

    c. _____

    d. _____

15. An apartment building with 45 units has a maximum gross annual income of $80,000 per year and an estimated vacancy rate of 5 percent. The management firm has computed an adjusted per-unit cost of $110 for the specific property. What percentage management fee should be charged?

    a.   6 percent   c.   7 percent
    b.   6.5 percent   d.   7.5 percent

Residential Rental Property

The preceding chapters examined the property manager's multifaceted role, one that includes analyzing market conditions, leasing space, communicating with tenants and owner, collecting rents, maintaining and staffing the premises, and providing the owner with financial reports on the operation of the property. The remaining chapters will demonstrate how the type of real property to be managed affects these management functions, beginning with the study of residential rental property.

Residential rental housing ranges from single-family houses to huge apartment projects of several thousand units and includes mobile home parks, time sharing resorts, government assisted housing, institutional housing, apartment hotels, and retirement communities. Apartment buildings house the largest majority of residential tenants, and techniques that are successfully employed in the management and administration of apartments are applicable to all types of rental housing. For this reason, this chapter will emphasize the management of apartment buildings.

Rent control laws have been passed in some areas of the country and present unique problems, mainly in the areas of financial operation, rent raises, and eviction of tenants. Therefore, the principles set forth in this chapter will have general application. Property managers operating under rent control laws should research and follow the regulations of the jurisdiction where the property is located.

TYPES OF APARTMENT COMPLEXES

As discussed in Chapter 1, there are several general categories of multifamily dwellings. Construction, design, location, facilities and amenities, and tenant type are the distinguishing characteristics of the different kinds of apartment buildings.

Garden apartments are designed for family living, usually in a sprawling two-story building or buildings in a project containing predominantly two- and three-bedroom units. Garden projects are often located in suburban areas or other regions where land is relatively inexpensive and large tracts are easily obtained. The *three-story walkup* building is usually found in urban areas and in older, more concentrated sections of the suburbs. It is preferred by couples and singles, and most units are either one- or two-bedroom apartments. *Multistory* elevator buildings containing efficiency and one-bedroom units are concentrated primarily on the edge of the downtown area of large cities although in recent years they have been built in suburban locations. These apartments are favored by unmarried working people who want to be close to their jobs. Also located either near the central city or in more affluent outlying areas are *highrise luxury properties,* which emphasize view, amenities, and prestigious addresses. Units in these buildings may have one, two, or three bedrooms, but all have relatively larger living areas than units in other types of apartment buildings. Higher-income families who seek the service and the comforts of a single-family home without the responsibilities of home ownership are the most common luxury highrise tenants.

Numerous facilities and services are available to apartment dwellers. Housing alternatives range from fully furnished units, where everything is supplied for the tenant, to unfurnished apartments that are equipped with only the floors and walls. These are the extremes of the spectrum, with the standard unit lying somewhere in between.

Garden-level complexes, multistory buildings, and highrise apartments might provide recreational facilities such as swimming pools, tennis courts, patios, and recreation rooms. These apartments usually have central air conditioning, the newest appliances, off-street parking areas, and sophisticated security systems. Luxury highrises offer doormen, window cleaning services, heated garages, grocery stores, banks, drugstores, and other conveniences located within the building. The walkup tenant probably receives the least in the way of extra services or facilities. Most of these units are rented unfurnished except for a stove and refrigerator. Traditionally, utility services—with the exception of electricity and telephone—were provided, but a shift has occurred over the past several years. Currently, many walkup, garden, and multistory apartments include only water and garbage removal as part of the monthly rent. The tenant is billed separately for all other utility services.

In any type of residential rental housing, the kind and number of facilities provided will have a direct effect on the property manager's work load, for swimming pools, laundry rooms, and parking areas increase the maintenance activities for the premises. Bear in mind, though, that facilities and services affect the overall desirability and influence the rental structure of any type of residential rental complex.

RESIDENTIAL MARKET ANALYSIS

Market surveys of economic conditions and comparable residential properties located in the immediate area are absolutely essential in gauging the viability of the property as an income-producing investment and in establishing a rental schedule for the apartments.

Rents should be based on two factors—comparable value and scarcity. Scarcity is measured in terms of the supply and demand relationship in the neighborhood. As explained in Chapter 2, the manager can identify the relative demand for a particular property by completing regional and neighborhood market analyses. Neighborhood boundaries must be determined in a residential market analysis because of the effect of attitudes of the community at large as to where certain social, cultural, or income groups ought to reside. The manager's market may be restricted by these arbitrary but very real preconceptions. The effect of employment levels of local industry, especially in a community dominated by a single type of industry, must also be analyzed, for layoffs of workers will be reflected in apartment occupancy rates.

Employment and income data should serve as a touchstone for setting the residential rental schedule. The accepted theory has been that people spend 25 percent of their income on housing, but this rule is no longer universally true. Because of rising costs, the increasing number of working couples, and the trend toward smaller families, many persons are willing to spend a higher percentage of their income on luxury living accommodations.

Census Bureau statistics will give the property manager a general idea of the population density within a particular neighborhood. However, it is not sufficient for the manager merely to be aware of the total number of persons in an area; he or she must also know the size of the average family in order to determine the type and number of housing units needed. For example, the financial prognosis for a highrise complex composed of studio and one-bedroom units would be quite different in an area of small families than it would be in a neighborhood of young singles or childless couples. Local marriage, birth, and divorce records give the residential property manager some indication of the family structure within a neighborhood.

Smaller families and the rapid increase in the number of single-person households will have a direct influence on the type and amount of residential rental space that will be required in the future. Between 1950 and 1959, the population of the U.S. grew at the rate of about 2.8 million persons per year. In recent year, the growth rate dropped to 1.7 million.

This decline in population growth predicts a decreasing need for new housing in the future. In the last decade, over 80 percent of the increase in the number of households consisted of single adults, young couples without children, and other one- or two-person households. These adult-oriented households tend to select an urban lifestyle over suburban living. Attempts to capitalize on this demographic trend have led to "adult only" residential rental facilities in many areas, which have produced charges of discrimination, with ensuing legislation or court decisions prohibiting these practices.

The manager must be aware not only of the family structure within a neighborhood, but also of current population shifts. Population shifts, which are a common phenomenon in our society today, are caused by changes in family styles and structures, increased mobility of the population, unsettled economic conditions, and increased longevity because of improved health care. When the manager detects an alteration in the composition of a neighborhood, he or she must carefully analyze the change in terms of land use and income level. There is a considerable difference between an increase that stems from an influx of middle-income families into an expanding community and one that is due to overcrowding in low-rent buildings. The implications for the future of the neighborhood and for the manager's property are quite different in each case.

Market surveys should also analyze the rental values of comparable properties in the area. A rental analysis of this nature measures and records data such as size, location, amenities, and rental structures for buildings similar to the subject property. The relative market value of the space can then be set and a base rental rate established for each type of apartment. This base rate should be adjusted to reflect preferential location, view, exposure, size, or design. An increase in the base rate might also be justified if the occupancy level in the neighborhood is 95 percent or better, indicating a heavy consumer demand.

MARKETING APARTMENT SPACE

Apartment space is a consumer good and, as such, can be marketed with promotional techniques like those used to sell cars or clothing. Even when the space itself is clean, attractively decorated, and in good condition, market conditions may be such that some units cannot be leased. An alert leasing manager quickly realizes which units are renting rapidly or are not moving fast enough and either adjusts the price or changes the method of advertising and display.

Price Adjustment

The goal in establishing a rental schedule is to realize the maximum market price for each unit. If each type of apartment is priced correctly, the different units will have the same rate of demand; that is, demand for studio, one-bedroom, and two-bedroom units will be equal and the manager will be able to achieve an occupancy rate of about 95 percent for all three types. However, this level of demand is the exception in the real market. More often than not, the manager will have to raise the base rent on the unit types that are fully occupied and decrease the rate for those units less in demand. An optimal price structure should assure the manager of a 95-percent occupancy level for all units. For this strategy to be economically sound, the revenue from the new 95-percent schedule must exceed the income that was collected when some types of units were fully occupied and others had tenant levels below 95 percent.

Show List

In order to establish a reasonable rental schedule, like the one outlined above, the manager must follow certain organizational procedures, such as compiling a show list. This list should enumerate the specific apartments in the building that are available for inspection by prospects. No more than three apartments of each type and size should be on the list at any one time, and whenever a unit is rented, it should be replaced by another vacated apartment that is ready for rental.

The manager can use the show list both as a control guide for the marketing program and as a source of feedback on its success or failure. The features of particular units are itemized on the list, so the manager can do a better and more informed selling job. The maintenance staff will have no problem keeping the 12 to 15 units on the list in top-notch condition, whereas it would be almost impossible for them to maintain all the vacancies in the building. Because the list is short and easy to read, the prospect is not unnecessarily delayed while the manager rifles through a pile of listing sheets looking for a vacant two-bedroom apartment. The limited number of show units suggests that space is at a premium and that a decision must be made quickly.

The show list should be reviewed weekly in order to determine which units are not moving. The manager should then inspect these units personally to find out why they are hard to rent. All curable flaws (worn carpeting, obsolete fixtures) should be corrected.

A particular unit may not rent after several showings to prospects because of poor "curb appeal," that is, a poor impression, created when the building is first seen from the street. Painting or cleaning up entry ways, cutting grass, trimming shrubs, etc., will often work wonders.

Advertising and Display

Even if the property is priced at the appropriate market level, the building may still struggle with a high vacancy rate if prospective tenants are not actively attracted to view the premises.

Classified Ads. Newspaper advertising is the major vehicle for renting apartments. When composing a classified advertisement, keep the needs of the prospective tenant in mind. For example, in a neighborhood where three-bedroom apartments are difficult to rent, an ad might appeal to a broader segment of the market if it offers a "two-bedroom apartment with den."

The classified advertisement should include the amount of rent, the size of the unit, the address of the property, and the phone number of the manager. If space costs and the advertising budget permit, the major amenities of the property should be mentioned. A typical small classified ad might read:

> $400/month for sunny, large 1-bdrm.
> apt; new carpet & drapes. Available
> 12-1. 1025 Webster/327-7083.

The purpose behind classified advertising is to attract the prospect's attention and induce him or her to telephone or come to look at the apartment. For this reason, variant typefaces and larger layouts are preferable when budgets permit. After the reader's attention is captured, his or her interest can be maintained by highlighting the location, size, and rent in an enlarged classified. The preceding ad could be redesigned for greater appeal to look like the sample below. The increased cost of this design will have to be evaluated by the manager on an individual basis.

> **De Paul University Area**
> Large 1-bedroom apt.
> New carpeting & appliances.
> Bright sunny living room.
> $400/Possession Dec. 1
> To see call 327-7083

Display Ads. More prestigious residential projects, especially when newly opened, often find it advantageous to use a display advertisement. These larger ads attract immediate attention, appeal to potential tenants' pride, and point up the many amenities offered by the building. The specifics of the rental schedule may be omitted in

deference to the status of the prospective clientele, as in the display ad below, but
a general indication of rent ranges is usually incorporated into the ad.

Reprinted with permission of Baird & Warner, Chicago, IL

Rental Centers. Because rental centers are not only costly to create but expensive to
staff and operate on an extended basis, they are rarely feasible for residential developments of less than 100 units. The basic purpose of a residential rental center is to rent
apartments more efficiently than otherwise possible. A center can shorten the rent-up
time during the initial stage of a project's development. After rent-up is complete, the
manager must decide whether there is a continued need for the center to sustain
occupancy levels through replacement rentals. If only 50 apartments are usually
vacant in any one year, a model apartment would serve the merchandising goal more
cost-effectively. However, if 200 apartments must be rented each year, the need for
a rental center would be indicated.

Older tenants are more stable than young ones. Larger apartments rented to families
do not have as high a turnover rate as studio or one-bedroom models. The manager
can determine the need for a rental center by identifying tenant types and projecting
the anticipated turnover. For example, a 350-unit development of predominantly
one-bedroom apartments might expect a 50-percent yearly turnover from its young,

single tenants. This means that 175 apartments (almost 15 units per month) must be rerented each year. A permanent rental center could be considered for such a project. For a similar size development of two-bedroom apartments tenanted mainly by families, the anticipated turnover rate might drop to about 15 percent, or 53 apartments annually. With only four or five apartments to be rented each month, a rental center cannot be considered cost-effective, although a model apartment might be used as a marketing tool.

APARTMENT LEASES AND TENANT RELATIONS

Chapter 5 outlined the rights and duties of the landlord and the tenants, as well as the legal remedies available to both parties in case of noncompliance with the lease terms. Figure 27 is a typical one-year gross lease and contains most of the major clauses described in Chapter 5. The clause that makes the tenant liable for his or her own utilities reflects the present trend toward individual metering for utility services.

Careful screening of lease applicants, as described in Chapter 6, should ensure that residents are able and willing to fulfill their obligations as stated in the lease agreement. By opening the lines of communication with tenants, the manager will build mutually satisfactory landlord-tenant relationships.

Property managers, resident managers, and leasing agents must be careful to observe not only the federal Fair Housing laws, but also similar state and local laws as well. While there may be certain exceptions in federal legislation, state and local laws have sometimes included many additional prohibitions.

Tenant Unions

Encouraged by the passage of landlord-tenant legislation in many states, an increasing number of tenant unions have formed, causing some anxiety about the possibility of explosive resident-management confrontations. Conflicts can be avoided, however, by implementation of a plan that brings management and residents together quickly in a controlled environment for the purpose of joint problem solving.

A relatively easy strategy is to establish formal, regularly scheduled meetings with representatives of tenant groups. Once a problem has been broached by the tenants, they should be confident that management will respond. If a win-lose atmosphere is avoided, a compromise can be reached through collective bargaining. A successful resolution is mutually beneficial. When it is arrived at in a businesslike manner, potentially destructive emotions can be kept in check and energy can then be channeled in a more productive direction.

In response to tenant demand, the county government of Prince George's County, Maryland, established a Landlord and Tenant Commission in 1973, which has exceptional authority over landlord and tenant relations. Prince George's County is a heavily populated area adjacent to Washington, D.C., in which it is estimated there are approximately 100,000 apartments. The County Landlord Tenant Act provides for licensing

Figure 27: LEASE AGREEMENT

APARTMENT LEASE — UNFURNISHED
(For Use In Illinois)

GEORGE E. COLE®
LEGAL FORMS

NO. L-17

APRIL 1980

CAUTION: Consult a lawyer before using or acting under this form.
All warranties, including merchantability and fitness, are excluded.

IF UNHEATED, CHECK HERE: _____
(SEE PARAGRAPH 11)

APARTMENT LEASE
UNFURNISHED

DATE OF LEASE	TERM OF LEASE		MONTHLY RENT	SECURITY DEPOSIT *
	BEGINNING	ENDING		
April 1, 1984	May 1, 1984	April 30, 1985	$500	$500

* IF NONE, WRITE "NONE" Paragraph 2 of this Lease then INAPPLICABLE.

LESSEE

NAME • J.P. Smithers

APT. NO. • 305

ADDRESS OF PREMISES • 248 West Windsor
Chicago, Illinois

LESSOR

NAME • Maddox Management

BUSINESS ADDRESS • 1309 45th. Street
Chicago, Illinois

In consideration of the mutual covenants and agreements herein stated, Lessor hereby leases to Lessee and Lessee hereby leases from Lessor for a private dwelling the apartment designated above (the "Premises"), together with the appurtenances thereto, for the above Term.

ADDITIONAL COVENANTS AND AGREEMENTS (if any)

LEASE COVENANTS AND AGREEMENTS

RENT

SECURITY DEPOSIT

1. Lessee shall pay Lessor or Lessor's agent as rent for the Premises the sum stated above, monthly in advance, until termination of this lease, at Lessor's address stated above or such other address as Lessor may designate in writing.

2. Lessee has deposited with Lessor the Security Deposit stated above for the performance of all covenants and agreements of Lessee hereunder. Lessor may apply all or any portion thereof in payment of any amounts due Lessor from Lessee, and upon Lessor's demand Lessee shall in such case during the term of the lease promptly deposit with Lessor such additional amounts as may then be required to bring the Security Deposit up to the full amount stated above. Upon termination of the lease and full performance of all matters and payment of all amounts due by Lessee, so much of the Security Deposit as remains unapplied shall be returned to Lessee. This deposit does not bear interest unless and except as required by law. Where all or a portion of the Security Deposit is applied by Lessor as compensation for property damage, Lessor when and as required by law shall provide to Lessee an itemized statement of such damage and of the estimated or actual cost of repairing same. If the building in which Premises are located (the "Building") is sold or otherwise transferred, Lessor may transfer or assign the Security Deposit to the purchaser or transferee of the Building, who shall thereupon be liable to Lessee for all of Lessor's obligations hereunder, and Lessee shall look thereafter solely to such purchaser or transferee for return of the Security Deposit and for other matters (including any interest or accounting) relating thereto.

CONDITION OF PREMISES; REDELIVERY TO LESSOR

3. Lessee has examined and knows the condition of Premises and has received the same in good order and repair except as herein otherwise specified, and no representations as to the condition or repair thereof have been made by Lessor or his agent prior to, or at the execution of this lease, that are not herein expressed or endorsed hereon; and upon the termination of this lease in any way, Lessee will immediately yield up Premises to Lessor in as good condition as when the same were entered upon by Lessee, ordinary wear and tear only excepted, and shall then return all keys to Lessor.

George E. Cole ® Legal Forms, reprinted with permission of Boise Cascade Corporation. This form applicable only in Illinois. No representations are made as to its legal sufficiency or accuracy due to the possibility it has become outdated as a result of changes in the law.

LEASE AGREEMENT—Cont.

LIMITATION OF LIABILITY

4. Except as provided by Illinois statute, Lessor shall not be liable for any damage occasioned by failure to keep Premises in repair, and shall not be liable for any damage done or occasioned by or from plumbing, gas, water, steam or other pipes, or sewerage, or the bursting, leaking or running of any cistern, tank, wash-stand, water-closet, or waste-pipe, in, above, upon or about the Building or Premises, nor for damage occasioned by water, snow or ice being upon or coming through the roof, skylight, trap-door or otherwise, nor for damages to Lessee or others claiming through Lessee for any loss or damage of or to property wherever located in or about the Building or Premises, nor for any damage arising from acts or neglect of co-tenants or other occupants of the Building, or of any owners or occupants of adjacent or contiguous property.

USE; SUBLET; ASSIGNMENT

5. Lessee will not allow Premises to be used for any purpose that will increase the rate of insurance thereon, nor for any purpose other than that hereinbefore specified, nor to be occupied in whole or in part by any other persons, and will not sublet the same, nor any part thereof, nor assign this lease, without in each case the written consent of the Lessor first had, and will not permit any transfer, by operation of law, of the interest in Premises acquired through this lease, and will not permit Premises to be used for any unlawful purpose or purpose that will injure the reputation of the same or of the Building or disturb the tenants of the Building or the neighborhood.

USE AND REPAIR

6. Lessee will take good care of the apartment demised and the fixtures therein, and will commit and suffer no waste therein; no changes or alterations of the Premises shall be made, nor partitions erected, nor walls papered, nor locks on doors installed or changed, without the consent in writing of Lessor; Lessee will make all repairs required to the walls, ceilings, paint, plastering, plumbing work, pipes and fixtures belonging to Premises, whenever damage or injury to the same shall have resulted from misuse or neglect; no furniture filled or to be filled wholly or partially with liquids shall be placed in the Premises without the consent in writing of Lessor; the Premises shall not be used as a "boarding" or "lodging" house, nor for a school, nor to give instructions in music, dancing or singing, and none of the rooms shall be offered for lease by placing notices on any door, window or wall of the Building, nor by advertising the same directly or indirectly, in any newspaper or otherwise, nor shall any signs be exhibited on or at any windows or exterior portions of the Premises or of the Building without the consent in writing of Lessor; there shall be no lounging, sitting upon, or unnecessary tarrying in or upon the front steps, the sidewalk, railing, stairways, halls, landing or other public places of the Building by Lessee, members of the family or others persons connected with the occupancy of Premises; no provisions, milk, ice, marketing, groceries, furniture, packages or merchandise shall be taken into the Premises through the front door of the Building except where there is no rear or service entrance; cooking shall be done only in the kitchen and in no event on porches or other exterior appurtenances; Lessee, and those occupying under Lessee, shall not interfere with the heating apparatus, or with the lights, electricity, gas, water or other utilities of the Building which are not within the apartment hereby demised, nor with the control of any of the public portions of the Building; use of any master television antenna hookup shall be strictly in accordance with regulations of Lessor or Lessor's agent; Lessee and those occupying under Lessee shall comply with and conform to all reasonable rules and regulations that Lessor or Lessor's agent may make for the protection of the Building or the general welfare and the comfort of the occupants thereof, and shall also comply with and conform to all applicable laws and governmental rules and regulations affecting the Premises and the use and occupancy thereof.

ACCESS

7. Lessee will allow Lessor free access to the Premises at all reasonable hours for the purpose of examining or exhibiting the same or to make any needful repairs which Lessor may deem fit to make for the benefit of or related to any part of the Building; also Lessee will allow Lessor to have placed upon the Premises, at all times, notice of "For Sale" and "To Rent," and will not interfere with the same.

RIGHT TO RELET

8. If Lessee shall abandon or vacate the Premises, the same may be re-let by Lessor for such rent and upon such terms as Lessor may see fit; and if a sufficient sum shall not thus be realized, after paying the expenses of such reletting and collecting, to satisfy the rent hereby reserved, Lessee agrees to satisfy and pay all deficiency.

HOLDING OVER

9. If the Lessee retains possession of the Premises or any part thereof after the termination of the term by lapse of time or otherwise, then the Lessor may at Lessor's option within thirty days after the termination of the term serve written notice upon Lessee that such holding over constitutes either (a) renewal of this lease for one year, and from year to year thereafter, at double the rental specified under Section 1 for such period, or (b) creation of a month to month tenancy, upon the terms of this lease except at double the monthly rental specified under Section 1, or (c) creation of a tenancy at sufferance, at a rental of _____ dollars per day for the time Lessee remains in possession. If no such written notice is served then a tenancy at sufferance with rental as stated at (c) shall have been created, and in such case if specific per diem rental shall not have been inserted herein at (c), such per diem rental shall be one-fifteenth of the monthly rental specified under Section 1 of this lease. Lessee shall also pay to Lessor all damages sustained by Lessor resulting from retention of possession by Lessee.

RESTRICTIONS ON USE

10. Lessee will not permit anything to be thrown out of the windows, or down the courts or light shafts in the Building; nothing shall be hung from the outside of the windows or placed on the outside window sills of any window in the Building; no parrot, dog or other animal shall be kept within or about the Premises; the front halls and stairways and the back porches shall not be used for the storage of carriages, furniture or other articles.

WATER AND HEAT

11. The provisions of subsection (a) only hereof shall be applicable and shall form a part of this lease unless this lease is made on an unheated basis and that fact is so indicated on the first page of this lease, in which case the provisions of subsection (b) only hereof shall be applicable and form a part of this lease.

(a) Lessor will supply hot and cold water to the Premises for the use of Lessee at all faucets and fixtures provided by Lessor therefor. Lessor will also supply heat, by means of the heating system and fixtures provided by Lessor, in reasonable amounts and at reasonable hours, when necessary, from October 1 to April 30, or otherwise as required by applicable municipal ordinance. Lessor shall not be liable or responsible to Lessee for failure to furnish water or heat when such failure shall result from causes beyond Lessor's control, nor during periods when the water and heating systems in the Building or any portion thereof are under repair.

(b) Lessor will supply cold water to the Premises for the use of Lessee at all faucets and fixtures provided by Lessor therefor. Lessor shall not be liable or responsible to Lessee for failure to furnish water when such failure shall result from causes beyond Lessor's control, nor during periods when the water system in the Building or any portion thereof is under repair. All water heating and all heating of the Premises shall be at the sole expense of Lessee. Any equipment provided by Lessee therefor shall comply with applicable municipal ordinances.

LEASE AGREEMENT—Cont.

STORE ROOM

12. Lessor shall not be liable for any loss or damage of or to any property placed in any store room or any storage place in the Building, such store room or storage place being furnished gratuitously and not as part of the obligations of this lease.

DEFAULT BY LESSEE

13. If default be made in the payment of the above rent, or any part thereof, or in any of the covenants herein contained to be kept by the Lessee, Lessor may at any time thereafter at his election declare said term ended and reenter the Premises or any part thereof, with or (to the extent permitted by law) without notice or process of law, and remove Lessee or any persons occupying the same, without prejudice to any remedies which might otherwise be used for arrears of rent, and Lessor shall have at all times the right to distrain for rent due, and shall have a valid and first lien upon all personal property which Lessee now owns, or may hereafter acquire or have an interest in, which is by law subject to such distraint, as security for payment of the rent herein reserved.

NO RENT DEDUCTION OR SET OFF

14. Lessee's covenant to pay rent is and shall be independent of each and every other covenant of this lease. Lessee agrees that any claim by Lessee against Lessor shall not be deducted from rent nor set off against any claim for rent in any action.

RENT AFTER NOTICE OR SUIT

15. It is further agreed, by the parties hereto, that after the service of notice or the commencement of a suit or after final judgment for possession of the Premises, Lessor may receive and collect any rent due, and the payment of said rent shall not waive or affect said notice, said suit, or said judgment.

PAYMENT OF COSTS

16. Lessee will pay and discharge all reasonable costs, attorney's fees and expenses that shall be made and incurred by Lessor in enforcing the covenants and agreements of this lease.

RIGHTS CUMULATIVE

17. The rights and remedies of Lessor under this lease are cumulative. The exercise or use of any one or more thereof shall not bar Lessor from exercise or use of any other right or remedy provided herein or otherwise provided by law, nor shall exercise nor use of any right or remedy by Lessor waive any other right or remedy.

FIRE AND CASUALTY

18. In case the Premises shall be rendered untenantable during the term of this lease by fire or other casualty, Lessor at his option may terminate the lease or repair the Premises within 60 days thereafter. If Lessor elects to repair, this lease shall remain in effect provided such repairs are completed within said time. If Lessor shall not have repaired the Premises within said time, then at the end of such time the term hereby created shall terminate. If this lease is terminated by reason of fire or casualty as herein specified, rent shall be apportioned and paid to the day of such fire or other casualty.

SUBORDINATION

19. This lease is subordinate to all mortgages which may now or hereafter affect the real property of which Premises form a part.

PLURALS; SUCCESSORS

20. The words "Lessor" and "Lessee" wherever herein occurring and used shall be construed to mean "Lessors" and "Lessees" in case more than one person constitutes either party to this lease; and all the covenants and agreements herein contained shall be binding upon, and inure to, their respective successors, heirs, executors, administrators and assigns and be exercised by his or their attorney or agent.

SEVERABILITY

21. Wherever possible each provision of this lease shall be interpreted in such manner as to be effective and valid under applicable law, but if any provision of this lease shall be prohibited by or invalid under applicable law, such provision shall be ineffective to the extent of such prohibition or invalidity, without invalidating the remainder of such provision or the remaining provisions of this lease.

WITNESS the hands and seals of the parties hereto, as of the Date of Lease stated above.

LESSEE: _J P Smithers_ (seal)   LESSOR: _J W Maddox_ (seal)

_____ (seal)   _____ (seal)

ASSIGNMENT BY LESSOR

On this _____, 19_____, for value received, Lessor hereby transfers, assigns and sets over to

_____ all right, title and interest in and to the above lease and the rent thereby reserved,

except rent due and payable prior to _____, 19_____.

_____ (seal)

_____ (seal)

GUARANTEE

On this _____, 19_____, in consideration of Ten Dollars ($10.00) and other good and valuable consideration, the receipt and sufficiency of which is hereby acknowledged, the undersigned Guarantor hereby guarantees the payment of rent and performance by Lessee, Lessee's heirs, executors, administrators, successors or assigns of all covenants and agrements of the above lease.

_____ (seal)

_____ (seal)

of apartment management companies and a complete process through which owners and consumers of rental housing may settle their disputes without resorting to the courts.

MAINTAINING THE APARTMENT BUILDING

As pointed out in Chapter 8, maintenance duties may be carried out by a large staff including a resident manager, janitorial staff, on-site maintenance crew, and various outside service contractors. The resident manager for a smaller property may have to assume maintenance responsibilities with no on-site support whatsoever. The precise duties of all employees involved in maintaining a property depend on the size and facilities of the building, the condition of the premises, and the terms of the management contract. In general, however, the resident manager is in charge of coordinating and executing the routine preventative and corrective maintenance for the building, while the property manager is responsible for supervising these functions. Minor repairs are usually handled by either the resident manager or maintenance staff employees. The resident manager should solicit bids on all large expenditures and obtain the approval of the property manager before engaging outside contractors for substantial amounts of work.

Resident Manager's Responsibilities

The resident manager is usually responsible for all maintenance activities. Grounds maintenance takes in pool cleaning; landscaping; rubbish removal; and upkeep of walkways, driveways, and parking areas. He or she also supervises housekeeping and maintenance of all common interior areas. Hallways, elevators, stairways, laundry rooms, recreation rooms, and entranceways are regularly inspected, as are the building's heating, ventilating, plumbing, and other major systems. The exterior residential inspection forms shown in Figure 28 illustrate some of the resident manager's typical concerns. An interior inspection report is also available from the Institute of Real Estate Management.

Routine jobs should be scheduled on a daily, weekly, or monthly basis. High-traffic areas require daily attention, as do lawns and swimming pools. Recreation and laundry rooms, parking areas, rubbish cans, and so forth can generally be inspected and cleaned on a semiweekly or weekly basis. Monthly activities might include fertilizing the lawn, fumigating the premises, and inspecting the heating and ventilating plant.

Minor plumbing, electrical repairs, and painting touch-up work can often be done at a great savings by the resident manager or on-site janitorial and maintenance staff. Clogged drains, leaky faucets, and inoperative toilet flush boxes may not require the attention of a $40-an-hour plumber. Light fixtures, bulbs, fuses, switch plates, and switches can be replaced by the building maintenance crew rather than by a skilled, expensive electrician.

Tenant requests for service should be entered on a three-copy form similar to that shown in Chapter 8. The top copy and a copy to be left in the apartment upon the completion of the work are assigned to the maintenance person answering the request. The third copy is kept by the manager until the job is completed.

FIG. 28 APARTMENT BUILDING INSPECTION REPORT

THE INSTITUTE OF REAL ESTATE MANAGEMENT
of the
NATIONAL ASSOCIATION OF REALTORS®

Form '40A

_____ 19___

APARTMENT BUILDING INSPECTION REPORT

Name of Property _____ Address _____

No. of Apts.: 1's_____ 1½'s_____

Type of Property _____

2's_____ 2½'s_____ 3's_____ 3½'s_____

No. of Stories _____ 4's_____ 4½'s_____ 5's_____ 5½'s_____

Report Submitted by _____ 6's_____ 7's_____ 8's_____ Total _____

EXTERIOR

Items	Character and Condition	Needs	Est. Expenses
Grounds			
1. Soil			
2. Grass			
3. Shrubs			
4. Flowers			
5. Trees			
6. Fences			
7. Urns			
8. Walks			
9. Cement flashings			
10. Parking curbs			
Brick and Stone			
11. Front walls			
A. Base			
B. Top			
C. Coping			
D. Tuck pointing			
E. Cleanliness			
12. Court Walls			
A. Base			
B. Top			
C. Coping			
D. Tuck pointing			
E. Cleanliness			
13. Side walls			
A. Base			
B. Top			
C. Coping			
D. Tuck pointing			
E. Cleanliness			
14. Rear walls			
A. Base			
B. Top			
C. Coping			
D. Tuck pointing			
E. Cleanliness			
15. Chimneys			

APARTMENT BUILDING INSPECTION REPORT—Cont.

GENERAL INTERIOR			
Items	Character and Condition	Needs	Est. Expenses
Vestibules			
1. Steps			
2. Risers			
3. Floors			
4. Marble slabs			
5. Walls			
6. Ceilings			
7. Door mats			
Vestibule Doors			
8. Glass			
9. Transoms			
10. Hinges			
11. Knobs			
12. Door checks			
13. Door finish			
14. Kick plates			
15. Handrails			
Mail Boxes			
16. Glass			
17. Doors			
18. Locks			
19. Name plates			
20. Intercom			
21. Signal buttons and connections			
Stair Halls			
22. Steps			
23. Landings			
24. Handrails			
25. Woodwork			
26. Carpets			
27. Walls			
28. Ceilings			
29. Skylights			
30. Windows			
31. Window coverings			
Rear Halls			
32. Steps			
33. Landings			
34. Walls			
35. Ceilings			
36. Handrails			
37. Garbage cans			
38. Waste-paper receptacles			
39. Windows			
40. Window coverings			

APARTMENT BUILDING INSPECTION REPORT—Cont.

Items	Character and Condition	Needs	Est. Expenses
Elevators			
41. Signal buttons			
42. Doors			
43. Cab floors			
44. Cab walls			
45. Cab ceilings			
46. Control mechanism			
47. Cables			
48. Pulleys			
49. Motor			
50. Shaft walls			
51. Shaft ceiling			
52. Shaft floor			
53. Floor numbers on doors			
Public Light Fixtures			
54. Entrance			
A. Brackets			
B. Fixtures			
C. Bulbs			
D. Switch			
55. Vestibule			
A. Brackets			
B. Fixtures			
C. Bulbs			
D. Switch			
56. Halls			
A. Brackets			
B. Fixtures			
C. Bulbs			

BASEMENT

Items	Character and Condition	Needs	Est. Expenses
Laundries			
1. Floors			
2. Walls			
3. Ceilings			
4. Washers			
5. Driers			
6. Vending machines			
7. Tubs & faucets			
8. Toilet bowls			
9. Lavatories			
10. Drains			
11. Windows			
12. Doors			
13. Window coverings			
Boiler Room			
14. Floor			
15. Pipes			
16. Fuel bin			
17. Fire hazards			

APARTMENT BUILDING INSPECTION REPORT—Cont.

Items	Character & Condition	Needs	Est. Expenses
Boiler Room (cont'd)			
18. Ceiling			
19. Walls			
20. Windows			
21. Doors			
22. Cleanliness			
23. Window coverings			
24. Trash containers			
Boiler			
25. Flues			
26. Tubes			
27. Valves			
28. Diaphragms			
29. Flange units			
30. Grates			
31. Ash pits			
32. Pointing on brickwork			
33. Motors			
34. Draft controls			
35. Chimney			
36. Thermostats			
37. Hydrostats			
38. Stoker			
39. Insulation			
40. Combustion chambers			
41. Water level			
Hot-Water Heater			
42. Tank			
43. Insulation			
44. Ash pit			
45. Incinerator			
46. Submerged system			
47. Hydrolator			
Pumps			
48. Motors			
49. Sump			
50. Pressure			
51. Circulating			
Lockers			
52. Floors			
53. Walls			
54. Ceilings			
55. Doors			
56. Fire hazards			
57. Aisles			
Central Air Conditioning			
58. Motors			
59. Cleanliness			
60. Accessibility			
General			
61. Plaster			
62. Trash and junk			
63. Screens			

The resident manager should thoroughly inspect each apartment after tenants vacate the premises. At best, the unit will have to be cleaned before it can be shown to prospective tenants. Only when all the required repairs have been completed can a tenant assume possession of the premises.

Property Manager's Responsibilities

The property manager prepares for seasonal conversions by inspecting the premises every spring and fall. Since the property manager is not usually in daily contact with each building, the resident manager should submit weekly reports on the condition of the property, the work performed that week, and the jobs anticipated for the upcoming week. When coupled with monthly inspection tours, these reports reveal a lot about the resident manager's performance and attitude.

APARTMENT OPERATING REPORTS

Owners of apartment buildings have the same need for operating reports as owners of commercial and industrial properties. The four reports described in Chapter 9 give the owner the raw data necessary to evaluate the property manager, determine the worth of the investment, and decide on the best course of action.

Additions to Monthly Income and Expense Report

Income from apartment buildings is derived primarily from rentals, although cleaning deposits, parking fees, and vending and laundry machines can provide additional revenue. Laundry leasing companies will install washers and dryers on a percentage basis. The percentage rate will depend upon the bargaining power of the manager and the overall expected revenue from the machines. Property managers of buildings that rent to families with children can usually negotiate for one-half the income from the laundry operations. An alternative is for the manager to buy laundry machines outright on behalf of the owner. This can be even more profitable.

Operating expenses for apartment buildings can be allocated to four major categories, as shown in the sample monthly income and expense report, Figure 29. This is an alternative to the form presented in Chapter 9.

Apartment Operating Budgets

Apartment occupancy rates are always subject to change because of economic conditions, such as employment cuts or the addition of new units to the market. Therefore, when preparing a budget, a property manager should determine if there are any predictable influences in the market for the coming budget year which might affect occupancy. For example, in periods of high occupancy, it is important to know what new projects are under construction, and when they will be available for leasing. Long periods of low vacancy rates in a community have usually caused new apartments to be constructed. A study of lease expiration dates in such situations should also be made to analyze the vulnerability of the manager's apartments to losses to newer units.

Figure 29: INCOME AND EXPENSE REPORT

Property:	Month: February		Year: 1984

Income

Gross Rent Schedule	$30,000	
less vacancy and rent loss	2,500	
effective rent		$27,500

Other Income

laundry	200	
vending	200	
parking	500	900

Total Receipts		$28,400

Expenses

Wages

property manager	$ 1,500	
resident manager	700	
staff	3,000	5,200

Variable Expenses

utilities	1,000	
maintenance	800	
professional fees	1,100	2,900

Fixed Expenses

property tax	650	
insurance	500	1,150

Capital Expenditures

rugs	650	
drapes		
paint	50	
appliances and fixtures	1,000	1,700

Total Expense		$10,950

Net Operating Receipts			$17,450

Debt Service		$ 8,000	

Cash Flow			$ 9,450

Figure 30: OPERATING BUDGET

Property:		Date: 1984
Income		
Gross Rent Schedule	$360,000	
less vacancy and rent loss	18,000	
effective rent		$342,000
Other Income		3,000
Total Receipts		$345,000
Expenses		
Wages		
property manager	$ 12,000	
resident manager	15,000	
staff	3,000	30,000
Variable Expenses		
utilities	32,000	
maintenance	12,000	
professional fees	3,000	47,000
Fixed Expenses		
property tax	32,000	
insurance	8,000	40,000
Capital Expenditures		
rugs	3,000	
drapes	2,000	
paint	1,000	
appliances and fixtures	4,000	10,000
Total Expense		$127,000
Net Operating Receipts		$218,000
Debt Service		$ 68,000
Cash Flow		$150,000

A sample operating budget for a medium-sized apartment building appears as Figure 30. Note that many expense items have been consolidated into the general categories of wages, variable expenses, fixed expenses, and capital expenditures. The format follows that for the income and expense reports. There are many alternate ways of itemizing income and expenses, but the manager should choose one format and use it consistently. This will simplify data for future comparisons.

Accurate and sufficient projections of all expenses, particularly variable expenses, are a vital part of the budget, so these costs should not be underestimated. Funds must be budgeted to preserve the physical condition of the property, weather adverse economic trends, or meet exceptionally high expenses during a particular year.

Cash Flow Analysis

Although cash flow projections often appear to be quite complex, they really deal only with previously used data, as discussed in Chapter 9. The cash flow analysis basically shows the effect that the investment property has on the owner's income in terms of tax benefits. The report allows the owner to analyze his or her actual return on investment after taxes and decide whether it is economically more advantageous to keep the property, invest more money in it, refinance it, or sell it.

For example, an older apartment building has a reliable gross income of $100,000 and an operating cost rate of 50 percent, including reserves. Its value is $400,000, and straight-line depreciation is computed based on an economic life of 25 years. The property has a $300,000 first mortgage at a 10-percent constant rate, which includes a 1-percent principal payback. If the owner is in a 50-percent tax bracket, the after-tax cash flow analysis would appear as follows:

Figure 31: AFTER-TAX CASH FLOW ANALYSIS

Gross Annual Income	$100,000
Operating Costs	− 50,000
Net Annual Income Before Debt Service	50,000
Mortgage Payments ($300,000 mortgage @ 10% constant)	− 30,000
Cash Flow After Debt Service	20,000
Principal Add-Back (@ 1%)	+ 3,000
Income Before Depreciation	23,000
Depreciation Allowance ($400,000 × .04; see Chapter 9)	− 16,000
Taxable Income	7,000
Tax Due (per owner's 50% tax bracket)	− 3,500
Net Income Return After Taxes	3,500
Deduct Principal Add-Back	− 3,000
Cash Flow Before Depreciation Add-Back	500
Depreciation Add-Back	16,000
After-Tax Cash Flow	$ 16,500

In calculating total return, investors will often add in the equity buildup from the reduction of the mortgage. Total return for this property would thus be $19,500.

Investment properties are expected to yield a satisfactory cash return on the investment (as shown by the after-tax cash flow in the preceding example) to ensure that the invested capital is not impaired, and to present the opportunity for value enhancement. These are goals that the owner will want to discuss with the manager when analyzing the cash flow statement and investigating economic alternatives to remedy unsatisfactory situations. If the cash return on the building in the previous example did not meet the owner's expectations, the manager might suggest that the owner refinance the property, raise the rents, or institute strict cost-accounting procedures to reduce costs.

Reducing Costs. While it is not advisable to increase present cash flow by deferring expenditures for real maintenance needs, an impressive savings may sometimes be made through volume buying or through an energy conservation program, both of which are discussed in Chapter 8. An energy conservation program in apartment property cannot be carried out successfully without the cooperation of the building staff and tenants, with the possible exception of programs in medium or highrise buildings. It is usually not feasible to install automatic or computerized controls in a small project or in a complex of many scattered buildings. However, the possibility for savings can be great because of the inefficient energy design of many older apartment projects, particularly in the southern states.

Short of a thorough energy-conservation analysis and cost reduction program, some common-sense precautions can be exercised to hold a ceiling on rising operating costs. All utility firms have energy consultants with whom the manager can confer. Utility rate schedules can be quite confusing to the uninitiated. Electric rates, for example, vary according to amount of power used, the time of day, the peak amount consumed at any one time, the use to which the electricity is put, and the cost of the fuel used to generate the electricity. A utility representative can determine the optimal type of service for the property and suggest ways of reducing waste.

Another simple method of reducing utility costs is to install timers or preferably photocell switches if possible, for hallway and outdoor lights. Higher-watt bulbs are often more efficient than smaller bulbs, and fluorescent lighting is most economical of all. Heating costs can be reduced by installing storm windows, caulking around doorways and windows, adding insulation to protect against heat loss through transference, installing automatic heating controls, and reducing heating hours.

Final Alternatives. When rents are as high as the market will allow, costs have been pared to the bone, and the property still is not showing a satisfactory return, the owner is faced with three final choices: subsidize, sell out, or make a major capital investment that will render the property more marketable. Central air conditioning could be installed, slow-renting units structurally converted to meet the market demand, or a swimming pool or other amenities added. Such expenditures should be made only after careful analysis. The increase in income will have to exceed the cost of the improvement when amortized over its economic life.

THE APARTMENT BUILDING STAFF

In general, the personnel guidelines set forth in Chapter 10 are fully applicable to the management of apartment projects. Because of round-the-clock involvement, the resident manager in particular occupies a pivotal position in maintaining residential properties and dealing with tenants. Dedication and fairness backed by training, strong selling and communication skills, good business judgment, and a working knowledge of record keeping are essential for a resident manager. Because the manager of residential property is much closer to tenants' personal lives than the manager of commercial property, apartment buildings seem to generate more problems than comparably sized office buildings. Needless to say, the resident manager in an apartment building must be tactful and patient. Several professional associations offer educational programs designed to develop the skills of a resident manager.

Professional Designations

Three professional real estate associations offer educational programs for apartment managers, which lead to a professional designation:

1. The Apartment Council of the National Association of Homebuilders (NAHB) offers the Registered Apartment Manager (RAM) program and the Executive Registered Apartment Manager program for supervisory managers.
2. The Institute of Real Estate Management (IREM) sponsors seminars, which lead to the designation of Accredited Resident Manager (ARM).
3. The National Apartment Association has three designation programs for its members—Certified Apartment Manager (CAM), Certified Apartment Property Supervisor (CAPS), and Certified Apartment Maintenance Technician (CAMT).

Good resident managers are not easy to find. Community colleges that provide formal training for this type of manager can be a source. Most often, however, the property manager will have to rely on referrals from other managers or on classified newspaper ads. In addition, a property manager can become acquainted with prospective resident managers through activity in local apartment associations.

A prospective manager should be required to fill out an employment application stating his or her education, experience, and references. The evaluation and selection of the resident manager is one of the property manager's most weighty tasks, and every effort must be made to perform it objectively. The ideal candidate should combine experience with a good employment history, a background similar to that of the tenant population, a stable work record, and a mature approach to the job. Some property managers choose to employ resident managers under a comprehensive contract that clearly specifies the compensation rate (including any apartment concessions), the hours of work, and the duties to be performed. It is standard policy to insert a clause in such contracts setting a dollar limit on expenditures the resident manager can make without first seeking the property manager's approval. Other property managers prefer a more simple contract on the grounds that neither party can foresee contingencies that might arise. As a minimum, wages and hours should always be in writing.

The resident manager must have the respect of the tenants in order to collect rents and deal with problems. The property manager should back up the resident manager whenever possible and should cultivate his or her good will by indicating that management appreciates the work he or she is doing. Whenever possible, the property manager should ask the resident manager's opinion of any changes or improvements made on the premises or operating plans. If the resident manager's advice is not followed, a reasonable explanation from the property manager is common courtesy and a gesture of team spirit.

SUMMARY

Multifamily dwellings differ from one another in size, structure, location, and number of amenities provided. Whereas garden apartments and luxury highrise units are usually fairly large (two or three bedrooms) and offer some recreational facilities, units in three-story walkup and multilevel elevator buildings are usually smaller and more modestly equipped. Garden apartments are commonly found in the more spacious suburban locations, while multistory and highrise buildings are concentrated near the downtown areas of large cities or in older, more densely populated suburbs. These differences exert a direct influence on an owner's economic policies and on the advertising techniques used to market each type of space.

The two most notable caveats in leasing residential space are to price each unit correctly for the market and to use the most effective advertising and promotional strategy for the particular property to be leased. In establishing a rent schedule, the property manager should first survey the rental schedules of comparable properties in the area and analyze the overall supply and demand relationship for apartments in the neighborhood. If the demand for the various types of apartments in his or her building is not even—that is, if there is a greater demand for one type of unit than for another—the manager may have to adjust the basic rental schedule accordingly, raising the base rent of the more desirable units while decreasing the rate for those that are less in demand.

A show list enumerating the apartments that are available for inspection can be invaluable to a property manager's marketing program. To create the impression that space is at a premium and to enable the maintenance staff to concentrate its efforts on the apartments currently being shown, the show list should not include all vacancies, but only two or three representative samples of each type of unit.

Because it reaches a large audience, newspaper advertising is the most widely used medium for renting apartments. A conventional listing should be brief but informative, appealing to the needs of the prospective tenant. Budget permitting, a manager might run larger display ads that highlight the amenities of available apartments. Display ads are usually limited to large, prestigious, or newly opened apartment complexes.

The cost-effectiveness of permanent rental centers is determined by the size and location of the building, the uniqueness of its services, the market demand, and tenant turnover. Generally speaking, permanent rental centers are worthwhile when large numbers of apartments must be rented over an extended period of time, as is usually the case with a young, mobile tenant population. Otherwise, temporary rental centers or model apartments are more economical alternatives.

The responsibility for the building's management is usually shared by the resident manager, who is immersed in the daily physical operation of the building, and the property manager, who oversees the general welfare of several buildings at once.

The resident manager must be diplomatic and responsive. Since he or she is responsible for the physical maintenance of the premises, a good resident manager must be systematic. The manager of a smaller property with little or no on-site staff should be versatile enough to make minor repairs around the building without calling in skilled but expensive laborers. The property manager, who is not in daily contact with each building in his or her care, relies heavily on maintenance reports from the resident manager. These should cover not only surface maintenance but upkeep of the building's vital plumbing, heating, and ventilating systems as well. Because the resident manager occupies such a pivotal position in the overall operation of the building, dealing with both owner and tenant, formal job training in this field is becoming more popular, and some community colleges offer such programs. The Apartment Council of the National Association of Homebuilders, the Institute of Real Estate Management, and the National Apartment Association offer courses of study which lead to the designations Registered Apartment Manager (RAM), Executive RAM, Accredited Resident Manager (ARM), Certified Apartment Manager (CAM), Certified Apartment Property Supervisor (CAPS), and Certified Apartment Maintenance Technician (CAMT).

In addition to leasing, supervising the resident manager, and inspecting the maintenance of the premises, the property manager must apprise the owner of the property's financial status. This is accomplished through the monthly *income and expense* reports and annual *profit and loss* statement. Both of these reports reflect rental and other income and show expenses arising from variable, fixed, capital, and wage expenditures. The property manager should be conservative in his or her annual *budget projections;* gross income should be projected on the basis of the past year's rental income. Funds should be budgeted in all four categories of expense—taxes, insurance, maintenance, and administration—so as to preserve the financial integrity of the property. The manager's *cash flow analysis* enables the owner to evaluate the return on his or her property investment. If the owner is dissatisfied, the property manager should suggest alternatives to the current management program. The after-tax cash flow on a property can sometimes be improved by an energy conservation program or other techniques for shaving operating costs. In other cases, the property might have to be refinanced, altered, or even sold.

The resident manager is the most important member of the apartment building staff. Cooperation and respect between the property manager and the resident manager can do much to further their common goal of financially sound and trouble-free building operations.

QUESTIONS: CHAPTER 11

1. The type of apartment building that provides the fewest amenities and services is the:

    a. garden apartment complex.
    b. walkup apartment.
    c. multistory elevator building.
    d. highrise luxury property.

2. Apartments with larger living areas and more bedrooms are found in:

    I.   highrise luxury properties.
    II. multistory elevator buildings.

    a. I only   c. both I and II
    b. II only   d. neither I nor II

3. List the two factors that the rental schedule for an apartment complex should be based on.

    a. _____
    b. _____

4. An apartment building is composed of 10 one-bedroom units that rent for $180, 10 two-bedroom units that rent for $210, and 10 three-bedroom units that rent for $240. All the one- and two-bedroom apartments are rented, but 4 of the three-bedroom units are vacant. The vacancy rate of the three-bedroom apartments can be expected to decrease by 10 percent (1 of the 4 vacant will rent) with a $10 rental cut. The property manager should establish this rental schedule:

    a. one-bedroom units $180   c. one-bedroom units $190
        two-bedroom units $210   two-bedroom units $220
        three-bedroom units $230   three-bedroom units $230
    b. one-bedroom units $190   d. the rental structure described in the
        two-bedroom units $220   problem should be maintained
        three-bedroom units $250

5. The show list of apartments to be rented:

    I.   should include all vacant apartments.
    II. benefits the maintenance staff.

    a. I only   c. both I and II
    b. II only   d. neither I nor II

6. In general the need for a rental center increases in apartment buildings with:

    I.   a younger tenancy.
    II. larger units (two and three bedrooms).

    a. I only   c. both I and II
    b. II only   d. neither I nor II

7. The lease agreement furnished in this chapter contains:

   I.   a confession of judgment clause.
   II. an item prohibiting the tenant from joining a tenant union.

   a. I only   c. both I and II
   b. II only   d. neither I nor II

8. Responsibility for controlling the daily operations of an apartment building rests with:

   a. the on-site janitor.   c. the resident manager.
   b. the property manager.   d. an on-site maintenance employee.

9. The physical condition and equipment of an apartment building should be inspected periodically by:

   I.   the property manager.
   II. the resident manager.

   a. I only   c. both I and II
   b. II only   d. neither I nor II

10. List the four major categories of operating expenses shown in this chapter on the sample monthly income and expense report for an apartment building.

   a. _____   c. _____
   b. _____   d. _____

11. An apartment complex has a gross annual income of $120,000 and an operating cost rate of 60 percent. Its total value is $500,000 and straight-line depreciation should be based on an economic life of 40 years. The property has a $350,000 mortgage at a 10-percent constant rate which includes a one-percent principal payback. If the owner is in a 30-percent tax bracket and a cash flow analysis is performed, the after-tax cash flow without the principal add-back will be:

   a. $ 700.   c. $16,500.
   b. $2,800.   d. $11,800.

12. When developing an operating budget, the astute property manager will be conservative in estimating:

   I.   income.
   II. expenses.

   a. I only   c. both I and II
   b. II only   d. neither I nor II

13.   If a property manager has several years' worth of income and expense reports and profit and loss statements on a property, as well as mortgage information, what two additional items are needed to develop a cash flow analysis?

    a.   _____

    b.   _____

14.   An apartment building is not yielding an acceptable return on investment, although rents are as high as possible and operating expenses have been shaved. List the three radical alternatives that are left to the owner.

    a.   _____

    b.   _____

    c.   _____

15.   Property managers explore several channels when hiring resident managers, but most are actually found through:

    a.   _____   c.   _____

    b.   _____   d.   _____

16.   There is a tendency in today's inflationary society for individuals and families to:

    a.   adhere to the standard 25-percent rule when seeking housing.

    b.   spend more than 25 percent of their income on housing.

    c.   spend less than 25 percent of their income on housing.

    d.   allow housing expenditures to be controlled by local market conditions in their neighborhood.

17.   A three-copy tenant service request form employs a copy for each of the following persons:

    a.   _____

    b.   _____

    c.   _____

Cooperatives and Condominiums

Cooperatives and condominiums are multiple-occupant properties in which the users of the premises have a vested interest in the building. While medical or office complexes and buildings wherein the occupants agree on objectives and advantages are suited to multiple ownership, most cooperative and condominium projects are residential properties. Therefore, this chapter will focus on residential cooperatives and condominiums.

From a management perspective, cooperatives and condominiums have almost all the maintenance and operating requirements of ordinary multiple-occupant structures. The only difference between residential cooperatives, condominiums, and apartment buildings is in their form of ownership and their tenancy. The property manager of a cooperative or condominium is working for a group of owner-occupants, whereas the apartment manager is representing the building owner to the tenants of his or her property.

Once occupancy has been established in a new cooperative or condominium project, management is most concerned with administrative duties and maintenance of the common areas, since each owner is responsible for the condition and upkeep of his or her own unit. Unlike the apartment manager, the manager of a cooperative or condominium has no responsibility for maintaining occupancy levels.

COOPERATIVES, CONDOMINIUMS, AND PUDs

Cooperative ownership of an apartment unit means that the apartment owner has purchased shares in the corporation (or partnership or trust) that holds title to the entire apartment building. The cooperative apartment owner is, in essence, a shareholder in a corporation whose principal asset is a building. In return for stock in the corporation, the owner receives a proprietary lease granting occupancy of a specific unit in the building. The owner occupies under lease but does not own the unit, and his or her interest is treated as personal property. Each unit owner must pay a pro rata share of the corporation's expenses, which includes any mortgage charges, real estate taxes, maintenance, payroll, etc. The owner can deduct for tax purposes a proportionate share of the taxes and interest charges (provided 80 percent of a cooperative's income is derived from tenant/owner rentals).

Condominium ownership estates in real property consist of an individual interest in an apartment or commercial unit and an undivided common interest in the common areas in the condo project such as the land, parking areas, elevators, stairways, and exterior structure. Each condominium unit is a statutory entity that may be mortgaged, taxed, sold, or otherwise transferred in ownership, separately and independently of all other units in the condo project. Units are separately assessed and taxed.

The *planned unit development* (called "PUD" from its acronym) is a relatively recent but highly popular concept in land development designed to produce a high density of building improvements and maximum utilization of open spaces. This efficient use of land allows greater flexibility for land development. It also usually results in lower-priced structures and minimum maintenance cost. The management of a planned unit development is very similar to that of a condominium in practice.

COOPERATIVE OWNERSHIP

Following World War I, and periodically since then until the 1950s, cooperative apartments were heavily promoted to combat high rents, particularly in Chicago, Los Angeles, New York, and Philadelphia. However, the basic principles involved in cooperatives go back much further in time and have a wider application. For instance, ownership of two- or four-family units by more than one of the occupants was common as far back as the 1880s in the U.S. and even earlier in Europe.

Structure of Cooperative Ownership

Cooperative ownership can be either trust or corporate in nature. A *trust cooperative* places legal ownership of the building in the name of a trust company, which issues beneficial *participation certificates,* or memberships, in the amount of the purchase price of the property (total cost minus mortgage). An individual with a membership certificate is granted the right to occupy a unit in the building subject to specific rules and regulations. This right is termed a *proprietary lease.* Officers of the trust share responsibility for managing the cooperative or hiring a professional property manager to assume these duties.

A *corporate cooperative* vests ownership of the property in a corporation. The corporation then issues stock of a total value equal to the purchase price of the cooperative, again figured by subtracting the amount of the mortgage from the cost of the property. This stock is allocated among the units of the building according to their relative value. Purchasers of stock in the corporation are then granted the right to occupy a unit under a proprietary lease. The proprietary lease lasts for the life of the corporation and is subject to rules and regulations established by the corporate charter and bylaws. Among these rules is the provision that the mortgage debt and the operating expenses for the property are divided among the occupants through monthly assessments. A board of directors, elected by the shareholders, is in charge of the operation of the property. The board has the power to engage the services of a professional property manager, if it so desires.

The Proprietary Lease

Share Allocation. Under the terms of the proprietary lease, the specific unit leased is inseparable from the shares of stock purchased. The number of shares allocable to a unit is determined by the size of the unit, its location in the building, and its features. The monthly charges to be paid as part of the lease agreement consist of a monthly assessment for operating costs based on the par value of the shares allocated to the unit, plus that unit's proportionate share of the total mortgage debt for the property.

For example, in the case of a 20-unit building worth $800,000 and subject to a $400,000 mortgage, the equity base held by the corporation totals $400,000 and could be represented by 4,000 shares of stock worth $100 each. The purchaser of 5 percent of the stock, or 200 shares, would hold a proprietary lease for a unit valued at $40,000 subject to a mortgage debt of $20,000. If the total monthly mortgage payment for the building was $4,000 and operating costs including payroll, property taxes, insurance, management fees, utilities, services, supplies, maintenance, and reserve funds totaled $6,000 per month, the holder of this lease would be assessed $500 per month ($4,000 $\times$ .05 = $200; $6,000 $\times$ .05 = $300).

Covenants. Several provisions in a proprietary lease differ from those in the standard rental agreement for an apartment. The care and maintenance of the interior of each unit is the responsibility of the lessee, as are all utilities for the apartment except water and sometimes heat. Corporate responsibilities include maintaining structural elements such as rough plumbing, electrical, and ventilating systems; cleaning exterior and interior public areas; and ensuring efficient services and the smooth operation of the property. The lease should also establish the lessee's liability for negligence and limit the lessor corporation's liability for damage and injury. The rental section of the proprietary lease provides for some token rental consideration, monthly assessments, and additional rent. In consideration of the costs borne by the corporation, the proprietary lease empowers the board of directors to adjust the monthly assessment as the need arises.

If some occupants are unable to meet their monthly assessments, or if they contract for services for which they are unable to pay, the remaining shareholders must bear the extra costs. Otherwise, the trust company or corporation will default on the mortgage, or a mechanic's lien might be filed against the title to the property. Hence, most proprietary leases provide remedies in the event of monthly payment defaults. The ultimate penalty is usually cancellation of the lease and forfeiture of all shares. The corporation would then own the unit and could sell or lease it. Prospective owners of cooperatives are often unwilling to accept the possibility of losing their apartments through default of the association. Consequently, the condominium form of ownership has become dominant.

As a further protection against defaults in assessments, a clause is often inserted in the lease to add a small amount to the monthly maintenance charge for the establishment of a reserve fund. Many proprietary leases state that the right of possession of the unit cannot be transferred without the consent of the board of directors. Others give the corporation the first right to purchase the stock or the certificate and lease of an occupant who wishes to sublet or sell out. This type of clause protects the financial integrity of the cooperative as a whole.

The accounting and information provisions of a proprietary lease usually provide that lessees will receive an audited operating statement at the end of the year, along with a forecasted operating budget for the next year. The lease also specifies that adequate insurance be carried on the property, an important item when dealing with cooperatives.

The Role of the Property Manager

The cooperative property manager's first responsibility is to fulfill corporate aims on behalf of the shareholders. This usually includes maintaining the physical integrity of the property, ensuring ongoing services to the occupants, and submitting regular operating reports to the board of directors. The precise services rendered can range from a periodic consulting opinion to full-time management services on a fixed-fee basis. The aims of the corporation and the services expected from the manager should always be spelled out in a detailed written contract. We will take a closer look at the management contract later in this chapter.

Cooperative owners seek the tax advantages, profitable equity position, and stabilized housing cost inherent in home ownership, but they also like to eliminate most maintenance responsibilities through centralized management. Costs for maintenance, services, and improvement of the property are borne proportionately by all shareholder-residents. The manager must make a realistic calculation of maintenance costs, one that provides for a contingency reserve fund to alleviate future increases in monthly payments. Since the property manager must operate within the economic confines imposed by the board of directors, he or she must have some input when the operating budget for the coming year is drawn up. In a financial sense as well as others, the manager acts as the real estate expert for the cooperative members.

One advantage to managing cooperatives (and condominiums) as opposed to apartment buildings is that cooperative members generally take more pride in their surroundings. A corollary of this fact is that they want to be more informed about management policies and practices. The manager should accommodate them by providing information, soliciting opinions both in person and through written questionnaires, and encouraging feedback. Also, the multiple-ownership structure tends to encourage factious differences of opinion that ultimately result in disgruntled shareholders or members, a stagnated corporation, needless expense, and reduced service. The property manager can avoid this pitfall of cooperative ownership; acting with the approval of the board of directors, he or she can assume full responsibility for the operation of the property, including employment decisions, maintenance functions, accounting reports, administration of corporate policy, and transference and registration of corporate stock. Properly structured and enforced, this system will discourage individual owners from trying to persuade the manager to handle requests for special treatment, which is always a problem in multiple-owner-occupied projects.

The manager should suggest a contract and a degree of compensation that will allow him or her to function as the secretary of the corporation—the person in charge of preparing the agendas for all meetings of the directors and stockholders, recording the minutes of these sessions, and providing the members with copies. To fulfill these obligations, the manager must be familiar with corporate law and have an experienced attorney available for consultation.

If the shareholders or members are to appreciate the property manager's skills, they must be apprised of operational programs and progress through periodic communications. The manager should submit an annual operating report, including a statement of the proportionate interest and taxes that are deductible items on an owner's individual tax return.

CONDOMINIUM OWNERSHIP

The condominium is perhaps the most revolutionary and rapidly growing development in real estate ownership during the last four decades. From a successful beginning in Puerto Rico in the 1950s, it is estimated that by 1994, condominium units will account for 50 percent of all new housing starts. The major difference between a cooperative and a condominium is that the occupants of a condominium own their individual units in fee simple. They also hold joint title to the common areas and the land on which the building sits. In a condominium, each owner finances his or her own unit, and real estate taxes are assessed on an individual basis. Condominiums are sometimes established in existing buildings by the tenants or an outside investor. In this case, each tenant purchases a unit plus a percentage of the common areas and the land from the present property owner or the investor, who acts as an intermediary. Most often, however, condominium projects are multifamily dwellings built by speculative developers for sale to individual buyers.

The dramatic shift toward condominium housing has received impetus from three factors. First, the interest rates on mortgage loans made over the last decade have favored condominium construction rather than the construction of rental apartment buildings. Construction mortgages for rental properties have been carrying interest rates about 1.5 percent higher than those for condominiums.

Secondly, the inflationary trend of recent years has made tenants fearful of steadily climbing rents. Faced with this grim prospect, many former renters sought the security of home ownership, only to find that inflation had placed most single-family homes beyond their limited financial means. Since many condominiums combine the advantage of home ownership with a more modest purchase price, many tenants either grouped together to purchase their present apartment building on a condominium basis or bought a unit in a new condominium development.

The third factor, which has influenced the development of condominiums, has been the time required in many large cities to travel from the central business district to single-family homes in the suburbs. Persons who want to avoid long rides on public transportation or long drives to work have purchased condominiums, either in the central city or in the near suburbs.

Conditions, Covenants, and Restrictions Declaration (CC&R "Declaration")

Laws have been enacted by most states to regulate the formation and control of condominiums. The CC&R declaration required to establish condominium ownership sets up an owners association following appropriate state law and defines the property, common elements, easements, and type of ownership. This body operates much like the board of directors for a cooperative. The rights, privileges, and limits of the association directors are controlled by the bylaws set forth in the CC&R declaration. It authorizes the association to designate the insurance liability of the association and the individual owners, prorate the common property tax bill among the units, regulate property use, establish a reserve fund for repairs and improvements, control landscaping, and decide upon the color of exterior paint. It also provides for the sale, lease, or transfer of rights in the property. The association is usually empowered to employ outside professional management.

Condominium regulations are less demanding than those for cooperative buildings. Because each owner holds fee simple title to a unit, failure by one unit owner to pay his or her mortgage does not endanger the financing of the entire project, as it would with a cooperative project. The association may regulate the resale of individual units. Resales are often subject to the right of first refusal by the other owners, minimum credit and reference criteria for the purchaser, or approval by the owners association. The regulation of resale condominiums must not be used as a facade for discrimination. For this reason, the restriction of resale rights to condominiums has been severely curtailed by the courts in recent years.

The Role of the Property Manager

The rapid expansion of the residential condominium market has opened new opportunities for property managers. Condominium management, like cooperative management, is concerned mainly with maintaining the integrity of the premises, ensuring ongoing service to occupants, and attaining other mutual goals of the owners. The manager maintains all common areas and advises the owners association. The cost data necessary to draw up an operating budget and make individual assessments for maintenance and reserves are usually provided by the property manager. Like the cooperative board of directors, the owners association is an elective body, not a permanent group. Acting with the consent of the association, the manager is often given full control of building operations in order to ensure stability and continuity of operation.

The need for professional management is becoming more pressing in the condominium field. Cashing in on the popularity of condominium ownership, developers are constructing thousands of multifamily buildings in desirable resort areas such as Hawaii, Florida, Arizona, the Gulf Coast, Colorado, and California. These units are predominantly used as second homes—that is, they are occupied by the owner for a portion of the year and then rented during the off-season. The absentee owners of resort condominiums are ideal candidates for the services of a year-round property manager. Frequently, the manager assumes responsibility for leasing the owners' apartments during their absence, in addition to his or her regular duties.

Contract. Because of the potentially broad range of responsibility for the property manager of a condominium, a written contract should be executed describing the rights and duties of each party. Areas that should be covered in detail are collection of assessments, accounting and budgeting, maintenance standards, personnel employ-

Figure 32: CONDOMINIUM MANAGEMENT AGREEMENT

OWNER _____

and

AGENT _____

For Property located at

_____

_____

Beginning _____ 19 ____

Ending _____ 19 ____

CONDOMINIUM MANAGEMENT AGREEMENT

THIS AGREEMENT, made and entered into this _____ day of

_____, 19 ____, by and between _____

_____

(the "DEVELOPER"), not individually but on behalf of all of the owners

from time to time of units in _____ (the "Condominium") and on behalf of the owners' association to be organized pursuant to Section _____

_____ or the not-for-profit corporation to be organized pursuant to Section _____ of said Act (the "OWNERS"), and _____ (the "AGENT");

WITNESSETH:

WHEREAS, under the provisions of the purchase contract with the purchaser of each condominium unit, the Declaration of Condominium Ownership and the By laws required under the provisions of the _____

Condominium Property Act, the OWNERS delegate the authority to manage the Condominium initially to the DEVELOPER and thereafter to an elected Board of Managers, which may be the Board of Directors of a not-for-profit corporation organized by the Owners (the "BOARD"); and

WHEREAS, under the provisions of the purchase contract with the purchaser of each condominium unit, the Declaration of Condominium Ownership and the By-laws required under the provisions of the _____

Condominium Property Act, the DEVELOPER is authorized to engage a management agent on behalf of the OWNERS under a contract to expire not later than _____ years after the first unit is occupied; and

WHEREAS, the DEVELOPER, on behalf of the OWNERS, desires to employ the AGENT to manage the Condominium, and the AGENT desires to be employed to manage the Condominium;

NOW, THEREFORE, it is agreed as follows:

1. The DEVELOPER on behalf of the OWNERS, hereby employs the AGENT exclusively to manage the Condominium for a period of _____ years, beginning on the date the first unit in the Condominium is occupied, and thereafter for yearly periods from time to time, unless on or before sixty days prior to the expiration of the initial term or on or before thirty days prior to the expiration of any such renewal period, either party hereto shall notify the other in writing that it elects to terminate this agreement, in which case this agreement shall be terminated at the end of said period.

CONDOMINIUM MANAGEMENT AGREEMENT—Cont.

2. The AGENT agrees to manage the Condominium to the extent, for the period, and upon the terms herein provided.

3. More particularly, the AGENT agrees to perform the following services in the name of and on behalf of the OWNERS, and the DEVELOPER, on behalf of the OWNERS, hereby gives the AGENT the authority and powers required to perform these services:

(a) The AGENT shall collect and, as necessary, receipt for all monthly assessments and other charges due to the OWNERS for operation of the Condominium and all rental or other payments from concessionaires, if any, provided that the AGENT shall have no responsibility for collection of delinquent assessments or other charges except sending notices of delinquency.

(b) The AGENT shall maintain records showing all its receipts and expenditures relating to the Condominium and shall promptly submit to the DEVELOPER or the BOARD a cash receipts and disbursements statement for the preceding month and a statement indicating the balance of deficit in the AGENT'S account for the Condominium on or before the _____ day of the following month.

(c) The AGENT shall prepare and submit to the DEVELOPER or the BOARD, on or before _____ of each year, a recommended budget for the next year showing anticipated receipts and expenditures for such year.

(d) Within _____ days after the end of each calendar year, the AGENT shall submit to the OWNERS a summary of all receipts and expenditures relating to the Condominium for the preceding year, provided that this service shall not be construed to require the AGENT to supply an audit. Any audit required by the OWNERS shall be prepared at their expense by accountants of their selection.

(e) Subject to the direction and at the expense of the OWNERS, the AGENT shall cause the common elements of the Condominium to be maintained according to appropriate standards of maintenance consistent with the character of the Condominium, including cleaning, painting, decorating and such other annual maintenance and repair work as may be necessary.

(f) On the basis of the budget, job standards and wage rates previously approved by the OWNERS, the AGENT shall hire, pay, negotiate collective bargaining agreements with, supervise and discharge engineers, janitors and other personnel required to maintain and operate the Condonimium properly. All such personnel shall be employees of the OWNERS and not of the AGENT. All salaries, taxes and other expenses payable on account of such employees shall be operating expenses of the Condominium.

(g) The AGENT shall execute and file all returns and other instruments and do and perform all acts required of the OWNERS as an employer under the Federal Insurance Contributions Act, the Federal Unemployment Tax Act, Subtitle C of the Internal Revenue Code of 1954 and the _____

Income Tax Act with respect to wages paid by the AGENT on behalf of the OWNERS and under any similar Federal, State or Municipal law now or hereafter in force (and in connection therewith the OWNERS agree upon request to execute and deliver promptly to the AGENT all necessary powers of attorney, notices of appointment and the like).

(h) Subject to the direction of the OWNERS, the AGENT shall negotiate and execute on behalf of the OWNERS contracts for water, electricity, gas, telephone and such other services for the common elements of the Condominium as may be necessary or advisable. The AGENT shall also purchase on behalf of the OWNERS such equipment, tools, appliances, materials and supplies as are necessary for the proper operation and maintenance of the Condominium. All such purchases and contracts shall be in the name and at the expense of the OWNERS.

(i) The AGENT shall pay from the funds of the OWNERS all taxes, building and elevator inspection fees, water rates and other governmental charges, and all other charges or obligations incurred by the OWNERS with respect to the maintenance or operation of the Condominium or incurred by the AGENT on behalf of the OWNERS pursuant to the terms of this agreement or pursuant to other authority granted by the OWNERS.

CONDOMINIUM MANAGEMENT AGREEMENT—Cont.

(j) **The AGENT** shall maintain appropriate records of all insurance coverage carried by the OWNERS. The AGENT shall cooperate with the DEVELOPER or the BOARD in investigating and reporting all accidents or claims for damage relating to the ownership, operation and maintenance of the common elements of the Condominium including any damage or destruction thereto.

(k) **The AGENT** coordinate the schedules of purchasers and other occupants of Condominium units for moving their personal effects into the Condominium or out of it and shall endeavor to schedule such movements so that there will be a minimum of inconvenience to other purchasers or occupants. However, the AGENT shall have no responsibility for procuring the completion of the work in units, for preparing or checking "punch-lists" for units or for otherwise acting as a liaison between the unit owners and the DEVELOPER.

4. In discharging its responsibilities under paragraph 3 hereof, the AGENT shall not make any expenditure nor incur any non-recurring contractual obligation exceeding $_____ without the prior consent of the DEVELOPER or the BOARD, provided that no such consent shall be required to repay any advances made by the AGENT under the terms of paragraph 6. Notwithstanding the limitations imposed by the preceding sentence, the AGENT may, on behalf of the OWNERS without prior consent, expend any amount, or incur a contractual obligation in any amount, required to deal with emergency conditions which may involve a danger to life or property or may threaten the safety of the Condominium or the OWNERS and occupants or may threaten the suspension of any necessary service to the Condominium.

5. Notwithstanding any other provision of this Agreement, the AGENT is given no authority or responsibility for maintenance of or repairs to individual dwelling units in the Condominium. Such maintenance and repairs shall be the sole responsibility of the OWNERS individually. Each individual dwelling unit owner may contract with the AGENT on an individual basis for the provision of certain maintenance and other related services which will be paid for in accordance with the agreement between the AGENT and the individual unit owner. Such shall not be considered to be a conflict of interest or otherwise obligate the agent to take any action except as he may agree to with the individual unit owner.

6. (a) **The AGENT** agrees that all monies collected by it on behalf of the OWNERS shall be deposited in a custodial account in a state or national bank where deposits are insured by the Federal Deposit Insurance Corporation separate and apart from AGENT's own funds. It is understood that such account may include other monies received by AGENT in a representative capacity on behalf of others than the OWNERS and that the balance in such account will usually exceed the insurance limits of the Federal Deposit Insurance Corporation for a single account. No interest shall be paid on such funds.

(b) All expenses of operation and management may be paid from the OWNERS' funds held by the AGENT, and the AGENT is authorized to pay any amounts owed to the AGENT by the OWNERS from such account at any time without prior notice to the OWNERS. The AGENT shall have no obligation to advance funds to the OWNERS for any purpose whatsoever.

(c) **The AGENT** agrees that all its employees who handle or are responsible for the safekeeping of any monies of the OWNERS shall be covered by a fidelity bond protecting the OWNERS, such bond to be in an amount and with a company determined by the AGENT.

7. **The OWNERS** shall pay the AGENT a management fee equal to the larger of $_____ per month or an amount calculated by multiplying the number of units conveyed to owners other than the DEVELOPER or occupied by a monthly charge of $_____ per unit. The management fee shall be paid monthly in advance. No further charge shall be made by the AGENT for the services of the building manager pursuant to paragraph 8, its services pursuant to paragraph 3 and the other services of the AGENT's professional staff, except as otherwise expressly provided in this Agreement. It is understood, however, that any clerical services performed for the DEVELOPER or the BOARD, such as preparation and circulation of notices and newsletters and general correspondence of the DEVELOPER or the BOARD shall be at the expense of the OWNERS.

CONDOMINIUM MANAGEMENT AGREEMENT—Cont.

7. (a) OTHER _____

_____

_____

_____

_____

_____

_____

8. The AGENT agrees that one of its employees shall be designated Building Manager for the Condominium. The Building Manager shall, upon not less than_____hours notice, attend meetings of the BOARD or the OWNERS as requested, provided that the OWNERS shall pay the AGENT $_____per hour for the Building Manager's attendance at each meeting. The Building Manager shall be custodian of the official records of the BOARD and the OWNERS' association, but shall not be required to record the minutes of meetings.

9. The DEVELOPER or the BOARD shall designate a single individual who shall be authorized to deal with the AGENT on any matter relating to the management of the Condominium. The AGENT is directed not to accept directions or instructions with regard to the management of the Condominium from anyone else. In the absence of any other designation by the BOARD, the President of the BOARD shall have this authority.

10. (a) The AGENT shall have no authority to make any structural changes in the Condominium or to make any other major alterations or additions in or to any building or equipment therein, except such emergency repairs as may be required because of danger to life or property or which are immediately necessary for the preservation and safety of the Condominium or the safety of the OWNERS and occupants or are required to avoid the suspension of any necessary service to the Condominium.

(b) The AGENT is given no responsibility for compliance of the Condominium or any of its equipment with the requirements of any ordinances, laws, rules, or regulations (including those relating to the disposal of solid, liquid and gaseous wastes) of the City, County, State, or Federal Government, or any public authority or official thereof having jurisdiction over it, except to notify the DEVELOPER or the BOARD promptly, or forward to the DEVELOPER or the BOARD promptly, any complaints, warnings, notices, or summonses received by it relating to such matters. The OWNERS represent that to the best of their knowledge the Condominium complies with all such requirements, and authorize the AGENT to disclose the ownership of the Condominium to any such officials, and agree to indemnify and hold harmless the AGENT, its representatives, servants and employees, of and from all loss, cost, expense and liability whatsoever which may be imposed on them or any of them by reason of any present or future violation or alleged violation of such laws, ordinances, rules or regulations.

11. The OWNERS further agree:

(a) To indemnify, defend and save the AGENT harmless from all suits in connection with the Condominium and from liability for damage to property and injuries to or death of any employee or other person whomsoever, and to carry at their own expense public liability, boiler, elevator liability (if elevators are part of the equipment of the Condominium), and workmen's compensation insurance naming the OWNERS and the AGENT and adequate to protect their interests and in form, substance and amounts reasonably satisfactory to the AGENT, and to furnish to the AGENT certificates evidencing the existence of such insurance. Unless the OWNERS shall provide such insurance and furnish such certificate within thirty days from the date of this agreement, the AGENT may, but shall not be obligated to, place said insurance and charge the cost thereof to the account of the OWNERS.

CONDOMINIUM MANAGEMENT AGREEMENT—Cont.

(b) To pay all expenses incurred by the AGENT including, without limitation, attorneys' fees for counsel employed to represent the AGENT or the OWNERS in any proceeding or suit involving an alleged violation by the AGENT or the OWNERS, or both, of any constitutional provision, statute, ordinance, law or regulation of any governmental body pertaining to environmental protection, fair housing or fair employment including, without limitation, those prohibiting or making illegal discrimination on the basis of race, creed, color, religion or national origin in the sale, rental or other disposition of housing or any services rendered in connection therewith or in connection with employment practices (unless, in either case, the AGENT is finally adjudicated to have personally and not in a representative capacity violated such constitutional provision, statute, ordinance, law or regulation), but nothing herein contained shall require the AGENT to employ counsel to represent the OWNERS in any such proceeding or suit.

(c) To indemnify, defend and save the AGENT harmless from all claims, investigations and suits with respect to any alleged or actual violation of state or federal labor laws. The OWNERS' obligation under this paragraph 11(c) shall include the payment of all settlements, judgments, damages, liquidated damages, penalties, forfeitures, back pay awards, court costs, litigation expense and attorneys' fees.

12. In the event it is alleged or charged that the Condominium or any equipment therein or any act or failure to act by the OWNERS with respect to the Condominium or the sale, rental or other disposition thereof or the hiring of employees to manage it fails to comply with, or is in violation of, any of the requirements of any constitutional provision, statute, ordinance, law or regulation of any governmental body or any order or ruling of any public authority or official thereof having or claiming to have jurisdiction thereover, and the AGENT in its sole and absolute discretion considers that the action or position of the OWNERS with respect thereto may result in damage or liability to the AGENT the AGENT shall have the right to cancel this agreement at any time by written notice to the OWNERS of its election so to do, which cancellation shall be effective upon the service of such notice. Such cancellation shall not release the indemnities of the OWNERS set forth in paragraphs 10 and 11 above and shall not terminate any liability or obligation of the OWNERS to the AGENT for any payment, reimbursement or other sum of money then due and payable to the AGENT hereunder.

13. This Agreement may be cancelled by the DEVELOPER or the BOARD before the termination date specified in paragraph 1 on not less than   days prior written notice to the AGENT, provided that such notice is accompanied by payment to the AGENT of a cancellation fee in an amount equal to   % of the management fee which would accrue over the remainder of the stated term of the Agreement. For this purpose the monthly management fee for the remainder of the stated term shall be presumed to be the same as that of the last month prior to service of the notice of cancellation.

14. Any notice required or permitted to be served hereunder may be served by registered mail or in person as follows:

(a) If to the AGENT:
Property Management Division
Firm_____
Address_____
City_____

(b) If to the OWNERS, to the DEVELOPER at its principal place of business or to the President of the BOARD at his or her home address.

Either party may change the address for notice by notice to the other party. Notice served by mail shall be deemed to have been served when deposited in the mails.

15. This Agreement shall be binding upon and inure to the benefit of the successors and assigns of the AGENT and the heirs, administrators, successors and assigns of the OWNERS. Notwithstanding the preceding sentence the AGENT shall not assign its interest under this Agreement except in connection with the sale of all or substantially all the assets of its business; in the event of such a sale, AGENT shall be released from all liability hereunder upon the express assumption of such liability by its assignee.

CONDOMINIUM MANAGEMENT AGREEMENT—Cont.

IN WITNESS WHEREOF, the parties hereto have affixed or caused to be affixed their respective signatures this_____ day of _____, 19 _____.

WITNESSES: OWNER:

_____   _____

_____   _____

_____   _____

_____

                                              AGENT:

                                              Firm _____

_____   By _____

Submitted by

POWER OF ATTORNEY

KNOW ALL MEN BY THESE PRESENTS, THAT

_____
(Name)

_____ located at
(State whether individual, partnership or corporation, etc.)

_____ has made,
(Address)
constituted and appointed, and, by these presents does hereby make, constitute and appoint, _____, a resident of the United States, whose address is _____, (its) true and lawful attorney for (it) (me) in (its) (my) name, place and stead to

execute and to file any Tax Returns due on and after_____

_____
under the provisions of the Social Security Act, now in force or future amendments thereto.

Dated at_____this_____day of_____, 19_____

                                    _____
                                    Signature of Taxpayer

                                    _____
                                    Title

Executed in presence of: _____
                                    Signature of Taxpayer

                                    _____
                                    Title

_____   _____
Witness   Signature of Taxpayer

_____   _____
Witness   Title

Acknowledged before me this_____day of_____, 19_____
NOTARIAL
SEAL

_____

ment, the legal status of the manager as an agent, emergency spending, and handling of owners' money. The management contract should also specify the amount of compensation to be paid and the terms of the agreement (hours, fees, cancellation). Because the owners association governing board is an elective body that changes constituency frequently, the manager should negotiate a contract for a guaranteed and reasonably long period of time. Otherwise, he or she may never receive adequate compensation for the time and effort expended in taking over the property. Figure 32 could be adapted for cooperative project management. Note, however, that the initial agreement for a new condominium is drawn up between the developer, acting on behalf of the owners, and the property manager. Not until the board of directors is elected does control pass from the developer into the hands of an owners organization.

In the past, unscrupulous developers have sought to maintain control of a condominium project in order to turn an additional profit. Under the terms of the construction mortgage financing for the project, the developer holds title to all units until purchasers take over responsibility for proportionate shares of the mortgage debt and receive title to the units bought. During the early stages of the condominium's development, the developer will still hold title to most of the units and enjoy the corresponding power to execute a contract with a property manager. By hiring a thinly disguised subsidiary company as manager for the project, the developer can retain considerable control over the property long after all the units are sold and the owners association should be functioning independently. Many states are now enacting legislation to ensure that the owners association has reasonable control by imposing a maximum allowable term for management contracts negotiated by developers.

On the national level, one source of condominium regulation is the Federal National Mortgage Association (Fannie Mae), which prescribes standards for mortgages to be sold on the secondary market. One Fannie Mae regulation requires that developers turn over a condominium association to the owners as soon as a specific percentage of units has been sold.

When the management contract is executed and the responsibility is transferred to the manager, he or she will require the general types of information and records discussed in Chapter 3. Cooperative managers need copies of the incorporation documents, the corporate seal, the stock journal, the bylaws, and minutes of previous board meetings. Condominium managers need copies of the conditions, covenants, and restrictions for the building's use; the bylaws; other controlling documents; and any warranties held by the developer and still in force.

Marketing Cooperatives and Condominiums

All too often, the property manager is not involved at the inception and initial sale of a cooperative or condominium. However, developers have begun to consult management at an earlier stage, partially because an experienced property manager can provide valuable planning input and partially because management is especially important when marketing condominiums and cooperatives. Since one of the major benefits to owners is freedom from maintenance, which is also one of the largest expense items in the property budget, the property manager should review all plans for such developments in terms of ease and cost of maintenance. The property manager can also be helpful in developing a realistic operating budget and assessments forecast and in educating the developer's sales personnel to the specific features of a property.

In general, cooperatives and condominiums are marketed in a manner similar to that used for prestige apartments and other luxury residences. Most developers use their own or outside sales agents for the initial sale of such properties, but the manager should be able to suggest marketing and publicity techniques if he or she is called upon to maintain the occupancy level. Most large condominium and cooperative projects are advertised in newspapers and local magazines, as illustrated in Figure 33. Media publicity can be a very cost-effective means of presenting the project to the buying public. Figure 34 shows the result of one successful publicity campaign of the kind a good professional property manager can provide.

Education for the Manager

The Community Associations Institute (CAI) is an independent, nonprofit research and education organization formed in 1973, which serves as a clearing house and research center on community associations. CAI does not represent any one profession or interest group; rather, it represents the process of creating and operating a successful viable community association. Its membership includes anyone involved with the process.

The CAI sponsors a professional management and development program consisting of five courses with a total of 100 hours of formal classroom training in every aspect of condominium and homeowner association operation. Successful completion of the course, coupled with three years of employment experience as a manager of a community association entitles an applicant to the designation of Professional Community Association Manager (PCAM).

OPERATING BUDGETS AND REPORTS

Condominium and cooperative managers generally use the same financial reporting system used by apartment managers, as discussed in Chapter 11. They must prepare an annual operating budget, monthly income and expense statements, and yearly cash flow reports. However, the more complex system of ownership and the fact that the residents are also the owners create unique budgeting problems for condominiums and cooperatives.

One common problem is underestimating utilities. In budget projections the manager must remember to make allowances for inflation *and* increasing rates, since the cost of all forms of energy is rising rapidly. A related concern is to allot enough money for maintenance expenses. Reserve funds should be budgeted for contingencies, the amount increasing as the property ages and more repairs are needed. It is a disservice to the community as a whole to create inadequate budgets in response to pressure from the owners association or to base any activity on political considerations.

On the whole, many condominiums and cooperatives suffer from a lack of long-range planning. A professional property manager can avoid the problems that often

Figure 33: CONDOMINIUM AD

WE BRING BACK THE DAYS OF MORTGAGE SECURITY

At Carriage Way Court, we give you the piece of mind and assurance of an old-fashioned, long-term interest rate.

That means when you buy one of the beautiful condominiums available in the second phase of our development, you don't ever have to worry about changing monthly payments, balloon payments or refinancing.

Plus, these rates are available with low down payments.

What's more, if need be, we'd be glad to talk about other ways to open the door to affordability.

Carriage Way Court is where the relaxed atmosphere of country living blends with the close-by convenience of exceptional shopping, recreation and transportation, and where classic Colonial and French architecture harmonizes with graciously-landscaped grounds. • One bedrooms from $42,400 • No closing costs • No service charges • Investor financing available • Models open: Daily 10-6, Weekends 11-5 • Directions: Located on Algonquin Road in Rolling Meadows, 1/4 mile east of Route 53 at 5000 Carriage Way Drive.

CARRIAGE WAY COURT
CONDOMINIUM

*Annual percentage rate

Baird & Warner
259-8230

Only a few one bedrooms remain

Broker Cooperation Invited

Reprinted with permission of Baird & Warner, Chicago, IL

A Sanctuary for buyers seeking drama

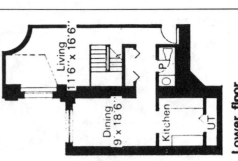

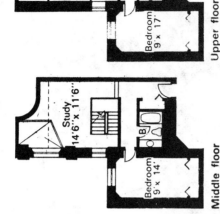

Upper floor

Middle floor

Lower floor

Loft 14'6" x 9'6"

Bedroom 9 x 17

B

Study 14'6" x 11'6"

Bedroom 9 x 14

B

Living 11'6" x 16'6"

Dining 9 x 18'6"

Kitchen

UT

P

FLOOR PLAN Judy Moore

Modern conveniences are being blended in an Old World setting at the Sanctuary, an historic landmark structure in Chicago's De Paul area.

The rental/condominium development at 2538 N. Sheffield was owned by the Little Sisters of the Poor, a Roman Catholic order of nuns founded in France in 1839. The structure originally was built in stages as St. Augustine's Home for the Aged from 1883 to 1898.

"We integrate living accommodations with the best of the old building. We bring in all-new hardwood floors, interior walls, plumbing, electrical, and individual forced-air furnaces and central air-conditioning you can control yourself," said Bruce Walko, vice president of marketing for Landmark Properties.

The firm, which specializes in restoring historically significant buildings, took over the project last August, after another developer's attempt ended in foreclosure.

"It was a real challenge since this building was not meant to be a residence," Walko said.

There are two portions of the Sanctuary: the renovat-ed original structure and a new courtyard with 17 town homes with underground parking on the Kenmore St. side. Investors will buy the condominiums, then rent them.

"People will buy them and get tax protection because they are certified properties," said Walko. But to realize the tax credit, the owner has to rent the unit to someone else.

Renters can participate in Landmark's rent/down payment savings plan, which allows some of the rent paid over five years to build equity toward purchase of the unit.

Dramatic living

Units 209 and 210, two of the most dramatic apartments in the renovated structure, are among the largest of 43 floor plans. Each has about 2,200 square feet of living space with two bedrooms, a study and a loft.

These two tri-level units with 35-foot church-style ceilings are being created from the old chapel and choir-loft area of the historic building. They overlook the courtyard and will be finished in mid-March to early April.

The purchase price starts at $240,000, subject to change. Optional underground parking is an additional $10,000. The rental fee will be from $2,000 to $2,100 per month.

"They are very dramatic units because they have a 16-foot arched window that extends from the living room, right up past the study, and up to the third floor loft," said Walko.

"Since the ceiling is part of the old chapel, it arches around the top. All these things are for the person who wants a unique apartment with a wide-open look to it. It is great for entertaining because there are three levels for various conversation areas,"

Inside each of these two units, a foyer leads to an 11½-by-16½-foot living room. There is also a 9-by-18½-foot dining room that is across from an 8-by-10-foot kitchen and connecting utility room with washer and dryer. A powder room and guest closet also are on the lower floor.

A central stairway leads to a 11½-by-14½-foot study that overlooks the living room below. A 9-by-14-foot bedroom and a full bath are also on the middle floor. More stairs lead to the third floor, where there is a 9½-by-14½-foot loft, a 9-by-17-foot bedroom and an adjacent full bath.

The renovated section of the Sanctuary will have 62 units, plus two units at the opposite end of the chapel that are smaller than the two just described. These tri-level units have 1,600 square feet, are priced from $160,000 and will rent for about $1,375 per month.

Custom design

"What is unique about these units is, you can tailor them to your needs," said Walko. "There is a lot of flexibility that is three floors high."

The study could be turned into a third bedroom and the loft used as an office area or whatever type of room best serve a need.

All the units will have washers, dryers, top-of-the-line appliances, hardwood floors, cathedral ceilings, marble-encased bathrooms and quarry-tile kitchen floors.

A floor plan of Unit 209 at the Sanctuary shows the three levels in the apartment created in the old chapel-choir loft area. The historic building at 2538 N. Sheffield is being developed by Landmark Properties.

arise when a condominium or cooperative development chooses inadequate service contractors in a misguided attempt to cut operating costs.

MANAGEMENT FEES

Condominium and cooperative management fees can be calculated using either the cost-per-unit method or the pricing worksheet explained in Chapter 10. With the per-unit method a surcharge should be added for the additional time spent satisfying a board of directors or an owners association rather than an individual owner. The manager must be service-oriented and diplomatic in reconciling the conflicting demands of several employers. A great deal of time is devoted to personal contact. If the manager assumes many other duties such as attending board or association meetings and developing a newsletter for circulation to stockholders or owners, he or she should charge an additional fee to cover the time expended in these activities. Condominiums and cooperatives that contract only for an accounting or consulting service can be charged a minimum fee, but there should be an additional charge for attendance at more than one board meeting per year.

When dealing with condominiums and cooperatives, the management fee should be quoted in gross dollars per month so it can be budgeted correctly. The board of directors or owners association can then allocate to each resident a prorated amount based on his or her share of ownership in the property. There are other, more compelling reasons why the management figure quoted should be a flat fee rather than a percentage of gross income, as is used for residential apartment fees. A percentage fee gives the residential manager extra profit when rents are raised or space is leased. The revenue from cooperatives and condominiums comes not from rents, but from monthly assessments to cover operating costs. If these managers contract for a percentage fee, they would profit more by allowing operating costs to skyrocket, since this would increase the monthly assessments, total revenue, and thereby the percentage management fee. They would also profit from increases in real property taxes and reserve funds. Since a percentage fee would place the owner and the manager in opposite camps, a flat fee should always be used when dealing with condominium and cooperative properties. In general, the manager should also quote a fee slightly higher than that on the estimate, since any increase in the management fee will have to come from negotiation with the board or association, at which time competitive bids will usually be solicited.

SUMMARY

From a management standpoint, cooperatives and condominiums have almost all the maintenance and operational needs of conventional multiple-occupant residences. The difference is in their form of ownership and tenancy. The manager of a cooperative or condominium works for a group of owner-occupants, who have slightly different goals than either apartment building owners or tenants. For the most part, the manager of a cooperative or condominium has no responsibility for occupancy levels or interior maintenance of individual units. The job entails maintaining common areas, ensuring the harmonious operation of the building, and submitting periodic operating reports to the occupants.

The most common form of cooperative ownership is the *corporate cooperative,* in which a corporation holds title to the property. Stockholders in the corporation are granted *proprietary leases* giving them the right to occupy a unit of the building subject to rules and regulations set forth in the corporate charter and bylaws. A board of directors, elected by the shareholders, is in charge of the operation of the premises and often hires a professional manager to assume this responsibility. *Trust cooperatives* are very similar to corporate cooperatives, except that the property is owned by a trust company. Individuals buy certificates or memberships instead of stock in order to receive a proprietary lease.

Under the terms of most proprietary leases, the care and maintenance of the interior of each unit is the responsibility of the unit owner, as are most of the utilities used by the occupant. Corporate responsibilities are preserving the major structural elements, maintaining equipment, cleaning exterior and interior common areas, ensuring operating efficiency, and providing services to the occupants.

Cooperative ownership often spawns differences of opinion that can interrupt the smooth operation of the property. The cooperative manager's major role is to implement the corporate aims of the shareholders. These aims typically include minimizing operating costs while preserving the property's value, comfort, convenience, and service. The precise services rendered by the manager can range from periodic consultations with the board of directors to full-time responsibility for operation of the property. Acting with the approval of the board of directors, the manager can take charge of staffing, maintenance work, accounting, administration of corporate policy, and transference of corporate stock. Thus, the professional property manager often holds the key to a successful cooperative by providing the centralized authority and control needed to serve the will of the majority.

The *condominium* is one of the fastest growing real estate phenomena. The purchaser of an apartment in a condominium receives *fee simple title* to the unit, plus joint title with the other residents to the common building elements and the land. Due to the rapid expansion in the condominium market, most states have enacted laws regulating their formation. The *conditions, covenants, and restrictions* declaration required to establish a condominium provides for an owners association. This association is usually empowered to regulate property use; prorate insurance bills among the owners; establish a reserve fund for maintenance and improvements; control landscaping and exterior decor; and hire professional management.

As in the management of cooperative units, condominium management is concerned primarily with maintaining the physical integrity of the premises and achieving the mutual goals of the owners. The owners association governing board is an elective body, like the corporate board of directors, and thus is not a permanent group. Acting with the consent of this association, the manager is often given full control of the operation of the premises. Absentee owners of condominiums in resort areas often employ a year-round property manager to maintain the premises and lease the units.

Because of the broad spectrum of duties open to a cooperative or condominium manager, it is important that a written contract be executed by the manager and the owners' representative body. This contract should specify the rights and duties of both parties, the fees to be charged, and the length of the contract term.

The Community Associations Institute offers an educational program for cooperative and condominium owners, association officers, and managers. CAI's program for managers leads to the designation of Professional Community Association Manager (PCAM).

Either the per-unit method of computing management fees or the management pricing worksheet can be used for cooperatives and condominiums, but additional charges should be included for the extra time involved in communicating with and satisfying multiple owners. The fee should also reflect extra services such as planning and attending board meetings, preparing special tax reports, administering corporate policy, or registering corporate stock. Management fees for condominiums and cooperatives should be flat fees, not percentages of revenue, and should be quoted in gross dollars per month so that they can be prorated easily among the owners and incorporated into owners' monthly assessments. The actual flat-rate management fee should be slightly higher than the manager's estimate in order to compensate for the fact that any increase in the fee will entail negotiation with the owners groups, at which time competitive bids will be solicited and the manager risks losing the account.

QUESTIONS: CHAPTER 12

1. Cooperatives which issue beneficial participation certificates are called:

   _____

2. Occupants can finance their units individually in a:

   I. cooperative.
   II. condominium.

   a. I only   c. both I and II
   b. II only   d. neither I nor II

3. Individuals who buy into a corporate cooperative receive two tangible proofs of participation. List them below.

   a. _____
   b. _____

4. Property taxes are assessed separately on each unit in a:

   I. cooperative.
   II. condominium.

   a. I only   c. both I and II
   b. II only   d. neither I nor II

5. A 50-unit corporate cooperative is worth $1,000,000 and is subject to a mortgage of $800,000. An individual who buys 2 percent of the stock would hold a proprietary lease for a unit:

   a. valued at $16,000.
   b. valued at $40,000 with a mortgage of $16,000.
   c. valued at $18,000.
   d. valued at $20,000 with a mortgage of $16,000.

6. A proprietary lease usually allocates to the cooperative as a whole:

   I. the right of first refusal on units to be sublet.
   II. the responsibility for maintaining common areas.

   a. I only   c. both I and II
   b. II only   d. neither I nor II

7. The benefits a professional property manager can offer a cooperative include:

    I.   centralizing authority and responsibility for the operations of the property.
    II. keeping shareholders or members informed of the financial status of the cooperative.

        a. I only   c. both I and II
        b. II only   d. neither I nor II

8. Condominium conditions, covenants, and restrictions declarations:

    I.   are more stringent than rules and regulations for most cooperatives.
    II. establish owners associations under most state laws.

        a. I only   c. both I and II
        b. II only   d. neither I nor II

9. Managers who deal with resort condominiums have an additional duty that is not part of their usual condominium responsibilities. This activity is:

    _____

10. The management fee for a condominium or cooperative:

    I.   is prorated among the occupants according to their interest in the property.
    II. should be expressed as a percentage of revenue.

        a. I only   c. both I and II
        b. II only   d. neither I nor II

11. Occupant-owners of condominiums and cooperatives have slightly different goals than do income apartment building owners. List three typical objectives that the property manager must help fulfill.

        a. _____
        b. _____
        c. _____

12. A corporate cooperative containing 150 units is valued at $75,000,000 and has a mortgage of $25,000,000. An individual who buys 5 percent of the stock would be granted a lease for a unit:

        a. valued at $333,333.
        b. valued at $500,000.
        c. valued at $3,750,000.
        d. with a mortgage of $166,667.

13.   The initial lease-up of cooperative and condominium properties:

   I.   is often handled by the developer.
   II.   is usually accomplished through display and classified ads.

      a.   I only   c.   both I and II
      b.   II only   d.   neither I nor II

14.   List three special budgeting problems a property manager should be aware of when dealing with cooperatives and condominiums.

      a.   _____
      b.   _____
      c.   _____

15.   A management firm with direct costs of $30,000 and indirect costs of $20,000 has the capability of handling 600 units. If a profit of 20 percent is desired, the approximate management fee for a cooperative of 200 units would be:

      a. $20,000 annually.   c. $40,000 annually.
      b. $60,000 annually.   d. $10,000 per month.

16.   Residential (and sometimes commercial) real estate development projects, which involve occupancy and ownership by several persons, but common management through an association, may take three forms:

      a.   _____
      b.   _____
      c.   _____

13
Office Buildings

By definition, an office is a building or room in which a particular service is supplied, as opposed to a place in which goods are manufactured or sold. The need for office space increased steadily over the past 50 years as the majority of American people left the agricultural and manufacturing segments of the economy. Presently, almost 75 percent of the work force is engaged in occupations other than farming or industry, and most require office space in which to operate.

A migration from rural communities to urban centers accompanied the shift in occupational patterns. As cities grew and business expanded, the demand for office space in areas of concentrated activity increased and land in such areas became scarce. This drive toward centralized locations and higher land costs combined with technical advances in construction methods to produce the multistory office buildings that are now predominant in large urban areas. Most of them contain a certain amount of retail space, usually on the ground floor. This chapter and the next suggest strategies for managing such retail properties.

Although the multistory office building dominates the metropolitan skyline, it is certainly not the only form of business space available. Thousands of firms are housed in one- to three-story buildings located in commercial shopping strips or industrial parks. In fact, the recent economic decline in many inner cities and the concomitant exodus of business to suburban locations have been a catalyst to the growth of smaller, outlying office complexes. Originally, most office property was owned by private investors, although a few office buildings were owned by their occupants or by small corporations formed by promoter-developers. Present increases in the costs of construction, equipment, services, and labor, though, have made it virtually impossible for an individual or small corporation to finance and maintain an average-sized office building in an urban area. As a result, many multistory office buildings today are owned by investment syndicates; large institutional investors such as Sears, IBM, John Hancock Insurance Co.; and other large conglomerates with the financial ability to develop and sustain the building over the initial years when cash return on the investment is minimal. Many small developers, unable to compete with corporate giants, have built office space in the suburban market.

Regardless of the size or type of office building, and whether it includes retail space or not, the property manager must take responsibility for the basic functions of marketing and leasing the space, maintaining the property, supervising the building staff, keeping operating costs down, and submitting financial reports to the owner. In order to market and lease office space successfully, the manager must study the product through market and property analyses. The property must then be vigorously promoted and a realistic rental schedule established for its units. As a negotiator, the manager will want to be well acquainted with typical office leases and their special clauses. The owner and the tenants must be apprised of operating and maintenance procedures. The manager's operating reports can measure the effectiveness of management activities.

MARKET ANALYSES

Regional and neighborhood analyses are especially relevant to commercial properties. Current economic trends are at least as significant as present market conditions when assessing the supply and demand for office space in an area. The manager must not overlook the number of new businesses in the area, the quantity of space a typical new business demands, and the number and type of tenants who want to move from their present location into newer facilities. The expansion of existing tenants must also be considered, for it has been estimated that in a growing community they will expand at a rate of ten or twenty percent a year. The *regional analysis* for an office building will emphasize the growing sectors of the regional economy, which may draw national firms to relocate there, or to open branch offices.

In analyzing demand for office space, the property manager must determine the absorption rate, or the number of square feet, which have historically been leased in the market area. If there are 3,000,000 square feet of vacant office space in a city, and the absorption has been 750,000 square feet per year, the city is said to have a four-year supply of leasable office space.

The *neighborhood analysis* emphasizes transportation, parking, and proximity to businesses and services when dealing with office properties. The prestige of the address should be highlighted, as should improvements, renovations, and new construction in the area.

Office space is often referred to as Class A, B, C, or D, based on unofficial guidelines published by the Building Owners and Managers Association International and used by BOMA in conducting its semiannual office market conditions survey. Although building class varies from city to city, it is usually determined by three major factors: age, location, and market position (rental rates).

The Class A building is relatively new in a prime location with a high occupancy rate, and its rental rates are high but competitive. Older buildings, fully renovated to modern standards, are designated Class B. They are in prime locations with high occupancy rates and competitive rental rates. A new building in a nonprime location may also be Class B. Class C includes older, unrenovated buildings in fairly good condition. They enjoy good occupancy, although possibly slightly lower than the city average. Their rental rates are moderate to lower. A building that is reaching the end of its functional life is designed Class D. Old and in poor condition, it survives with low rental rates and low occupancy.

The vacancy rate of other office buildings in the area is a revealing statistic. To avoid misinterpretation, the market should be broken down into segments and buildings grouped according to rating—Class A, B, C, or D as outlined above, and according to age, condition, location, facilities, and amenities. An average market vacancy rate of 12 percent is misleading, for example, unless the manager realizes that vacancies in newer buildings are as low as 2 percent, while older buildings have vacancy rates of 16 percent to 20 percent. Analysis of the movement of tenants from older to newer properties indicates the degree to which new properties can be expected to feed off older buildings and may also reveal other uses for older properties. Space vacated by tenants moving to newer quarters is often occupied by businesses having relatively little customer contact. The prestige of their office locale means less to these firms than convenient layout and reasonable rent. Once the demand pattern for an area has been analyzed, the rent schedule for a specific building within that market can be determined.

PROPERTY ANALYSIS

Property analysis gives the manager a basis for setting a rental schedule, estimating income and expense for the property, and anticipating the reactions of prospects. A survey published in the *Journal of Property Management* identified four key factors influencing the selection of office facilities. On the average, cost was the overriding concern for most respondents, followed by bus and highway accessibility, environment of the property, and labor market, in that order.

When the survey responses were broken down according to size of the firm, the same factors assumed prominence, but their ranking was slightly different. Although cost comes first for all three groups, larger firms place more emphasis on labor market and bus and highway accessibility than do smaller ones. This suggests that smaller firms are less dependent on their employees for productivity than are larger businesses. Environment was valued equally by all three groups.

The Building Owners and Managers Association International has developed a standard method of floor measurement that has been in use since 1915. The BOMA method measures construction, rentable, usable, and storage areas in an office building. The BOMA Standard has been accepted and approved by The American National Standards Institute.

Construction area of a floor is computed by measuring to the outside finished surface of permanent outer building walls. It includes the area of all enclosed floors of the building, basements, mechanical equipment floors, and penthouses. This procedure is sometimes called the New York method.

Rentable area of a floor is computed by measuring to the inside finished surface of the dominant portion of the permanent outer building walls. "Dominant portion" means that portion of the inside finished surface of the permanent outer building wall which is 50% or more of the vertical floor-to-ceiling dimension measured at the dominant portion. If there is no dominant portion, or if the dominant portion is not vertical, the measurement for area shall be to the inside finished surface of the permanent outer building wall where it intersects the finished floor. Excluded are any major vertical penetrations of the floor, such as utility shafts, stairwells, and elevators. No deductions are made for building columns or projections necessary to the building. Included in rentable area, however, are restrooms, janitor closets, and rooms such as electrical rooms, which are necessary to the operation of the building.

When comparing *office space,* a prospective tenant will want to know the number of square feet that can actually be occupied. This space under the BOMA method is known as usable area. The **usable area** is computed by measuring to the finished surface of the office side of corridor and other permanent walls, to the center of partitions that separate the office from adjoining usable areas, and to the inside finished surface of the dominant portion of the permanent outer building walls. Not included in usable area are those portions of the building normally associated with the core of the building such as corridors, lobbies, restrooms, major penetrations of the floor, and rooms containing equipment for the building.

In determining the **rentable area** of any particular office on a floor, the rentable/usable ratio (R/U Ratio) is first computed. The conversion formula for computing the R/U Ratio is as follows:

$$\frac{\text{Rentable Area}}{\text{Usable Area}} = \text{Rentable/Usable Ratio (``R/U Ratio'')}$$

$$\text{Usable Area} \times \text{R/U Ratio} = \text{Rentable Area}$$

$$\frac{\text{Rentable Area}}{\text{R/U Ratio}} = \text{Usable Area}$$

The conversion formula is used for a *multiple-tenancy* floor. Where a floor is rented to a single tenant, the rentable area is taken as the area chargeable to the tenant (restrooms and corridors on that floor are considered part of the tenant's space), and there is no necessity for conversion.

Areas used for *retail stores* in an office building are measured by the definition of store area. The number of square feet in a ground floor store area is computed by measuring from the building line in the case of street frontages, and from the inner surface of other outer building walls and from the inner surface of corridor and other permanent partitions and to the center of partitions that separate the premises from adjoining rentable area. No deductions are made for vestibules inside the building line or for columns or projections necessary to the building. No additions are made for bay windows extending outside the building line.

The ratio of rentable space to usable space is sometimes called *loss factor,* a reflection of the efficiency of space utilization on a single-tenancy floor. On a multiple-tenancy floor, this relationship is referred to as the *load factor.*

The loss or load factor is figured into the cost of usable space. For example, if 22,000 rentable square feet are offered at $8 per square foot, but only 19,125 square feet are usable, the loss factor is 1.15 (22,000 ÷ 19,125 = 1.15). The real cost to the tenant per usable square foot is $9.20 ($8 × 1.15 = $9.20), or a difference of $1.20 per square foot from the rent quotation. The efficiency of space utilization should be considered when constructing the rental schedule for the building. Spaces with a high loss factor should compensate with a lower base rent.

Setting the Rental Schedule

As noted earlier, rental cost is a pertinent factor in the selection of office space. A uniform and realistic rent schedule capitalizes on all the features tenants customarily consider part of rental value.

The first step in setting a rental schedule is determining the absolute minimum that can be charged for space in the property in order to cover the operating expenses and provide some return on investment to the owner. The following formula may be used to calculate the minimum rental rate:

$$\frac{\text{operating expenses} + \text{mortgage payments} + \text{owner's return on equity}}{\text{rentable area of building}} = \text{minimum rent}$$

For example, an office building with a market value of $4 million contains 64,000 square feet of rentable space. The owner put 20 percent down on the property and has mortgage payments totaling $90,000 a year. Operating expenses are about $300,000 per year, and the owner needs to get at least a 10-percent return on the investment or equity. Following the above formula for computing the minimum rental rate:

$$\frac{\$300,000 + \$90,000 + (10\% \text{ of } \$800,000 \text{ down payment})}{64,000 \text{ sq. ft.}} = \begin{array}{l} \$7.34 \text{ per sq. ft.} \\ \text{minimum rent} \end{array}$$

This figure represents the absolute minimum that can be charged for economic survival. It does not take into account contingencies such as vacancy loss, and it does not bear any relation to the current market, which is the most important determining factor in setting a rental schedule. Nonetheless, this computation can ensure that the base rental rate suggested by the market and property analyses is high enough to cover the basic costs.

The next step is to establish a realistic base rate per square foot for a typical space within the building. The base rate should be significantly higher than the minimum rate arrived at earlier. It should also reflect the features of the property and its current value relative to similar buildings in the area. Thus the schedule is dependent on general building features such as exterior appearance, style of the lobby, elevator service, condition of corridors, management services, and the present tenant population. Once the base rate has been established for typical office space in the building, a specific rental schedule for each type of space must be developed. Depending on its features, each office space is graded as above-standard, standard, or below the base rate. Ultimately, the rental schedule will reflect variables such as height above street level, floor location relative to elevators, interior layout and decor, natural lighting, and view.

Another method of measuring and charging for office space is known as the *New York method*. Under the New York method, all of the construction area of a floor or building in a shopping center is used in determining the rent. For instance, if a building or floor measures 100 feet by 100 feet, the area which must be allocated to tenants in renting the space is 10,000 square feet. As administered by some landlords, tenants in multiple-story buildings may also be charged a pro rata share of ground-floor lobby space. In this way all the space in a building is accounted for. Rents will tend to be less per square foot than under the BOMA method. This method is not popular in some areas, due to the difficulty of convincing prospective tenants that they should pay for space such as stairwells, elevator shafts, etc., which they cannot actually occupy.

MARKETING OFFICE SPACE

The marketing of office space requires a systematic and continuing program to attract prospective occupants, analyze their space needs, and show them units that are suited to their budget and space requirements. Although there are several ways to merchandise office space, a thorough knowledge of the area market and the specific property is essential to each. Four general points can be raised to convince prospects to relocate: a substantial *price advantage, increased efficiency, prestige,* and *economy* in a new location.

Advertising the Property

The most commonly used methods of attracting prospective tenants to office buildings are signs, brochures, display ads, direct mail, publicity and public relations efforts, referrals, canvassing, leasing agents, and rental centers. The property manager must decide which techniques are best suited to each type of office space and how to develop an advertising strategy that captures the prospect's interest and enhances his or her desire for the space.

Signs. A sign directing inquiries to the manager should be posted on all office buildings.

Brochures. Because there are more people involved in it, and an office move is generally for a long term, the decision to rent office space is usually not as spontaneous as the selection of an apartment. It is a good idea, therefore, to give prospects a brochure after they have seen the space. Figure 35 is an example of one effective approach.

Ads. Although classifieds are rarely used to market office space, well-placed institutional display ads can be effective. Figure 36 is a good example. Display advertisements in well selected out-of-town target area newspapers, trade magazines, or the *Wall Street Journal* reach a select audience over a wide metropolitan or regional area. These ads address themselves to the decision makers and their influence groups within prospective tenant organizations, emphasizing the prestige and value of the space.

Direct Mail. The quickest way to lease a large new building is to generate movement within the current market. This can be accomplished by addressing the latent portion of the market. Firms that are not actively looking for new offices are not generally

St. Charles Office Park

When you work
in pleasant surroundings
you and your employees work more efficiently
...and enjoy life too.

CMD

Courtesy of CMD Midwest, Inc., Chicago, Illinois

Prestigious New Office Space in a parklike environment

The St. Charles Office Park has been designed to provide the highest standard of quality throughout the buildings—quality assured by CMD's 78 year reputation as a leader in real estate development.

The parklike setting, with green areas and building aesthetics, is in keeping with the natural charm of the Fox River Valley.

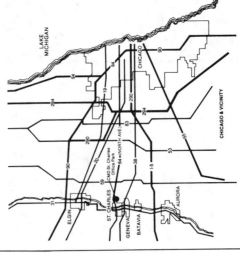

The community of St. Charles is linked to O'Hare Airport, downtown Chicago and other Illinois communities by major thoroughfares and highways. Nearby is Du Page County Airport, one of the best in the Middle West for business, pleasure and charter aircraft.

St. Charles is part of Chicago's business and commercial community, yet is far enough away in the Fox River Valley to be a distinctive community.

An outstanding residential environment, St. Charles is actively pursuing the location of corporate and regional offices. An abundance of cultural, educational, recreational and commercial attractions, featured on the map on the back page, confirm the vitality and prosperity of the community.

St. Charles is a desirable location for your new office. A properly designed working environment achieves increased profits through attracting better employees, increasing productivity and reducing employee turnover. The St. Charles Office Park is designed to meet today's needs of today's businesses.

Developed, owned and managed by the nation's most experienced real estate developer, the St. Charles Office Park is located within CMD's 675 acre St. Charles Industrial Park.

Entry is through the Office Park's own attractively designed stone gateway into an environment totally landscaped and beautifully maintained by CMD. There is parking adjacent to individual suites. The buildings offer a flexible office concept, with space planning service available for your needs. Model offices, in various sizes, can be seen to help with your decision on the ideal suite for you.

Developed by CMD, the pacesetter in planned industrial communities

A few words about the developer will assure you of the quality of the St. Charles Office Park. CMD originated the concept of planned industrial communities in the United States in 1902. Today, CMD properties in the Chicago area, in Phoenix, Arizona and in Sacramento, California are servicing large corporations such as Motorola, Swift & Co., Du Kane Corp., American Hospital Supply and other distinguished firms, as well as hundreds of smaller companies. CMD maintains an ownership position in all of its developments and establishes a permanent business relationship with the community and its clients. This relationship protects your investment and environment, as well as CMD's.

For an office tenant, responsible and experienced management is an important consideration. CMD manages its own properties and also manages over one hundred properties owned by other investors. This is ample confirmation of CMD's experience and capability. The standards for quality and prestige set by CMD are the highest in the industry and have been maintained for 78 years.

The St. Charles
Office Park Concept

The pleasant feeling of country air and green areas is carried into the building through use of atriums, interior glass walls and skylights.

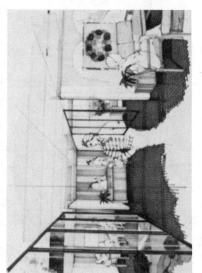

The image of your company is reflected in your office with space planning for your needs and building integrity assured by CMD's long-standing reputation.

As a prestige environment for your office, the first phase of the CMD Park consists of contemporary one-story buildings located on 10.8 landscaped acres. Each building is planned to have 49,712 square feet and is designed to be subdivided into suites of 800 to 2,000 square feet or more.

Project Amenities

- All masonry building
- Flexible office design
- Individual heating and air conditioning controls for all suites
- Private entry for exterior suites
- Private washroom facilities
- Atriums and skylights
- The latest in energy efficient HVAC systems
- Fully automatic fire prevention sprinkler system
- Totally landscaped environment
- Exterior building illumination
- Energy efficient—
    Double glazed insulated tinted glass
    Heavily insulated exterior walls and roof
- Parking adjacent to individual suites
- Full height solid core doors
- Ceiling heights—9 ft.
- Numerous custom options available
- On-site management

Building Standard

- Self-contained gas heating system and central air conditioning maintained by landlord
- Modular fluorescent lighting system
- Acoustic tile—suspended ceiling
- Draperies
- Wall to wall carpeting
- Duplex outlets and telephone locations
- Private office partitioning

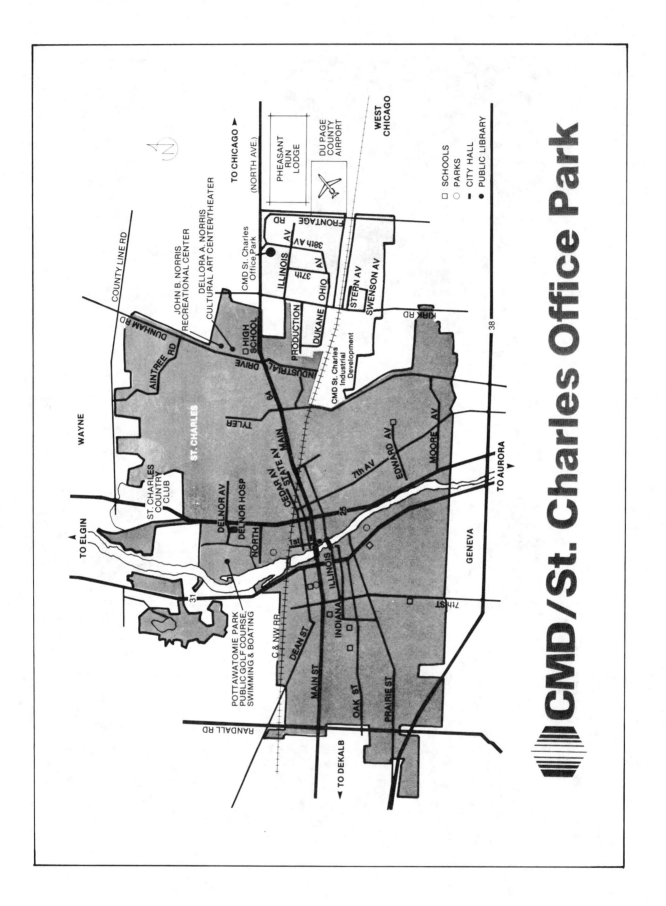

CMD/St. Charles Office Park

Figure 36: INSTITUTIONAL ADVERTISEMENT

When looking for an office broker, there's one important sign to watch for.

As a major office broker, we're proud of the firm we've built. The clients we've represented. The number of leases we've engineered.

So if you're someone who may need to select a broker, is there anything more telling than success? We think there is.

Because many of the clients you see here, we've seen before. With large needs and small. Downtown, in the suburbs or both. In Chicago and beyond. Relationships that last a lifetime.

If you're looking into real estate, look at us. You'll see there's no end to what we'll do for you.

Bennett & Kahnweiler Associates
Corporate Real Estate

Downtown: 312/559-0808 • Suburban: 312/671-7911

Reprinted with permission by Bennett & Kahnweiler Associates

influenced by signs, ads, or leasing agents, but they may be responsive to direct-mail pieces that offer a better value or location than their present office space. A list of potential tenants can be culled from sources like the *Dun & Bradstreet Reference Book,* which lists companies according to the nature of their business. *The Dunhill International List* provides names of law, accounting, and brokerage firms, as well as small businesses. Letters to members of the latent market should be accompanied by printed materials about the building and a reply card.

Public Relations. A well-executed public relations program can be a cost-effective supplement to advertising, direct-mail campaigns, and other marketing techniques, particularly when dealing with newly constructed multistory office buildings. News items like Figure 37 are invaluable publicity for an office building.

Referrals. Good will is a powerful leasing tool. Local government officials and representatives of utility companies are often in a position to provide leads. An ambitious office manager will cultivate these sources and become active in the local chamber of commerce, professional associations, and other service groups.

Canvassing. Canvassing is probably the best prospecting method for leasing office space, and most productive when the list of prospects has been qualified to some extent. The Dun & Bradstreet directory and others published by the local chamber of commerce will furnish the manager with names of firms which, by their nature, might be interested in the particular space being marketed. The financial section of the newspaper often contains articles on firms that are enjoying rapid financial growth, acquiring subsidiaries, or planning for expansion. Though time-consuming, phone calls to area firms can generate business from the latent market as well as from companies with admitted space needs.

Canvassing efforts should begin in areas closest to the subject property and progress outward in concentric circles around the property. Managers of large office buildings often allow leasing agents or sales representatives to perform this function on their behalf.

Rental Center. Like large residential developments, new multistory office buildings often use rental centers.

Qualifying the Tenant

Advertising and promotion provoke inquiries about space, but the real marketing of the property is done by personal contact with the prospect at the building. Much valuable time can be saved if the prospect is qualified before being shown any space. In fact, spatial requirements should be one of the first areas of qualification. Preliminary space planning convinces prospective tenants that the manager cares about their requirements and is rendering professional service. The manager should keep a permanent record of all the information obtained when qualifying a prospect.

Space Planning. The starting point for a needs assessment is an understanding of the nature of the prospect's business, the types of staff positions it demands, the number of people in each position, and the tasks that each performs. Ths business life-style

FIG. 37: OFFICE PUBLICITY

Shiny 40-story tower proposed for Oakland

Grubb & Ellis has been selected as the exclusive leasing agent for the dramatic new 40-story Kaiser Center Tower on the shore of Lake Merritt, Grand and Harrison, Oakland.

Harold A. Ellis Jr., president of the real estate firm, said: "Grubb & Ellis is confident that Kaiser Center Tower will be a landmark office building attracting companies and businesses that want a premier location in a beautiful setting."

At 40 stories, the building designed by the architectural firm of Skidmore, Owings and Merrill will be the tallest in the Eastbay and its offices will command sweeping panoramic views of Lake Merritt, the Oakland Hills, San Francisco and the Bay.

A distinctive feature of the building's design is its curving frontage that affirms an affinity for Lake Merritt which it faces. The building's sides and back, facing Grand Avenue and Kaiser Plaza, by contrast are straight-sided.

The exterior aluminum metallic finish and wide floor-to-ceiling windows take on a bluish tone reflecting the waters of Lake Merritt.

John L. Guillory, vice president and district manager for Grubb & Ellis Commercial Brokerage, said: "We at Grubb & Ellis are confident that Oakland's popularity will greatly assist our leasing efforts. Kaiser Center is already established as a significant financial center because of the friendly business climate in Oakland and we are looking forward to leasing up the Kaiser Center Tower."

Richard O. Clark, vice president and sales manager for the Commercial Brokerage office, added that Kaiser Center is a premier location for business. "It is unique because of its superb transportation network and proximity to financial institutions in Oakland and San Francisco. Yet here is an office building that has beautiful Lake Merritt right at its front door and a park to enjoy. Running, jogging, it's just a great place and Kaiser Center Tower is absolutely dynamite."

The building is enhanced by a tree-lined landscaped plaza with terracing and plans for a pedestrian skyway system to link the tower with future build-

Oakland, CA
(Alameda Co.)
Tribune
(Cir. D. 165,413)
(Cir. S. 183,341)

JUL 17 1985

Proposed 40-story Kaiser Center Tower on Lake Merritt

ings in the complex and the existing Kaiser and Ordway Building.

The new tower will continue the development of the Kaiser Center in Oakland. Kaiser Center is an affiliate of Kaiser Development Company, which is owned by Kaiser Aluminum & Chemical Corporation.

Kaiser Center encompasses six contiguous blocks between Lake Merritt and Webster, Grand and 20th. The city-approved master plan calls for three additional office towers, linked by landscaped plazas and pedestrian bridges. the existing world-famous roof garden at the Kaiser Center will serve as a model for future gardens at the center.

Located strategically at Grand and Harrison, the proposed building is within three blocks of the 19th Street BART station and is close to all major freeways. AC Transit provides continuous bus service to Jack London Square, other parts of downtown Oakland, the Oakland International Airport and SFO International Airport. AC Transit also links residential communities in the Eastbay with the Kaiser Center.

Reprinted with permission of Grubb & Ellis Commercial Brokerage and the Oakland Tribune, Inc.

and hierarchical structure also shape the space allocation plan. The need for office space will vary from the secretarial to the managerial level. Some positions and processes require nonstandard space usage, such as a photo reproduction lab or a computer room.

From this information, four categories of space usage have been identified. *Single office space* refers to enclosed or semienclosed areas serving a single occupant and including a circulation area to provide access to the office. Unit office spaces can vary in size from a private office of about 100 square feet, suitable for middle managers, to a 345-square-foot private office large enough to accommodate a company president.

Multipersonnel areas are open or closed workspaces for more than one person. The standard allowances for closed areas range from 55 to 90 square feet per person, depending on the status of the individual, company policy, and the number of workers sharing one closed space. In general, when a number of workers share a space, the square footage allotted to each may be reduced. These standards provide sufficient space so that work stations do not interfere with one another and traffic can circulate to and through the work area.

Open spaces allow greater flexibility with larger groups. Open-area requirements can range from approximately 45 square feet each for 15 or more workers to 80 square feet per person for 6 employees or less.

Special facilities are workspaces for one or more persons which are designed to accommodate the special equipment used by these workers in the course of their jobs. Since this category takes in a diverse group of special-use areas, standard space allotments are difficult to determine. Guidelines have been established, however, for the special facilities most often required by businesses. For example, a conference room for four people requires about 200 square feet of space. A reception area for three visitors and a receptionist would require the same. A lunchroom for four should contain 250 square feet.

Miscellaneous areas are spaces designed for other special facilities. In this category of space, which does not include permanently assigned work areas, are libraries, supply rooms, mailrooms, vaults, and computer rooms. The two most universal and essential miscellaneous areas are filing space and allowances for traffic flow. Corridors and other interior circulation requirements are often estimated at 15 percent of the total office area, while 5 percent is usually added for filing space. Access circulation needs can be determined later on a situational basis, with allowance for interior traffic flow.

Although the space standards mentioned above are not meant to yield precise square footage requirements, prospective tenants will evaluate a space in terms of its ability to satisfy their current needs. Therefore, it is wise for the manager or leasing agent to analyze prospects' space requirements before showing them any specific office areas.

Other Factors in Space Planning. While determining the prospect's quantitative needs, the manager should also discover what quality of office space is desired. The business image of the tenant firm will be influenced by the physical appearance of the space.

The *floor population* and the *clerical-executive mix* also must be considered when exploring the quality of space that a prospect desires.

Most prestige-oriented business tenants want tenants of comparable status in close proximity, whether they are competitive firms or not. They are sensitive to the visiting clientele for the other tenants on the floor. Tenants providing a specialty service, such as lawyers, usually prefer not to be placed next to a rival firm. The ideal situation is to have each floor leased by tenants who are involved in different businesses but who enjoy the same level of prestige.

The best way to gauge a prospect's spatial requirements and other needs is to visit the space the firm is presently occupying and study its current operations, together with any changes or expansions the prospect desires. There is no substitute for this first-hand knowledge and the flexibility it can provide.

Additional Areas of Qualification. Having determined the prospect's spatial requirements, the manager will then seek related information—motives for moving, rental budget, parking and transportation needs, preferences for amenities and alterations, projected moving date, and special lease clauses needed. It is also important to qualify the representative of the prospect firm with regard to that person's status in the company and authority to make decisions.

Sometimes, an executive who is looking for space will not give the manager all the information needed for proper qualification until he or she is interested in a particular property. In such cases, the manager must show space that corresponds to the prospect's stated specifications. When a suitable space is found, the manager must backtrack and qualify the prospect thoroughly in order to accommodate the firm's actual requirements.

Figure 38 is an information sheet to be used when leasing office space. The following questions should be asked of all prospective tenants:

- When does your present lease expire?
- How long have you been in your present space?
- What is your current rent?
- Are you interested in new space?
- Do you need more, less, or an equal amount of space?
- What is your budget for new space?
- What is your financial strength?
- Why do you want to move?
- When do you need the new space?
- How many employees will you move?
- What kind of improvements and amenities are needed?
- How much parking is required? Is it paid by the company or the employee?
- Do you have any specific transportation needs?
- Who will make the decisions?
- Who can sign the lease? Where is this person located?
- Where do you want to locate? Why?
- When can you see the space?
- Are you interested in buying?

Figure 38: LEASING INFORMATION, OFFICE SPACE

Date:_____

Organization: _____

Address:_____Phone:_____

Service/Product:_____Market Area:_____

Yrs. in Bus:_____No. of Employees:_____Hrs. Oper:_____

Decision Maker/Position:_____

Lease

Starting Date:_____ Length:_____ Options:_____

Price (pr. sq. ft.)_____ Month:_____ Year _____

Other Expenses: _____

Location

Preferred Locations: (1) _____

(2)_____ (3)_____ (4)_____

Specific Locational Requirements (freeways, other businesses, etc.): _____

_____

Access to Public Transportation: _____

Other: _____

Facility

Type of Building:_____

Quality:_____ Total Sq. Ft.:_____

Specifications:

reception _____ private offices _____

open area _____ work area _____

storage area _____ conf. room _____

parking _____ other _____

Previous Viewing

space seen	shown by	date
a)_____	_____	_____
b)_____	_____	_____
c)_____	_____	_____
d)_____	_____	_____

Are you interested in new space?

If yes:

When do you need to be in the new space? _____

How many employees will you move? _____

What kind of improvements do you require?_____

Who will make the decision to move?_____

Who can sign the lease?_____

Will you buy?_____

Other Information

_____

_____

_____

_____

Showing the Space

The space itself is usually the deciding factor in transforming a prospective tenant into a tenant. If the space is not skillfully presented and its advantages highlighted, the preliminary advertising and qualification efforts will be wasted.

Every large office building should have a manager's office to handle the building operations and to receive prospective tenants and outside leasing agents. It is essential that the management office be attractively furnished, for it is the first office the prospect will see.

Before being shown any units, the prospect should be familiarized with the features of the building's locale, as brought out in the manager's area and neighborhood analyses. If traffic patterns, transportation, and parking are major concerns, benefits in these areas should be emphasized. The manager should help the prospect visualize his or her firm in the space and should listen carefully to the prospect's reactions to specific features and benefits. In the case of a prospective commercial tenant, it is worthwhile for the manager (or the leasing agent) to note both positive and negative reactions. Client responses tell the manager what adaptations are needed to make the space suitable for the prospect. This information is indispensable as the merchandising process moves into its final and most critical stage—negotiation of the lease agreement.

Making every effort to close the prospect, the manager should begin discussing lease terms after showing the office space. If a prospect lacks the authority to negotiate terms or requires more time, brochures about the property are a useful source of information for the prospect. The manager should provide as much additional material as possible and follow up with phone calls or personal contact.

When dealing with an agent or branch office of a large corporation located in another city, the manager can expedite the transaction by offering to get all pertinent data to the decision maker in the home office. This might be accomplished by mailing the brochures, plans, and specifications to the decision maker; by discussing the matter over the telephone; or by traveling to the home office to present the benefits of the space in person. However, the manager must be sure that the local representative of the prospect is sold on the space and wants the manager to do so. The manager must appear to be helping the local prospect, not going over his or her head.

NEGOTIATIONS AND THE LEASE

The standard office lease is a written contract between the tenant and the building manager (or owner) which defines the rights and duties of each party over a specified period of time. The object of negotiation is to achieve a signed lease, beneficial to both parties, in the shortest possible period of time. The general rules for negotiation outlined in Chapter 6 include acting in a professional manner, inspiring confidence, cooperating with outside leasing agents, and excluding attorneys from initial negotiations. The manager must be knowledgeable concerning the property, the market, the owner's objectives, and the tenant's need in order to strike a satisfactory agreement between the parties.

A new office building that comes on the market in a depressed economic cycle may take a long time to lease to breakeven occupancy. The real skill of the manager in reading economic trends comes into play in these instances. As a protection, the manager should attempt to negotiate leases on a staggered basis, or for terms that will hold the tenant in the building beyond the time of known competitive expansion.

The office lease itself is subject to the requirements for a legal contract and usually contains at least the basic clauses mentioned in Chapter 5. Figure 39 is a typical example. Of special importance are clauses defining the responsibilities of each party in the event of damage to the other's property from water, fire, explosion, or other cause. Many office leases contain escalation clauses, and are known as index leases. Four sections have special legal or economic importance and merit a closer examination: the escalation clause, assignment and subletting, provision for services, and the possession clause.

Escalation Clause

Because most office leases run for terms in excess of one year, an escalation clause, or "pass-through" clause, is usually incorporated into the terms of the agreement. The purpose of a pass-through clause is to cover the unavoidable annual increases in real estate taxes and operating expenses. While the principle of the escalation clause is fairly standard and generally understood, methods of computation vary greatly. Increases in taxes and expenses above the figures for the stipulated base year can be prorated, based upon the tenant's percentage of the total space occupied, and billed and paid as a separate charge; in other cases, the base rental rate can be adjusted directly.

Some leases compute increases in reference to a base-year figure that has been adjusted to reflect full occupancy. This is most advantageous for the tenants, especially when the base year is the first year of a building's life, when leasing is still in progress. For example, if base-year expenses totaled $500,000 for a building only half-occupied, and the operating expenses from the first comparison year at 75-percent occupancy came to $1,250,000, the amount of increase prorated among the tenants would be $750,000. However, if the base-year figure is adjusted to $1,000,000 in order to reflect full occupancy, the amount to be prorated after the first year would only be $250,000, a substantial savings for the tenants.

Assignment and Subletting

The right to assign or sublet the leased premises often becomes a point for negotiation, since this can be vital to a tenant. It protects the tenant from rapid expansion or collapse in business. The tenant's liability in no way decreases when the space is assigned or sublet, but he or she may vacate the premises without major financial loss. Many leases provide that a tenant may sublet or assign the premises only after obtaining the landlord's written approval and giving sufficient notice. Some require that any increases of sublet rental rates over the tenant's rate be shared with the landlord. This allows the landlord to maintain control over the constituency of the tenant population while leaving the tenant an alternative.

Figure 39: OFFICE LEASE, INDEXED

ASSIGNMENT

For value received, the undersigned Lessee hereby assigns all the Lessee's right, title and interest in and to the within lease from and after _____

_____unto_____

the premises to be used and occupied for_____and for no other purpose.   It is expressly

agreed this assignment shall not release or relieve the undersigned, as Original Lessee, from any liability under the covenants of the lease, nor from the provisions of paragraph (e) of Section 15 of this lease.

LESSEE } _____[SEAL]
_____[SEAL]

Dated_____, 19

ACCEPTANCE OF ASSIGNMENT

In consideration of the above assignment and the written consent of the Lessor thereto, the undersigned Assignee (binding also the Assignee's heirs, legal representatives and successors), hereby assumes the obligations of said lease imposed on the Lessee and promises to make all payments and to keep and perform all conditions and covenants of the lease by the Lessee to be kept and performed commencing_____, expressly adopting for the undersigned the provisions of paragraph (e) of Section 15 of the lease as though here restated.

ASSIGNEE } _____[SEAL]
_____[SEAL]

Dated_____, 19

OFFICE LEASE

No._____

Rent:

To: 19

From: 19

Term:

Premises:

Lessee:

Lessor:

SORG PRINTING COMPANY OF ILLINOIS

CONSENT TO ASSIGNMENT

Lessor hereby consents to the above Assignment upon the express condition that Original Lessee shall remain liable for the prompt payment of the Rent and the keeping and performance of all conditions and covenants of the lease by the Lessee to be kept and performed. The Lessor does not hereby consent to any further Assignment or to any subletting of the premises.

LESSOR } _____[SEAL]
_____[SEAL]

Dated_____, 19

GUARANTY

In consideration of the making of the above lease by the Lessor with the Lessee at the request of the undersigned and in reliance on this guaranty, the undersigned hereby guarantees the payment of the Rent to be paid by the Lessee and the performance by the Lessee of all the terms, conditions, covenants and agreements of the lease, and the undersigned promises to pay all the Lessor's expenses, including reasonable attorney's fees, incurred by the Lessor in enforcing all obligations of the Lessee under the lease or incurred by the Lessor in enforcing this guaranty.   The Lessor's consent to any assignment or assignments, and successive assignments by the Lessee and Lessee's assigns, of this lease, made either with or without notice to the undersigned, or a changed or different use of the demised premises, or Lessor's forbearance, delays, extensions of time or any other reason whether similar to or different from the foregoing, shall in no wise or manner release the undersigned from liability as guarantor.

WITNESS the hand and seal of the undersigned at the date of the above lease.

_____[SEAL]

OFFICE LEASE—FORM B—(Revised 1976)

THIS INDENTURE, made   19   , **Witnesseth:**

                                                                                          Lessor,

hereby leases unto

                                                                                          Lessee,

and the Lessee accepts the **Premises**, known as

Chicago, Illinois, for the **Term** of

commencing   , 19   , and ending   , 19   , unless sooner terminated as provided herein, to be occupied and used by the Lessee for

In Consideration Thereof, the Parties Covenant and Agree: 1. Rent. Lessee shall pay to the Lessor, or to

in the United States of America, at   , in coin or currency which, at the time or times of payment, is legal tender for public and private debts

the sum of   or as directed from time to time by the Lessor's notice,

in installments as follows: Dollars ($)

payable one each in advance promptly on the first day of every calendar month of the term and at the current rate for fractions of a month if the term shall be terminated on any day other than the last day of any month.   Unpaid rent shall bear interest at 7% per annum from the date due until paid.

2. Service: The Lessor shall provide: (a) **Janitor Service** in and about the premises, Saturdays, Sundays and holidays excepted.   The Lessor shall not provide any janitor service without the Lessor's written consent.   If the Lessor's consent be given, such janitor service shall be subject to the Lessor's supervision but at the Lessee's sole responsibility.   The Lessee shall not provide any janitor service in the premises except through a janitor contractor or employees who are, and shall continuously be, in each and every instance satisfactory to the Lessor.   (b) **Heat** daily from 8 a.m. to 5 p.m. (Saturdays to 1 p.m.), Sundays and holidays excepted, whenever heat shall, in the Lessor's judgment, be required for the comfortable occupation and use of the premises.   (c) **Water** from City of Chicago mains for drinking, lavatory and toilet purposes, drawn through fixtures installed by the Lessor or by the Lessee with the Lessor's written consent.   The Lessee shall pay, at rates fixed by the Lessor, for water used for air conditioning, refrigerating or any purpose other than drinking, lavatory and toilet purposes.   (d) **Passenger Elevator Service** in common with other tenants daily from 8 a.m. to 6 p.m. (Saturdays to 1 p.m.), Saturdays, Sundays and holidays excepted.   Elevator service at other times shall be optional with the Lessor and, if provided, shall never be deemed a continuing obligation of the Lessor.   The Lessor may change manually operated and controlled elevators to operatorless, automatic elevators operated and controlled by passengers without liability of the Lessor to the Lessee and without impairing any obligation of the Lessee under this lease.   (e) **Electricity** if and so long as the Lessor shall generate or distribute electric current for light and power in the Building, the Lessee shall obtain all current used in the premises

from the Lessor and pay the Lessor's charges therefor, within five days after the rendering of each statement of account unless otherwise specified in the Lessor's statement of account.   The Lessee's failure to pay promptly the Lessor's charges for electricity shall entitle the Lessor, upon not less than ten days' notice, to discontinue furnishing current to the Lessee, and no such discontinuance shall be deemed an eviction or disturbance of the Lessee's use of the premises or render the Lessor liable for damages or relieve the Lessee from performance of the Lessee's obligations.   Upon not less than thirty days' notice, the Lessor may cease to furnish electricity to the Lessee without any responsibility to the Lessee except to connect, within the thirty day period, the electric wiring system of the premises with another source of supply of electricity.   Electrical service may be changed, upon thirty days' notice, from direct current to alternating current, without liability of the Lessor to the Lessee.   All electricity used during janitor service, alterations and repairs in the premises shall be paid for by the Lessee.

    The Lessor does not warrant that any of the services above mentioned will be free from interruptions caused by war, insurrection, civil commotion, riots, acts of God or the enemy or Government action, repairs, renewals, improvements, alterations, strikes, lockouts, picketing, whether legal or illegal, accidents, inability of Lessor to obtain fuel or supplies, or any other cause or causes beyond the reasonable control of the Lessor.   Any such interruption of service shall never be deemed an eviction or disturbance of the Lessee's use and possession of the premises or any part thereof, or render the Lessor liable to the Lessee for damages, or relieve the Lessee from performance of the Lessee's obligations under this lease.

3. Lessor's Title: The Lessor's title is and always shall be paramount to the title of the Lessee, and nothing herein contained shall empower the Lessee to do any act which can, shall or may encumber the title of the Lessor.

4. Certain Rights Reserved to the Lessor: The Lessor reserves the following rights: (a) to change the name or street address of the Building without notice or liability of the Lessor to the Lessee; (b) to install and maintain a sign or signs on the exterior of the Building; (c) to have access for the Lessor and the other tenants of the Building to any mail chutes located on the premises according to the rules of the United States Post Office; (d) to designate all sources furnishing sign painting and lettering, ice, drinking water, towels and toilet supplies used on the premises; (e) during the last ninety days of the term or any part thereof, if during or prior to that time the Lessee vacates the premises, to decorate, remodel, repair, alter or otherwise prepare the premises for reoccupancy; (f) to constantly have pass keys to the premises; (g) to grant to anyone the exclusive right to conduct any particular business or undertaking in the Building; (h) to exhibit the premises to others and to display "For Rent" signs on the premises; (i) to take any and all measures, including inspections, repairs, alterations, additions and improvements to the premises or to the Building, as may be necessary or desirable for the safety, protection or preservation of the premises or the Building or the Lessor's interests, or as may be necessary or desirable in the operation of the Building.

The Lessor may enter upon the premises and may exercise any or all of the foregoing rights hereby reserved without being deemed guilty of an eviction or disturbance of the Lessee's use or possession and without being liable in any manner to the Lessee.

5. Default Under Other Lease: If the term of any lease, other than this lease, made by the Lessee for any premises in the Building shall be terminated or terminable after the making of this lease because of any default by the Lessee under such other lease, such fact shall empower the Lessor, at the Lessor's sole option, to terminate this lease by notice to the Lessee.

6. Liability for Acts or Neglect: If any damage whether to the demised premises or to the building, or any part thereof, or whether to the Lessor or to other tenants in the building, results from any act or neglect of the Lessee, or of the Lessee's agents or employees, the Lessor may, at the Lessor's option, repair such damage and the Lessee shall, upon demand by the Lessor, reimburse the Lessor forthwith for the total cost of such repairs. Neither the Lessor nor the Lessee shall be liable for any damage caused by its act or neglect if the Lessor or the Lessee or a tenant has recovered the full amount of the damages from insurance. All property belonging to the Lessee or any occupant in the building shall be at the risk of the Lessee and such other person only and the Lessor shall not be liable for damage thereto or theft or misappropriation thereof.

7. Holding Over: If the Lessee retains possession of the premises or any part thereof after the termination of the term by lapse of time or otherwise, the Lessee shall pay the Lessor rent at double the rate of rental specified in Section 1 for the time the Lessee thus remains in possession, and in addition thereto, shall pay the Lessor all damages sustained by reason of the Lessee's retention of possession. If the Lessee remains in possession of the premises, or any part thereof, after the termination of the term by lapse of time or otherwise, such holding over shall, at the election of the Lessor expressed in a written notice to the Lessee and not otherwise, constitute a renewal of this lease for one year. The provisions of this Section do not waive the Lessor's rights of reentry or any other right hereunder.

8. Assignment and Subletting: The Lessee shall not (a) assign or convey this lease or any interest under it; (b) allow any transfer hereof or any lien upon the Lessee's interest by operation of law; (c) sublet the premises or any part thereof, or (d) permit the use or occupancy of the premises or any part thereof by any one other than the Lessee.

9. Condition of Premises: The Lessee's taking possession shall be conclusive evidence as against the Lessee that the premises were in good order and satisfactory condition when the Lessee took possession. No promise of the Lessor to alter, remodel or improve the premises or the Building and no representation respecting the condition of the premises or the Building have been made by the Lessor to the Lessee, unless the same is contained herein, or made a part hereof. This lease does not grant any rights to light or air over property, except over public streets kept open by public authority. At the termination of this lease by lapse of time or otherwise, the Lessee shall return the premises in as good condition as when the Lessee took possession, ordinary wear and loss by fire excepted, failing which the Lessor may restore the premises to such condition and the Lessee shall pay the cost thereof. The Lessee may remove any floor covering laid by the Lessee, provided (a) the Lessee also removes all nails, tacks, paper, glue, bases and other vestiges of the floor covering, and restores the floor surface to the condition existing before such floor covering was laid, or (b) the Lessee pays to the Lessor, upon request, the cost of restoring the floor surface to such condition. If the Lessee does not remove the Lessee's floor coverings, from the premises prior to the end of the term, the Lessee shall be conclusively presumed to have abandoned the same and title thereto shall thereby pass to the Lessor without payment or credit by the Lessor to the Lessee.

10. Alterations: The Lessee shall not make any alterations in or additions to the premises without the Lessor's advance written consent in each and every instance. The Lessor's decision to refuse such consent shall be conclusive. If the Lessor consents to such alterations or additions, before commencement of the work or delivery of any materials onto the premises or into the Building, the Lessee shall furnish the Lessor with plans and specifications, names and addresses of contractors, copies of contracts, necessary permits and indemnification in form and amount satisfactory to Lessor and waivers of lien against any and all claims, costs, damages, liabilities and expenses which may arise in connection with the alterations or additions. All additions and alterations shall be installed in a good, workmanlike manner and only new, high-grade materials shall be used. Whether the Lessee furnishes the Lessor the foregoing or not, the Lessee hereby agrees to hold the Lessor harmless from any and all liabilities of every kind and description which may arise out of or be connected in any way with said alterations or additions. Before commencing any work in connection with alterations or additions, the Lessee shall furnish the Lessor with certificates of insurance from all contractors performing labor or furnishing materials insuring the Lessor against any and all liabilities which may arise out of or be connected in any way with said additions or alterations. The Lessee shall pay the cost of all such alterations and additions and also the cost of decorating the premises occasioned by such alterations and additions. Upon completing any alterations or additions, the Lessee shall furnish the Lessor with contractors' affidavits and full and final waivers of lien and receipted bills covering all labor and materials expended and used. All alterations and additions shall comply with all insurance requirements and with all ordinances and regulations of the City of Chicago or any department or agency thereof and with the requirements of all statutes and regulations of the State of Illinois or of any department or agency thereof. The Lessee shall permit the Lessor to supervise construction operations in connection with alterations or additions if the Lessor requests to do so. All additions, hardware, non-trade fixtures and all improvements, temporary or permanent, in or upon the premises, whether placed there by the Lessee or by the Lessor, shall, unless the Lessor requests their removal, become the Lessor's property and shall remain upon the premises at the termination of this lease by lapse of time or otherwise without compensation or allowance or credit to the Lessee. If, upon the Lessor's request, the Lessee does not remove said additions, hardware, non-trade fixtures and improvements, the Lessor may remove the same and the Lessee shall pay the cost of such removal to the Lessor upon demand. The Lessee shall remove the Lessee's furniture, machinery, safe or safes, trade fixtures and other items of personal property of every kind and description from the premises prior to the end of the term, however ended. If not so removed, the Lessor may request their removal, and if the Lessee does not remove them, the Lessor may do so and the Lessee shall pay the cost of such removal to the Lessor upon demand. If the Lessor does not request their removal, all such items shall be conclusively presumed to have been conveyed by the Lessee to the Lessor under this lease as a bill of sale without further payment or credit by the Lessor to the Lessee.

11. Use of Premises: (a) The Lessee shall occupy and use the premises during the term for the purpose above specified and none other. (b) The Lessee shall not exhibit, sell or offer for sale on the premises or in the Building any article or thing except those articles and things essentially connected with the stated use of the premises without the advance written consent of the Lessor. (c) The Lessee will not make or permit to be made any use of the premises which, directly or indirectly is forbidden by public law, ordinance or governmental regulation or which may be dangerous to life, limb or property, or which may invalidate or increase the premium cost of any policy of insurance carried on the Building or covering its operations. (d) The Lessee shall not display, inscribe, print, paint, maintain or affix on any place in or about the Building any sign, notice, legend, direction, figure or advertisement, except on the doors of the premises and on the Directory Boards, and then only such name or names and matter, and in such color, size, style, place and material, as shall first have been approved by the Lessor in writing. (e) The Lessee shall not advertise the business, profession or activities of the Lessee conducted in the Building in any manner which violates the letter or spirit of any code of ethics adopted by any recognized association or organization pertaining to such business, profession or activities, and shall not use the name of the Building for any purpose other than that of business address of the Lessee, and shall never use any picture or likeness of the Building in any circulars, notices, advertisements or correspondence without the Lessor's express consent in writing. (f) The Lessee shall not obstruct, or use for storage, or for any purpose other than ingress and egress, the sidewalks, entrances, passages, courts, corridors, vestibules, halls, elevators and stairways of the Building. (g) No bicycle or other vehicle and no dog or other animal or bird shall be brought or permitted to be in the Building or any part thereof. (h) The Lessee shall not make or permit any noise or odor that is objectionable to other occupants of the Building to emanate from the premises, and shall not create or maintain a nuisance thereon, and shall not disturb, solicit or canvass any occupant of the Building, and shall not do any act tending to injure the reputation of the Building. (i) The Lessee shall not install any piano, phonograph, or other musical instrument, or radio or television set in the Building, or any antennae, aerial wires or other equipment inside or outside the Building, without, in each and every instance, prior approval in writing by the Lessor. The use thereof, if permitted, shall be subject to control by the Lessor to the end that others shall not be disturbed or annoyed. (j) The Lessee shall not place or permit to be placed any article of any kind on the window ledges or on the exterior walls, and shall not throw or permit to be thrown or dropped any article from any window of the Building. (k) The Lessee shall not undertake to regulate any thermostat, and shall not waste water by tying, wedging or otherwise fastening open any faucet. (l) No additional locks or similar devices shall be attached to any door or window. No keys for any door other than those provided by the Lessor shall be made. If more than two keys for one lock are desired by the Lessee, the Lessor may provide the same upon payment by the Lessee. Upon termination of this lease or of the Lessee's possession the Lessee shall surrender all keys of the premises and shall make known to the Lessor the explanation of all combination locks on safes, cabinets and vaults. (m) The Lessee shall be responsible for the locking of doors and the closing of transoms and windows in and to the premises. (n) If the Lessee desires telegraphic, telephonic, burglar alarm or signal service, the Lessor will, upon request, direct where and how connections and all wiring for such services shall be introduced and run. Without such directions, no boring, cutting or installation of wires or cables is permitted. (o) If the Lessee desires and the Lessor permits blinds, shades, awnings, or other form of inside or outside window covering, or window ventilators or similar devices, they shall be furnished, installed and maintained at the expense of the Lessee and must be of such shape, color, material and make as approved by the Lessor. (p) All persons entering or leaving the Building between the hours of 6 p. m. and 8 a. m., Monday through Friday, or at any time on Saturdays, Sundays or holidays, may be required to identify themselves to a watchman by registration or otherwise and to establish their rights to enter or leave the Building. The Lessor may exclude or expel any peddler, solicitor or beggar at any time. (q) The Lessee shall not overload any floor. The Lessor may direct the routing and location of safes and other heavy articles. Safes, furniture and all large articles shall be brought through the Building and into the premises at such times and in such manner as the Lessor shall direct and at the Lessee's sole risk and responsibility. The Lessee shall list all furniture, equipment and similar articles to be removed from the Building, and the list must be approved at the Office of the Building or by a designated person before building employes will permit any article to be removed. (r) Unless the Lessor gives advance written consent in each and every instance, the Lessee shall not install or operate any steam or internal combustion engine, boiler, machinery, refrigerating or heating device or air conditioning apparatus in or about the premises, or carry on any mechanical business therein or use the premises for housing accommodations or lodging or sleeping purposes, or do any cooking therein, or use any illumination other than electric light, or use or permit to be brought into the Building any inflammable oils or fluids such as gasoline, kerosene, naphtha and benzine, or any explosives or other articles deemed extra hazardous to life, limb or property. (s) The Lessee shall not place or allow anything to be against or near the glass of partitions or doors of the premises which may diminish the light in, or be unsightly from, halls or corridors. (t) The Lessee shall not install in the premises any equipment which uses a substantial amount of electricity without the advance written consent of the Lessor. The Lessee shall ascertain from the Lessor the maximum amount of electrical current which can safely be used in the demised premises, taking into account the capacity of the electric wiring in the building and the premises and the needs of other tenants in the building and shall not use more than such safe capacity. The Lessor's consent to the installation of electric equipment shall not relieve the Lessee from the obligation not to use more electricity than such safe capacity. (u) The Lessee shall not lay linoleum or other similar floor covering so that such floor covering shall come in direct contact with the floor of the premises, and if linoleum or other similar floor covering is used, an interliner of builder's deadening felt shall first be affixed to the floor by paste or other material soluble in water. The use of cement or other similar material is prohibited. (v) In addition to all other liabilities for breach of any covenant of this Section 11, the Lessee shall pay to the Lessor all damages caused by such breach and shall also pay to the Lessor an amount equal to any increase in insurance premium or premiums caused by such breach. The violation of any covenant of this Section 11 may be restrained by injunction.

12. Repairs: Subject to the provisions of Section 13, the Lessee shall, at the Lessee's own expense, keep the premises in good order, condition and repair during the term, including the replacement of all broken glass with glass of the same size and quality, with signs thereon, under the supervision and with the approval of the Lessor. If the Lessee does not make repairs promptly and adequately, the Lessor may, but need not, make repairs, and the Lessee shall pay promptly the cost thereof. At any time or times, the Lessor, either voluntarily or pursuant to governmental requirement, may, at the Lessor's own expense, make repairs, alterations or improvements in or to the Building or any part thereof, including the premises, and, during operations, may close entrances, doors, corridors, elevators or other facilities, all without any liability to the Lessee by reason of interference, inconvenience or annoyance. The Lessor shall not be liable to the Lessee for any expense, injury, loss or damage resulting from work done in or upon, or the use of, any adjacent or nearby building, land, street or alley. The Lessee shall pay the Lessor for overtime and for any other expense incurred in event repairs, alterations, decorating or other work in the premises are not made during ordinary business hours at the Lessee's request.

13. Untenantability: If the premises or the Building are made untenantable by fire or other casualty, the Lessor may elect (a) to terminate this lease as of the date of the fire or casualty by notice to the Lessee within thirty days after that date, or (b) to repair, restore or rehabilitate the Building or the premises at the Lessor's expense within one hundred twenty days after the Lessor is enabled to take possession of the injured premises and undertake reconstruction or repairs, in which latter event the lease shall not terminate but rent shall be abated on a per diem basis while the premises are untenantable. If the Lessor elects so to repair, restore or rehabilitate the Building or the premises and does not substantially complete the work within the one hundred twenty day period, either party can terminate this lease as of the date of the fire or casualty by notice to the other party not later than one hundred thirty days after the Lessor is enabled to take possession of the injured premises and undertake reconstruction or repairs. In the event of termination of the lease pursuant to this Section 13, rent shall be apportioned on a per diem basis and be paid to the date of the fire or casualty.

14. Eminent Domain: If the Building, or any portion thereof which includes a substantial part of the premises, or which prevents the operation of the Building, shall be taken or condemned by any competent authority for any public use or purpose, the term of this lease shall end upon, and not before, the date when the possession of the part so taken shall be required for such use or purpose, and without apportionment of the condemnation award. The Lessee shall have no right to share in such award. Current rent shall be apportioned as of the date of such termination. If any condemnation proceeding shall be instituted in which it is sought to take or damage any part of the Building, or the land under it, or if the grade of any street or alley adjacent to the Building is changed by any competent authority and such change of grade makes it necessary or desirable to remodel the Building to conform to the changed grade, the Lessor shall have the right to cancel this lease upon not less than ninety days' notice prior to the date of cancellation designated in the notice. No money or other consideration shall be payable by the Lessor to the Lessee for the right of cancellation, and the Lessee shall have no right to share in the condemnation award or in any judgment for damages caused by the change of grade

15. Lessor's Remedies: All rights and remedies of the Lessor herein enumerated shall be cumulative, and none shall exclude any other right or remedy allowed by law.

(a) If any voluntary or involuntary petition or similar pleading under any section or sections of any bankruptcy act shall be filed by or against the Lessee, or any voluntary or involuntary proceeding in any court or tribunal shall be instituted to declare the Lessee insolvent or unable to pay the Lessee's debts, and in the case of an involuntary petition or proceeding, the petition or proceeding is not dismissed within thirty days from the date it is filed the Lessor may elect, but is not required, and with or without notice of such election, and with or without entry or other action by the Lessor, to forthwith terminate this lease, and, notwithstanding any other provision of this lease, the Lessor shall forthwith upon such termination be entitled to recover damages in an amount equal to the then present value of the rent specified in Section 1 of this lease for the residue of the stated term hereof less the fair rental value of the premises for the residue of the stated term.

(b) If the Lessee defaults in the payment of rent, and Lessee does not cure the default within five days after demand for payment of such rent, or if the Lessee defaults in the prompt and full performance of any other provision of this lease, and the Lessee does not cure the default within twenty days (forthwith if the default involves a hazardous condition) after written demand by the Lessor that the default be cured unless the default involves a hazardous condition, which shall be cured forthwith upon the Lessor's demand, or if the leasehold interest of the Lessee be levied upon under execution or be attached by process of law, or if the Lessee makes an assignment for the benefit of creditors, or if a receiver be appointed for any property of the Lessee, or if the Lessee abandons the premises, then and in any such event the Lessor may, if the Lessor so elects but not otherwise, and with or without notice of such election and with or without any demand whatsoever, either forthwith terminate this lease and the Lessee's right to possession of the premises or, without terminating this lease, forthwith terminate the Lessee's right to possession of the premises.

(c) Upon any termination of this lease, whether by lapse of time or otherwise, or upon any termination of the Lessee's right to possession without termination of the lease, the Lessee shall surrender possession and vacate the premises immediately, and deliver possession thereof to the Lessor.

(d) If the Lessee abandons the premises or otherwise entitles the Lessor so to elect, and the Lessor elects to terminate the Lessee's right to possession only, without terminating the lease, the Lessor may, at the Lessor's option enter into the premises, remove the Lessee's signs and other evidences of tenancy, and take and hold possession thereof as in Paragraph (c) of this Section 15 provided, without such entry and possession terminating the lease or releasing the Lessee, in whole or in part, from the Lessee's obligation to pay the rent hereunder for the full term, and in any such case the Lessee shall pay forthwith to the Lessor, if the Lessor so elects, a sum equal to the entire amount of the rent specified in Section 1 of this lease for the residue of the stated term plus any other sums then due hereunder. Upon and after entry into possession without termination of the lease, the Lessor may, but need not, relet the premises or any part thereof for the account of the Lessee to any person, firm or corporation other than the Lessee for such rent, for such time and upon such terms as the Lessor in the Lessor's sole discretion shall determine, and the Lessor shall not be required to accept any tenant offered by the Lessee or to observe any instructions given by the Lessee about such reletting. In any such case, the Lessor may make repairs, alterations and additions in or to the premises, and redecorate the same to the extent deemed by the Lessor necessary or desirable, and the Lessee shall, upon demand, pay the cost thereof, together with the Lessor's expenses of the reletting. If the consideration collected by the Lessor upon any such reletting for the Lessee's account is not sufficient to pay monthly the full amount of the rent reserved in this lease, together with the costs of repairs, alterations, additions, redecorating and the Lessor's expenses, the Lessee shall pay to the Lessor the amount of each monthly deficiency upon demand; and if the consideration so collected from any such reletting is more than sufficient to pay the full amount of the rent reserved herein, together with the costs and expenses of the Lessor, the Lessor, at the end of the stated term of the lease, shall account for the surplus to the Lessee.

(e) The Lessee hereby constitutes and irrevocably appoints any attorney of any court to be the true and lawful attorney of the Lessee, and, in the name, place and stead of the Lessee, to appear for and on behalf of the Lessee in any court of record at any time in any suit or suits brought against the Lessee for the enforcement of any right hereunder by the Lessor, to waive the issuance and service of process and trial by jury, and, from time to time, to confess judgment or judgments in favor of the Lessor and against the Lessee for any rent and interest thereon due hereunder by the Lessee to the Lessor and for costs of suit and for a reasonable attorney's fee in favor of the Lessor to be fixed by the court, and to release all errors that may occur or intervene in such proceedings, including the issuance of execution upon any such judgment, and to stipulate that no appeal shall be prosecuted from such judgment or judgments, or that no proceedings in chancery or otherwise shall be filed or prosecuted to interfere in any way with the operation of such judgment or judgments or of any execution issued thereon or with any supplemental proceedings taken by the Lessor to collect the amount of any such judgment or judgments, and to consent that execution on any judgment or decree in favor of the Lessor and against the Lessee may issue forthwith.

(f) Any and all property which may be removed from the premises by the Lessor pursuant to the authority of the lease or of law, to which the Lessee is or may be entitled, may be handled, removed or stored by the Lessor at the risk, cost and expense of the Lessee, and the Lessor shall in no event be responsible for the value, preservation or safekeeping thereof. The Lessee shall pay to the Lessor, upon demand, any and all expenses incurred in such removal and all storage charges against such property so long as the same shall be in the Lessor's possession or under the Lessor's control. Any such property of the Lessee not removed from the premises or retaken from storage by the Lessee within thirty days after the end of the term, however terminated, shall be presumed to have been conveyed by the Lessee to the Lessor under this lease as a bill of sale without further payment or credit by the Lessor to the Lessee.

(g) The Lessee shall pay upon demand all the Lessor's costs, charges and expenses, including the fees of counsel, agents and others retained by the Lessor, incurred in enforcing the Lessee's obligations hereunder or incurred by the Lessor in any litigation, negotiation or transaction in which the Lessee causes the Lessor, without the Lessor's fault, to become involved or concerned.

16. Subordination of Lease: The rights of the Lessee under this lease shall be and are subject and subordinate at all times to the lien of any mortgage or mortgages now or hereafter in force against the Building or the underlying leasehold estate, if any, and to all advances made or hereafter to be made upon the security thereof, and the Lessee shall execute such further instruments subordinating this lease to the lien or liens of any such mortgage or mortgages as shall be requested by the Lessor.

17. Notices: In every instance where it shall be necessary or desirable for the Lessor to serve any notice or demand upon the Lessee, it shall be sufficient (a) to deliver or cause to be delivered to the Lessee a written or printed copy thereof, or (b) to send a written or printed copy thereof by United States certified or registered mail, postage prepaid, addressed to the Lessee at the demised premises, in which event the notice or demand shall be deemed to have been served at the time the copy is posted, or (c) to leave a written or printed copy thereof with some person above the age of ten years in possession of the demised premises or to affix the same upon any door leading into the demised premises, in which event the notice or demand shall be deemed to have been served at the time the copy is so left or affixed. All notices or demands shall be signed by or on behalf of the Lessor.

18. Miscellaneous: (a) No receipt of money by the Lessor from the Lessee after the termination of this lease or after the service of any notice or after the commencement of any suit, or after final judgment for possession of the premises shall renew, reinstate, continue or extend the term of this lease or affect any such notice, demand or suit.

(b) No waiver of any default of the Lessee hereunder shall be implied from any omission by the Lessor to take any action on account of such default if such default persists or be repeated, and no express waiver shall affect any default other than the default specified in the express waiver and that only for the time and to the extent therein stated. The invalidity or unenforceability of any provision hereof shall not affect or impair any other provision.

(c) In the absence of fraud, no person, firm or corporation, or the heirs, legal representatives, successors and assigns, respectively, thereof, executing this lease as agent, trustee or in any other representative capacity shall ever be deemed or held individually liable hereunder for any reason or cause whatsoever.

(d) The words "Lessor" and "Lessee" wherever used in this lease shall be construed to mean Lessors or Lessees in all cases where there is more than one lessor or lessee, and the necessary grammatical changes required to make the provisions hereof apply either to corporations or individuals, men or women, shall in all cases be assumed as though in each case fully expressed.

(e) The Lessor shall have the right to terminate this lease on the thirtieth day of April in any year if the Lessor proposes or is required, for any reason, to remodel, remove or demolish the Building or any substantial portion of it, or if the Lessor decides to sell the Building and the land under it, or if the Lessor's stockholders decide to sell sixty-six and two-thirds percent or more of the Lessor's capital stock (if the Lessor is a corporation), or if the Lessor decides to convey the prime leasehold (if any), or to make a ground lease, or to lease to one tenant for a term of ten years or more either all the Building or all the Building except the ground floor. Such termination shall become effective and conclusive by notice of the Lessor to the Lessee not less than ninety days prior to the thirtieth day of April fixed in the notice. No money or other consideration shall be payable by the Lessor to the Lessee for this right and the right hereby reserved to the Lessor shall inure to all purchasers, assignees, lessees, transferees and groundlessees, as the case may be and is in addition to all other rights of the Lessor.

(f) Provisions inserted herein or affixed hereto shall not be valid unless appearing in the duplicate original hereof held by the Lessor. In event of variation or discrepancy, the Lessor's duplicate shall control.

(g) Each provision hereof shall extend to and shall, as the case may require, bind and inure to the benefit of the Lessor and the Lessee and their respective heirs, legal representatives and successors, and assigns in the event this lease has been assigned with the express, written consent of the Lessor.

(h) The headings of sections are for convenience only and do not limit or construe the contents of the sections.

(i) Submission of this instrument for examination does not constitute a reservation of or option for the premises. The instrument becomes effective as a lease upon execution and delivery by both Lessor and Lessee.

(j) All amounts (other than rent) owed by the Lessee to the Lessor hereunder shall be paid within ten days from the date the Lessor renders statements of account therefor and shall bear interest at the rate of 7% per annum thereafter until paid.

(k) Provisions typed on the back of this lease and signed by the Lessor and the Lessee and all riders attached to this lease and signed by the Lessor and the Lessee are hereby made a part of this lease as though inserted at length in this lease.

(l) If the Lessee shall occupy the premises prior to the beginning of the term of this lease with the Lessor's consent, all the provisions of this lease shall be in full force and effect as soon as the Lessee occupies the premises. Rent for any period prior to the beginning of the term of this lease shall be fixed by agreement between the Lessor and the Lessee.

In Witness Whereof, the parties hereto have caused this indenture to be executed under their seals, on the date first above written.

LESSOR

By..(SEAL)

LESSEE

Lessee should sign name
in full as written in the
body of this lease.

......................(SEAL)
......................(SEAL)
......................(SEAL)
......................(SEAL)

Some office leases include a *recapture provision* within the assignment and subletting clause. This provision gives the landlord the right to recover any space that the tenant is unable to occupy or sublease. The landlord can then re-lease the space to a tenant of his or her own choice. Reaction to a recapture provision will vary with the tenant's size, financial strength, and space requirements. A tenant who sees a possibility of subleasing the space for a higher rent than that called for in the lease may object. On the other hand, the landlord is justified in keeping maximum control of the length of the tenants' leases and the economic terms of the tenancy agreements. Any disagreement concerning a clause or provision in the lease should be brought up during the negotiation period, before the lease is signed.

Services

The landlord's obligation to provide utility services should be explicitly stated, as this can have an important economic effect on both tenant and landlord. Some leases will specify that the landlord supply heating and air conditioning during business hours only. More favorable from the tenant's perspective are leases wherein the landlord agrees to furnish heating and air conditioning at a reduced, but comfortable, level during nighttime hours and over the weekend. After-hours heating and cooling are sometimes available to the tenant at cost. In these cases, the basis for the charges must be explicit in the lease.

The responsibility for electrical service also should be established. Landlords of large office buildings frequently supply electrical service without charge up to certain specified limits. In other cases, electricity may be resold by the landlord to the tenants, or each tenant could be separately metered and billed.

Possession

An office lease does not usually become void if the landlord fails to deliver possession of the premises on the date stated. Due to the magnitude of the work involved in fitting up an area to suit a particular tenant's needs, some leeway in meeting construction deadlines should be allowed. The owner's desire for income and high-quality tenants serves as a silent guarantee that possession will be surrendered as soon as circumstances allow. Tenants may insist, however, on a time limit on such delay.

The tenant's cooperation is vital in the initial alteration of space. Some leases allow the landlord to accelerate the beginning of the rental obligation period if the tenant delays in delivering the firm's space utilization plans.

Office Lease Concessions

Concessions are common in leasing office space. They are simply negotiable points in the lease terms that are decided in the prospective tenant's favor. They may involve almost any clause in the rental agreement. In order to be attractive, a concession must alleviate a basic problem or satisfy a particular desire of the prospect. On the other hand, concessions mean money to the owner and affect the total economic value of the lease. When negotiating lease terms, the property manager must balance the prospect's wants and needs with the owner's objectives in terms of the market situation.

Every leasing situation has its own bargaining criteria. As negotiator, the property manager must determine what priorities the concessions under consideration have in the minds of both parties. Negotiation is a process of give and take, and the first prerequisite of a successful negotiator is knowing which concessions will be sacrificed by one party in return for others deemed of greater value. When leasing office properties, the manager will find that prolonged negotiations are the rule rather than the exception.

Remodeling Office Space. One area of negotiation that reflects the impact of economic conditions is initial tenant alteration and remodeling. In the past, when space was at a premium, incoming tenants bore the expense of fitting up, or altering, an area to suit their needs. However, when the exodus to the suburbs began, many downtown office centers were left with vacancies. These tenant-hungry properties brought the situation full cycle; landlords became willing to pay the cost of extensive tenant alterations to get tenants into their buildings. These recurring cycles of tenant advantage—landlord advantage—tenant advantage are a normal phenomenon in the office building industry. They occur because of the long lead time required to plan, construct, and lease an office building.

Most large multistory office buildings have prescribed criteria for tenant alteration allowances, which may be expressed in terms of dollars per square foot that are available for alterations. Prospective tenants usually should not be told the dollar figure. They should be aware only of the *building standard,* a specific combination of amenities and alterations that the owner is willing to make free for the incoming tenant. The building standard might include any or all of the following items:

- two coats of paint on walls and interior partitions
- one telephone jack for every 150 square feet of rentable space
- one double 115-volt electrical outlet per 100 square feet of rentable space
- up to one linear foot of interior partitioning for each 15 square feet rented
- one door per each 30 linear feet of interior partitions
- decorator venetian blinds on all windows
- carpeting in enclosed areas; asbestos tile in open- and high-traffic areas
- acoustic tile ceiling
- air conditioning.

Tenants requiring alterations or additions beyond those itemized on the standards list must contract and pay for these services independently, after receiving approval from the landlord.

Many larger buildings with ongoing alteration and remodeling activity have their own construction crews or an administrative group that is responsible for contracting, coordinating, and supervising the work of engineers, architects, and construction workers for the remodeling project. In such cases, a schedule of cost estimates for the most frequent remodeling jobs can be made available to the tenant. Credit against construction costs will usually be given to the tenant for any of the building-standard allowance not used. The tenant is also often given the option of amortizing the construction costs over the term of the lease.

MAINTENANCE AND STAFFING OF OFFICE BUILDINGS

Once the negotiating process has been successfully completed and the new tenant has signed the lease and taken possession of the premises, the property manager should focus on maintaining good relations with the tenant. A high turnover rate means greater expense for the owner in terms of marketing space, remodeling costs, and lost rentals. Efficient maintenance is the best way to keep a tenant population happy and thereby avoid the high costs of turnover. Proper maintenance also preserves the worth of the property, another of the owner's foremost objectives.

A comprehensive preventative maintenance program should be set up according to the procedures described in Chapter 8. Regular inspections and preventative maintenance can cut repair and replacement costs and ensure uninterrupted service to tenants. Inspection forms for both the interior and exterior of office buildings are available through the Institute of Real Estate Management.

Unique Maintenance Requirements

Three areas of maintenance assume added significance when an office property is involved. Elevator operation, routine cleaning, and new construction in office properties differ from the same jobs in residential buildings. An additional consideration is that boilers and other large heating and air conditioning units must be maintained by highly skilled personnel. Often, local building codes will require certain equipment to be attended on a 24-hour basis.

Elevator Operation. In general, multistory office buildings are taller than their residential counterparts. Elevators in office buildings travel more miles and require more constant maintenance to ensure good service and cleanliness. The two principal concerns of the office property manager are a satisfactory schedule of elevator service and the efficient movement of large numbers of people during morning and evening rush hours. A minimum summons interval between elevators can be established for each floor by regularly dispatching cabs from both the ground floor and the top of the shaft.

Most buildings today are equipped with fully automated elevators. The traditional elevator operator has been replaced by the building receptionist or information officer. This person works the automated controls for the elevators and serves as a traffic director and general source of information. Modern automatic elevator installations are so complicated and expensive that most office building managers contract the maintenance of the elevators, shafts, and machinery to an outside firm specializing in this type of work. The contractor is then responsible for maintenance functions such as lubrication, cleaning, repair, and replacement.

Housekeeping. Unlike residential properties, office buildings endure heavy traffic during the day. Therefore, most public areas must be cleaned during night hours. This does not imply, however, that janitorial services are not needed during normal daytime hours to maintain washrooms, lobbies, corridors, and other public areas. In small buildings, the day janitor should also take care of minor repairs that tenants might request.

The other distinguishing feature of office properties is that management is usually responsible for having tenants' interior spaces cleaned. Night janitors are charged with cleaning the individual offices if neither the manager nor the tenants have separate service contracts with outside firms for office cleaning. The night crew is also responsible for janitorial jobs that cannot be performed during the day, such as washing and waxing common areas and vacuuming or mopping the lobby and elevator cabs. Most office buildings will require two shifts of janitorial personnel, a supervisor for each shift, and a general maintenance superintendent to coordinate the efforts of all janitorial crew members. A chief engineer is usually engaged to care for the physical plant and equipment.

Security. Security is becoming an increasingly important responsibility of management for all types of property. Office buildings, particularly large structures, present unique problems because of the high concentrations of occupants above ground level. Emergency procedures must be prepared for fires, power failures, water line breaks, explosions, bomb threats, and serious injuries or heart attacks to persons in the building. All these procedures and available security personnel must be coordinated with the building's electrical, mechanical, communication, and control equipment. The total security arrangements for such a wide scope of emergencies are sometimes referred to as the life support system of the building, but the term is not common among professional building managers. Advances in safety and security devices are occurring daily, and the professional property manager needs to keep informed of developments in this critical area of responsibility.

New Construction. The office manager is faced with the prospect of new construction each time a tenant moves in, since most tenants require some special alteration of the space to suit their needs. Again, depending on which alternative is economically advantageous, the manager may choose either to contract out for such work or to maintain a skilled on-site crew. In any case, the manager should cultivate a good working relationship with contractors or the supervisor of the construction crew since time is often of the essence when preparing space to lease.

Many office managers supplement revenue from the property by selling construction and remodeling work to existing tenants. Tenants often require minor alterations that must be undertaken at their own expense, and it is quite convenient for them to buy services through the manager's on-site crew or outside contracting firm. The services can be sold at a slight markup or provided at cost as an additional benefit to the tenant.

In general, building maintenance and operating personnel must fit into an efficient and cost-effective pattern. The need for permanent staff painters, window cleaners, carpenters, electricians, plumbers, garage keepers, and security guards will depend upon the size of the building and the needs of the tenants. Many of these jobs can be performed more economically on a contract basis. In recent years, an increasing number of office buildings have been turned over to specialized contracting firms that perform all the janitorial work.

The Building Owners and Managers Institute International (BOMI) has a training program available for building engineers and maintenance personnel, which covers all aspects of large equipment operation and maintenance. Completion of these courses leads to the designations of Systems Maintenance Technician (SMT) and Systems Maintenance Administrator (SMA).

MANAGEMENT ADMINISTRATION AND ACCOUNTING

Regardless of a building's size, a central office should be set up to oversee the management of the operating policy for the property. In small buildings where a resident manager or a business office is not economically viable, tenants and others involved in the operation of the property should be told where to reach the superintendent and the property manager. In larger buildings, the business office should be centrally located, tastefully decorated, and adequately staffed, following the guidelines set out in Chapter 10. Administrative procedures for data recording, filing, and expense accounting should conform to the general patterns outlined in Chapters 9 and 10. Because of the number of variables which must be accounted for and charged to tenants, office building administration requires close supervision on the part of the property manager.

One of the most comprehensive standardized systems of income and expense accounting available to the property manager has been developed by the Building Owners and Managers Association International. The advantage of this standard accounting method is that it discloses essential controls and facilitates intra-industry comparisons.

The BOMA Chart of Accounts provides a format for internal consistency of management accounting within a firm and facilitates comparison of the manager's operations with those of others locally and nationwide. BOMA also publishes an annual *Experience Exchange Report* containing local, regional, and national averages of operating income and expenses, plus other information, for office buildings of various sizes. Using the standard BOMA Chart of Accounts, the operating reports for a property can be checked against normative statistics compiled from industry experience. The property manager can then identify any areas of expense that seem too high and rate his or her own operating efficiency against that of other management operations.

SUMMARY

The need for office space has increased steadily over the past 50 years, during which time most American workers have left the agricultural and manufacturing segments of the economy. Today, a variety of business space is available. Predominant in metropolitan areas are multistory office buildings, usually owned by large institutional investors who are able to finance high construction and operating costs. Smaller developers have subsidized more modest office buildings of one to three stories in shopping centers, industrial parks, and suburban areas. Regardless of ownership or the size of the office building, the manager shoulders the responsibility for marketing and leasing space, maintaining the property, minimizing operating costs, and submitting financial reports to the owner.

In order to set a valid rental schedule and lease space effectively, the manager must conduct detailed regional, neighborhood, and property analyses. Building managers should give most attention to the demand for space by new businesses in the area, the expansion rate of existing tenants, and the number and type of tenants who wish to move into newer facilities. The rental prognosis for a specific building depends not only on the demand pattern for the area, but also on the building's condition, special features, and competition.

A uniform and realistic rental schedule reflects tenant preferences. The property manager needs to know the absolute minimum rent that can be charged to cover expenses and provide a return on investment. Then, by studying the market and rental schedules of comparable properties in the area, he or she can establish a base rent for a typical office space in the building. This base rent should be significantly higher than the minimum rent computed earlier. Finally, all office space in the building should be graded as superior or inferior to the standard space, depending on individual features, and priced accordingly.

The BOMA method of measuring rentable space may be used to determine how much actual occupiable space a prospective tenant will be paying for. Two factors have been devised to measure efficiency of space utilization. On a single-tenancy floor, the ratio of rentable to usable space is referred to as the *loss factor;* on a multiple-tenancy floor, this relationship is called the *load factor.* These factors should be taken into account when constructing a rental schedule.

Office space may be marketed in several ways: signs may be posted on the premises; brochures may be distributed; display ads may be placed in newspapers and magazines; or a direct-mail campaign may be developed to address the latent portion of the market. Public relations programs aimed at decision makers in prospective tenant organizations are often useful, as are referral networks including current tenants, business acquaintances, key contacts, and personal friends. Canvassing efforts and on-site rental centers are other methods of leasing space.

The first thing the manager must do is qualify the prospect in terms of spatial requirements. He or she must also analyze the nature of the prospect's business, the types of staff positions in the firm, the number of persons in each position, and the tasks that each performs. This information can be gathered on a visit to the tenant's current space.

The four basic categories of space usage that can be identified are single office space, multipersonnel areas, special facilities, and miscellaneous areas. The quality of the office space is at least as important as the quantity. Floor population, clerical-executive mix, and client image will determine the quality of space the prospect desires.

A skillful presentation of the available office space is imperative. All its advantages should be pointed out and the prospect's positive or negative reactions noted for future reference in negotiating the lease agreement. Office lease negotiations are usually complex and time consuming. Almost every clause in the lease agreement is a potential point for negotiation. It is especially important that the manager determine whether or not the prospective tenant requires the right to assign or sublet the space, and how he or she will react to a recapture provision. The landlord's obligation to provide heating, air conditioning, and electrical service should be carefully examined, as should be the method of calculating the escalation clause, if one is included. To protect the owner's best interests, the lease should contain a clause stating that the contract is not void if possession is delayed for a short period. The tenant, likewise, has a responsibility to deliver to the landlord without delay his or her space utilization plans so that the work involved in fitting up an area can be initiated.

Another lease point that must be negotiated to the satisfaction of both tenant and landlord is office space remodeling or alteration. Most large multistory office buildings now have prescribed criteria for tenant alteration allowances. Tenants who need alterations beyond the ones itemized in these building standards must absorb the cost themselves.

In office buildings, as in all rental properties, a preventative maintenance program is the surest way to promote favorable landlord-tenant relations. Office property maintenance entails elevator operation, cleaning services, and new construction. Elevators in office buildings are more heavily used than their residential counterparts, so cleanliness, a satisfactory schedule of service, and efficiency must be ensured. A night shift of janitorial personnel is responsible for major cleaning of public areas and individual offices, while a day shift cleans the washrooms, lobby, and corridors.

Tenant alteration or remodeling, a common requirement in office space, can be performed either by a skilled on-site crew or by an outside firm.

Management, direction, and operating policies for the building must be provided by a central office. The format and accounting system developed by BOMA to standardize financial reports on office properties can help the manager prepare operating reports and can facilitate intraindustry comparisons. Under the BOMA Chart of Accounts, income is divided into rental income, service income, and miscellaneous income. The categories of expense include operations, alterations, fixed charges, and financial expenses. Statements utilizing the standard BOMA format can then be compared to normative local, regional, and national income and expense statistics published in BOMA's annual *Experience Exchange Report.*

QUESTIONS: CHAPTER 13

1. Space on the third floor of an office building rents for $7.80 per square foot and has a loss factor of 1.2, while space on the fourth floor rents for $7.90 per square foot and has a loss factor of 1.1 The third floor space:

   I. is less expensive than the space on the fourth floor.
   II. would cost $205,920 for 22,000 square feet of *usable* space.

   a. I only   c. both I and II
   b. II only   d. neither I nor II

2. Office space which rents for $6.80 per square foot has a loss factor of 1.12; thus:

   I. 18,000 square feet of rentable space would contain 16,071 square feet of usable space.
   II. it would cost $167,552 per year to obtain 22,000 square feet of usable space.

   a. I only   c. both I and II
   b. II only   d. neither I nor II

3. A regional analysis for a subject office property:

   I. is unnecessary if the neighborhood analysis is thorough.
   II. usually contains the vacancy rates for comparable buildings.

   a. I only   c. both I and II
   b. II only   d. neither I nor II

4. Studies have shown that there are four key factors that influence most prospect firms to select office space. List them below in order of decreasing importance.

   a. _____   c. _____
   b. _____   d. _____

5. The base rate for an office building:

   I. should reflect the amenities of the space and competition in the area.
   II. is the lowest possible dollar-per-square foot figure; the actual rental schedule is always higher.

   a. I only   c. both I and II
   b. II only   d. neither I nor II

6. Write the equation for calculating the loss factor of office space below.

   _____

7. According to the BOMA method of measuring office space:

   I. rentable space includes elevator shafts and lobbies.
  II. columns used to support the building are deducted from the total area.

    a. I only   c. both I and II
    b. II only   d. neither I nor II

8. List four types of advertising that are especially effective when leasing office space.

    a. _____   c. _____
    b. _____   d. _____

9. List three additional methods of obtaining leads and prospective tenants.

    a. _____
    b. _____
    c. _____

10. Which advertising medium should a manager use when addressing the latent market for office space?

    _____

11. When calculating a prospect's spatial requirements, the manager should include filing space and an allowance for traffic circulation:

   I. at about 5 percent and 15 percent of the total office space, respectively.
  II. only if the prospect will be on a multitenant floor.

    a. I only   c. both I and II
    b. II only   d. neither I nor II

12. List the four general arguments a property manager can use to arouse a prospective tenant's interest in an office building.

    a. _____   c. _____
    b. _____   d. _____

13. An escalation clause in an office lease:

   I. provides that the rental rate will be increased annually by a specified standard dollar amount.
  II. is used to compensate for inflation and rising operating costs.

    a. I only   c. both I and II
    b. II only   d. neither I nor II

14. Tenant alterations and remodeling expenses in an office property:

    a.   are usually charged to the lessor.
    b.   are usually charged to the lessee.
    c.   are charged to the lessor when over the building standard.
    d.   can be amortized over the terms of the lease.

15. Maintenance of office properties differs significantly from residential property maintenance in that:

    I.   offices need more cleaning and routine housekeeping.
    II. new construction is less frequent in office space, but the jobs are usually larger.

    a.   I only   c.   both I and II
    b.   II only   d.   neither I nor II

16. The generally accepted method for measurement of floor area in an office building is:

    I.   the American National Standard of the Building Owners and Managers Association International (BOMA).
    II. the New York method.

    a.   I only   c.   both I and II
    b.   II only   d.   neither I nor II

14
Shopping Centers and Retail Property

As discussed in Chapter 1, retail space is the second major classification of commercial property. Retail establishments are places where commodities are sold in small quantities directly to the consumer. This chapter will focus on the predominant type of retail establishment—specialty and department stores.

Traditionally, retail merchants have tended to congregate in areas that were accessible to a large number of people. The historical result of this trend was the establishment of a central urban business district located at the focal point of public transportation facilities. The larger metropolitan areas also supported secondary concentrations of retail stores at outlying transportation junctures.

Mass production of automobiles during the 1920s not only changed the lifestyle of American families, but also brought about a shift in the location pattern of residences and retail centers. Slowly throughout the 1930s, and then with increased rapidity after World War II, mobile Americans began to move farther from the central business district and to rely less upon public transportation.

To capitalize on this automotive revolution, investors and retailers began to build freestanding sets of stores with facilities for on-site parking. These served as convenient retail outlets for the burgeoning residential neighborhoods on the fringes of the cities. A typical small shopping center of this type might contain a grocery store, a drugstore, and several other small retail establishments. Neighborhood and community center construction proliferated after the war years, and more ambitious projects were planned. By the 1950s, large retail and department stores realized that their economic survival depended on following the customers to the suburbs. At this point, the emphasis in retailing shifted from merely satisfying neighborhood demands to catering to the merchandise needs of trade areas covering miles rather than blocks. The large regional shopping center became prevalent.

The field of retail property management runs the gamut from small neighborhood stores to large shopping complexes. Small shopping centers of 4 to 10 stores usually require only exterior maintenance and financial administration from the manager, with the tenant assuming responsibility for interior upkeep. Major regional shopping centers, however, offer one of the greatest challenges in property management. Much of this chapter is devoted to the broader aspects of shopping center management.

CLASSIFICATION OF CENTERS

Shopping centers can be grouped by market area, pattern, or ownership. Whichever method is used, the major tenant of the center serves as the guide for classification. The retail store that serves as the focal point for a center is termed the *key tenant,* or *anchor store.*

Market Area Classifications

Categorization by market area is relatively simple because the size of the market area that a shopping center serves is reflected in the size of the center. Most commercial *strip centers* are located on the edge of urban areas or in the suburbs. They consist of approximately 10,000 to 30,000 square feet (4 to 10 retail spaces) on a main thoroughfare and are primarily for convenience shopping. The typical design for these districts is a straight line of stores set back far enough from the street to allow for perpendicular parking. These strip developments often are owner-managed, even if the owner is not one of the occupants, which is also common.

The *neighborhood center* is designed to provide convenience shopping for customers within a 1½-mile radius. It usually incorporates 15 to 20 stores located on about 3 acres of land and anchored by a supermarket. The neighborhood center usually contains a drugstore, a dry cleaner, and other small stores that need about 1,000 families to support their activities. In size, it will contain up to approximately 100,000 square feet.

The *community center,* anchored by a junior department store, usually occupies about 10 acres and includes from 20 to 70 stores. It draws customers from a 5-mile trading radius and depends on a minimum of 5,000 families for its support. In addition to the apparel and other goods offered by the department store, community centers usually have one or two supermarkets, a variety store, and small convenience stores. In sparsely populated areas of the country, a community center may serve customers from a wide geographical area. The square footage in a community normally ranges from 150,000 to 300,000 square feet, according to studies by the Urban Land Institute.

The *regional center* varies in size from 70 to 225 stores, serves a radius of 10 to 50 miles, and is supported by 50,000 to 150,000 families. Depending upon its size, the regional center houses as many as six major department stores, accompanied by food stores, satellite stores offering a range of general merchandise, restaurants, and banks.

The Urban Land Institute in its publication *Dollars & Sense of Shopping Centers* has designated the regional center as the second largest type of center, calling the largest type of shopping center a *super regional center,* although this nomenclature is not yet in widespread use. The largest centers may house as much as 1 million square feet or more of shops and appurtenant areas.

When leasing a retail location, the manager must find the tenant who is best suited to the available space and who will thus enjoy the greatest chance of success. The type of center will suggest guidelines to follow, although these conventions need not be accepted unquestioningly. A market analysis of the surrounding area will disclose the composition of the population within the trading radius, the median income of the families, the traffic patterns for the area, and the competition. It is quite possible that less than 1,000 families could support a neighborhood center if all had above-average incomes. On the other hand, the prognosis would be bleak for a community center located in an area where most of the 5,000 families needed for its support were on welfare.

Pattern Classifications

Several basic design patterns, illustrated on the next page, have emerged during the 40-year evolution of the shopping center. One type, the neighborhood *strip center,* was mentioned earlier. A variation on it is the *L-shaped center.* Anchor tenants (shown as shaded portions in the illustrations) are usually located at the end of each leg of the L.

Another spin-off from the straight strip center is the *U-shaped center,* formed by a line of stores at right angles to each end of the strip. Because they are larger, U-shaped centers often serve entire communities and can have as many as three key tenants— one at each end of the U, with the major anchor store in the middle of the strip.

The stores in a *cluster-design* shopping center form a rectangle bounded by parking facilities on all four sides. The anchor store usually occupies one side of the rectangle and extends from the periphery to the center of the cluster. Cluster-design centers may be open or enclosed and may serve a local community or a region, depending on size.

Three anchor stores can be accommodated by either a *T-design* or *triangle center.* Both patterns provide for parking on all sides and can be either open or enclosed areas. They may serve a community or an entire region.

Regional centers are most often of the *dumbbell* design. Basically, this pattern consists of two strips of stores that face each other along a mall, with an anchor tenant at each end and parking on all four sides. The *double-dumbbell* center accommodates four key tenants. One dumbbell runs longitudinally and the other latitudinally. The malls for each dumbbell segment meet to form a central court. Dumbbell centers can be either single- or multilevel, open or enclosed. Split-level, enclosed double-dumbbell centers are now the preferred regional type.

Owner Classifications

A shopping center can be owned by a single individual, a group of persons forming a partnership, or by a corporation. Almost all shopping centers are financed by one or more long-term mortgages; in fact, it is not unusual for large centers to have several types of ownership and debts in their financial structure. The land, for instance, may be owned by one entity and the stores by another. In most cases, large shopping centers are financed partly by the key tenants and partly by the owner or developer. Major chain department stores often own their buildings and lease or purchase the land for them from the developer or shopping center owner. Several department stores might agree to finance, as a joint venture, the construction of a large enclosed mall.

Figure 40: PATTERN CLASSIFICATIONS

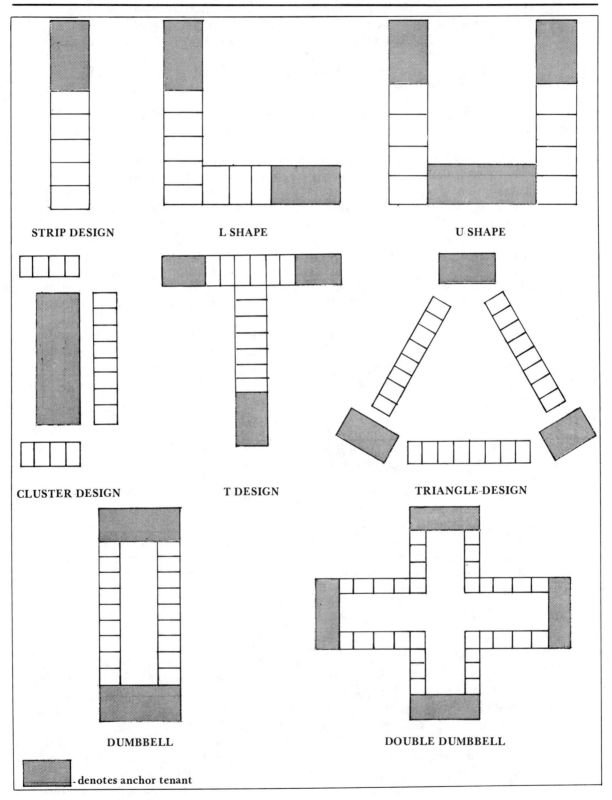

STRIP DESIGN   L SHAPE   U SHAPE

CLUSTER DESIGN   T DESIGN   TRIANGLE DESIGN

DUMBBELL   DOUBLE DUMBBELL

- denotes anchor tenant

Corporations are subject to different tax regulations than individuals, and not all owners have the same overall financial objectives for their investments. Thus, it is essential for the manager to know the nature of the debt relationship, the type of ownership, and the implications these have for the operation of the center.

MARKETING RETAIL SPACE

Leasing is one of the retail property manager's most critical activities. Because each retail outlet in a shopping center depends on the traffic generated by other outlets, and because percentage leases giving the owner a vested interest in the success of the retailer are often used, quality tenants and the proper mix of types of stores are a must in retail space.

Vacant stores cannot be leased unless prospective tenants are being attracted to the premises. As with other types of property, retail space can be advertised by signs, ads, radio spots, brochures, and letters. The most widely used strategies are brochures, direct-mail campaigns, and personal contact with prospective tenants. Broker referral campaigns and in-house or outside leasing agents are other sources of qualified tenants.

Advertising

Most people who are interested in retail space do not look for leasing sites in the newspaper. They drive through the area where they wish to locate and scout for signs on available locations.

Display ads are usually placed in the financial section of metropolitan papers to promote large retail properties.

Display advertising in selected periodicals and trade journals is a practical marketing tactic for some types of retail space. A large new regional shopping mall, for example, might run display ads in the regional issues of news weeklies to create a prestigious image that will attract potential tenants. Even more to the purpose is display advertising done in *Shopping Center World, National Mall Monitor,* and *Chain Store Age*— trade journals that are read by tenants, owners, and managers. One can detect the appeal to status and prestige in the sample ad, Figure 41. This kind of advertising is most potent during the initial lease-up of a newly developed center. Advertising spots aired over local radio stations are a viable advertising method for very large commercial developments.

Brochures

A concise, readable, and tastefully designed brochure should be distributed to a select group of potential tenants. It may highlight a single property or an entire shopping center. Location maps and layout diagrams will interest leasing agents as well as potential tenants. Lease terms should not be spelled out, for fear of leading a prospect to make a premature judgment before understanding the property's advantages. Parts of one effective brochure appear as Figure 42.

We've set our sites on San Diego.

As one of the nation's leading shopping center developers for nearly four decades, we pride ourselves on choosing the finest locations for the innovative and responsive retail projects we have become known for.

We think San Diego is the place to be.

An ideal climate and an expanding economic base has helped make San Diego the fastest growing city in the West. It's one of the reasons we moved our corporate headquarters here in 1982. And it's also the reason that by the end of the year we will be building or expanding regional retail centers on three prime sites in San Diego county.

Horton Plaza, San Diego
Designed to be a comprehensive urban center in the heart of downtown San Diego, Horton Plaza will feature Nordstrom, Robinson's, The Broadway and Mervyn's; theatres, restaurants and a myriad of business and personal services when it opens in mid-1985. Shops and boutiques as individual as the proprietors who own them will provide the character and further the appeal of this 900,000-square-foot multi-use complex. A daily "bazaar" of events with sidewalk vendors, noon concerts, street plays and art exhibits will delight San Diego shoppers and visitors.

University Towne Centre, La Jolla
Since opening in 1977, University Towne Centre has consistently been one of the Hahn company's most successful centers. Now, upscale expansion plans, including a new Nordstrom, will provide additional opportunities on two levels of specialty shops and restaurants with outdoor deck areas for dining and community activities.

North County Fair, Escondido
This two-level climate-controlled complex in Escondido will feature six department stores — JCPenney, May Co., Robinson's, The Broadway, Nordstrom and a sixth to be named — in addition to 165 specialty shops, restaurants and extensive community facilities such as multi-screen movie theatre, bicycle trails and a family fitness center. Scheduled opening is fall 1985.

For leasing information, contact John Visconsi, Hahn Development Leasing, 569-4949.

▦ Ernest W. Hahn, Inc.

3666 Kearny Villa Road San Diego, CA 92123 (619) 569-4949

Ernest W. Hahn, Inc. is one of the nation's largest shopping center developers, with 42 centers in operation around the United States. Reprinted with permission.

Figure 42: RETAIL BROCHURE

Reprinted with permission of Morris & Fellows, Inc.

THE CENTER

Ashby's Village is a unique specialty retail center combining ease of access, a decidedly pleasant shopping environment and a merchandise mix targeted to the upscale, sophisticated market. The traditional architectural statement is carefully tailored to market tastes and designed to direct the shoppers' attention to each store front.

Ashby's Village offers to Greenville a convenient and complete shopping experience featuring fashion apparel and accessories, home furnishings and decorative items, gifts, leisure and recreational goods and personal services.

THE MAJOR

The center is anchored by Ashby's, an upscale branded ladies clothier selling nationally recognized labels and designer fashions at least 20% below retail. A subsidiary of Best Products, Ashby's adds this 13,000 square foot store to locations throughout Virginia, the Carolinas and Florida. An aggressive merchandiser and advertiser, Ashby's prides itself in creating exceptional retail sales volumes in beautifully appointed stores with emphasis on efficient and friendly customer service. Ashby's will set the tone of a merchandise blend geared to the market's elevated lifestyle and taste levels.

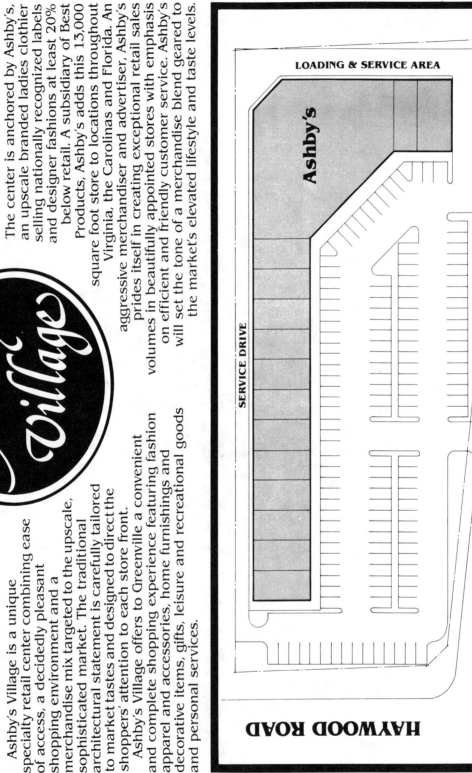

31,000 SQ. FT. • 140 SPACES

THE MARKET

Affluence and activity are the hallmarks of the Greenville marketplace. The Greenville County trade area contains 280,311 residents, with 178,397 people living within a ten minute drive of the center. Greenville is nationally noted for its high quality of life. Area industry creates an employment base of white collar and skilled technical personnel. Traditional southern values, a family orientation and high cultural and educational awareness combine to create a strong sense of community.

The primary market mean income of $24,896, well in excess of national norms, is expected to grow to $32,721 by 1987, an increase of 31.5%. Households earning above $50,000 annually will increase by 118% in that same period.

This situation signifies a healthy and growing discretionary income available for retail expenditure. The market residents' average age of 27.6 combines with the elevated personal income levels to create an active consumer lifestyle. Forty-four percent of the market population falls into the desirable "high needs" age group of 21 to 49 years old. This valuable group traditionally exhibits spending patterns in positive disproportion to its share of the population base.

Ashby's Village enjoys a highly visible site exposed to 40,000 cars per day. The site is adjacent to a major Interstate interchange, between affluent residential areas and major shopping magnets.

GREENVILLE, SOUTH CAROLINA PRIMARY MARKET PROFILE
1987 Forecast

AGE		HOUSEHOLD INCOME	
0-17	29%	-$10,000	3%
18-20	4%	$10,000-14,999	6%
21-29	15%	$15,000-24,999	39%
30-39	18%	$25,000-49,999	32%
40-49	12%	$50,000+	20%
50-64	12%		
65+	9%		
Mean Age 32.2		Mean Income $32,721	

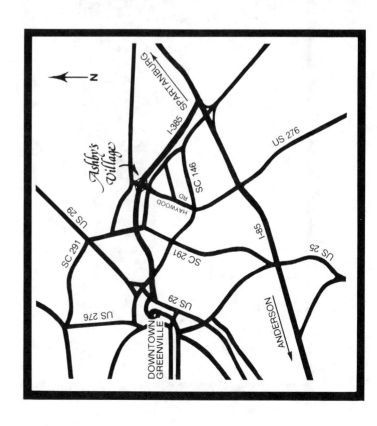

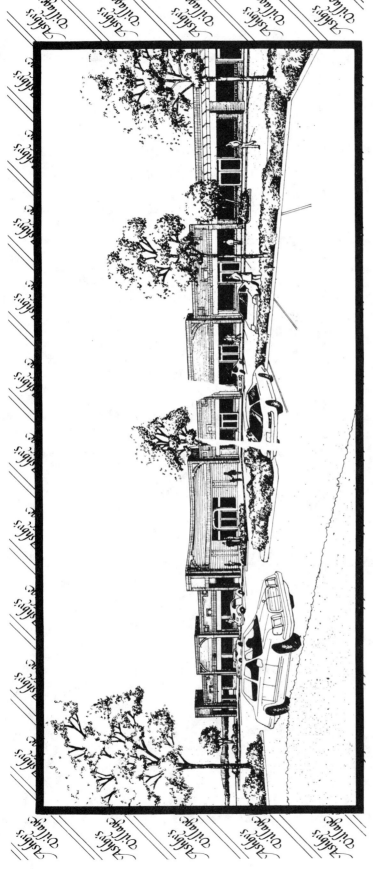

THE DEVELOPER

Retail Properties Group, Ltd., was founded for the purpose of developing high quality commercial real estate throughout the Southeast, with emphasis on retail properties. The development experience of the company principals encompasses site selection and land assembly, financing, project design and construction supervision and leasing. A diverse and extensive real estate history includes development of office complexes, redevelopment and adaptive re-use of older properties, assembly and acquisition of land for office, retail and mixed-use facilities, and management of real estate portfolios for major financial institutions. Special assignment brokerage skills have been instrumental in selecting retail, office and apartment sites for premier national developers. Retail experience includes all facets of shopping center development, and all sizes of centers, including super-regional malls of 1,000,000 square feet. From the location and assessment of development opportunities to the supervision of design, construction, operations and marketing functions, Retail Properties Group is a solid, creative and dependable real estate resource.

For leasing information contact:

David Glenn   803/271-3894
710 E. McBee Avenue,
Greenville, SC   29601

R. Kent Rose   404/255-9266
290 Carpenter Drive, Building 300,
Atlanta, GA   30328

Direct Mail

Direct mailings are the most popular vehicle for advertising retail centers. Mailing lists should include only those companies most likely to become tenants. Names can be obtained from the Yellow Pages, or from a more sophisticated source such as the *Dun & Bradstreet Reference Book* or the *Retail Tenant Prospect Directory* published by the *National Mall Monitor.*

Publicity and Public Relations

A unique characteristic of retail properties is that individual tenants must advertise and publicize the property in an effort to attract consumers for their goods. Advertisements taken out by an individual merchant or a group of merchants in one center draw attention to that shopping center. The added exposure gained from these ads increases sales for existing tenants and enhances the property's appeal to prospective tenants. An ongoing promotional effort is so integral to the success of a retail store or shopping complex that many leases contain a provision establishing a merchants association. Tenants must pay a membership fee based on square footage and spend a percentage of gross sales on joint advertising for the center.

Some regional shopping centers publish their own newspaper sections containing advertisements paid for by individual tenants. These may be distributed as supplements to local papers, either by direct mail or carrier. Since the tenants are required in their leases to advertise in this newspaper periodically, the shopping center reaps the benefits of free publicity while making newspaper advertising more affordable for its tenants and enlarging the trade area.

In general, community centers are the smallest type of shopping complex to require sustained or joint promotional programs, while all regional centers will certainly feel the need for organized, full-time promotion. Promotional programs for large regional centers often are under the control of a salaried on-site director who may organize flower and plant shows, art exhibits, antique shows, and seasonal events to be held in the shopping center.

When deciding whether to hire a salaried on-site person for promotion or an outside advertising agency, the manager should remember the basic principle that advertising costs should not exceed 20 percent of the total operating budget for the center.

Leasing Agents

Besides serving as a source of information to prospective tenants, brochures and direct-mail pieces can solicit the cooperation of outside brokers and leasing agents. The manager can encourage key commercial space brokers in the area to bring prospects to the building by offering a commission split or other financial incentive. Broker referral campaigns such as this can increase the property's exposure in the market. Many retail property management firms use in-house leasing agents in the initial rent-up of a new development. They are usually paid on a salaried basis and spend much of their time contacting proprietors of prosperous shops in the area and canvassing for other desirable tenants.

International Council of Shopping Centers

The International Council of Shopping Centers (ICSC) is a special-interest organization composed of retail property owners, managers, and users. Since most large chain stores and other prospective tenants are ICSC members, this organization can be serviceable to managers who are leasing retail space. ICSC publishes a directory of its members and sponsors an annual convention where retail tenants and managers can meet. It also sponsors two training programs, leading to designations of: Certified Shopping Center Manager (CSM) for managers and Certified Marketing Director (CMD) for center marketing professionals.

PERCENTAGE LEASE NEGOTIATIONS

Retail merchants must be qualified in much the same manner as office tenants are screened. The prospect firm must be financially solvent and compatible with other tenants in the center. With retail space, the *mix* of tenant types and locations is a prevailing concern. Stores should be placed so that traffic generated by one benefits the others, and so that competition is not a detriment. In many cases, two or more businesses of the same kind in a center stimulate competition and add to the total volume of business transacted. In other situations, customer traffic is merely divided between the two retail outlets, and neither profits. For example, if a strip center already has one grocery store, a second supermarket located in that center probably would fail. A cleaning establishment or a laundromat would be a more likely candidate for the center.

The manager must know the market and exercise good judgment when deciding on tenant mix in the shopping center. Industry statistics compiled by the International Council of Shopping Centers show the percentage of total shopping center space typically allotted to each type of store (department store, drugstore, women's specialty shop, tobacco shop, shoe store, etc.). For example, more than 7 percent of the total space in most regional shopping centers is used by food stores, about 23 percent by clothing stores, 6 percent by shoe stores, and 4 percent by gift and specialty shops. These figures can guide the retail manager in selecting the tenant population and the best tenant mix.

The location of the vacant space within the shopping center also has an impact on tenant selection. In a large regional center, a men's clothing store is more suitably situated between a men's shoe store and a tobacco shop than between an ice cream parlor and a women's dress shop. Customers attracted to the shoe store, the tobacco shop, or the clothing store will overflow into the other two outlets, increasing sales for all three merchants.

After evaluating a merchant in terms of tenant mix in the center, the manager should take a serious look at the prospect's needs. Are the parking facilities, gross amount of leasable space, and customer market in the area suitable for the prospect's type of business? These questions and others are raised in Figure 43, the retail tenant requirement worksheet. The manager should be certain that the prospect is the best possible merchant for the particular space and that, given the market, he or she will do the highest possible volume of business at that location. Financial backing is also

Figure 43: RETAIL CLIENT REQUIREMENTS

DATE: _____

COMPANY: _____ ADDRESS: _____

CONTACT: _____ POSITION: _____ PHONE: _____

TYPE OF BUSINESS: _____

LAND REQUIREMENTS

Maximum Price Per Square Foot $ _____
Minimum Square Feet Required _____
Dimensions _____ By _____
Corner Location _____ Yes __·__ No _____
Desired Parking Ratio _____ To _____

BUILDING REQUIREMENTS

Typical Building Size (Square Feet) _____
Dimensions _____ By _____
Typical Building Costs ($/Sq. Ft.) _____

ACQUISITION REQUIREMENTS

Buy — Yes ☐ No ☐
Ground Lease — Yes ☐ No ☐
   Minimum _____ Years
   Percent to Investor _____ %
   Subordination _____ Yes ☐ No ☐
Build-To-Suit — Yes ☐ No ☐
   Maximum Lease Term _____ Years
   Annual Rent $ _____ Gross ☐ Net ☐
   Financial Strength of Lease Signature $ _____
Preferred Developers _____

SHOPPING CENTER LOCATION Yes ☐   No ☐

Neighborhood ☐   Community ☐   Regional ☐   Freestanding ☐
Desired Co-Tenants _____

EXISTING OPERATION DATA

Areas Presently Operating In _____
Number of Units _____ Attach List of Addresses of Existing Units

DEMOGRAPHICS REQUIRED

Trading Area Radius _____ Miles
Distance Between Units _____
Population In Trading Area _____
Average Household Income ($/Yr.) _____

EXPANSION PLANS

Primary Areas _____

_____ Quota _____

ACTION TO TAKE & ACTION TAKEN

_____
_____
_____
_____
_____

SALESMAN

_____

DISTRIBUTION

Name _____

Office _____

FORM #327

OTHER PERTINENT DATA

Reprinted with permission by Grubb & Ellis Commercial Brokerage

important. The tenant must be solid enough to pay for or obtain financing for tenant alterations, fixtures, inventory, advertising, rent, percentage rent, insurance, maintenance, and other operating expenses.

A merchant's success in a given location hinges upon accurate qualification. After being qualified, the tenant is shown the space, and the leasing process moves into the final negotiating stages.

Percentage Leases

Whether or not a percentage lease can be negotiated with a prospective tenant will depend primarily upon the attraction of a location to retail trade. Because it is difficult to forecast future rental value, a percentage lease usually is used to lease retail space for more than 3 to 5 years. Most percentage leases require payment of either a *fixed minimum rental* or a *percentage rent* based on gross sales, whichever is greater. For example, if the fixed minimum rental is $500 per month and the percentage rent is 5 percent of gross sales, a tenant who has a sales volume of $12,000 would pay $600 rent for that month ($12,000 × .05 = $600). However, if gross sales fell to $8,000 in the following month, the tenant would pay the $500 minimum rent, since 5 percent of $8,000 in gross sales is only $400. Such leases are often called *minimum-guaranteed* percentage leases.

There are several other types of percentage leases: straight percentage, variable scale, and maximum. Under a *straight percentage* lease, the rental rate is based solely on a percentage of the gross income of the business, with no minimum guaranteed rent. This type of lease is uncommon, and it is employed only in unusual circumstances, such as distressed property, or for interim or seasonal occupancy.

With a *variable scale,* the percentage rental rate changes according to the volume of business done. If, for example, the percentage rate is 6 percent of the first $10,000 income per month and 4 percent of all income over that amount, the lease is on a decreasing variable scale, like Figure 44.

Conversely, a lease might specify a rental schedule of 5 percent on sales up to $10,000 and 5.5 percent on sales over $10,000. This increasing variable schedule reflects the fact that a retailer's costs do not necessarily increase in proportion to the sales volume. It allows the lessor to share in the extra profits of higher gross sales. A *maximum* percentage lease has a clause setting a ceiling on the amount of rent to be paid.

The advantage of a percentage lease from the tenant's point of view is that it is a long-term lease with a fair minimum rental, obligating the tenant to pay additional amounts *only* when business volume justifies an increase. From the manager's and owner's perspective, the percentage lease implies that any new business is due to the tenant's location. The owner is allowed to share in the increasing value of the business volume and the location.

Negotiation

The percentage lease contains most of the standard rights and obligations of landlord and tenant stipulated in other lease forms. The negotiation process usually centers

Figure 44: PERCENTAGE STORE LEASE

No._____

STORE LEASE
PERCENTAGE RENTAL

Lessor:_____

_____

_____

Lessee:_____

_____

_____

Premises:_____

_____

_____

Term:_____

From_____ 19____

To_____ 19____

Rent per Month, $_____

Rent per Annum, $_____

Rent per Term, $_____

SORG PRINTING COMPANY OF ILLINOIS

© Building Managers Association of Chicago. Reprinted
with permission.

STORE LEASE—PERCENTAGE RENTAL—FORM A (Revised 1976)

THIS INDENTURE, made ...., 19........, **Witnesseth:** ....

.... **Lessor,**

hereby leases unto ....

.... **Lessee,**

and Lessee accepts the **Premises** known as ....

....

....

for the **Term** of ....

commencing ...., 19........, and ending ...., 19........, unless sooner terminated as provided herein, to be occupied and used by Lessee for

....

In Consideration Thereof, the Parties Covenant and Agree: 1. RENT: Lessee shall pay to Lessor, or ....

.... in coin or currency which, at the time or times of payment, is legal tender for public and private debts in the United States of America,

at .... or elsewhere as designated from time to time by Lessor's notice:

(a) **Fixed Rental:** the sum of ....Dollars ($..........................)

in installments as follows: ....

....

....

....

....

....

.... payable one each in advance on the first day of every calendar month

.... of the term and at the current rate for fractions of a month if the term shall end or be terminated on any day other than the last day of any month;

(b) **Percentage Rental:** the further sums promised in the "PERCENTAGE RENTAL PROVISIONS," incorporated herein as part of this Section 1;

(c) **All Other Sums** payable hereunder within ten days after Lessor renders statements of account therefor unless otherwise provided therein; and

(d) **Interest** at 7% per annum from due date of and upon each defaulted obligation until paid.

All of said sums and the interest thereon constitute RENT accruing hereunder.

To exhibit the premises to prospective tenants, purchasers or others; (d) To display during the last ninety days of the term without hindrance or molestation by Lessee "For Rent" and similar signs on windows or elsewhere in or on the premises; (e) During the last ninety days of the term or at any time after Lessee abandons the premises, to enter and decorate, remodel, repair, alter or otherwise prepare the premises for reoccupancy; (f) To take any and all measures, including inspections, repairs, alterations, additions and improvements to the premises or to the building as may be necessary or desirable for the safety, protection or preservation of the premises or of the Building or Lessor's interests, or as may be necessary or desirable in the operation of the building.

Lessor may enter upon the premises and may exercise any or all of the foregoing rights hereby reserved without being deemed guilty of an eviction or disturbance of Lessee's use or possession and without being liable in any manner to Lessee.

5. DEFAULT UNDER OTHER LEASE: If the term of any lease, other than this lease, made by Lessee with Lessor be terminated or terminable after the making of this lease because of any default by Lessee under such other lease, that fact shall empower Lessor, at Lessor's sole option, (a) to terminate this lease, or (b) to add any sums due to Lessor under the other lease to the Rent payable under this lease. The exercise of above rights becomes effective by Lessor's notice only.

6. WAIVER OF CLAIMS: To the extent permitted by law, Lessee releases Lessor and Lessor's agents and servants from, and waives all claims for damage to person or property sustained by Lessee or any occupant of the Building or premises resulting from the Building or premises or any part of either or any equipment or appurtenance becoming out of repair, or resulting from any accident in or about the Building, or resulting directly or indirectly from any act or neglect of any tenant or occupant of the Building or of any other person, including Lessor's agents and servants. This Section 6 shall apply especially, but not exclusively, to the flooding of basements or other sub-surface areas, and to damage caused by refrigerators, sprinkling devices, air-conditioning apparatus, water, snow, frost, steam, excessive heat or cold, falling plaster, broken glass, sewage, gas, odors or noise, or the bursting or leaking of pipes or plumbing fixtures, and shall apply equally whether any such damage results from the act or neglect of Lessor or of other tenants, occupants or servants in the Building or of any other person, and whether such damage be caused or result from any thing or circumstance above mentioned or referred to, or any other thing or circumstance whether of a like nature or of a wholly different nature. If any such damage, whether to the demised premises or to the Building or any part thereof, or whether to Lessor or to other tenants in the Building, result from any act of neglect of Lessee, Lessor may, at Lessor's option, repair such damage and Lessee shall, upon demand by Lessor, re-imburse Lessor forthwith for the total cost of such repairs. Lessee shall not be liable for any damage caused by its act or neglect if Lessor or a tenant has recovered the full amount of the damage from insurance and the insurance company has waived in writing its right of subrogation against Lessee. All property belonging to Lessee or any occupant of the premises that is in the Building or the premises shall be there at the risk of Lessee or other person only, and Lessor shall not be liable for damage thereto or theft or misappropriation thereof.

7. HOLDING OVER: If Lessee retains possession of the premises or any part thereof after the termination of the term by lapse of time or otherwise, Lessee shall pay Lessor rent at double the rate of rental and interest thereon, specified in section 1, for the time Lessee thus remains in possession, and in addition thereto, shall pay Lessor all damages sustained by reason of Lessee's retention of possession. If Lessee remains in possession of the premises or any part thereof after termination of the term by lapse of time or otherwise, such holding over shall, at the election of Lessor, expressed in a written notice to Lessee and not otherwise, constitute a renewal of this lease for one year. Lessor's acceptance of any rent after holding over does not renew this lease. The provisions of this section do not waive Lessor's rights of reentry or any other right hereunder.

8. SUBLETTING OR ASSIGNMENT OR TRANSFER OF CONTROL: Lessee shall not allow or permit any transfer of this lease or any interest under it or any lien upon Lessee's interest by operation of law or assign or convey this lease or any interest under

2. SERVICE: Lessor shall furnish: (a) Heat (unless by special provision herein Lessee shall furnish heat) whenever, in Lessor's judgment, necessary for the comfortable use of the premises, in so much thereof as at the date of this lease is equipped for heating, daily except Sundays and holidays during the customary business hours for Lessee's stated use of the premises in the vicinity, but not earlier than 8 a.m. or later than 6 p.m. on any day unless specifically stated herein.

(b) Water from city mains through existing pipes, for which Lessee shall pay at rates fixed by Lessor.

(c) Electricity from existing wiring and connections if and so long as Lessor shall generate or distribute electric current in the building. So long as Lessor furnishes electric current, Lessee shall obtain all current used in or about the premises from Lessor and shall pay Lessor therefor at the prevailing public utility rates and charges for similar services as measured by meter; provided, however, that direct current demand charges may, at the election of Lessor, be estimated on any reasonable basis; and provided further, that Lessor shall not be obligated to furnish light bulb service. Lessee shall give Lessor written notice of any error of any type whatever in any statement of account for electric current within sixty days from the date of each such statement. Unless such notice is given, the statement of account shall be deemed correct and Lessor shall not be obligated to make refund to Lessee for any error therein. Upon not less than thirty days notice, Lessor may cease to furnish electricity to the premises without any responsibility to Lessee except to connect, within the period of notice, the wiring system of the premises with another source of supply of electricity, either direct or alternating current. Lessor may change electrical service and supply, upon at least thirty days notice, from direct current to alternating current without any liability of Lessor to Lessee.

Lessee shall pay Lessor's charges for water and electricity within five days after the billing therefor unless otherwise stated in the statements of account. Lessee's failure to pay promptly any such charge shall entitle Lessor, upon not less than five days' notice, to discontinue furnishing the service not paid for, and no such discontinuance shall be deemed an eviction or disturbance of Lessee's use of the premises or render Lessor liable to Lessee for damages or relieve Lessee from performance of Lessee's obligations hereunder. Lessee shall pay for all electricity and water used during alterations, repairs, and decorating made in the premises during the term, or made at any time in consequence of any default by Lessee. Lessor provides no janitor service in the premises and does not warrant that any of the services above mentioned will be free from interruptions caused by war, insurrection, civil commotion, riots, acts of God or the enemy or Government action, repairs, renewals, improvements, alterations, picketing, whether legal or illegal, accidents, inability of Lessor to obtain fuel or supplies or any other cause or causes beyond the reasonable control of the Lessor. Any such interruption shall never be deemed an eviction or disturbance of Lessee's use and possession of the premises or any part thereof, or render Lessor liable to Lessee for damages, or relieve Lessee from full performance of Lessee's obligations under this lease.

3. LESSOR'S TITLE: Nothing herein contained shall empower Lessee to do any act which can, may or shall cloud or encumber Lessor's title. Lessee's rights are and shall always be subordinate to the lien of any mortgage or mortgages now or hereafter placed upon the Building or any underlying leasehold estate and to all advances made or hereafter to be made upon the security thereof, and Lessee shall execute such further instruments subordinating this lease to the lien or liens of any such mortgage or mortgages or to any such underlying lease or leases as shall be requested by Lessor. Lessor's demise, if any, of subsidewalk space, or of any space outside the lines of the lot or lots whereon the Building stands, conveys only Lessor's rights thereto. If, at any time during the term, any municipality or public authority shall (a) take possession of all or any part of such space, this lease shall continue without abatement or diminution of Rent; (b) require compensation for such space, Lessee will pay to Lessor amount or amounts equal thereto during compensable portions of the term hereof. This lease does not grant any rights to light or air over any property except over public streets, alleys or ways kept open by public authority.

4. RESERVED RIGHTS: Lessor reserves the following rights: (a) To change the name or street address of the building without notice or liability of Lessor to Lessee; (b) To install and maintain a sign or signs on the exterior of the building; (c)

it, or sublet the premises or any part thereof, or permit the use or occupancy of the premises or any part thereof by any one other than Lessee. If Lessee is a corporation and if, during the term of this lease, the ownership of the shares of stock which constitute control of Lessee changes by reason of sale, gift or death, Lessor may at any time thereafter terminate this lease by giving Lessee written notice of such termination at least sixty days prior to the date of termination stated in the notice. The receipt of rent after such change of control shall not affect Lessor's rights under the preceding sentence.

9. CONDITION OF THE PREMISES: Lessee has examined the premises before signing this lease and is satisfied with the condition thereof, excepting only such alterations, improvements, repairs, decorating and cleaning, if any, which are specifically provided for herein. Lessee's taking possession shall be conclusive evidence as against Lessee that the premises were in good order and satisfactory condition when Lessee took possession hereunder. No promise of Lessor to alter, remodel, improve, repair, decorate or clean the premises or any part thereof, and no representation respecting the condition of the premises or the Building, has been made by Lessor to Lessee, unless the same is contained herein or made a part hereof. At the termination of this lease by lapse of time or otherwise, Lessee shall return the premises and all equipment and fixtures therein in as good condition as when Lessee took possession, ordinary wear and tear excepted, failing which Lessor may restore the premises, equipment and fixtures to such condition and Lessee shall pay the cost thereof upon request.

10. ALTERATIONS: Lessee shall not make any alterations in or additions to the premises without Lessor's advance written consent in each and every instance. Lessor's decision to refuse such consent shall be conclusive. If Lessor consents to such alterations or additions, before commencement of the work or delivery of any materials onto the premises or into the Building, Lessee shall furnish Lessor with plans and specifications, names and addresses of contractors, copies of contracts, necessary permits and indemnification in form and amount satisfactory to Lessor and waivers of lien against any and all claims, costs, damages, liabilities and expenses which may arise in connection with the alterations or additions. Whether Lessee furnishes Lessor the foregoing or not, Lessee hereby agrees to hold Lessor harmless from any and all liabilities of every kind and description which may arise out of or be connected in any way with said alterations or additions. All additions and alterations shall be installed in a good, workmanlike manner and only new, high-grade materials shall be used. Before commencing any work in connection with alterations or additions, Lessee shall furnish Lessor with certificates of insurance from all contractors performing labor or furnishing materials insuring Lessor against any and all liabilities which may arise out of or be connected in any way with said additions or alterations. Lessee shall pay the cost of all such alterations and additions and also the cost of decorating the premises occasioned by such alterations and additions. Upon completing any alterations or additions, Lessee shall furnish Lessor with contractors' affidavits and full and final waivers of lien and receipted bills covering all labor and materials expended and used. All alterations and additions shall comply with all insurance requirements and with all ordinances and regulations of the City of Chicago or any department or agency thereof and with the requirements of all statutes and regulations of the State of Illinois or of any department or agency thereof. Lessee shall permit Lessor to supervise construction operations in connection with alterations or additions if Lessor requests to do so. All additions, alterations, hardware, non-trade fixtures and all improvements, temporary or permanent, in or upon the premises, whether placed there by Lessee or by Lessor, shall, unless Lessor requests their removal, become Lessor's property and shall remain upon the premises at the termination of this lease by lapse of time or otherwise without compensation or allowance or credit to Lessee. If, upon Lessor's request, Lessee does not remove said additions, hardware, non-trade fixtures and improvements, Lessor may remove the same and the Lessee shall pay the cost of such removal to Lessor upon demand. If Lessee does not remove Lessee's furniture, floor coverings, trade fixtures and other personal property of all kinds from the premises

If Lessee furnishes heat, Lessee shall maintain the temperature in the premises high enough to prevent the freezing of water in plumbing fixtures and all other damage caused by low temperature. (s) Unless Lessor gives advance written consent, neither Lessee, nor any trustee, receiver, assignee or any other person acting for or on behalf of Lessee, Lessee's estate or creditors, shall conduct an auction in the premises. (t) In addition to all other liabilities for breach of any covenant of this Section 11, Lessee shall pay to Lessor all damages caused by such breach and shall also pay to Lessor an amount equal to any increase in insurance premium or premiums caused by such breach. The violation of any covenant of this Section 11 may be restrained by injunction.

12. REPAIRS AND MAINTENANCE: Subject to the provisions of Section 13, Lessee shall, during the term, at Lessee's own expense, keep the premises in good order, condition and repair, including the replacement of all broken glass with glass of the same size and quality, under the supervision and with the approval of Lessor. The Lessor shall procure full coverage insurance covering the cost of the replacement of all broken glass in the premises with glass of the same size and quality and the Lessee shall upon demand pay to the Lessor the cost of such insurance. If Lessee does not make repairs promptly and adequately, Lessor may, but need not, make repairs, and Lessee shall pay promptly the reasonable cost thereof, including overtime and other expense if Lessor, at Lessee's request, makes such repairs, including decorating, at times other than ordinary business or labor hours. At any time or times, Lessor, either voluntarily or pursuant to Governmental requirement, may do all things necessary in connection therewith, all without any improvements in or to the Building or any part thereof including the premises, and, during operations, may do all things necessary in connection therewith, all without any liability to Lessee by reason of interference, inconvenience, annoyance or loss of business. Lessor shall not be liable to Lessee for any expense, injury, loss or damage resulting to Lessee from work done in, upon, along, or the use of, any adjacent or nearby building, land, street, alley or way.

13. UNTENANTABILITY: If the premises or the Building are made wholly untenantable by fire or other casualty, Lessor may elect (a) to terminate this lease as of the date of the fire or casualty by notice to Lessee within thirty days after that date, or (b) to repair, restore or rehabilitate the Building or the premises at Lessor's expense within one hundred twenty days after Lessor is enabled to take possession of the injured premises and to undertake reconstruction or repairs, in which latter event the lease shall not terminate but fixed Rent shall be abated on a per diem basis while the premises are untenantable. If Lessor elects so to repair, restore or rehabilitate the Building or the premises, and does not substantially complete the work within the one hundred twenty day period, either party can terminate this lease as of the date of the fire or casualty by notice to the other party not later than one hundred thirty days after Lessor is enabled to take possession of the injured premises and to undertake reconstruction or repairs. In event of termination of the lease pursuant to this Section 13, fixed Rent shall be apportioned on a per diem basis and be paid to the date of the fire or casualty. If the demised premises shall be partially damaged by fire or other casualty without the fault or neglect of Lessee, Lessee's servants, employees, agents, visitors or licensees, the premises shall be repaired, restored or rehabilitated by and at the expense of Lessor, and fixed Rent until the damaged portion of the premises is ready for occupancy by Lessee shall be apportioned according to the part of the demised premises which is usable by Lessee. In all cases, due allowance shall be made for reasonable delay which may be caused by adjustment of insurance, strikes, labor difficulties or any cause beyond Lessor's control.

14. EMINENT DOMAIN: If the building, or any portion thereof which includes a substantial part of the premises, or which prevents the operation of the building, shall be taken or condemned by any competent authority for any public use or purpose, the term of this lease shall end upon, and not before, the date when the possession of the

prior to the end of the term, however ended, Lessee shall be conclusively presumed to have conveyed the same to Lessor under this lease as a bill of sale without further payment or credit by Lessor to Lessee.

11. USE OF PREMISES: (a) Lessee shall occupy and use the premises during the term for the purpose above specified and none other, conducting Lessee's customary business activity therein during all usual days and hours for the business in the vicinity except when prevented by strikes, fire, casualty or other causes beyond Lessee's reasonable control and except during reasonable periods for the repair, cleaning and decorating the premises. (b) Unless specifically provided herein and then only upon strict compliance with such provisions, Lessee shall not manufacture, distribute, store, sell or give away any alcoholic liquor, as defined in the Illinois Liquor Control Act approved January 31, 1934 as amended. (c) Lessee shall not exhibit, sell or offer for sale, use, rent or exchange on the premises or in the building any article, thing or service except those ordinarily embraced within the stated use of the premises. (d) Lessee will not make or permit to be made any use of the premises which, directly or indirectly, is forbidden by public law, ordinance or governmental or municipal regulation or order, or which may be dangerous to life, limb or property, or which may invalidate or increase the premium cost of any policy of insurance carried on the building or covering its operations. (e) Lessee will comply with all requirements to state, municipal or other governmental inspections, licenses and permits and will promptly pay all proper fees and charges in connection therewith, failing which Lessor may, but need not, pay any and all such fees and charges for the account of Lessee; (f) Lessee shall keep all first floor street frontage show windows brightly lighted during the term from dusk of each day until _____ P.M., including Sundays and holidays. (g) Lessee shall not display, install, inscribe, paint or affix any sign, picture, advertisement or notice inside or outside the premises or the building except in such place or places and of such color, size, design, style and material as shall have advance written approval by Lessor, and, upon expiration of the term, whether by lapse or otherwise, Lessee shall remove all such signs, pictures, advertisements and notices. At the request of Lessor, Lessee shall remove any and all signs, pictures, advertisements and notices which Lessor shall consider objectionable or injurious to the building or premises. (h) Lessee shall not use the name of the building for any purpose other than Lessee's business address and shall never use any picture or likeness of the building or premises in any advertisements, notices or correspondence without Lessor's advance written consent. (i) Lessee shall remove snow and ice from the sidewalks in front of, adjoining and in the rear of premises, and shall keep all such sidewalks and all entrances, passages, courts, corridors, vestibules, halls, approaches, exits, elevators and stairways free from all obstructions of every kind, and from ashes, garbage, litter and refuse of every kind, and in a clean and sanitary condition. (j) Lessee shall keep all windows of the premises clean and shall maintain the front or fronts of the premises in an attractive condition. (k) Lessee shall not make or permit any noise or odor that is objectionable to the public, to other occupants of the building, or to Lessor, to emanate from the premises and shall not create or maintain a nuisance thereon, and shall not disturb, solicit or canvass any occupant of the building, and shall not do any act tending to injure the reputation of the building or the premises. (l) Lessee shall not place or permit any radio or television or antenna, loud speakers, sound amplifiers or other similar devices on the roof or outside of the building. (m) Lessee shall not waste water by tying, wedging or otherwise fastening open any faucet. (n) Upon termination of the lease or of Lessee's possession, Lessee shall surrender all keys to the premises to Lessor at the place then fixed for the payment of rent and shall make known to Lessor the explanation of all combination locks on safes, cabinets and vaults in the premises. (o) If Lessee desires awnings, shades, Venetian blinds or window or door coverings of any kind, whether inside or outside, Lessee shall furnish and maintain the same in good and attractive condition at Lessee's expense and risk, and all shall be of such shape, color, design and material, quality and make as shall first be approved by Lessor in writing. (p) Lessee shall not overload any floor; Lessor may direct the routing and location of safes and all heavy articles. (q) Unless Lessor gives advance written consent, Lessee shall not use the premises or any part thereof for housing accommodations or for lodging or sleeping purposes, and shall not do any cooking therein and shall not use any illumination other than electric light. (r) Lessee shall not take or permit to be taken any supplies, merchandise, fixtures, equipment or appliances in or out of the premises or the building except through proper service doors,

part so taken shall be required for such use or purpose, and without apportionment of the condemnation award. Lessee shall have no right to share in such award. Current Rent shall be apportioned as of the date of such termination. If any condemnation proceeding shall be instituted in which it is sought to take or damage any part of the building, or the land under it, or if the grade of any street or alley adjacent to the building is changed by any competent authority and such change of grade makes it necessary or desirable to remodel the building to conform to the changed grade, Lessor shall have the right to cancel this lease upon not less than ninety days' notice prior to the date of cancellation designated in the notice. No money or other consideration shall be payable by Lessor to Lessee for the right of cancellation, and Lessee shall have no right to share in the condemnation award or in any judgment for damages caused by the change of grade.

15. REMEDIES: All rights and remedies of Lessor herein enumerated shall be cumulative and none shall exclude any other right or remedy allowed by law.

(a) If any voluntary or involuntary bankruptcy petition or similar pleading under any section or sections of any bankruptcy act shall be filed by or against Lessee, or any voluntary or involuntary proceeding in any court or tribunal shall be instituted to declare Lessee insolvent or unable to pay the Lessee's debts, and in the case of an involuntary petition or proceeding, the petition or proceeding is not dismissed within thirty days from the date it is filed Lessor may elect, but is not required, and with or without notice of such election, and with or without entry or other action by Lessor, to forthwith terminate this lease, and, notwithstanding any other provision of this lease, Lessor shall forthwith upon such termination be entitled to recover damages in an amount equal to the then present value of the rent specified in Section 1(a) of this lease for the residue of the stated term hereof, less the fair rental value of the premises for the residue of the stated term.

(b) If Lessee defaults in the payment of Rent and such default continues for five days after Lessor's notice thereof to Lessee as provided in Section 16, or if Lessee defaults in the prompt and full performance of any other provision of this lease, and the Lessee does not cure the default within twenty days (forthwith if the default involves a hazardous condition) after written demand by the Lessor that the default be cured, Lessor may, if Lessor so elects, but not otherwise, forthwith terminate this lease and Lessee's right to possession of the premises, one or both. If the leasehold interest of Lessee be levied upon under execution or be attached by process of law, or if Lessee makes an assignment for the benefit of creditors, or if a Receiver be appointed for any property of Lessee, or if Lessee abandons the premises, then and in any such event Lessor may, if Lessor so elects but not otherwise, and with or without notice of such election and with or without any demand whatsoever either forthwith terminate this lease and Lessee's right to possession of the premises, or without terminating this lease, forthwith terminate Lessee's right to possession of the premises.

(c) Upon any termination of this lease, whether by lapse of time or otherwise, or upon any termination of Lessee's right to possession without termination of the lease, Lessee shall surrender possession and vacate the premises immediately, and deliver possession thereof to Lessor.

(d) If Lessee abandons the premises or otherwise entitles Lessor so to elect, and Lessor elects to terminate Lessee's right to possession only, without terminating the lease, Lessor may at Lessor's option enter into the premises, remove Lessee's property and other evidences of tenancy, and take and hold possession thereof as in paragraph (c) of this Section 15 provided, without such entry and possession terminating the lease or releasing Lessee, in whole or in part, from Lessee's obligation to pay the Rent hereunder for the full term, and in any such case Lessee shall pay forthwith to Lessor, if Lessor so elects, a sum equal to the entire amount of the Rent specified in Section 1(a) of this lease for the residue of the stated term plus any other sums then due hereunder. Upon and after entry into possession without termination of this lease, Lessor may, but need not, relet the premises or any part thereof for the account of Lessee to any person, firm or corporation other than Lessee for such Rent, for such time and upon such terms as Lessor in Lessor's sole discretion shall determine. Lessor shall not be required to accept any tenant offered by Lessee or to observe any instructions given by Lessee about such reletting. In any such case, Lessor may make repairs, alterations and additions in or to the premises, and redecorate the same to the extent deemed by Lessor necessary or desirable, and Lessee shall, upon demand, pay the cost thereof, together with Lessor's expenses of the reletting. If the consideration collected by Lessor upon any such reletting for Lessee's account is not sufficient to pay monthly the full amount of the Rent reserved in this lease, together with the costs of repairs, alterations, additions, redecorating and Lessor's expenses, Lessee shall pay to Lessor the amount of each monthly deficiency upon demand; and if the consideration so collected from any such reletting is more than sufficient to pay the full amount of the Rent reserved herein, together with the costs and expenses of Lessor, Lessor, at the end of the stated term of the lease, shall account for the surplus to Lessee.

(e) Lessee hereby constitutes and irrevocably appoints any attorney of any court to be the true and lawful attorney of Lessee, and, in the name, place and stead of Lessee, to appear for Lessee in any court of record at any time in any suit or suits brought against Lessee for the enforcement of any right hereunder by Lessor, to waive the issuance and service of process and trial by jury, and, from time to time, to confess judgment or judgments in favor of Lessor and against Lessee for any fixed rental and interest thereon due hereunder by Lessee to Lessor and for costs of suit and for a reasonable attorney's fee in favor of Lessor to be fixed by the court, and to release all errors that may occur or intervene in such proceedings, including the issuance of execution upon any such judgment, and to stipulate that no appeal shall be prosecuted from such judgment or judgments, and that no proceedings in chancery or otherwise shall be filed or prosecuted to interfere in any way with the operation of such judgment or judgments or of any execution issued thereon or with any supplemental proceedings taken by Lessor to collect the amount of any such judgment or judgments, and to consent that execution on any judgment or decree in favor of Lessor and against Lessee may issue forthwith.

(f) Lessee shall pay upon demand all Lessor's costs, charges and expenses, including the fees of counsel, agents and others retained by Lessor, incurred in enforcing Lessee's obligations hereunder or incurred by Lessor in any litigation, negotiation or transaction in which Lessee causes Lessor, without Lessor's fault, to become involved or concerned.

(g) In event any lien upon Lessee's title results from any act or neglect of Lessee, and Lessee fails to remove said lien within ten days after Lessor's notice to do so, Lessor may remove the lien by paying the full amount thereof or otherwise and without any investigation or contest of the validity thereof, and Lessee shall pay Lessor upon request the amount paid out by Lessor in such behalf, including Lessor's costs, expenses and counsel fees.

16. NOTICES: In every instance where it shall be necessary or desirable for Lessor to serve any notice or demand upon Lessee, it shall be sufficient (a) to deliver or cause to be delivered to Lessee a written or printed copy thereof, or (b) to send a written or printed copy thereof by United States certified or registered mail, postage prepaid, addressed to Lessee at the demised premises, in which event the notice or demand shall be deemed for all purposes to have been served at the time the copy is mailed, or (c) to leave a written or printed copy thereof with some person above the age of ten years in possession of the demised premises or to affix the same upon any door leading into the demised premises, in which event the notice or demand shall be deemed to have been served at

the time the copy is so left or affixed. All notices shall be signed by or on behalf of Lessor.

17. MISCELLANEOUS.

(a) No receipt of money by Lessor from Lessee after the termination of this lease or after the service of any notice or after the commencement of any suit, or after final judgment for possession of the premises, shall renew, reinstate, continue or extend the term of this lease or affect any such notice, demand or suit.

(b) No waiver of any default of Lessee hereunder shall be implied from any omission by Lessor to take any action on account of such default if such default persists or be repeated, and no express waiver shall affect any default other than the default specified in the express waiver and that only for the time and to the extent therein stated. The invalidity or unenforceability of any provision hereof shall not affect or impair any other provision.

(c) In the absence of fraud, no person, firm or corporation, or the heirs, legal representatives, successors and assigns, respectively, thereof, executing this lease as agent, trustee or in any other representative capacity, shall ever be deemed or held individually liable hereunder for any reason or cause whatsoever.

(d) The words "Lessor" and "Lessee" whenever used in this lease shall be construed to mean Lessors or Lessees in all cases where there is more than one Lessor or Lessee, and the necessary grammatical changes required to make the provisions hereof apply either to corporations or individuals, men or women, shall in all cases be assumed as though in each case fully expressed.

(e) Provisions inserted herein or affixed hereto shall not be valid unless appearing in the duplicate original hereof held by Lessor. In event of variation or discrepancy, Lessor's duplicate shall control.

(f) Each provision hereof shall extend to and shall, as the case may require, bind and inure to the benefit of Lessor and Lessee and their respective heirs, legal representatives and successors, and shall bind assigns in the event this lease has been assigned with the express written consent of Lessor.

(g) Submission of this instrument for examination does not constitute a reservation of or option for the premises. The instrument becomes effective as a lease upon execution and delivery both by Lessor and Lessee.

(h) The headings of sections of the lease are for convenience only and do not define, limit or construe the contents of the sections.

(i) All amounts (other than rent) owed by Lessee to Lessor hereunder shall be paid within ten days from the date Lessor renders statements of account therefor and shall bear interest at 7% per annum thereafter until paid.

(j) Provisions typed on the back of this lease and signed by Lessor and Lessee and all riders attached to this lease and signed by Lessor and Lessee are hereby made a part of this lease as though inserted at length in this lease.

(k) If Lessee shall occupy the premises prior to the beginning of the term of this lease with Lessor's consent, all the provisions of this lease shall be in full force and effect as soon as Lessee occupies the premises. Rent for any period prior to the beginning of the term of this lease shall be fixed by agreement between Lessor and Lessee.

PERCENTAGE RENTAL PROVISIONS

(b-1) PERCENTAGE RENTAL: Lessee shall pay to Lessor sums of money equal to the following percentages of Gross Sales:

(b-2) GROSS SALES: The term "Gross Sales" includes the total of all sales of merchandise, all charges for services for which charge is made, and the gross receipts from all business transacted, in, upon and from the premises during the term by Lessee and all others occupying the premises or any part thereof.

The term "Gross Sales" excludes bona fide refunds and credits for returns of merchandise, and the amounts turned over by Lessee to the State of Illinois on account of the "Retailers' Occupation Tax Act" of Illinois, approved June 28, 1933, and amendments thereto.

The Percentage Rental Provisions apply to all Gross Sales made for cash or upon credit, or partly for cash and partly upon credit, regardless of collections of charges for which credit is given, and to all sales, charges for services and business transacted for whether orders are taken in or upon the premises during the term regardless of whether the merchandise is delivered, wholly or in part, and whether the services are rendered and the business is transacted in, from or upon the premises. Each sale, charge or business transaction upon installments, or a contract therefor, shall be treated as a gross sale for the full price or charge in the month during which such sale, charge or contract shall be made.

(b-3) RECORDS: Lessee shall keep and preserve full, complete and true records of all Gross Sales, including all cash register tapes, in manner and form satisfactory to Lessor for at least two years following the close of each year of the lease; shall permit Lessor or Lessor's representative to examine or audit the records at any and all reasonable times, and shall, upon Lessor's request, explain the methods of keeping the records.

(b-4) MONTHLY STATEMENTS: On or before the tenth day of _____ 19......, and on or before the tenth day of each and every calendar month during the remainder of the term, and also on or before the tenth day of _____ 19......, Lessee shall prepare and deliver to Lessor at the place then fixed for the payment of Rent a sworn statement of Gross Sales during the preceding calendar month. The statement shall be sworn to by Lessee, if an individual; by a partner of Lessee, if a partnership and by an executive officer of Lessee, if a corporation.

(b-5) Annual Statements: On or before the fifteenth day of _____, 19......, and on or before the same day of each _____ during the remainder of the term, and also on or before the same day of _____, 19......, Lessee shall deliver to Lessor at the place last fixed for the payment of Rent a statement prepared and certified by an accountant licensed under the laws of the State of Illinois, showing Gross Sales during the year of the term ended on the last day of the last previous month. The accountant's certificate to the statement shall certify that he made a complete examination of the books, Federal income tax return or returns and cash register tapes of Lessee; that he compared the Gross Sales shown in the statement to the Illinois Retailers' Occupation tax and Use tax returns and that the statement is prepared In accordance with accepted accounting principles. If Section (b-1) or any other provision of this lease, or the enforcement thereof by Lessor, requires an accounting for Gross Sales and payment of Percentage Rental for a period less than one year (hereafter referred to as a "short period") or if Lessor and Lessee desire to adjust the accounting period to Lessee's fiscal year which is different from the lease year and a short period thereby results at the beginning or end of the term of the lease, such short period shall be dealt with as follows: If such short period is less than six months in length, it shall be added to the previous year, or if no previous year, to the next succeeding year, and the total period shall be considered as a single period in calculating percentage rental. If such short period is six months or more in length, it shall be considered a separate year. The Annual Statement required by this section shall be filed on the fifteenth day of the _____ month following the expiration of such total or short period, as the case may be. With each such Annual Statement or statement of a short period Lessee shall pay to Lessor any and all sums due hereunder and then remaining unpaid for the entire period covered by such statement.

(b-6) CONTESTING LESSEE'S STATEMENTS: If Lessor is not satisfied with any Monthly, Annual or other Statement, Lessor shall serve notice upon Lessee of Lessor's dissatisfaction within one hundred eighty days after Lessor's receipt of the Statement complained of, and it shall not be necessary for Lessor to specify therein the grounds for Lessor's dissatisfaction. Unless within ten days after service of Lessor's notice of dissatisfaction Lessee satisfies Lessor with respect to such statement, Lessor shall have the right to make an audit of all books and records of Lessee, including Lessee's bank accounts, which in any way pertain to or show Gross Sales. Such audit shall be made by an accountant to be selected by Lessor, and all expenses of the audit shall be paid by Lessee if the report of the accountant shows the statement complained of to have contained error prejudicial to Lessor's receipt of Rent in an amount equal to or greater than 2% of the amount of Rent reported by the Lessee's statement for the period of the audit; otherwise to be paid by Lessor. The final audit of the accountant made pursuant to this Section (b-6) shall be conclusive upon the parties, and Lessee shall pay to Lessor within five days after a copy of the public accountant's final report has been delivered to Lessee the amount, if any, shown thereby to be due to Lessor. If Lessor makes any such audit, all Statements made by Lessee after the Statement complained of and until ten days after Lessor receives the final report of the public accountant shall be subject to Lessor's notice of dissatisfaction. "Accountant" as used in this section means an accountant licensed under the laws of Illinois.

(b-7) FAILURE TO DELIVER STATEMENTS: If Lessee omits to prepare and deliver promptly any Monthly, Annual or other Statement required by the Percentage Rental Provisions, Lessor may elect to treat Lessee's omission as a substantive breach of this lease entitling Lessor to terminate this lease and Lessee's right to possession of the premises, or to make an audit of all books and records of Lessee, including Lessee's bank accounts, which in any way pertain to or show Gross Sales, and to prepare the Statement or Statements which Lessee failed to prepare and deliver. Such audit shall be made and such Statement or Statements shall he prepared by a public accountant to be selected by Lessor. The Statement or Statements, so prepared, shall be conclusive on Lessee, and Lessee shall pay all expenses of the audit and other services.

(b-8) CONDUCT OF BUSINESS: Lessee shall, during the entire term, continuously use the demised premises for the purpose stated in this lease, carrying on therein Lessee's business undertaking diligently, assiduously and energetically. Lessee shall maintain on the premises a substantial stock of goods, wares and merchandise and equipment, adequate to assure successful operation of Lessee's business, and shall employ clerks, salesmen and others sufficient for the service and convenience of customers. Lessee shall keep the premises open and available for business activity therein during all usual days and hours for such business in the vicinity except when prevented by strikes, fires, casualty or other causes beyond Lessee's reasonable control and except during reasonable periods for repairing, cleaning and decorating the premises. Lessee shall include the address and identity of its business activity in the demised premises in all advertisements made by Lessee in which the address and identity of any other local business activity of like character conducted by Lessee shall be mentioned, and shall not divert elsewhere any trade, commerce or business which ordinarily would be transacted by Lessee in or from the demised premises.

(b-9) RESTRICTION: During the term of this lease, Lesse shall not, without Lessor's advance written consent, engage or participate, directly or indirectly, as owner, principal, employee or agent, or furnish financial or other aid or support to, any business enterprise or undertaking which is in any manner or degree competitive with the stated use of the demised premises for which this lease is made and which business enterprise or undertaking is situated within a radius of two city blocks (not less than 600 feet) in all directions from the Building in which the demised premises are located.

(b-10) LIMITATION: By this lease, Lessor does not acquire any right, title or interest in or to any property of Lessee except such rights as are specifically stated in the lease. Lessor is not and never shall be liable to any creditor of Lessee or to any claimant against the estate or property of Lessee for any debt, loss, contract or other obligation of Lessee. The relationship between Lessor and Lessee is solely that of landlord and tenant, and is not and never shall be deemed a partnership or joint venture.

In Witness Whereof, the parties hereto have caused this indenture to be executed under their seals, on the date first above written.

LESSOR

......................................[SEAL.]

LESSEE

......................................[SEAL.]

......................................[SEAL.]

......................................[SEAL.]

......................................[SEAL.]

......................................[SEAL.]

GUARANTY.

In consideration of the making of the above lease by the Lessor with the Lessee at the request of the undersigned and in reliance on this guaranty, the undersigned hereby guarantees the payment of the Rent to be paid by the Lessee and the performance by the Lessee of all the terms, conditions, covenants and agreements of the lease, and the undersigned promises to pay all the Lessor's expenses, including reasonable attorney's fees, incurred by the Lessor in enforcing all obligations of the Lessee under the lease or incurred by the Lessor in enforcing this guaranty. The Lessor's consent to any assignment or assignments, and successive assignments by the Lessee and Lessee's assigns, of this lease, made either with or without notice to the undersigned, or a changed or different use of the demised premises, or Lessor's forebearance, delays, extensions of time or any other reason whether similar to or different from the foregoing shall in no wise or manner release the undersigned from liability as guarantor.

WITNESS the hand and seal of the undersigned at the date of the above lease.

....[SEAL]

ASSIGNMENT BY LESSOR.

For value received, the undersigned Lessor hereby sells, transfers, sets over and assigns unto .... all Lessor's right, title and interest in and to the within lease from and after ...., 19......, together with all the Rents, issues and profits and other payments by Lessee required to be made for use and occupancy of the premises therein described.

Dated.., 19........

....(SEAL)

....(SEAL)

(Lessor)

ASSIGNMENT BY LESSEE.

For value received, the undersigned Lessee hereby assigns all the Lessee's right, title and interest in and to the within lease from and after .... unto .... and for the premises to be used and occupied for .... and for no other purpose. It is expressly agreed this assignment shall not release or relieve the undersigned, as Original Lessee, from any liability under the covenants of the lease.

Dated.., 19........

....(SEAL)

....(SEAL)

(Lessee)

ACCEPTANCE OF LESSEE'S ASSIGNMENT.

In consideration of the above assignment and the written consent of the Lessor thereto, the undersigned Assignee (binding also the Assignee's heirs, legal representatives and successors), hereby assumes the obligations of said lease imposed on the Lessee and promises to make all payments and to keep and perform all conditions and covenants of the lease by the Lessee to be kept and performed commencing ...., expressly adopting for the undersigned the provisions of paragraph '(e) of Section 15 of the lease as though here restated.

Dated.., 19........

....(SEAL)

....(SEAL)

(Assignee)

CONSENT TO LESSEE'S ASSIGNMENT.

The Lessor hereby consents to the above Assignment upon the express condition that the Original Lessee shall remain liable for the prompt payment of the Rent and the keeping and performance of all conditions and covenants of the lease by the Lessee to be kept and performed. The Lessor does not hereby consent to any further Assignment or to any subletting of the premises.

Dated.., 19........

....(SEAL)

....(SEAL)

(Lessor)

around the computation and method of rental payment. The amounts of the minimum and percentage rentals; the definition of gross sales; methods of reporting sales and paying percentage rentals; geographical restrictions on business operations; requirements as to business hours, inventory, and personnel; and a recapture provision are all open for discussion during the negotiation of a percentage lease.

Setting Rental Rates. The first step in the negotiation process is to arrive at an acceptable minimum rental based on rates for comparable space in the area market. The minimum rental must then be related to the percentage rental rate.

Every type of business has a different percentage ratio of rental rate to business volume. This ratio is determined by each industry's cost of doing business, profit margin, and stock turnover rates. In general, slow turnover indicates lower business volume and higher profit margins, as with a jewelry store. Rapid turnover of stock is accompanied by high volume of sales and a low profit margin, as in a discount store or a supermarket. Accordingly, the percentage rental for a jeweler would be higher than for a grocer, since the sales volume is lower. A general guide when negotiating lease terms is the percentage lease tables published by the International Council of Shopping Centers, the Urban Land Institute, and other real estate management organizations. Tables like the following display a range of percentage rents applicable to particular types of business throughout the country.

Figure 45: PERCENTAGE LEASE RANGES

PERCENTAGE LEASE RANGES	
Automobile Dealers	1–3%
Automobile Accessories	2–5
Automobile Parking	40–70
Barber Shops	8–10
Beauty Shops	6–10
Books and Stationery	5–8
Candy Shops	6–10
Cigar Stores	6–10
Department Stores	2–3
Drugs—Independent	4–6
Drugs—Chains	2–4
Electrical Appliances	3–6
Florists	7–10
Furs	6–8
Furniture	4–6
Hardware	3–6
Jewelers	6–10
Liquor Stores	3–6
Men's Clothing	4–8
Theaters	8–12
Restaurants	5–10
Shoes—Retail	5–8
Shoes—Repair	8–10
Sporting Goods	5–8
Women's Wear	4–8

Many landlords include tax participation clauses in their percentage leases to provide more income stability. With property taxes rising so rapidly, long-term leases should ask the tenant to pay any increases in taxes or assessments above the rates for a specified base year. The tax participation clause is sometimes accompanied by a further provision that excess taxes paid by the tenant will be credited against the total percentage rental due for the lease year. Whether or not this provision is included depends mainly on the amount of the minimum rent and the percentage of gross sales to be paid. The parties usually agree upon a gross sales total that must be reached before a credit is given.

In the case of large regional shopping centers, similar participation provisions are sometimes included for insurance, common area maintenance, security services, contributions to a merchants association, or joint promotional efforts.

Gross Sales. The standard definition most often acceptable to both parties is "the gross amount of all sales made on, from, or at the leased premises, whether for cash or on credit, after deducting the sales price of any returned merchandise where a cash refund is given." The tenant must maintain records of all transactions subject to the percentage rate and furnish monthly statements of gross sales. At the expiration of the lease, the tenant may have to submit a statement of gross income for the entire lease term prepared by an independent certified public accountant.

The lease should specify the owner's right to have the tenant's financial records audited during business hours. Because of the cost, most managers audit only the tenants they are suspicious of, and then only once a year. If an audit shows a tenant's records of gross sales to be accurate, most leases will make the landlord pay for the audit. However, if the audit discloses that the tenant owes rent in excess of a specified percent of the amount that was actually paid for that period, the tenant must pay for the audit as well as the amount of rent as determined by the audit.

Method of Payment. Most percentage leases (including the sample on the preceding pages) require gross sales to be reported by the tenant in writing on a monthly basis, with any amount due to be paid within 10 days of the report. Many businesses are seasonal, though, and tenants with great seasonal variations in gross sales will insist on some type of adjustment provision. A luggage outlet, for example, which might have very low sales for the first 10 months of the year, probably will have to pay the minimum rent because it is a higher figure than the percentage of income. In November and December, when business flourishes and more than compensates for the previous lack of revenue, the tenant is expected to pay a percentage of this overage income.

The most common method of adjustment in such cases requires the appropriate minimum or percentage rate to be paid each month, with the additional provision that if the total rent paid during a 12-month period exceeds the agreed-upon percentage of total volume when computed over the entire year, the tenant will receive a refund or credit for the excess rent paid. Other leases provide that the percentage amount be paid only at the end of each lease year, while still others establish payment periods based on the expected variations in volume.

Operating Methods. To protect their percentage of gross sales from erosion by sales from a branch store, most owners will not allow a tenant to open another store within a certain radius. Clauses like this sometimes do not hold in court, so they are becoming obsolete.

Other provisions in the percentage lease also are aimed at regulating tenant operations that affect gross sales volume. Tenants must be encouraged to expand their businesses as much as possible if the owner is to receive maximum profits from their use of the property. If a tenant in an open mall agrees to extend its hours of operation beyond the normal business day in order to increase sales volume, thereby incurring added overhead costs, the landlord might consider a slight reduction in the percentage rental. If the percentage rate is decreased, however, the minimum rental should be raised proportionately to guarantee the owner adequate compensation in spite of the percentage reduction. For security purposes, tenants in enclosed malls cannot remain open after mall hours or on days when the mall is closed. Each lease should at least specify that the tenant will not close before the normal closing time of the mall (uniform hours). Depending upon the tenant's reputation and financial status, lease covenants may stipulate its business hours, its staff composition, and the size of its inventory in order to assure maximum gross sales. The tenant may be asked to spend a certain portion of income on advertising, as mentioned earlier.

Recapture. The landlord usually retains the right to terminate a percentage lease at the end of an acceptable period of time if gross sales have not reached the level anticipated during negotiations. This is known as a *recapture clause* and is incorporated in the lease terms dealing with consideration. The tenant may request a further provision that keeps the lease in effect by increasing the minimum rent to the amount the owner would have received had the expected sales volume been achieved. This type of recapture clause must not be confused with the recapture provision mentioned in Chapter 13 in discussing an assignment and subletting clause, for each is used in a different situation.

Tenant Improvements. Most retail space consists simply of four unfinished walls, a floor, and a ceiling, with very few improvements or alterations performed by the landlord. Although this point is open to negotiation, the tenant generally contracts for and finances the alterations needed for his or her operations. Negotiation of tenant improvement expenditures in older centers, where a new tenant is moving into previously occupied space, is complicated by the fact that it is difficult to differentiate between expenses for deferred maintenance, building improvements, and alterations that accrue to the tenant's advantage *only* on the one hand, and those that correct deferred maintenance or increase the inherent value of the property itself on the other.

Negotiations will center around the independent value and tax advantages of the improvement for both parties. If the owner performs the work and can prove that it is being done for a particular tenant *only,* with no salvage value for future tenants, he or she can expect a short-term tax write-off for depreciation during the lease term. But, since it is not easy to prove that new flooring is for the sole benefit of the present tenant, the owner usually has to allocate this and other improvement costs to increasing the capital value of the property, thereby lengthening the period for depreciation write-off. Tenants encounter fewer problems in verifying their right to depreciate their improvements over the term of a lease. The fact that tenants ordinarily garner a greater tax break from improvements than does the owner must be considered during negotiations. Regardless of who actually pays for the improvements, an amount should be added to the base rent to compensate for taxes or insurance costs resulting from them.

The building rules incorporated into leases for retail space are quite stringent. The manager should keep control over the architecture, facades, signs, and other specifications of the tenants' outlets even though the owner is not financing such construction.

MAINTENANCE OF RETAIL PROPERTY

The retail property manager's maintenance duties are complex because of the center's size and the necessity to determine the tenant's share of the common area maintenance. Strip centers usually require maintenance only of the exterior of the building, its structural elements, and parking facilities. Enclosed regional centers, with their common areas and central utility system, demand more of the manager's attention.

An enclosed center is actually one multiple-occupancy building, much like a cooperative or condominium, in which the obligations of the landlord, co-owners, and tenants overlap. Customarily, these overlapping obligations are set forth in the basic documents establishing the center, primarily in the reciprocal easement agreement. It is usually lengthy, but plats which accompany it will help in clarifying the rights among the various tenants. The manager must understand the implications of any reciprocal easement agreements between the prime owner of the center and other owners such as major department stores. He or she must also be acquainted with the terms of the leases.

Like any manager of a large multitenant building, the retail center manager must be familiar with the heating, air-conditioning, utility distribution, waste disposal, and electronic security systems. The manager need not know how to maintain these systems personally, but he or she must know enough about them to set up maintenance procedures and to hire contractors or building employees to perform the work. If maintenance work is performed exclusively on a contract basis, at least one person is usually employed full-time by a large center to act as a liaison agent. This person should also be able to handle routine maintenance jobs that are costly when done by an outside contractor on a one-time basis.

Preventative maintenance programs and routine inspections of the building, grounds, and equipment are especially important for retail properties because of the heavy use they endure. A full set of physical inspection checklists can be obtained from the International Council of Shopping Centers. These lists, entitled *Library of Shopping Center Forms for Management and Operations,* resemble those seen previously for apartment building inspection. A small strip center can be checked easily by the manager. Large regional centers, however, may require experts to examine their more complex operating equipment.

SECURITY OF RETAIL PROPERTY

Security measures necessary for the protection of a shopping center will vary according to the size of the center. In a small strip center, generally the merchants will handle security problems; however, in larger centers, the on-site manager may be the sole security. The efforts of the on-site manager may be reinforced during busy shopping seasons by the addition of one or more security officers. In a large mall center, a security director with a force of security officers will be in direct charge of security measures, but ordinarily the security director will report to the mall manager.

A decision must be made as to whether the security force will be visible with uniforms, etc., or will be dressed in distinctive blazers, which may be more in keeping with the tone of the center.

The International Association for Shopping Center Security (IASCS) has developed a program for certification of shopping center officers through a combination of training and experience. The Certified Security Officer (CSO) program is sponsored by the IASCS.

ADMINISTRATIVE RESPONSIBILITIES

The retail property manager's administrative responsibilities are governed by the owner's objectives. When a large corporation or association is the owner-employer, its objectives and the manager's responsibilities are clearly spelled out in the organization's bylaws. In other cases, the corporate owner of one or more shopping centers may sign a management contract delegating all authority to the manager, who becomes the primary decision maker for the property. The manager then must formulate a plan for attaining the owner's goals.

In either case, the manager will be unable to perform effectively without considering the tax consequences of his or her decisions and their effect on the owner's income. The manager need not know the intimate details of the prime owner's income, but channels for reporting financial data must be set up and maintained if the owner's objectives are to be met and the manager is to receive adequate direction.

Financial Reports

Due to variations in shopping center size, function, layout, ownership, and tenancy, it is impossible to establish a uniform system of financial reporting for retail properties. It is possible, though, to classify and describe common reports in general terms. Basically, the owner wants two types of information about the property—its current financial status and its economic future. A *Standard Manual of Accounting for Shopping Center Operations,* published by the Urban Land Institute (ULI), provides retail property managers with a standardized system for reporting income and expense. The method is adaptable to both large and small centers and permits intraindustry cost comparisons. This accounting system is similar to BOMA's standardized method for office building accounting.

Under the standardized accounting method for shopping centers, there are five major *rental income items:* minimum rental guaranteed by the tenants' leases; overage rent based on percentage clauses; rental income from rent escalation clauses; income from sale of services to tenants; and income from sale of utilities. These income items should be realistic estimates of actual income, with the rent loss and vacancy factors built in. The most difficult source of income to predict is the overage rental income based on percentage or escalation clauses. Overage income information must be gathered whenever the retail property manager prepares a forecast, budget, or financial statement. To acquire this information, the manager obtains a statement of sales volume from all tenants at the times specified in their leases. As a supplementary report, the manager should compare each tenant's figures for the current period with its past performance and determine the percent of increase or decrease for the current year. Conferences with store managers may reveal sales projections for the coming year. The historical record of each tenant's performance permits comparison of one tenant with another and with the group as a whole. Obviously, such reports are most illuminating during the lease renewal negotiations.

Expense items under the standard method of accounting for retail property are charged to one of the following categories: building maintenance, public area maintenance, utilities, office area maintenance, financing, advertising and promotion, real estate taxes, insurance, or administrative costs. Building maintenance expenses take in employee wages and supplies for all retail space within the shopping center. Public area maintenance (parking lot, mall, grounds, etc.) and office area maintenance are in separate categories. In the utility expense category is the cost of all forms of energy as well as the labor involved in supplying heat, lighting, and air conditioning to tenants. Under the standard system of accounting for shopping centers, financing costs are simply the *interest* on outstanding loans, since any amount applied to reduce the loan principal should not be expensed. Insurance costs include insurance against fire and other damage, boiler and equipment insurance, liability insurance, rental value insurance, and employee bonds. Management fees, the building office payroll, other office expenses, and professional fees are considered administrative expenses.

Operating Budget. The format of a retail center operating budget is similar to that used for other forms of income property. The major difference is that capital expenditures must be broken out and listed in a separate budget.

Another significant aspect of the retail property operating budget is its rigidity. The major expenses are those for mortgage payments and real estate taxes, neither of which is subject to short-term attempts at cost control. Therefore, only a relatively small portion of the total budgetary allotment can be influenced by economy measures.

The *capital expenditures budget* includes income from the sale of assets, payments on the principal of a mortgage or other debt, and yearly expenses for repairs or additions that will be depreciated over several years. The capital expenditures budget must be prepared along with the operating budget, since the two reports are closely interrelated. However, the manager must adopt a different frame of reference when preparing the capital budget. Unlike the operating budget, the capital expenditures budget must look several years into the future.

Capital expenditures can be divided into two major categories governed by different economic principles. Money spent for *preservation* is not meant to generate new income, but to protect the facilities that are already in existence. Repairing the asphalt surface of a shopping center parking lot would be classed as a capital expense for preservation. Tenants often absorb some of the cost of such an expense through a common area maintenance charge.

Income-producing capital expenditures either produce more gross income or increase present net income by reducing operating expenses. For example, capital expenditures for expansion or for installation of a more efficient heating plant could be considered income-producing. Before incurring any expense of this nature, the manager should prepare a detailed cost analysis of the proposed investment to determine if the initial cash outlay will be recovered in the long run.

Monthly Cash Flow Forecast. After the owner has approved the annual budget, the manager should prepare a monthly forecast of cash flow to serve as a reference point for fiscal management in the upcoming year. For the purposes of this report, cash flow is simply the difference between money received and money spent each month (total income minus operating expense and debt service).

The monthly forecast is necessary because of the uneven flow of cash during the year. Peaks in expenses must be anticipated so that there is cash on hand when the bills fall due. To some degree, income also fluctuates due to vacancies and the fact that percentage rents are not payable on a single time schedule. These variables are reflected in Figure 46, the monthly cash flow forecast. To prepare the monthly forecast, the manager must estimate when total annual income will be received and expenses paid out. The estimates are then calendared by month and broken down into the standard income and expense categories contained in the operating budget. The forecast should be reviewed in depth at least quarterly. If obvious discrepancies are found, the manager should adjust the forecast for the remainder of the year or identify the reason for the discrepancies and try to remedy them.

Monthly Income and Expense Statement. The frequency with which the manager must submit interim operating reports will depend upon the owner's needs and the size of the shopping center. The monthly income and expense statement should compare the income and expenses for the month with the cash flow forecast for that month. The statement should make a running tabulation of actual income and expenses for the year to date and should compare these figures to the budgetary allotment for this period. The ULI form, Figure 47, illustrates this process.

Profit and Loss Statement. Besides correlating actual results with forecasted amounts, the year-end profit and loss statement should supply any supplementary information needed for the owner's tax returns, such as depreciation charges, capital improvement costs, and the total amount of debt reduction. The data may be displayed in three columns—one for the budgeted amount, another for the actual figures, and a third expressing the variance between budget estimates and real costs. An additional column showing the figures for the preceding year could be included as a frame of reference for the owner.

Industry Statistics. Another benefit of using the standardized system of accounting described in this section is that it follows the format of the industrywide compilation of financial reports on shopping centers published by the Urban Land Institute. Called *Dollars and Sense of Shopping Centers,* the survey is published every 3 years. From it the retail property manager can identify new trends and determine how well the shopping center is doing compared to similar centers.

Figure 46: MONTHLY CASH FLOW FORECAST

Property: Date:

Income	January	February	March	April	May	June	July	August	September	October	November	December
Minimum rental income	100,000	100,000	100,000	90,000	60,000	70,000	80,000	90,000	98,000	100,000	100,000	100,000
Overage rent	20,000	18,000	18,000	17,000	18,000	18,000	18,000	20,000	30,000	25,000	30,000	40,000
Rental income from escalation	1,000	1,100	1,250	1,500	1,800	2,200	2,500	2,750	3,000	3,300	3,600	4,000
Services to tenants	9,000	9,000	9,000	9,000	9,000	9,000	9,000	9,000	9,000	9,000	9,000	9,000
Sale of utilities	7,000	7,000	7,000	7,000	7,000	7,000	7,000	7,000	7,000	7,000	7,000	7,000
Other income	1,000	1,000	1,500	1,500	2,000	1,500	1,500	1,500	1,500	1,000	1,000	1,000
Total	$138,000	$136,100	$136,750	$126,000	$97,800	$107,700	$118,000	$130,250	$148,500	$145,300	$150,600	$161,000
Expense												
Building maintenance	1,000	1,000	1,000	2,000	2,000	2,000	2,000	2,000	1,000	1,000	1,000	500
Public area maintenance	9,000	9,000	9,000	9,000	9,000	9,000	9,000	9,000	9,000	9,000	9,000	9,000
Utilities	6,000	6,000	5,000	5,000	5,000	6,000	6,000	6,000	5,000	6,000	6,000	6,000
Office area maintenance	1,000	1,000	1,000	1,000	1,000	1,000	1,000	1,000	1,000	1,000	1,000	1,000
Financing and payments on loan principal	48,000	48,000	48,000	48,000	48,000	48,000	48,000	48,000	48,000	48,000	48,000	48,000
Advertising and promotion	1,500	1,500	1,500	1,000	1,000	1,500	1,000	1,500	1,500	1,000	1,500	1,500
Real estate taxes	—	—	—	—	—	72,000	—	—	—	—	—	72,000
Insurance	—	—	4,000	—	—	4,000	—	—	4,000	—	—	4,000
Administrative	5,500	5,500	5,500	4,600	4,100	4,600	4,600	5,100	6,100	6,000	6,100	6,300
Miscellaneous	5,000	5,000	5,000	5,000	5,000	5,000	5,000	5,000	5,000	5,000	5,000	5,000
Total	$77,000	$77,000	$80,000	$75,600	$75,100	$153,100	$76,600	$77,600	$80,600	$77,000	$77,100	$153,300
Cash Flow	$61,000	$59,100	$56,750	$50,400	$22,700	($45,400)	$41,400	$52,650	$67,900	$68,300	$73,500	$7,700

Figure 47: ULI REPORT OF OPERATING INCOME (LOSS) AND CASH FLOW

Report of Operating Income (Loss) And Cash Flow

Month Of _____

	Current Month			Year to Date		
	Plan	Actual	Over (Under) Plan	Plan	Actual	Over (Under) Plan
Income						
01 Rental Income—Minimum Rent						
02 Rental Income—Overages						
03 Rental Income—Rent Escalation Charges						
07 Income for Common Area Services						
08 Income from Sale of Utilities						
09 Miscellaneous Income						
TOTAL INCOME						
Expenses						
10 Building Maintenance						
20 Parking Lot, Mall and Other Public Areas						
25 Central Utility Systems						
30 Office Area Services						
40 Financing Expense						
50 Advertising and Promotion						
60 Depreciation and Amortization of Deferred Costs						
70 Real Estate Taxes						
80 Insurance						
90 General and Administrative						
TOTAL EXPENSES						
NET INCOME (LOSS)						
Add: Depreciation and Amort. of Deferred Costs						
Deduct: Mortgage and Other Loan Principal Payments						
NET CASH FLOW						

From the *Urban Land Institute Standard Accounting Manual.* Used by permission.

Special Aspects of Insurance for Shopping Centers

Before any insurance can be purchased, the owner's legal liabilities must be clearly distinguished from the tenants'. Although the land or buildings for the center may have different owners, they function as a single entity, and a loss in one owner's section may impede operations in another's.

Roadways, sidewalks, and parking areas also may have more than one owner and may be within an area leased by a specific tenant. These facilities are available to shoppers as a group, with no demarcation of different ownership interests, so it is often difficult to determine the liability for a personal injury claim arising from an accident in a public area.

A good general rule for the manager to follow in securing public liability coverage for the center is to have all owners and/or tenants named as coinsureds on all policies even remotely affecting their interests. For added protection, the property manager and merchants association should also be named as insureds on liability policies. Insurance policies should be purchased to cover all the major areas of risk outlined in Chapter 9. Plate glass insurance should be the responsibility of the tenant.

Each merchant in the shopping center will want to carry adequate insurance on inventory and improvements, plus product liability insurance, general liability insurance, workmen's compensation, and other policies suited to the type of business. Again, the owner, manager, and merchants association should be named as coinsureds on public liability insurance purchased by the tenants. The two most expensive types of policy are general liability insurance and fire and extended coverage. The cost of the former has skyrocketed during the past few years, especially for retail properties.

SUMMARY

Any place where goods are sold or exchanged can be classified as a retail establishment. Retail space, the second major type of commercial property, is remarkably complex in its various types.

Mass production of automobiles, beginning in the 1920s, changed the lifestyle of most American families. No longer dependent on public transportation, families deserted the city's central business district for life in less congested suburban areas. Retail merchants followed their customers, and during the 1930s small shopping centers of 4 to 10 stores began to spring up on the fringes of cities to serve the consumer needs of these new residential neighborhoods. After World War II, the suburban exodus increased in intensity, and larger shopping complexes serving many square miles of suburbs became common.

The retail property management field ranges from centers with only a few retail outlets to large regional complexes. Obviously, the demands on the manager's time and talents vary with the type of property involved. Small centers usually require only exterior maintenance from the manager, while major shopping complexes, with their sophisticated equipment and large common areas, test the executive and administrative skills of the most experienced manager.

Shopping centers can be grouped by market area, pattern, and ownership. Market area categorization is usually reflected in the size of the center. The *strip center* consists of 4 to 10 stores and has the smallest market area. The *neighborhood center* includes 15 to 20 stores and is designed to provide convenience shopping for customers within a 1½-mile radius. The *community center* usually has a junior department store plus other convenience outlets and draws customers from a 5-mile radius. *Regional centers* can vary greatly in size (70 to 225 stores), but all have at least one major department store as their key tenant. Customers come from 10 to 50 miles to take advantage of the full range of merchandise and services offered by the major stores and the many satellite establishments located in the regional center.

During the evolutionary period for the shopping center, a number of basic design patterns have developed to accommodate key and subsidiary tenants. These patterns include linear strip centers, L-shaped centers, U-shaped centers, clusters, T-design groups, triangles, dumbbell centers, and double-dumbbell centers.

Vacant retail space cannot be leased unless prospective tenants are being attracted to the premises. As with other types of property, retail space can be advertised through signs, ads, brochures, and direct-mail pieces. Broker referral campaigns, leasing agents, and publicity efforts also can increase the exposure of the property. Retail property advertising generally relies most heavily on brochures, direct-mail packages, and leasing agents.

When qualifying a prospect for retail space, the manager must assess his or her financial capabilities, compatibility with existing tenants, spatial and parking needs, preferences in amenities, and customer requirements. A retail outlet's location within a shopping center has a great effect on the success or failure of the business. Competitors should not be situated next to each other, but allied businesses or services should be grouped together so that each benefits from the customer traffic to and from the neighboring stores. The manager's objective is to find the merchant who will do the largest volume of business in each retail location.

Because it is difficult to forecast future rental value, a percentage lease is often used when space is leased for more than 3 to 5 years. Most percentage leases are *minimum-guaranteed* percentage leases, requiring periodic payment of either a fixed minimum rent or a percentage rent based on gross sales, whichever is greater. The other three types of percentage lease types are *straight percentage, variable-scale,* and *maximum* percentage leases.

The percentage lease must specify most of the standard rights and obligations of landlord and tenant as well as the more complex financial considerations involved in negotiating a percentage lease. The amounts of the minimum and percentage rentals, the definition of gross sales, methods for reporting sales and paying percentage rentals, and inclusion of tax and insurance participation clauses must be determined. Geographical restrictions on business operations; requirements as to business hours, inventory, and personnel; extent of tenant alterations; and a recapture provision also are open to discussion during the negotiation of a percentage lease.

The amount of work involved in the physical maintenance of retail properties depends on the center's size, geographical location, and the tenants' share of common area maintenance. Strip centers usually require only maintenance of the building's exterior and preservation of its structural integrity. The enclosed, multitenant regional center, however, poses maintenance problems similar to those found in any large multitenant office building.

Housekeeping and routine cleaning of common elements are a major expense item in the maintenance budget for retail properties. Shopping centers demand rigorous preventative maintenance programs and routine inspections of the physical structure, grounds, interior, and equipment. Inspection checklists can be obtained from the International Council of Shopping Centers. Repairs, replacements, and other corrective maintenance should be scheduled carefully. In setting up a maintenance program, the shopping center manager has the option of using outside contractors or permanent building staff for diverse tasks. In each instance, this decision should only be made after a cost comparison of the alternatives.

Because of the great variations in shopping center size, function, layout, and tenancy, it is impossible to establish a uniform system of financial reporting that meets the needs of every type of retail property. It is possible, though, to classify and describe common financial reports in general terms. Basically, the owner wants two types of information about the property—its current financial status and predictions of events which are likely to influence the future of the shopping center.

The *Standard Manual of Accounting for Shopping Center Operations,* published by the Urban Land Institute, provides a standardized system for drawing up operating and capital expenditure budget forecasts, monthly cash flow forecasts, actual monthly cash flow statements, and a year-end profit and loss statement. These standardized accounting methods allow the manager and the owner to make intraindustry comparisons of the center's productivity.

Shopping centers need protection against all the major risks brought out in Chapter 9. However, retail property insurance is complicated by the fact that shopping centers, which function as a single entity, often are owned by more than one person, group, or corporation. Although roadways, sidewalks, malls, and other common areas may be within the area leased to a specific tenant, these facilities are made available to shoppers as a group. Thus, it is often difficult to determine liability for a personal injury claim arising from an accident in a public area. A good general rule for the manager to follow when purchasing liability insurance coverage for the center is to have owners, tenants, the manager, and the merchants association named as coinsureds on all liability policies even remotely affecting the interests of any other party. The manager should also require each tenant to name all owners, the manager, and the merchants association as coinsureds on liability insurance taken out by the individual tenant.

The International Council of Shopping Centers (ICSC) is a professional real estate association composed of persons interested in the shopping center industry. ICSC sponsors two training programs leading to the designations of Certified Shopping Center Manager (CSM) and Certified Marketing Director (CMD).

QUESTIONS: CHAPTER 14

1. List the four market areas of shopping center classifications.

   a. _____   c. _____
   b. _____   d. _____

2. Most regional shopping centers are:

   a. U-shaped.   c. T-shaped.
   b. cluster-design.   d. dumbbell.

3. Sketch a cluster-design shopping center below, indicating the placement of one key tenant.

4. In general, retail property is best advertised by:

   a. classified ads.   c. radio.
   b. direct mail.   d. display ads.

5. A brochure advertising retail space should include:

   I. information on parking and traffic flow.
   II. lease terms.

   a. I only   c. both I and II
   b. II only   d. neither I nor II

6. Most promotional programs for shopping centers:

   I. are entirely subsidized by the manager.
   II. benefit both tenants and manager.

   a. I only   c. both I and II
   b. II only   d. neither I nor II

7. List the four major types of percentage leases.

   a. _____   c. _____
   b. _____   d. _____

8. The sample percentage lease in Chapter 14 contains a:

   I.   rental variable with sales volume.
   II. tax participation clause.

     a.   I only   c.   both I and II
     b.   II only   d.   neither I nor II

9. A retail store with a low business volume generally has:

   I.   lower profit margins.
   II. lower percentage rental rates.

     a.   I only   c.   both I and II
     b.   II only   d.   neither I nor II

10. A merchant signs a lease that sets a minimum monthly rental rate of $600, or 6 percent of gross sales. If rent is computed on a monthly basis, what is the total amount of rent paid in the first quarter if gross sales were $8,000 in January; $11,000 in February; and $12,000 in March?

     a. $1,860   c. $1,920
     b. $1,800   d. $1,980

11. A variable-scale percentage lease sets the monthly rental rate at 6 percent of gross sales up to and including $15,000, *plus* 5 percent of gross sales in excess of $15,000 but not in excess of $30,000, *plus* 4 percent of gross sales in excess of $30,000. What would the rental payment be if gross monthly sales were $42,000?

     a. $1,650   c. $2,100
     b. $2,130   d. $2,070

12. A shopping center that draws customers from a 5-mile radius would be considered a:

     a.   neighborhood center.   c.   community center.
     b.   regional center.   d.   strip center.

13. A shopping center has an annual income of $1,700,000 and expenses of $1,250,000. The value of this retail property is $5,000,000. If comparable properties have capitalization rates of 8 percent, then:

   I.   the center is turning an above-average profit.
   II. the center's capitalization rate is 8.5 percent.

     a.   I only   c.   both I and II
     b.   II only   d.   neither I nor II

14. A property manager has two prospective tenants for a particular retail space. Bijou is a jewelry store that expects to do $72,000 in annual gross sales. This prospect is willing to sign an increasing variable-scale lease for 7 percent on income up to and including $50,000 per year and 8 percent on any income over this amount. Trade Winds, an import boutique, would have reliable annual gross sales of $97,000 in the same space. Trade Winds is willing to sign a straight percentage lease at 6 percent. All other factors being equal, which prospect is more desirable?

---

15. A community center of 200,000 square feet has the following tenant constituency:

food and food services: 39,950 sq. ft.   furniture: 7,975 sq. ft.
general merchandise: 96,025 sq. ft.   financial: 8,100 sq. ft.
clothing and shoes: 25,900 sq. ft.   offices and services: 16,050 sq. ft.
dry goods: 5,000 sq. ft.

There is also a vacant retail space of 1,000 square feet located between a shoe store and a soda shop. The recommended tenant mix for this type of shopping center by gross leasable area is as follows:

food and service: 20 percent   furniture: 4 percent
general merchandise: 48 percent   financial: 4 percent
clothing and shoes: 13 percent   offices and services: 8 percent
dry goods: 3 percent

What type of tenant should be probably be solicited for the vacant space?

    a.   food store   c.   bank
    b.   dry goods store   d.   furniture store

16. Security measures in a shopping center:

  I.   will vary according to size.
  II. require a decision as to whether a visible security force will wear police uniforms or distinctive attire such as blazers in a large center.

    a.   I only   c.   both I and II
    b.   II only   d.   neither I nor II

15
Industrial Property

Industrial real estate includes all land and buildings used or suited for use by industry. Industry encompasses all activities involved in the production, storage, and distribution of *tangible goods* as opposed to intangible services. It refers to the transformation of raw materials or components into finished products and extends to the packaging, warehousing, distribution, and transporting of these finished products.

NATURE OF INDUSTRIAL REAL ESTATE

Classifications

An industrial site is any location at which industrial activity occurs. Buildings or improvements on the land must provide the most efficient environment for the industrial operations of the tenant. Depending on their adaptability, both industrial land and buildings can be classified as general-purpose, special-purpose, or single-purpose.

General-purpose buildings have a wide range of alternate uses. These properties can be used for storage or adapted for light manufacturing or assembly plants. *Special-purpose buildings* have certain physical characteristics that limit the scope of their use. For example, only a few industrial enterprises require heavily insulated storage facilities. Buildings suitable for only one type of operation, or even one firm, are termed *single-purpose* industrial properties. A steel mill, for instance, cannot be converted readily to an alternate use.

Characteristics

The unique features of industrial real estate have a direct bearing on the management of such property. Industrial properties generally require heavy investment capital. Although many large corporations prefer to locate a site and build a plant to meet their exact specifications, these activities can tie up a substantial portion of the firm's operating funds. Because these corporations prefer to invest their capital in their own business operations rather than in real estate, they will seek an investor who wants to put money into a property with a guaranteed long-term lease. The corporation will then sell the chosen site to the investor and simultaneously execute a long-term lease. This is termed a *sale-leaseback agreement;* it returns the capital investment of the firm so that the funds can be reinvested in the business. Since this arrangement is profitable for both parties, industrial real estate is often investment property, with the manufacturer-tenant paying rent to the investor-owner.

In addition, the specialized nature of some industrial buildings and the large size of others make industrial property a slow-moving commodity in the real estate market. The nonliquidity of the property increases the owner's investment risk, which, in turn, leads the owner to place more demands on the industrial tenant.

To an even greater degree than with commercial shopping centers, the *value of industrial property is closely intertwined with the profitability of the firm renting the space*. The integration of the property with the machinery and inventory of the tenant firm makes it difficult for the manager to distinguish between the value of the owner's facilities and the tenant's equipment. Once the equipment is installed, the *customized quality* of the property makes the functioning of the tenant's machinery an indispensable part of the owner's capital investment.

Technological changes make heavy or specialized industrial facilities very susceptible to *rapid functional obsolescence*. This threat increases the owner's investment risk and challenges management to plan carefully for the future in order to minimize the chances of structural or functional obsolescence of the building or its tenants. Warehouses and storage space are an exception to this rule. Since this general-purpose industrial space requires less customization, it presents less danger of functional obsolescence. Tenants in warehouses and distribution facilities tend to relocate more frequently; hence, the investment risk of such property is lower and the liquidity higher.

Most industrial tenants have comparatively long lease terms, ranging from 10 to 25 years or more. The high cost of moving heavy machinery and maintaining large inventories is not conducive to yearly changes in location, so the selection of a suitable site is critical. Since industrial tenants are not expected to be experts in the real estate market, the responsibility for matching tenant and property rests largely on the shoulders of the industrial property manager.

THE INDUSTRIAL REAL ESTATE MARKET

Trends in the Industrial Real Estate Market

Paralleling the postwar shifts in other sectors of the real estate market, the industrial segment has shown increased mobility since the end of World War II. Despite the high cost of relocation, more firms are leaving the traditional bastions of industrial activity in the northeastern U.S. for locations in the southwest. A number of factors, including lower property taxes, a better labor market, lower pay scales for workers, fewer unions, lower construction costs, and a better climate have fostered this trend.

There is also a counter trend to the movement of industrial firms from the older industrial cities to new locations in other parts of the country. Since older industrial communities have already paid for roads, highway networks, ample utilities, and good sewage systems, industry is beginning to find very competitive location offers from older areas. The large inventory of vacant industrial buildings and high unemployment have also softened rigid union requirements in these areas, and some observers believe this trend will accelerate.

Transportation. In tandem with this latest shift in industrial location is the tendency for new establishments and branch facilities to be located in suburbs. The move to the suburbs has received impetus from changes in the nation's transportation patterns. The labor force, once dependent on urban transportation systems, can now use the automobile to commute to work in outlying areas. The most dramatic change in these patterns has been the rapid emergence of the freight trucking industry due to construction of interstate highways and expressway systems. Industrial firms are no longer forced to locate near rail facilities and are free to leave the congested metropolitan areas. These factors, combined with the lower cost of land in suburban locations, have been a catalyst for the construction of industrial developments in outlying areas.

Plant Size and Features. When industrial firms relocate in outlying areas, they tend to prefer one-story buildings. The reason is simple: there is more total usable space in a one-story building, and the cost of construction is generally lower. Also, the single-level plant provides flexibility of spatial layout and ease in moving goods into and out of the plant. Thanks to pallet storage and forklift moving equipment, goods can be moved more quickly on one level than they could be in elevators in a multi-level building.

Technological changes in material handling, from delivery of raw materials to shipment of finished products, have made it necessary to redesign the shipping and receiving facilities of industrial properties. Standard-sized shipping containers have increased the capacity and flexibility of material handling operations. Plants using this new method require specialized docking and loading facilities, another need that the industrial property manager must try to accommodate.

Industrial property managers must also be aware of alternative uses for their properties. One of the most profitable is multiple-tenancy. Although most firms would prefer to reserve an entire building for their use, the economic advantages of multiple-tenancy can be attractive to small and young enterprises. When establishing multiple-tenancy, managers should give some thought to the rental schedule and the compatibility of the tenants.

Land-Use Patterns. The most important new development in industrial land use is the planned *industrial park*. Although these parks first appeared before World War II, they did not gain prominence until after the war. In actuality, an industrial park is simply a suburban industrial subdivision designed to offer land in outlying areas with good accessibility to comparatively small users. Industrial parks attract businesses that formerly occupied lofts because they allow the tenant to combine office, manufacturing, and storage space in a one-story building. In many cases, the land is sold to an industrial concern, which then builds its own plant. There is little need for professional property management in these parks.

Industrial parks have been made possible in large part through liberalized zoning ordinances in growing communities. Since they view industry as a source of employment, income, and tax revenue, they are willing to pass the types of legislation industry wants, including open-occupancy laws, to attract unskilled labor to the suburban location.

In addition to industrial parks, many cities have areas where there is a concentration of office-warehouse buildings. Generally, these consist of one-story units, located in areas having easy access to the Interstate Highway System. Quite often, developers will build several of these buildings on a speculative basis and sell them to individual owners.

Figure 48: BUILDING INFORMATION FORM

INDUSTRIAL BUILDING INFORMATION

Size _____   Dimensions_____

Location_____

Date Available _____   Monthly Rent _____

Ground Area _____   Parking_____ Cars

Lot Dimensions Frontage_____ Depth_____

Zoning _____ In City _____ Out of City_____

Type Construction _____ # of Stories _____

Elevators _____Capacity (Tons) _____

Electric Power (Quantity) _____ Natural Gas _____

Roof Construction _____ Truck Docks_____

Office Space (Describe) _____

Restrooms _____ Heating _____

A.C._____ Sprinklers_____

Column Spacing_____ Drains_____

Clearance (Minimum Constant) _____ Taxes _____

Tax District _____ Topography _____

Rail Access_____ Labor Force _____

Distance from Highways_____

Market and Property Analyses. While general industrial trends provide a useful frame of reference, the industrial property manager's objective is to match a particular property with a specific firm. This process requires a detailed study of the physical aspects of the property, local supply and demand, and each prospect's needs.

The demand for industrial properties is not an independent factor, but relies upon consumer demand for the product of the industrial process. To determine the market demand for a particular type of industrial property the manager must know something about the nature of industrial processes and the character of industrial growth and development in his or her area. The first step in advertising, showing, leasing, and managing an industrial property is to study its features and the prospect's reactions to them. The manager should keep a written record of such information, perhaps on a form similar to Figure 48.

In order to interpret the demand for industrial space accurately, the manager must know why industries select one location over another. When selecting plant sites, an industrial firm will try to minimize production costs (rent, wages, taxes) and transportation costs for both raw materials and finished goods. The firm will also assess the site's profitability, perhaps by comparing demand and income factors in the local market. In a highly competitive market, the location with the lowest transportation and production costs may not be the most profit-producing. Profit may be determined by the location of competitors, the importance of customer proximity, the extent of the market area, and the responsiveness of product demand to price changes.

Industry Classification by Locational Preference. Three major categories of industry can be identified, based upon the criteria for selecting space. *Market-oriented* industries sell to private or industrial consumers. Industries of this type rely upon a large consumer population and are sensitive to growth trends or shifts in the marketplace. Market-oriented industries prefer to be located near points of distribution in order to reach their customers more quickly and economically.

Resource-oriented industries need to be located near their source of raw materials or supplies in order to minimize materials transportation costs. Plants using large amounts of fuel or bulky raw materials such as iron ore are usually resource-oriented.

Labor-oriented industries, especially those using unskilled workers, are concerned with the availability and cost of the labor pool. An automobile manufacturer will center itself in an area market that offers semiskilled and unskilled workers. Also, firms have located on the U.S.-Mexican border to take advantage of cheap labor-intensive operations conducted in Mexico, with final assembly or packaging in the United States.

Surveying the Local Market. The property manager should analyze the local market in light of the industrial site-selection factors discussed above. An industrial firm looking for space will usually want factual data about the economic base of the community and the population, including family size and composition, average age, income level, predominant occupations, and education. Potential industrial tenants will request data on local transportation services and on the skills, training, and turnover rate of the local labor force. The market survey should look into the availability, price, and source of utilities and fuel, as well as into the financial stability, services, and attitude of local government. Income tax rates, local tax rates and assessment policies, municipal services, and zoning ordinances are vital pieces of information to prospective industrial tenants. The information is available to the property manager through public sources such as the Census Bureau, local tax rolls, and the local unemployment office. Other data can be gathered from the files of banks, local development groups, municipal agencies, utility companies, and university departments of social research and urban studies.

The availability of financing through the issuance of tax-free industrial revenue bonds will often be a consideration in determining whether an industry will locate in a particular city. An investigation of this financing source should be part of the market analysis. Also, a property manager should determine whether or not the chamber of commerce or a similar group has organized an industrial park. These organizations typically subsidize the sale of land for industrial plants at prices well below market rates to attract new industries to the city. In such cases, private investors may not be able to compete.

MARKETING INDUSTRIAL SPACE

Most industrial managers and industrial firms rely heavily on outside leasing agents, called industrial brokers, to market or locate properties since the most distinctive feature of industrial space marketing is its specialization. The industrial property manager and broker must be in command of much technical knowledge about the property and about industries that may be good prospects for the properties. Industrial prospects are most interested in the utility of the property, not its amenities or prestige, and they usually ground their decisions firmly in economic facts.

Since the planning, financing, and construction of industrial property requires a long lead time, developers in many areas where demand is heavy have been successful in building speculative industrial buildings. Under this method of operation, shell buildings are constructed in the most popular sizes. After signing a lease with a tenant, investors can finish a building in a short time, usually no more than 90 days. This system has been particularly successful in areas experiencing a rapid increase in population.

Industrial Advertising and Promotion

Managers of industrial properties usually use signs and brochures to draw prospects to a building. Ordinarily, industrial brochures contain a picture of the premises, brief copy highlighting the special features of the space, and an area map. This type of advertisement is sent to a select group of firms that constitutes the market for a particular property. The list of prospects must reflect the manager's knowledge of the subject property and the types of industry that would be suited to it. Dun & Bradstreet and other directories are helpful in compiling such lists. The *Standard Industrial Classification Manual* is another valuable reference tool that groups related industries and firms. By looking up one company that is particularly suited for a property (such as a previous tenant), the manager can find related firms with similar equipment, space, and locational requirements. These firms might be interested in the vacant space and should be added to the direct-mail list.

As mentioned earlier, cooperation with outside brokers and leasing agents is the most common and productive method of marketing industrial space. The marketing and leasing of an industrial property often are accomplished before the property manager becomes involved in the transaction. If this is not the case, the industrial manager should develop a mailing list of key brokers. Professional organizations such as the Society of Industrial Realtors® can act as referral networks.

Tenant Qualification

After industrial prospects have been attracted, the manager must assess their space, transportation, and labor needs. As suggested by Figure 49, a sample industrial client requirement worksheet, there are several avenues of investigation for the manager to pursue when qualifying a prospect.

Total Land Area Required. A plant site includes the total land area within the property boundaries, both open acreage and the area covered by buildings, parking lots, landscaping, docks, and so forth. Custom-service, market-oriented industrial firms generally require less than 10 acres of land. These industries rely heavily on their proximity to a concentration of manufacturers that serve as potential consumers for their special products: precision tools, electronic components, and so on. On the other hand, heavy industries like automobile or aircraft manufacturers usually need 100 acres or more. Industries requiring large amounts of land tend to be resource- or labor-oriented.

Land-Employment Densities. One of the things a manager looks at when qualifying a prospective tenant is the number of employees on the major shift during normal plant operation. Employment density is expressed as the ratio of the number of major shift employees to total land area. Industries with a *low* ratio of employees per acre (10 or less) usually require plant facilities with a large area. These are called *labor-extensive* industries, most of which process raw materials. A chemical plant is a good example of this type of industry. *Labor-intensive* industries, on the other hand, show a *high* concentration of employees per acre. Electronics firms and other operations using highly skilled professional personnel may have as many as 75 workers per acre.

Employment density is a measure of the prospective tenant's parking needs. However, since it is based only on the number of workers on the major shift, the figure must be adjusted to allow for shift overlap, which swells the number of vehicles on the premises. In general, the manager can figure that vehicle storage will account for 60 percent of the total space needed for parking, with the other 40 percent allowed for traffic flow.

Building-Employment Density. Though it is virtually impossible to forecast a prospective tenant's total floor area needs by the nature of its business alone, some generalizations can be made. Labor-intensive industries employing highly skilled personnel—drug manufacturers, for instance—usually require 25,000 square feet of floor space or less. Labor-extensive industries, however, often need over 100,000 square feet of area to accommodate their heavy industrial activities.

Figure 49: INDUSTRIAL CLIENT REQUIREMENTS

Date _____

Company _____ Address _____

Type of Business/Mfg _____ Dist. _____ Employees _____
Area _____ N/S to _____ E/W to _____
Timing _____ Lease Expiration _____

Warehouse

Area _____ sq. ft.   Dim _____ Expanded to _____
Clg. Hgt. _____ Concrete _____ Concrete Block _____ Steel _____ Other _____
Clear span: y☐ n☐ Posts _____ ft. centers   Skylights: y☐ n☐   Crane: y☐ n☐ ___ton
Floor Drains: y☐ n☐ Sprinklers Required: y☐ n☐ Desirable: y☐ n☐
Rail spur: y☐ n☐   No. of Spots _____
Parking _____ spaces   Employees _____ Visitors _____
Floor load: Normal _____ Heavy _____ lbs/sq. ft. _____
Elec. Power: 110V _____ 240V _____ 480V _____ single/3 phase _____ Amps
Heat: y   n   Number _____ BTUs _____
Light: Normal _____ Heavy _____ Foot Candles _____ Fluorescent: y☐ n☐
Front Truck Doors: DI _____   DH _____ Rear Truck Doors: DI _____   DH _____
Side Truck Doors: DI _____   DH _____   Truck Well: y☐ n☐

Office

Total Area _____ sq. ft.   A/C: y☐ n☐   Mess.: y☐ n☐ _____ lbs/sq. ft.
Private Offices _____ Sizes _____
Conference _____ x _____   Lunchroom _____ x _____ ft.
Reception _____ x _____   Other _____ x _____ ft.
Restrooms   _____ Ladies Lounge _____
Heat: F/A _____ Wall _____ ADT _____

Yard

Area _____ sq. ft.   Paved _____
Fenced _____ L.F.   Expansion _____ sq. ft. _____
L/B Ratio _____   Landscaping _____

Miscellaneous

Lease Term _____   Option _____
Parent Company _____   Address _____
Phone _____ Contact _____
Budget _____   Net Worth _____

Dun & Bradstreet: y   n   Date _____

Other _____
_____
_____
_____
_____
_____

Gross floor area is the total of all floor space within the exterior walls of the building, with no allowance for structural projections. To be classified as part of the gross floor area, a space must have a ceiling height of at least 7½ feet. Unenclosed areas such as loading platforms should not be included in the gross floor area.

Structural Density. The ratio of the total ground floor area of a building to the total land area is termed *structural density.* For example, a 100,000-square-foot site on which a plant with a ground floor of 25,000 square feet is located has a structural density of 25 percent. Standard structural density ratios have been decreasing steadily since 1945, when sites in the central city had ratios as high as 80 percent. The average density for a general-purpose industrial building in today's market should be between 25 and 33 percent.

Access. Manufacturers in heavy industry usually require direct access to major trucking routes, air cargo transport, railroads, or even deep-water ports. Major thoroughfares to residential areas inhabited by the work force are also crucial. Wholesalers and distributors need access to trucking routes and to a major street system capable of handling traffic flow for incoming goods and outgoing deliveries.

Financial Capability. As with commercial tenants, the property manager should study an industrial tenant's past profit records, financial resources, and backing to be sure that the firm will become a viable, productive tenant. Industrial tenants who want a sale-leaseback arrangement must demonstrate a strong fiscal position before a developer will agree to become involved in the transaction as the owner-lessor; the property manager working for another type of owner should be no less careful. Once an industrial tenant leases and takes possession of property, it is difficult to remedy any problems that arise if the tenant is not suited to the space or does not have the operating capital to be successful there.

Showing the Property

If a property is not zoned for the type of industrial activities the prospective tenant engages in, or if the utility service is below the minimum needs of the firm's operation, then it may be a waste of time to bring the prospect to the site. The manager should simply explain the situation and try to build a rapport with the prospective tenant so that he or she can be placed in another property at a later date. When the prospective tenant's land area, space, density, and other requirements match the specifications of the property, the manager can feel more secure about the prognosis for the firm's economic success at the location and should show the available space.

Most of the general rules presented in preceding chapters for exhibiting residential, office, and commercial properties apply to the presentation of industrial space as well. When showing industrial space, the manager should remember to stress features and benefits that are important to the industrial prospect. These include an adequate sprinkler and fireproofing system, covered truck docks, adaptability of layout, and often, high ceilings.

The industrial property manager often has to show a building to a group. Invariably, members of the group will split up to explore their separate concerns. Since the manager cannot follow everyone and note down individual responses, he or she should go with the person in charge. It is likely that subordinates will voice their objections to the decision maker, giving the manager the opportunity to respond to their remarks, too. If the manager will arrange an appropriate debriefing session after the tour, over coffee or at a lunch, he will have an opportunity to answer all objections which have been raised by members of the group.

Prequalifying the prospect is imperative in industrial leasing. It is the only way to prepare for fielding objections and answering questions at the site. By knowing the firm's actual needs and willingness to make building modifications, the manager can save time and facilitate completion of the transaction. Another essential factor in leasing industrial property is good follow-up. The manager must take the initiative in contacting the prospect, obtaining further information, and making presentations to all involved parties. By diplomatically overcoming any minor problems and following through on the transaction, the manager will arrive at the final step in the marketing process—negotiating the lease for the premises.

Lease Negotiations

The industrial lease (Figure 50) includes a description of the premises, lease term, rent, security deposit, use of the premises, and the legal responsibilities and remedies of both parties—all the typical provisions of residential, office, and commercial property leases. However, the terms and conditions involving taxes, insurance, maintenance, and other legal matters are highly individualized in industrial leases and must be negotiated separately between each landlord and tenant. Then an attorney must formalize the agreement.

Net Leases. As discussed in Chapter 5, a net lease demands that the tenant pay some or all of the basic property expenses such as real estate taxes and assessments, insurance, utilities, and maintenance costs. In theory, there are three standard forms of net lease. The *straight net lease* requires the tenant to pay for some or all of the real estate taxes and assessments in addition to the rental obligation. Under a *net-net lease* the tenant must generally pay the taxes and assessments *plus* the insurance premiums set forth in the lease agreement. The *net-net-net,* or *triple-net, lease* holds the tenant liable for taxes and assessments, insurance premiums, *and* the cost of repairs and maintenance work stipulated in the lease terms.

A cost-conscious prospect will prefer a gross lease. The landlord, wanting safety, stability, and a reasonable level of income, will press for a net lease. Very few industrial leases are gross leases; the landlord and tenant usually compromise on some form of net lease agreement. Many owners prefer to retain the obligation to pay taxes and carry fire insurance (but with reimbursement by the tenant in many cases) so that they know their property will not be taken for unpaid taxes or destroyed by fire without reimbursement. Leases in such cases should carry a tax participation clause and a clause directing the tenant to share in increasing insurance premiums.

The annual rental rate for an industrial property is usually based on the owner's *rent factor,* which is calculated using the percentage of gross return the owner wants to earn on the investment. If the owner paid $600,000 for the building and wants a

Figure 50: NET INDUSTRIAL LEASE

Parties

AGREEMENT OF LEASE, made as of the _____ day of _____ , 19 _____ ,
between _____ ,
a corporation organized under the laws of the state of _____ ,
with its principal place of business at _____
_____ , hereinafter referred to as
Lessor, and _____ ,
a corporation organized under the laws of the state of _____ ,
with its principal place of business at _____
_____ , hereinafter referred to as Lessee.

WITNESSETH:

Leased Premises

1. Lessor hereby leases to Lessee and Lessee hereby hires from Lessor the land and all buildings erected thereon, known as _____
_____ ,
and more particularly described as set forth on Exhibit A attached hereto, subject to all matters set forth on Exhibit B attached hereto.

Term

2. This lease is for a term of _____ years, commencing _____ and terminating _____ .

Cash Rental

3. Lessee covenants and agrees that it will pay to Lessor at the address herein specified, or to such other person or at such address as Lessor may from time to time designate by written notice to Lessee, an aggregate rental of $ _____ for the term, payable in lawful money of the United States of America in equal monthly installments of $ _____ each on the _____ day of _____ , 19 _____ . Lessor shall have the right to assign its interest in the lease and in the rentals payable by the Lessee hereunder.

Taxes and Assessments

4. As additional rent, Lessee agrees and covenants to pay and discharge, before they become delinquent, all ad valorem taxes, general and special assessments and other taxes levied or assessed against the leased premises or arising in respect to the occupancy, use or possession of the leased premises, and which are assessed or become a lien or become due and payable during the term of this lease. This obligation of Lessee shall include the obligation, imposed by any law, ordinance or regulation now in existence or hereafter enacted or adopted, to pay any taxes, assessments or charges for public improvements or services levied or imposed in whole or in part as a capital or other levy against the leased premises or on the rents hereunder, or in substitution for ad valorem taxes, charges or assessments for public improvements or services as now imposed by law, but Lessee shall not be required to pay any income, gross receipts, corporate franchise or any inheritance, transfer, estate or succession taxes of Lessor. Lessee shall, within thirty (30) days following the last day on which any such taxes or assessments may be paid without incurring any interest or penalty, furnish to Lessor receipts or other evidence demonstrating payment thereof. There shall be an apportionment of all such taxes between Lessor and Lessee with respect to the first and last year of the term hereof. Lessee may, in good faith and in a lawful manner and upon giving notice to Lessor of its intention so to do, contest any tax, assessment or charge against the leased premises, but all costs and expenses incident to such contest shall be paid by Lessee and in case of an adjudication adverse to Lessee, then Lessee shall promptly pay such tax, assessment or charge. Lessee shall indemnify and save Lessor harmless against any loss or damage arising from such contest and shall, if necessary to prevent a sale or other loss or damage to Lessor, pay such tax, assessment or charge under protest and take such other steps as may be necessary to prevent any sale or loss.

Maintenance and Repair

5. Lessee agrees to keep and maintain the buildings and all other improvements on the leased premises, and parking areas and ways used in connection with the leased premises, in as good a state of repair as the same are turned over to it, ordinary wear and tear excepted, and

NET LEASE—Cont.

in a clean, safe and sanitary condition, and agrees to make all necessary repairs, interior, exterior and structural, to said building and other improvements, and to pay and hold Lessor free and harmless from bills or assessments for light, heat, water, gas, sewer rentals or charges, vault taxes or rentals and any other expenses arising out of or incidental to the occupancy of said leased premises. Lessee further releases and agrees to save Lessor harmless from any and all damages and liability which may occur to the contents of any portion of said leased premises during the term of this lease. Lessee agrees to repair and restore all improvements on the demised premises following any damage to or loss or destruction of the premises or any part thereof from any cause whatsoever, at Lessee's expense and without cost to Lessor.

Offsets

6.   No claim the Lessee may have against the Lessor for any reason shall be offset against the rentals due from Lessee to Lessor.

Lessee's Improvements

7.   Lessee, during the full term of this lease, shall have the right, at any time and from time to time, at its own and sole expense and liability, to place or install on the leased premises such improvements, buildings and fixtures it shall desire, all of which shall be and remain, from the time of construction or installation, the property of Lessor, without payment or offset; provided that Lessee shall first obtain the prior written consent of Lessor if any such improvements or buildings shall involve any structural changes in the improvements existing at the commencement of this lease, and provided further that upon the termination of this lease for any reason Lessee shall, if required by Lessor, promptly remove all such improvements, buildings and fixtures and place the leased premises in the same condition as at the commencement of the term of this lease, and provided further that no such installation or construction shall violate any lawful rule or regulation, plat or zoning restriction or other law, ordinance or regulation applicable thereto, and shall be done and performed in a good and professional manner. All costs of any such improvements shall be paid in cash by Lessee and Lessee shall allow no liens for labor or materials to attach to the leased premises by virtue thereof. If the estimated costs of such buildings or improvements shall exceed $, Lessee shall submit drawings and specifications to Lessor for Lessor's approval, and no work shall be commenced until Lessor has approved such drawings and specifications and the contracts, contractors, performance and payment bonds and the sureties thereon.

Insurance

8.   The Lessee agrees to pay as additional rental all premiums required during the term hereof to provide and keep in force policies of:

a. Fire and extended coverage insurance in some insurance company or companies authorized to do business in the state of _____ in an amount not less than _____ percent of the full insurable value of the buildings and other improvements now constructed or to be constructed on the said leased premises, and in any event not less than an amount sufficient to prevent the insured from becoming a coinsurer under any applicable coinsurance clause, and to keep such insurance in full force and effect for and during the time any buildings and improvements are located on the leased premises, or are being constructed on the leased premises and thereafter during the term of this lease. For the purposes hereof "full insurable value" shall mean the replacement cost of the improvements without allowance for depreciation but excluding footings, foundations and other portions of improvements which are not insurable. A determination of full insurable value shall be made at least once every 3 years at Lessee's expense by a firm of qualified fire insurance appraisers satisfactory to Lessor and to fire insurance companies generally. Lessee may provide policies containing a_____ percent coinsurance clause. Such policy or policies shall insure Lessor and Lessee and, so long as an institutional investor holds a first lien on the premises under a mortgage, shall contain a standard mortgagee clause providing for payment of proceeds to such mortgagee.

b. Public liability and property damage insurance with limits of not less than $__for injury or death of any one person, $__for injury or death in any one accident or occurrence and property damage in the amount of $__insuring Lessor and Lessee.

c. Such other types of insurance, and in such amounts, as Lessor may reasonably require, provided such other insurance is commonly carried in connection with properties

NET LEASE—Cont.

similar to the leased premises or businesses similar to that being conducted on the leased premises.

All policies required by this paragraph shall be carried in such companies and upon such forms as both parties hereto from time to time approve. No policies shall be subject to cancellation or material modification except after ten (10) days' written notice to Lessor and Lessor's mortgagee and each policy shall so provide. All policies required to be furnished hereunder (or certificates in the event insurance is provided under a blanket policy) shall be deposited with Lessor prior to the commencement of the term hereof, and renewals thereof or evidence of the payment of premium to continue the coverage in force shall be deposited with Lessor not less than 30 days prior to the date on which such insurance would expire.

Restoration Following Loss

9. Upon the occurrence of any loss, Lessee will give written notice thereof to Lessor and promptly commence and will diligently complete, or cause to be commenced and diligently completed, the repair and restoration of the premises so that, insofar as possible, upon the completion of such repair or restoration the improvements will constitute an entire architectural unit which will have a commercial value at least as great as prior to the damage or loss. If the estimated cost of repair or restoration shall exceed $_____, Lessee shall submit to Lessor for Lessor's approval the drawings and specifications; and all contracts, contractors, performance and payment bonds and the sureties thereon shall be subject to Lessor's prior approval. If the loss, damage or destruction results from a casualty covered by a policy or policies of insurance, the insurance proceeds recovered shall be paid to Lessee to reimburse it for its expenses incurred in repairing and restoring the premises upon submission by Lessee of evidence of completion of and payment for the work. In the event such proceeds are inadequate to reimburse Lessee for the cost of such repair or restoration, Lessee shall pay any additional amounts required from its own funds. Any sums remaining after such repair or restoration shall be the property of the Lessor.

Abatement

10. The Lessee's obligations to pay rent and to perform all of the other covenants and agreements which Lessee is bound to perform under the terms of this lease shall not terminate, abate or be diminished during any period that the premises or any part thereof are untenantable, regardless of the cause of such untenantability, except as provided in Paragraph 17 hereof.

Compliance with Laws, etc.

11. Lessee, in the use and occupancy of the leased premises, and in the prosecution and conduct of its business and activities, shall at its own cost and expense secure and maintain all necessary licenses and permits required for the conduct of its business, and shall at all times comply with all laws and ordinances and all lawful rules and regulations issued by any legally constituted authority, and with the applicable orders, regulations and requirements of any Board of Fire Underwriters, and observe all plat and deed restrictions of record, including in such compliance any required changes in the improvements, structural or otherwise, but may, within such limits, use the leased premises for any lawful purpose.

Waste; Use; Liens

12. Lessee agrees not to do nor suffer any waste to the leased premises, nor cause, suffer or permit any liens to attach to or to exist against the leased premises by reason of any act of Lessee or by reason of its failure to perform any act required of it hereunder. Provided, however, Lessee shall not be required to pay or discharge any lien against the leased premises so long as Lessee has given Lessor notice of its intent to contest such lien and Lessee is in good faith contesting the validity or amount thereof and has given to Lessor such security as Lessor has requested to assure payment of such lien and to prevent the sale, foreclosure or forfeiture of the leased premises by reason of nonpayment. On final determination of the lien or claim for lien Lessee will immediately pay any judgment rendered, and all costs and charges, and shall cause the lien to be released or satisfied. Lessee will not use or permit the use of the leased premises in any manner which would result, or would with the passage of time result, in the creation of any easement or prescriptive right.

Lessor's Performance of Lessee's Duties

13. If Lessee should default in the performance of any covenant on its part to be performed by virtue of any provision of this lease, Lessor may, after any notice and the expiration of any period with respect thereto as required pursuant to the applicable provisions of this lease,

NET LEASE—Cont.

perform the same for the account of Lessee, and Lessee hereby authorizes Lessor to come upon the leased premises and while on the leased premises to do anything necessary to accomplish the correction of such default. If Lessor, at any time, is compelled to pay or elects to pay any sum of money by reason of the failure of Lessee, after any notice and the expiration of any period with respect thereto as required pursuant to the applicable provisions of this lease, to comply with any provision of this lease, or if Lessor is compelled to incur any expense, including reasonable attorneys' fees, in instituting, prosecuting or defending any action or proceeding instituted by reason of any default of Lessee hereunder, the sum or sums so paid by Lessor, with all interest, costs and damages, shall be deemed to be additional rental hereunder, and shall together with interest thereon at the rate of 6 percent per annum be due from Lessee to Lessor on the first day of the month following the incurring of such respective expense, except as otherwise herein specifically provided.

Notice to Mortgagee and Right to Cure Lessor's Default

14. So long as there remains of record a first mortgage of Lessor's interest in the premises, and Lessee has been given written notice of the identity and address of such mortgagee, no notice provided for herein shall be deemed to have been given unless a copy thereof is given to such mortgagee at the same time and in the same manner as the original was given to the other party to this lease. Lessee agrees that if in any notice to Lessor the performance of some act is required or compliance with some provision hereof is requested and Lessor does not, within the allotted time, perform such act or comply with such provision, Lessee will so notify the mortgagee and mortgagee shall have sixty (60) days after receipt of such notice in which to perform such act or comply with such provision for and on behalf of Lessor, and Lessee shall have no right to terminate this lease if the mortgagee shall perform and comply as and within the time herein provided. In the event the act or thing to be complied with is of such a nature that it cannot be performed or complied with within said 60-day period, mortgagee shall be deemed to have complied herewith in the event it commenced the performance or compliance within said 60-day period and thereafter completes the same with due diligence. The granting to the mortgagee of additional time in which to comply shall not be deemed in any manner to release or relieve Lessor from the obligations of Lessor under this lease. The said mortgagee is hereby authorized to enter upon the leased premises and while on the leased premises to do anything necessary to correct such default.

Covenant of Peaceful Possession

15. Upon performance of all of the conditions, covenants and agreements herein contained on the part of the Lessee, Lessor shall provide Lessee quiet and peaceful possession of the leased premises during the full term hereof, without hindrance or molestation from anyone claiming rights or interest therein through or against the Lessor.

Assignment and Subletting

16. Lessee shall not assign, mortgage or encumber this lease nor sublet the leased premises, or any part thereof, without the written consent of the Lessor, provided, however, that such consent shall not be arbitrarily nor capriciously withheld. Lessee shall in any event continue to be liable hereunder following any assignment or subletting.

Condemnation

17. In the event all of the leased premises, or so much thereof as to cause the premises not taken to be unsuitable for Lessee's purposes even after restoration and repair, are permanently taken or condemned for a public or quasi-public use, this lease shall terminate. Lessee's interest in any award made with respect to such taking shall be subordinate to the extent of an amount, if any, which when added to the amount to which Lessor is entitled to receive is necessary to pay fully the then unpaid balance of any first mortgage on the leased premises.

In the event less than all of the leased premises are taken or condemned for a public or quasi-public use and the portion of the premises not taken may be made reasonably suitable for Lessee's use by repair or restoration, this lease will not terminate. Lessee shall, in such event, promptly commence and diligently complete the repair and restoration of the premises so that upon completion the premises will constitute a complete architectural unit with an appearance, character and commercial value as nearly as possible equal to the value of the premises immediately prior to the taking. There shall be an abatement of rental after such taking, and during the balance of the term hereof, in the proportion that the floor area of the

NET LEASE—Cont.

building taken bears to the total floor area of the building immediately prior to such taking. Lessee shall be reimbursed for its costs of repair and restoration to the extent of the amount of the award received on account of such taking. In repairing and restoring the leased premises, the drawings and specifications, contracts, contractors, bonds and the sureties thereon, shall all be subject to Lessor's approval. Any award remaining after Lessee has been fully reimbursed for its costs of repair and restoration shall be the property of the Lessor.

Merger of Estates

18. Lessee agrees that it will not, so long as there is a first mortgage lien upon the leased premises, convey or transfer its interest in this lease directly or indirectly to the Lessor, or accept a conveyance of the Lessor's interest in this lease; and that in the event of any happening which by operation of law would cause a merger of the estates of Lessor or Lessee with the result that this lease would terminate, Lessee covenants and agrees for the benefit of any mortgagee of Lessor's interest in the leased premises, and with the intention that any mortgagee may rely hereon, that Lessee will assume and agree to pay the remaining amount of the indebtedness, both principal and interest, secured by any such mortgage, and will assume and agree to perform the undertakings of the mortgagor in said mortgage.

Lessor Indemnified

19. Lessee agrees to indemnify and save Lessor harmless from any and all liability, damage, expense, cause of action, suits, claims or demands (unless due to the acts, omissions, negligence or fault of the Lessor) arising from injury to persons or damage to property on the leased premises, or upon the abutting sidewalks or curbs, and to save Lessor harmless from any and all liabilities arising from Lessee's failure to perform any of the terms, conditions and covenants of the lease required to be performed by Lessee.

Inspection of Premises

20. Lessee agrees to permit Lessor and its agents, and any mortgagee of the leased premises, to come upon and inspect the premises at all reasonable times, and to come upon the premises if necessary to perform any act which Lessee has failed to perform, as provided in Paragraph 13 hereof.

Defaults and Remedies

21. If one or more of the following events (herein called "defaults") shall happen and be continuing, namely:

a. default shall be made in the punctual payment of any rent herein agreed to be paid and such default shall continue for a period of fifteen (15) days after written notice is given Lessee by Lessor of such default;

b. Lessee makes an assignment for the benefit of creditors;

c. Lessee files a petition in bankruptcy or for relief under the Federal Bankruptcy Law or any other applicable statute, or makes an assignment for the benefit of creditors;

d. an attachment or execution is levied upon the Lessee's property in or interest under this lease, which is not satisfied or released or the enforcement thereof stayed or superseded by an appropriate proceeding within thirty (30) days thereafter;

e. an involuntary petition in bankruptcy or for reorganization or arrangement under the Federal Bankruptcy Law is filed against Lessee and such involuntary petition is not withdrawn, dismissed, stayed or discharged within ninety (90) days from the filing thereof;

f. a Receiver or Trustee is appointed for the property of Lessee or of Lessee's business or assets and the order or decree appointing such Receiver or Trustee shall have remained in force undischarged or unstayed for thirty (30) days after the entry of such order or decree;

g. Lessee shall vacate or abandon the leased premises, or shall fail to perform or observe any other covenant, agreement or condition to be performed or kept by the Lessee under the terms and provisions of this lease, and such failure shall continue for thirty (30) days after written notice thereof has been given by Lessor to the Lessee; then and in any such event Lessor shall have the right, at the option of the Lessor, then or at any time thereafter while such default or defaults shall continue, to elect either (1) to cure such default or defaults at its own expense and without prejudice to any other remedies which it might otherwise have, any payment made or expenses incurred by Lessor in curing such default with interest thereon at 6 percent per annum to be and become additional rent to be paid by Lessee with the next installment of rent falling due thereafter, or (2) to re-enter the

NET LEASE—Cont.

leased premises by force or otherwise, without notice, and dispossess Lessee and anyone claiming under Lessee by summary proceedings or otherwise, and remove their effects, and take complete possession of the leased premises and either (i) declare this lease forfeited and the term ended, or (ii) elect to continue this lease in full force and effect, but with the right at any time thereafter to declare this lease forfeited and the term ended. In such re-entry the Lessor may, with or without process of law, remove all persons from the premises, and Lessee hereby covenants in such event, for itself and all others occupying the leased premises under Lessee, to peacefully yield up and surrender the leased premises to the Lessor. Should Lessor declare this lease forfeited and the term ended, the Lessor shall be entitled to recover from Lessee the rental and all other sums due and owing by Lessee to the date of termination, plus the costs of curing all of Lessee's defaults existing at or prior to the date of termination, plus the worth as of the termination of the lease of an amount equal to the then value of the excess, if any, of the aggregate of rent and charges equivalent to rent reserved in this lease for the balance of the term over the then reasonable rental value of the leased premises for the balance of the term, discounted at a rate of 4 percent per annum. Should Lessor, following default as aforesaid, elect to continue this lease in full force, Lessor shall use its best efforts to rent the premises on the best terms available for the remainder of the term hereof, or for such longer or shorter period as Lessor shall deem advisable. Lessee shall remain liable for payment of all rentals and other charges and costs imposed on Lessee herein, in the amounts, at the time and upon the conditions as herein provided, but Lessor shall credit against such liability of the Lessee all amounts received by Lessor from such reletting after first reimbursing itself for all costs incurred in curing Lessee's defaults and in re-entering, preparing and refinishing the premises for reletting, and reletting the premises.

No re-entry by Lessor or any action brought by Lessor to oust Lessee from the premises shall operate to terminate this lease unless Lessor shall give written notice of termination to Lessee, in which event Lessee's liability shall be as above provided. No right or remedy granted to Lessor herein is intended to be exclusive of any other right or remedy, and each and every right and remedy herein provided shall be cumulative and in addition to any other right or remedy hereunder or now or hereafter existing in law or equity or by statute. In the event of termination of this lease, Lessee waives any and all rights to redeem the premises either given by any statute now in effect or hereafter enacted. Any holding over by Lessee after the termination of this lease shall create a tenancy from month to month, on the same terms and conditions and at the same rental as herein provided applicable during the term hereof, and such tenancy may be terminated by Lessor on sixty (60) days' written notice to Lessee.

Condition of Premises upon Termination

22. Upon termination of this lease, Lessee covenants and agrees to remove all of its property from the premises, and Lessee shall also remove any improvements made by Lessee upon the premises (which, prior to removal, shall be the property of the Lessor) if such removal is requested by Lessor, and Lessee shall repair any damage caused by the removal thereof, and shall leave the premises in good and clean condition and repair.

Successors and Assigns

23. The obligations and responsibilities shall be binding upon and the rights and benefits shall inure to the successors and assigns of the parties hereto; but the liabilities of any successor to the interest of the Lessor hereunder shall be limited to the performance of those obligations which arise and accrue during the period of ownership of the leased premises by any such successor.

Notices

24. Any notices or inquiries regarding this lease shall be delivered to Lessor at _____ _____and to Lessee at _____ _____ or to such other address as the parties may designate in writing. Notice may be given by registered or certified mail, and in such event the date of service shall be the date on which notice is deposited in a United States post office properly stamped and addressed.

NET LEASE—Cont.

No Oral Agreements

25. It is expressly agreed between Lessor and Lessee that there is no verbal understanding or agreement which in any way changes the terms, covenants and conditions herein set forth, and that no modification of this lease and no waiver of any of its terms and conditions shall be effective unless made in writing and duly executed by the authorized officers of the necessary parties or party.

Subordination to Mortgage; Nondisturbance of Lessee

26. This lease shall be, at the election of the holder of any first mortgage, subject and subordinate to that mortgage, whether now existing or hereafter placed upon the leased premises and to all renewals, modifications, consolidations, replacements and extensions thereof, and Lessee will, at the request of the holder of such mortgage, promptly execute any instrument or instruments for delivery to any such mortgagee or mortgagees, specifically providing for such subordination, but such subordination is and shall be on the condition that so long as Lessee pays all rentals and performs all other obligations imposed upon it in this lease, in the time and manner specified, neither Lessee's use and occupation of the leased premises nor the continuance of this lease shall in any way be terminated, affected or prejudiced by the holder of such mortgage, by foreclosure proceedings or otherwise, and neither the Lessee nor the mortgagee shall have the right to terminate this lease following foreclosure of the mortgage.

No Implied Waiver

27. The failure of Lessor to insist, in one or more instances, upon the strict performance by Lessee of any of the provisions of this lease shall not be construed as a waiver of any future breach of such provisions. Receipt by Lessor of rent with knowledge of the breach of any provision hereof shall not be deemed a waiver of such breach.

Warranties of Lessee

28. Lessee warrants to and for the benefit of any mortgagee of the leased premises that as of the date of execution of this lease it neither has nor claims any defense to this lease nor any offset against the rentals payable or other obligations required of Lessee hereunder, and Lessee warrants that it has not paid any rental in advance for a period of more than one month and covenants that it will not, without such mortgagee's written consent, at any time during the term hereof prepay any rental for a period longer than one month.

Maintenance of Corporate Existence and Assets; Merger and Consolidation

29. Lessee covenants that it will maintain its corporate existence and that it will not during the term hereof sell, transfer or assign all or substantially all of its assets, or merge into or consolidate with any other corporation unless the surviving corporation shall have a net worth at least equal to the net worth of Lessee immediately prior to such merger or consolidation and unless such surviving corporation shall execute and deliver to Lessor and to any mortgagee of the leased premises a written assumption of the obligations of Lessee under this lease.

Expense Obligations

30. It is the intention of the parties that Lessor shall receive the cash rental specified in Paragraph 3 hereof as a net rental, free from all taxes, charges, expenses, damages and deductions of every description, and that Lessee shall pay all taxes, charges, expenses, damages and deductions which, except for this lease, would have been chargeable against the leased premises or Lessor. Lessee shall not, however, be under any obligation to pay any franchise, estate, inheritance, payroll or income tax payable by Lessor or upon the income or profits of Lessor, by reason of any law now in effect or hereinafter enacted, unless such taxes are a result of a shift of the incidence of taxation now and ordinarily imposed on realty, in which event Lessee shall be liable for the payment of such tax only if such tax is imposed in lieu of real property taxes and then only to the extent of the decrease in real property taxes as a result of such substitution.

IN WITNESS WHEREOF, the parties have executed this agreement each by their respective officers thereunto duly authorized and have caused their respective seals to be hereto affixed, all as of the day and year first above written.

10 percent return, the rental rate will be around $60,000 per year. Naturally, this figure is then modified by factors such as the economic pressure on the owner, the desirability of the tenant, the urgency of the tenant's need for suitable quarters, competition, the specifics of the lease, and general market conditions. The total annual rental amount is then broken down into a dollar-per-square-foot figure for the tenant's analysis during negotiations.

The manner of rent payment varies greatly under industrial leases. Rent may be paid monthly, quarterly, semiannually, or annually at either the beginning or end of the lease period. Payments may be equal throughout the lease term or subject to adjustment at dates specified in the lease. The amount of rent and the method of payment are negotiable items. Neither the rent factor nor the per-square-foot rental figure is stated in the lease. It usually specifies only the total amount of rent to be paid and the rental rate over the term of the lease.

Longer lease terms, option clauses, and building modifications are also open to negotiation. The impact of these factors on the outcome of the transaction will depend on the manager's skill in assessing the position of each party and on what issues each is willing to compromise to gain on another front.

For example, a prospective tenant's demand for additional dock space and a sprinkler system might be satisfied by a small rent reduction. Likewise, the tenant's willingness to sign a longer lease might encourage the landlord to lower the rent factor. The longer period gives the landlord more time over which to amortize the mortgage on the property, thereby reducing monthly loan payments and decreasing the annual cost of the property. If the yearly gross return on the investment were increased, it would be in the owner's best interests for the manager to adjust the rent factor on the property. It is the manager's job to know these facts and to bring owner and tenant to mutually satisfactory terms.

Although much time and effort are spent negotiating industrial leases, they have relatively long terms and provide a very worthwhile financial return.

MAINTENANCE OF INDUSTRIAL PROPERTY

The manager of industrial property is most involved in leasing space and enforcing the terms of the lease agreement. Under the various forms of net lease, the tenant assumes some or all of the maintenance responsibilities for the property. The tenant's upkeep of his or her equipment accounts for much of the interior building maintenance that might otherwise fall to the manager. Many tenants hire their own janitorial crew to maintain the premises as stipulated in the lease. Others, especially those located in industrial parks, contract with a professional service agency for maintenance work at their plant.

Upkeep of the grounds and the building's exterior is often the only maintenance responsibility that is not assumed by the tenant under the lease terms or covered by routine equipment care. These tasks become the province of the property manager. The steps involved in the upkeep of industrial property are basically the same as those for residential, office, or commercial property. The vigilant property manager will inspect the property periodically to detect lease violations and ensure that the owner's investment is being protected.

SECURITY OF INDUSTRIAL PROPERTY

Security of office-warehouses and small free standing industrial buildings is provided during business hours by the presence of the tenant and by security alarm systems when the buildings are closed for the day. Large industrial parks and plants, which may occupy hundreds of acres, will have a separate security force which may resemble the police department of a small city. Security of industry on this scale is generally a separate department of the industrial organization responsible for the facility. The American Society for Industrial Security (ASIS), a professional association of industrial security personnel, sponsors a training program leading to the designation Certified Protection Professional (CPP).

SUMMARY

Industrial sites include all land and buildings where activities related to the production, storage, and distribution of *tangible goods* take place. Industrial sites fall into three major classifications, based upon their adaptability to other uses.

General-purpose buildings have a wide range of uses but are most often adapted for light manufacturing or assembly plants. The physical characteristics of *special-purpose buildings* limit their use. Buildings that are suitable for only *one* purpose and cannot be converted readily to any alternate use are termed *single-purpose properties.*

In general, industrial properties require heavy investment capital, are slow moving in the real estate market, and are susceptible to rapid functional obsolescence. Another distinctive characteristic of industrial property is the relative fixity of industrial tenants, who are restricted from frequent changes in location by the high cost of moving their equipment and inventories. Because of the nature of industrial property, it is essential that the manager match tenant and location by analyzing the market and qualifying prospective tenants.

Like other sectors of the real estate market, industrial firms have shown increased mobility since the end of World War II. As the freight trucking industry developed in the 1950s, industrial firms were no longer tied to the rail facilities of the congested central metropolitan areas and began to relocate in suburban areas. At the same time, the labor force began to commute to work in automobiles instead of on urban transport systems. The increased availability of labor encouraged industrial relocation to outlying areas.

One of the most promising new developments in industrial land use is the planned industrial park. This type of suburban industrial subdivision offers land in outlying areas with good accessibility to comparatively small users of space.

The demand for industrial property is related to local demand for the product of the industrial process. Industries that prefer to be located near consumers or users are *market-oriented.* Industries that locate near their major supplier or source of raw materials are *resource-oriented. Labor-oriented* industries are concerned with the existence and cost of a sufficient labor pool. To determine the demand for a particular type of industrial property and to assess its suitability for a specific tenant, the manager must be familiar with the nature of various industrial processes and the character of industrial growth and development in his or her market.

Industrial property is usually leased by means of signs, brochures, and industrial brokers. This process demands much more technical and specialized knowledge than marketing commercial or residential space. Negotiations are usually prolonged and complex, but since industrial leases are long-term, leasing efforts need not be made very frequently.

An industrial firm looking for space will want detailed facts about the economic base of the community and a profile of its population. It will also need data on the skills, education, and turnover rate of the local labor force and on local transportation facilities, utilities, taxes, zoning, and government regulations.

The property manager must qualify the prospect firm in terms of space, transportation, and labor needs. By knowing the firm's actual needs and willingness to make building modifications, the manager can avert minor problems that might block progress toward the next step in the leasing process—negotiating the lease for the premises.

Industrial leases are generally net leases. Depending upon the terms of the agreement, a *net lease* requires the tenant to pay some or all of the basic expenses of the premises, such as real estate taxes, assessments, property insurance, and maintenance costs. Thus, although the standard industrial lease includes many of the typical provisions encountered in leases for other types of property, the terms and conditions involving real estate taxes and assessments, insurance premiums, and maintenance cost responsibilities are highly individualized and must be negotiated separately between each manager and tenant.

The initial bargaining position of the manager is usually based on the *rent factor,* or the percentage of gross return the owner wants from the property. It is also in the owner's favor to obtain a completely net lease, with the tenant paying as many expenses for the property as possible. The manager may grant concessions or even lower the rent during the negotiation process. Pertinent factors in this decision are the economic pressure on the owner, the desirability of the tenant, the urgency of the tenant's need for suitable quarters, and general market conditions.

Under the various forms of net lease, the tenant usually assumes most or all of the maintenance responsibilities for the property; those not assumed by the tenant become the province of the property manager. Since the tasks involved in the upkeep of industrial property are basically the same as those for residential, office, or commercial property, the maintenance and inspection techniques discussed in preceding chapters are adaptable to the needs of the industrial property manager.

QUESTIONS: CHAPTER 15

1. A warehouse would be an example of a:

   a. general-purpose building.
   b. special-purpose building.
   c. limited-purpose building.
   d. single-purpose building.

2. Storage space has:

   I. greater liquidity than light assembly plants.
   II. a great investment risk due to the instability of tenancy.

   a. I only
   b. II only
   c. both I and II
   d. neither I nor II

3. List the three categories of industry based on the criteria firms use in selecting a location.

   a. _____
   b. _____
   c. _____

4. Industrial space is particularly suited to which marketing method?

   a. classified ads
   b. display ads
   c. direct mail
   d. radio commercials

5. A plant occupying 200,000 square feet is located on a site containing 600,000 square feet. The structural density of the property is:

   a. 30 percent.
   b. 33 percent.
   c. 40 percent.
   d. 12 percent.

6. A labor-intensive industry:

   I. has a high ratio of employees per acre.
   II. usually requires plant facilities with a large area.

   a. I only
   b. II only
   c. both I and II
   d. neither I nor II

7. When measuring industrial space, gross floor area:

   I. must have a ceiling height of 8½ feet.
   II. does not include structural projections supporting the building.

   a. I only
   b. II only
   c. both I and II
   d. neither I nor II

8. Structural density of industrial properties:

I. is the total land area of the property divided by the ground floor area of the building.
II. has increased steadily since 1945.

    a. I only
    b. II only

    c. both I and II
    d. neither I nor II

9. List four types of property expenses that may be charged to the tenant under a net lease.

    a. _____
    b. _____

    c. _____
    d. _____

10. Write the equation for determining an owner's rent factor.

    _____

11. An industrial building of 11,000 square feet cost $370,500, and the owner wants a 12 percent annual return on the investment. The minimum rent per square foot the manager should obtain for the space is:

    a. $2.22.
    b. $4.04.

    c. $6.23.
    d. $3.37.

12. Drug manufacturers:

I. are usually considered labor-intensive firms.
II. generally require over 100,000 square feet of area in their plants.

    a. I only
    b. II only

    c. both I and II
    d. neither I nor II

13. Industry in the United States is currently shifting to:

I. suburban locations.
II. the northwest.

    a. I only
    b. II only

    c. both I and II
    d. neither I nor II

14. What is the gross floor area of a one-story plant with a constant ceiling height of 11 feet and the following floor plan?

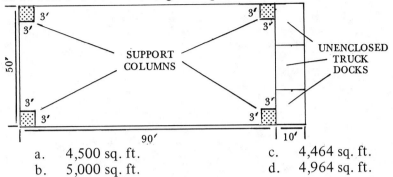

    a.   4,500 sq. ft.   c.   4,464 sq. ft.
    b.   5,000 sq. ft.   d.   4,964 sq. ft.

15. Speculative construction of shell industrial buildings:

    I.   permits tenants rapid occupancy to their specifications once their lease is signed.
    II.   has not been successful in areas experiencing rapid population growth.

    a.   I only   c.   both I and II
    b.   II only   d.   neither I nor II

16
Subsidized Housing

One of the most revolutionary activities in the real estate market is urban renewal. By 1945, almost every city and town in our nation was littered with deteriorated buildings. Depression years, followed by wartime emergencies and expenditures, had encouraged bypassing of building and housing codes to the point where properties in some areas were so overcrowded and unsafe as to be virtual slums. This condition was so widespread that the federal government was forced to begin rehabilitating these unsafe, undesirable neighborhoods. Wherever feasible, however, large-scale urban rehabilitation or redevelopment programs were meant to be initiated and financed at the local level. Such programs involved all types of urban property, both residential and commercial.

The term *urban renewal* encompasses three possible approaches to improving a blighted area—conservation, correction, or clearance and redevelopment. Buildings that are beginning to deteriorate but that still have substantial economic use remaining call for blight prevention, or *conservation.* This is the least expensive approach, involves less radical physical changes, and does not have a detrimental impact on surrounding areas. It consists simply of minor repairs, preventative maintenance, and frequent inspections.

Blight *correction,* or rehabilitation, is an appropriate solution for properties where decay has made substantial inroads, but only if expenditures for capital improvements can reverse the trend. Correction involves major repairs of the physical structure, equipment, and working systems of the building. The manager must consider the projected capital investment in terms of the remaining economic life of the building and improvements before pursuing this approach.

When deterioration has progressed so far that properties have become unsalvageable and decay encourages the substandard living habits characteristic of slums, the structures should be razed to make way for redevelopment. This is slum *clearance.* The local government has the power to condemn the properties in a slum area, buy the land, and offer it for sale to developers who will build low- to middle-income housing on the site. Although private builders and developers actually construct the subsidized housing, the federal government often finances or subsidizes the construction of new projects on such sites.

Professional property managers are vital to the federal and local government agencies involved in urban renewal. It is not enough that new public housing is built in these areas; it must also be operated efficiently. An experienced manager of multitenant residential properties can guide the development of functional housing for low-income families. Once the projects are built, the manager can oversee their operation so that the needs of the residents are met.

FEDERAL HOUSING PROGRAMS

The actual construction and operation of public housing projects for low-income families has traditionally been the responsibility of local governments. The federal government either loaned the money needed to finance a project or made annual contributions to permit the housing complex to operate with affordable rental rates.

Up until the mid 60s, most public housing projects were newly constructed units built for precisely that purpose. In 1965 Congress authorized the Department of Housing and Urban Development (HUD) to provide financial assistance to local housing authorities for the acquisition and operation of existing buildings or privately constructed new housing for low-income tenants. The Housing and Urban Development Act was passed in 1968 as a comprehensive piece of legislation.

Under the 1968 Housing Act, the Federal Housing Administration (FHA), an agency of HUD, was created to encourage private participation in the development and construction of housing for low-income families through rental and mortgage insurance programs. FHA-insured mortgages and government subsidies were awarded to nonprofit cooperative groups for the construction of low-income housing.

Apartments in public housing buildings covered under the HUD Section 8 Housing Assistance Payments Program are rented on a subsidized basis. A tenant pays up to 30 percent of his or her adjusted monthly income; HUD pays the difference between that figure and market rent. The eligible income for occupants of public housing varies according to geographical area and the number of dependents in the family. Note how rental payments are broken down in the HUD Section 8 Housing Assistance Payments contract shown on the following pages.

In addition to public housing, the local housing authority in some cities will contract with private investors for housing for eligible recipients. This presents an opportunity for owners to obtain tenants who have been screened by HUD. Often, single-family homes are needed, which are suitable for large families. Part of an agreement between a local housing authority and a private investor is shown as Figure 51.

HUD has developed several standard lease forms to be used exclusively with public housing. One of its residential lease forms is reproduced as Figure 52. The manager of public housing must be willing to work within the framework established by this government agency.

Legislation pertaining to subsidized housing changes constantly. An informed manager stays abreast of changes in local, state, and national laws and programs. Despite the variables of rental rates, income levels, and program details, all of these subsidized

Figure 51: HOUSING AUTHORITY AGREEMENT

U.S. DEPARTMENT OF HOUSING AND URBAN DEVELOPMENT
SECTION 8 HOUSING ASSISTANCE PAYMENTS PROGRAM
EXISTING HOUSING

PART I OF THE

HOUSING ASSISTANCE PAYMENTS CONTRACT

MASTER SECTION 8 ACC NUMBER:	EXISTING HOUSING ACC PART I NUMBER AND DATE	CONTRACT NUMBER:

This Housing Assistance Payments Contract ("Contract") is entered into between the Owner, **Urban America Property**, and the PHA, **Chicago Housing Authority**, which is a public housing agency as defined in the United States Housing Act of 1937 ("Act"). The PHA is entering into this Contract pursuant to an Annual Contributions Contract ("ACC") with the United States of America ("Government") (see Section 2.3 of this Contract).

The purpose of this contract is to enable the Lower-Income Family identified in Section 1.1 to lease a Decent, Safe, and Sanitary dwelling unit pursuant to the Section 8 Housing Assistance Payments Program.

The Owner and the PHA agree as follows:

1.1   CONTRACT UNIT, FAMILY, AND LEASE.

(a)   Contract Unit and Family. The following described dwelling unit ("Contract Unit") is leased by the Owner under a lease approved by the PHA ("Lease") to the following Lower-Income Family ("Family"):

Contract Unit: _____
(Address of Unit, including Apt. No. if any)

Family: _____
(Name of Person(s) Signing Lease)

(b)   Lease. The Lease shall at all times contain the Required Lease Provisions set forth in Appendix VI of the Existing Housing Regulations, 24 CFR, Part 882, but shall not contain the Prohibited Lease Provisions set forth in Appendix VII of the Regulations. A copy of the Required Lease Provisions and of the Prohibited Lease Provisions shall be made available by the PHA to the Owner at the Owner's request in advance of execution of this Contract.

1.2   CONTRACT RENT, FAMILY PORTION OF RENT, ASSISTANCE PAYMENTS.

(a)   Amount of Contract Rent. The total rent payable to the Owner for the Contract Unit ("Contract Rent") is $ __300.00__ per month.

(b)   Family Portion of Rent. The amount payable by the Family toward the Contract Rent is $ __140.00__ per month.

(c)   PHA Assistance Payment. The PHA shall pay on behalf of the Family a housing assistance payment of $ __160.00__ per month. This amount is equal to the difference between the Contract Rent and the Family portion of the Contract Rent. Neither the PHA nor the Government has assumed any obligation whatsoever for the Family portion of the Contract Rent, or for the satisfaction of any claim by the Owner against the Family, except in accordance with Section 1.5 of this Contract. The financial obligation of the PHA is limited to making housing assistance payments on behalf of the Family in accordance with this Contract.

(d)   Adjustments. The Family portion of the Contract Rent and the amount of the housing assistance payment are subject to change by reason of changes in (1) Family income or composition, (2) the extent of exceptional medical or other unusual expenses, or (3) the Allowance for Utilities and Other Services, all as determined by the PHA, effective as of the date stated in a notification by the PHA of such change to the Family and the Owner.

(e)   Termination of Payments Due to Family Ineligibility.

(1)   The Family's eligibility for housing assistance payments continues until the amount payable by the Family equals the total Contract Rent plus any applicable Allowance. However, the termination of eligibility at such point shall not affect the Family's other rights under its Lease nor shall such termination preclude resumption of payments as a result of subsequent changes in income or rent or other relevant circumstances during the term of this Contract. However, (i) if this Contract terminates at a time when the Family is ineligible for housing assistance payments, the Contract shall not be renewed and (ii) if one year has elapsed since the date of the last housing assistance payment on behalf of the Family, this Contract shall be terminated even though the termination date under Section 1.3 has not yet been reached.

(2)   The PHA may determine, after having given the Family reasonable notice (with a copy to the Owner) and opportunity to respond, that the Family is ineligible for further housing assistance payments because of failure to comply with the Family's obligations under the Certificate of Family Participation. The PHA shall notify the Family and the Owner of such determination. This notification shall state that housing assistance payments on behalf of the Family shall terminate as of the date of the notification and that this Contract shall also terminate as of that date. However, if the Owner proceeds to evict the Family as quickly as possible, this Contract shall continue in effect solely for the purpose of enabling the Owner to receive further housing assistance payments for the period of the tenant's occupancy pending eviction until commencement of occupancy by another tenant, not to exceed a period of 60 days, in accordance with and subject to the conditions and limitations of Sections 1.4(a), (b), and (c) not inconsistent with such purpose.

HOUSING ASSISTANCE PAYMENTS CONTRACT—Cont.

1.3   TERM OF CONTRACT.

The term of this Contract shall be _____ years [the term of the Lease] beginning on _____ , 19_____ ; Provided, however, that if the Family continues in occupancy, after the expiration of the term, on the same terms and conditions as the original Lease, the Contract shall continue in effect for the duration of such tenancy, but the total duration of the Contract shall in no case extend beyond the term of the ACC.

1.4   PAYMENT FOR VACATED UNITS.

Housing assistance payments shall be made by the PHA to the Owner, under the terms and conditions of this Contract, only for the period during which the Contract Unit is leased or occupied by the Family during the term of the Contract (see Section 1.3), except as follows:

(a)   If the Family vacates its unit in violation of the provisions of the Lease or tenancy agreement, the Owner shall receive housing assistance payments in the amount of 80 percent of the Contract Rent for a vacancy period not exceeding 60 days or the expiration or other termination of the Lease or tenancy agreement, whichever comes first; Provided, however, that if the Owner collects any of the Family's share of the rent for this period in an amount which, when added to the 80 percent payments, results in more than the Contract Rent, such excess shall be payable to the Government or as the Government may direct; and provided further that if the vacancy is the result of action by the Owner, the Owner shall not receive any payment under this Section 1.4 if the action was in violation of the Lease or the Contract or any applicable law. (See Section 2.6.)

(b)   The Owner shall not be entitled to any payment under this Section 1.4 unless he (1) immediately upon learning of the vacancy, has notified the PHA of the vacancy or prospective vacancy, (2) has taken and continues to take all feasible actions to fill the vacancy including, but not limited to, contacting applicants on his waiting list, if any, requesting the PHA and other appropriate sources to refer eligible applicants, and advertising the availability of the unit, and (3) has not rejected any eligible applicant except for good cause acceptable to the PHA.

(c)   The Owner shall not be entitled to housing assistance payments with respect to vacant units under this Section 1.4 to the extent he is entitled to payments from other sources (for example, payments for losses of rental income incurred for holding units vacant for relocatees pursuant to Title I of the Housing and Community Development Act of 1974 or payments under Section 1.5).

1.5   SECURITY DEPOSITS. [This section is applicable only if the Owner has required the Family to pay a security deposit.]

(a)   The Family has paid the Owner a security deposit in an amount equal to the amount payable by the Family toward one month's Gross Rent. If the Family vacates the unit, the Owner, subject to State and local law, may utilize the deposit as reimbursement for any unpaid rent or other amount owed under the Lease. If the amount of the security deposit is insufficient for such reimbursement, the Owner may claim reimbursement from the PHA, not to exceed an amount equal to the remainder of one month's Contract Rent. Any reimbursement under this Section shall be applied first toward any unpaid rent. If the Family vacates the unit owing no rent or other amount under the Lease, or if such amount is less than the amount of the security deposit, the Owner shall refund the full amount or the unused balance, as the case may be, to the Family.

(b)   In those jurisdictions where interest is payable by the Owner on security deposits, the refunded amount shall include the amount of interest payable. The Owner shall comply with all State and local laws regarding interest payments on security deposits.

1.6   OTHER CONDITIONS FOR HOUSING ASSISTANCE PAYMENTS.

The rights of the Owner to receive housing assistance payments under this Contract shall be subject to his compliance with all the provisions of this Contract, including Part II which contains provisions on matters including, but not limited to, the requirements for obtaining payments, the provision of required services, and maintenance of the Contract Unit in Decent, Safe, and Sanitary condition.

1.7   ENTIRE AGREEMENT. This Contract, including Part II hereof, contains the entire agreement between the parties hereto, and neither party is bound by any representations or agreements of any kind except as contained herein. No changes in this Contract shall be made except in writing signed by both the Owner and the PHA.

1.8   OWNER'S WARRANTY OF LEGAL CAPACITY. . The Owner warrants that he has the legal right to execute this Contract and to lease the dwelling unit covered by this Contract.

PHA __CHICAGO HOUSING AUTHORITY_____   OWNER _____

By _____   By _____

_____   _____
             (Official title)   *(Official title)*

Date _____   Date _____

Figure 52: HUD LEASE FORM

HUD-9620
December 1971
(Formerly FHA-2372
Multi-Family)

U.S. DEPARTMENT OF HOUSING AND URBAN DEVELOPMENT
PROPERTY DISPOSITION PROGRAM

LEASE

COMPLETE AS APPLICABLE:
PROJECT:
Lease Code and Number:

This agreement, made in quadruplicate, this _____ day of _____ 19 ____ , between the Secretary of Housing and Urban Development, acting under the provisions of the National Housing Act, as amended, as LANDLORD, and _____ as TENANT.

WITNESSETH, that the LANDLORD leases to the TENANT, and the TENANT hires from the LANDLORD, premises known as

for the term commencing on the _____ day of _____ , 19 ____ , and ending on the last calendar day of _____ , 19 ____ , at the rental of _____ Dollars ($ _____) per month. Said rent shall be payable monthly in advance on or before the first calendar day of each month during the term. In the event the TENANT shall, with the consent of the LANDLORD, hold over after the term of this lease, he shall become a hold-over TENANT of said premises for a further definite term of 1 month only at the same rental, payable in advance on the first day of said renewed term. It is expressly agreed that unless either party notifies the other to the contrary at least 30 days prior to the expiration date or any hold-over term of this lease, said term shall automatically extend for a definite term of one month at the stated monthly rental. Said rent shall be payable at the office of

or to such other person and at such other place as the LANDLORD shall, from time to time, by written notice designate.

The agreed rental includes services and equipment as specified hereinafter, with the express understanding that temporary failure to furnish such services or temporary mechanical failure of such equipment shall give TENANT no claim for damages or for statement of rent.

1. The TENANT for himself and his heirs, executors, administrators, and assigns, agrees as follows: (a) To pay the rent herein stated promptly when due, without any deductions whatsoever and without any obligation on the part of the LANDLORD to make any demand for the same; (b) To pay all charges for utilities, except as noted hereinafter, as they become due; (c) To use the premises for no unlawful purposes, but to occupy the same only as a dwelling; (d) Not to assign or sublet the premises without the LANDLORD's written consent; (e) To keep the premises in a clean and sanitary condition, and to comply with all laws, health and police requirements, with respect to said premises and appurtenances, and to save the LANDLORD harmless from all fines, penalties, and costs for violation or noncompliance with any of said laws, requirements, or regulations, and from all liability arising out of any such violation or noncompliance; (f) Not to use said premises for any purposes deemed hazardous by insurance companies carrying insurance thereon; (g) That if any damage to the property shall be caused by his acts or neglect, the TENANT shall forthwith repair such damage at his own expense, and should the TENANT fail or refuse to make such repair within a reasonable time after the occurrence of such damage, the LANDLORD may at his option make such repair and charge the cost thereof to the TENANT, and the TENANT shall thereupon reimburse the LANDLORD for the total cost of all damages so caused; (h) To permit the LANDLORD, or his agents, to post "FOR RENT" and "FOR SALE" signs and to exhibit the premises to prospective purchasers or tenants at reasonable hours and to enter the premises for the purpose of making reasonable inspections and repairs.

2. The TENANT by the execution of this agreement admits that the premises are in a tenantable condition and agrees that at the end of said term to deliver up and surrender said premises to the LANDLORD in as good condition as when received, reasonable wear and tear thereof, excepted.

3. It is further agreed that the LANDLORD will make all necessary repairs to said property except repairs necessary to be made caused by the acts or neglect of the TENANT. No alteration, addition, or improvements shall be made in or to the premises without the consent of the LANDLORD in writing, and all additions and improvements made by the TENANT shall belong to the LANDLORD.

4. The TENANT further agrees that if he should fail to pay the rent herein stipulated promptly when due or should fail to comply with any and all other provisions of this agreement, then in any of said cases, it shall be lawful for the LANDLORD, at his election or option, to reenter and take possession, the TENANT hereby expressly waiving any and all notices to vacate said premises, and thereupon this demise shall absolutely terminate; however, nothing in this agreement shall constitute or be construed as a waiver or relinquishment of any right accruing to the LANDLORD under this agreement by virtue of law. Tenant agrees to pay all costs of proceedings by the Landlord for recovery of rents or for recovery of the possession of the premises, or for the enforcement of any of the terms and conditions of this lease, including a reasonable attorney's fee.

5. All goods and chattels placed or stored in or about the premises are at the risk of the TENANT.

6. The TENANT further agrees to abide by the RULES and REGULATIONS attached to and considered a part of this lease and any amendments thereto provided by the LANDLORD.

7. The failure of the LANDLORD to insist upon the strict performance of the terms, covenants, agreements and conditions herein contained or any of them, shall not constitute or be construed as a waiver or relinquishment of the LANDLORD'S right thereafter to enforce any such term, covenant, agreement, or condition, but the same shall continue in full force and effect.

LEASE—Cont.

8. The TENANT warrants that no person or agency has been employed or retained to solicit or secure this lease upon an agreement or understanding for a commission, percentage, brokerage, or contingent fee, excepting bona fide employees or bona fide established commercial agencies retained by the TENANT for the purpose of securing business. For breach or violation of this warranty, the LANDLORD shall have the right to annul this lease without liability or in its discretion to require the TENANT to pay, in addition to the rentals and other amounts payable hereunder, the full amount of such commission, percentage, brokerage, or contingent fee.

9. No Member of or Delegate to Congress, or Resident Commissioner, shall be admitted to any share or part of this contract or to any benefit that may arise therefrom, but this provision shall not be construed to extend to this contract if made with a corporation for its general benefit.

This lease contains the entire agreement between the parties hereto, and neither party is bound by any representations or agreement of any kind except as herein contained.

Secretary of Housing and Urban Development, Landlord

WITNESS:

_____   BY _____
                                                                              TITLE

_____   _____

_____   _____
                                                                              TENANT

_____   _____

NOTE: No changes are to be made in the printed provisions of this agreement. In the event any alteration is required it must be submitted to the Office of Property Disposition, Department of Housing and Urban Development at Washington, D.C. 20413, for approval.

public housing developments have a common need for ongoing management. The nonprofit or government organization that initiates the project and sees it through construction cannot maintain the necessary constant supervision, so someone must be there to look after the property and the tenants.

Because private sponsors of housing projects such as churches or charitable organizations are usually neophytes in the real estate field, they are often unable to anticipate or cope with the management problems of large multitenant buildings. Financial crises often arise when rents, which may have been overestimated, are found to be inadequate to cover the underestimated operating costs. Nonprofit private sponsors seldom provide for tenant relations specialists, youth organizers, or the additional maintenance staff and funds required in buildings housing large families with many children.

Since its inception, low-income public housing in many cities has suffered from both inadequate property management and bureaucratic mismanagement. Public housing tenants are no different from other tenants in their desire for decent living conditions, although many are unaccustomed to caring for their living surroundings. The manager must help them develop pride of ownership and a greater sense of responsibility for their surroundings.

Problems and unrest in housing projects often stem from the fact that the local housing authorities are representatives of government agencies. Restricted by their budget-oriented structure, the housing authorities are unable to communicate with the tenants. Accentuating this traditional lack of understanding is the wide economic and social gap between the two parties. Because housing authority groups are not schooled in property management, tenants are often frustrated by negative or slow responses to their requests for repairs and service. The better tenants eventually leave, and the property deteriorates. Vacancies and rent delinquencies increase, vandalism begins, and the property goes into the downward spiral of decay.

HUD is attempting to correct the lack of trained management by conducting management courses, sometimes in connection with local colleges, and by certifying managers who have graduated from HUD-approved management courses, such as CAM or RAM, discussed in Chapter 11.

SUCCESSFUL MANAGEMENT APPROACHES

Subsidized housing is a new field of endeavor for property managers who enjoy dealing with people and are not afraid of hard work. Low-income housing is managed in much the same way as other types of housing, except that the larger dwelling units and greater population density create heavy use and significantly higher maintenance costs. Tenant turnover, vacancy rates, rent loss, and collection costs are higher in this type of housing.

Managers who work as independent contractors for the Federal Housing Administration are usually employed under a 3-year contract. Called Area Management Brokers (AMB), their principal duties include taking over the property, preparing repair specifications, soliciting repair bids from contractors, coordinating and inspecting repair

Figure 53: FHA SUMMARY ACCOUNTING REPORT FORM

U. S. DEPARTMENT OF HOUSING AND URBAN DEVELOPMENT FEDERAL HOUSING ADMINISTRATION **BROKER'S SUMMARY ACCOUNTING REPORT**	**INSTRUCTIONS:** Prepare original and two copies by typewriter. Mail original with attachments to the Multifamily Mortgage Branch. Office of the Comptroller. Federal Housing Administration. Washington. D.C. 20412. Mail duplicate copy to the local area or insuring office with attachments as instructed by HM 4309.1. Accounting Handbook for Acquired Properties. Retain triplicate copy for broker's file.

Name of Broker		Contract No.	Date of Preparation
Identification of Property (ies) and Address *(City and State)*		Period Covered by Report	

Attached are Broker's Report of Collections. FHA Form No. 2700a. and Broker's Report of Disbursements. FHA Form No. 2700b. (with supporting data) covering the operations of the above property (ies) during the period indicated. Also attached is FHA Form No. 2751 as at the last day of the prior reporting period.

COLLECTIONS *(From Form 2700a)*		$
DISBURSEMENTS *(From Form 2700b)*		
★BALANCE		$
AMOUNT DUE FHA	*{Check attached drawn payable to "Federal Housing Administration"}*	$
AMOUNT DUE BROKER	*{Original (1034) and three copies (1034a) Public Voucher attached.}*	$

★Show amount in brackets. if Disbursements exceed Collections.

The undersigned certifies that this is a true and correct statement of collections and disbursements for the operation of the above property (ies); that all bills are just and correct and have been paid; the statement is in accordance with the contract identified above; that the amount due broker. if any. has not been previously claimed or paid; and that any adjustment found to be necessary as a result of any subsequent review by any authorized official of the Department of Housing and Urban Development or of the Comptroller General of the United States will be effected as prescribed by FHA.

Signature of Broker or Authorized Representative	Official Title

WARNING: Section 1010 of Title 18. U.S.C.. "Department of Housing and Urban Development and Federal Housing Administration transactions," provides: "Whoever, for the purpose of . . . influencing in any way the action of such Department . . . makes, passes, utters, or publishes any statement, knowing the same to be false . . . shall be fined not more than $5,000 or imprisoned not more than two years, or both."

Section 1012 of Title 18. U.S.C.. "Department of Housing and Urban Development transactions," provides: "Whoever, with intent to defraud . . . makes any false report or statement to or for such Department; . . . receives any compensation, rebate, or reward, with intent to defraud such Department or with intent unlawfully to defeat its purposes; . . . Shall be fined not more than $1,000 or imprisoned not more than one year, or both."

Remarks:

Figure 54: FHA REPORT OF DISBURSEMENTS FORM

U.S. DEPARTMENT OF HOUSING AND URBAN DEVELOPMENT

HOUSING - FEDERAL HOUSING COMMISSIONER

MANAGER'S REPORT OF DISBURSEMENTS

INSTRUCTIONS: Prepare by typewriter in quadruplicate in accordance with the procedures contained in Handbook 4309.1, Accounting Handbook for Acquired Properties. Distribute copies as instructed on Form 2700, "Manager's Summary Accounting Report". Briefly describe each disbursement as well as indicating the appropriate account number.

DOUBLE SPACE AFTER EACH ENTRY

PROJECT NO.	CONTRACT NO.	IDENTIFICATION OF PROPERTY(IES)	PERIOD COVERED

The disbursements itemized below were made for the account of the above identified property(ies). The pre-numbered checks bore the dates and amounts shown, and were drawn payable to the vendors, contractors, individuals, etc., identified below.

PAYEE	PURPOSE OF EXPENDITURE	PAID			
		ACCOUNT NUMBER	AMOUNT	CHECK NUMBER	DATE OF CHECK

TOTAL *(Or Subtotal if this is not the final page)*

ACCOUNT NUMBERS AND LINE ITEMS

Acct. No.	Description	Acct. No.	Description	Acct. No.	Description	Acct. No.	Description
	Expenses-Administrative		**Expenses-Maintenance**		**Expenses-Utilities**		**Expenses-Taxes & Insurance**
6210	Advertising	6410	Elevator	6420	Heating Fuel	6710	Real Estate Taxes
6310	Office Employee Payroll Costs	6430	Janitor and Cleaning	6450	Electricity	6711	Other Taxes
		6461	Exterminating	6451	Water	6720	Insurance/Bond Premium
6311	Office Expenses	6470	Garbage Removal	6452	Gas		
6320	Management Fees	6510	Security				
6330	Resident Manager Payroll Costs	6520	Grounds		**Expense-Total Operating**		**Expenses-Decent, Safe and Sanitary Housing**
		6530	Maintenance Employees Payroll Cost				
6340	Legal Expenses	6541	Routine Repair	6000	Total Operating Expenses	6538	Exterior
6360	Telephone Expenses	6561	Decorating			6549	Interior
6390	Miscellaneous Administrative	6570	Vehicle			6557	Energy Efficiency
		6590	Miscellaneous Maintenance			6591	Miscellaneous

Figure 55: HUD RECONDITIONING PROGRESS SURVEY

U.S. DEPARTMENT OF HOUSING AND URBAN DEVELOPMENT
PROPERTY DISPOSITION PROGRAM
RECONDITIONING PROGRESS SURVEY

Project Name _____   Contract No. _____

Address _____   Case/Project No. _____

Name of Contractor _____

INSTRUCTIONS

A. CONTRACT INSPECTOR. Submit this form weekly in accordance with the Agreement for Construction Inspection Services between the local HUD Office Contracting Officer and the Contractor.

B. STAFF INSPECTOR. Prepare this form in conjunction with every contractor's request for payment, and for every interim inspection made to assure that work is being performed in accordance with the contract for the construction services.

I. Inspection during contract (including delayed completion) reveals:

A. Variations from drawings and specifications
- (1) ☐ Planning or design
- (2) ☐ Workmanship
- (3) ☐ Materials
- (4) ☐ Supervision deficient
- (5) ☐ Other

B. Correction of previously recorded variations
- (1) ☐ Not started
- (2) ☐ In progress
- (3) ☐ Completed
- (4) ☐ Subject of contract change request

C. Uninstalled material
- (1) ☐ Not as specified
- (2) ☐ Stored off site
- (3) ☐ Unsuitably protected

D. ☐ Noteworthy occurrences or delays
E. ☐ Inspection by other
F. ☐ Premature occupancy
G. ☐
H. ☐

II. EXPLANATION:

Enter significant activities, explanation of statements marked above and actions taken or recommended.

_____

_____

_____

_____

_____

_____

_____

_____

_____

_____

_____

Estimated percent
of completion _____

Signed _____

☐ Staff Insp. _____ ☐ Contr. Insp. _____

Date _____

Figure 56: HUD PURCHASE ORDER FORM

U.S. DEPARTMENT OF HOUSING AND URBAN DEVELOPMENT
PROPERTY DISPOSITION PROGRAM

**PURCHASE ORDER AND
PAYMENT AUTHORIZATION**

*(Pertaining To Expense On Acquired Properties
See Handbooks 4310.5, 4312.1, and 4320.1)*

INSTRUCTIONS TO FIELD OFFICES: For payment to contractor by Treasury check, forward Parts 1, 2, and 3 to Office of Finance and Accounting. For payment from special Bank Account, Area Management Broker or Project Managers will transmit Part 1 with original accounting report and Part 2 and 3 with duplicate and triplicate report copies. See HUD Handbook 4045.1, Chapter 11, for detailed instructions.

**FOR OFFICE OF FINANCE
AND ACCOUNTING
USE ONLY**

1. Bureau Voucher No.

2. Bureau Schedule No.

3. TO: Contractor and Payee

Payee's Account No.

Name Control | Rpt. Code

4. Street Address

7. Field Office *(City only)*

8. Order No. | 9. Date

5. City | 6. State | Zip Code

10. Discount Terms

11. Time for Delivery

Subject to conditions printed on the reverse side hereof, you are hereby requested and authorized to perform the services and/or deliver the articles below *(or on attached)* according to terms of your quotation. The information indicated in items 7, 8, and 9 must appear on all packages, papers, correspondence, etc., relating to this transaction.

12. Ordered by *("HUD" or Area Management Broker/Project Manager's Name and Address)*

13. Consignee *(Address of property or project office)*

14. Signature | 15. Title

16. AUTHORIZED BY ──────▶ | Signature

(For completion by Field Office when articles/services ordered by Area Management Broker or Project Manager)

Title | Date

17. ITEM NO.	18. ARTICLES AND/OR SERVICES (If this information is itemized on bid specifications, attach a copy and show below "IN ACCORDANCE WITH ATTACHED")	19. QUAN-TITY	UNIT PRICE		22. AMOUNT
			20. Cost	21. Per	

If above space insufficient, use Purchase Order and Payment Authorization Continuation Sheet, Form 2542A.

TOTAL–INCLUDING CONTINUATION SHEET | $

23. CONTRACTOR'S CERTIFICATION OF COMPLETION

The undersigned hereby certifies that (a) all services stipulated under this purchase order have been completed or supplies delivered, as of the date shown, in accordance with the specifications, and (b) that all claims of laborers or others performing services or furnishing materials in the performance of the services have been paid. In addition, furnished herewith are all manufacturer warranties with respect to materials and equipment relative to performance hereunder.

Contractor_____ Date_____

Per _____ Title _____
(Signature)

When this form is signed in the name of a company or corporation, the name of the person writing the company or corporate name, as well as the capacity in which he signs, must appear. For example: "John Doe Company, per John Smith, Secretary".

24. AREA MANAGEMENT BROKER OR PROJECT MANAGER'S CERTIFICATE *(IF APPLICABLE)*

Date First Inspected | I certify that I (or my representative) personally inspected this property on the dates shown and to the best of my knowledge and belief all specifications have been met and all repairs have been made and payment therefor has not heretofore been made. | Signature | Date Final Inspection and Acceptance

25. CHIEF PROPERTY OFFICER'S *(OR DESIGNEE'S)* CERTIFICATION

Payment Approved For

$ _____ on basis of _____ ▶

☐ Acceptance of Area Management Broker or Project Manager's Inspection for Repairs (Form HUD–9519 on file in Local Office)

☐ Staff Inspection Report (Form HUD 9519 on file in Local Office)

Signature | Title | Date

26. AUTHORIZED CERTIFYING OFFICER'S CERTIFICATION

Pursuant to authority vested in me, I certify that this Purchase Order and Payment Authorization is correct and proper for payment.

Signature | Authorized Certifying Officer's Stamp

WARNING: Section 1001 of Title 18, U.S.C. Statements or entries generally. Whoever, in any matter within the jurisdiction of any department or agency of the United States knowingly and willfully falsifies, conceals or covers up by any trick, scheme, or device a material fact, or makes any false, fictitious or fraudulent statements or representations, or makes or uses any false writing or document knowing the same to contain any false, fictitious or fraudulent statement or entry, shall be fined not more than $10,000 or imprisoned not more than five years or both.

work, supervising maintenance and security, and submitting financial reports. Figure 53, The Broker's Summary Accounting Report, and Figure 54, the Report of Disbursements, are official FHA forms that must be completed as income and expense statements. HUD has created the Reconditioning Progress Survey (Figure 55) and the Purchase Order and Payment Authorization (Figure 56) to maintain control over new construction or repairs done on acquired properties. These are a few of the numerous reports required by this government agency. Managers of privately owned housing projects usually develop their own methods for handling the property entrusted to them.

The key to success for the manager of subsidized housing lies in his or her ability to be firm, available, and responsive to tenants while instilling in them a reciprocal sense of responsibility for the condition of the property. The manager's skill at developing a workable plan of operation for the property is also critical.

Firmness

Good management-resident relations stem from mutual understanding, trust, and respect. The expectations and obligations of both parties should be clear at the beginning of the relationship. All residents should receive a copy of the building regulations. The manager must then be firm in enforcing those regulations, particularly the ones concerning pets, maximum number of residents per apartment, security precautions, garbage handling, noise, and prompt rental payments. To be fair, rules must be enforced consistently. For the sake of tenant morale, penalties for infractions of the regulations must be applied without discrimination.

Initial tenant screening can eliminate many of the problems arising from noncompliance with building rules. There are agencies that run checks on rental applications filled out by prospective tenants for public housing. Investigation of recent past residences yields information on the prospect's pattern of rent payment, behavior, history of property damage, noise complaints, or other breach of a previous lease agreement.

The system for rent collection should be inflexible. If the rent is not paid within a month of its due date, appropriate legal action should be initiated. This may sound harsh, but there are compelling reasons for management to insist on prompt rental payments.

If rent delinquencies are tolerated, payments on the mortgage and utilities for the building will be delayed and late penalties incurred. The manager who follows a lax collection procedure does a disservice to delinquent tenants by allowing them to pile up a larger debt than they can afford to repay. The manager also is being unfair to residents who pay their rent promptly, for rental rates will eventually have to be raised to cover the delinquencies. If the paying residents discover that they are carrying the burden for delinquent tenants, nonpayment or slow payments of rents may spread throughout the building as a form of tenant protest.

Responsiveness

Repairs should be made as quickly as possible, no matter how often tenants make demands. Good repair service shows that management is sincere about maintaining the building. This display of good faith should be accompanied by fines for residents who are responsible for property damage.

It is the responsibility of the property manager to determine tenants' needs by asking for their suggestions and to fulfill all reasonable requests. Since residents want to live in a building that is efficiently operated and maintained, they can often devise a better way of coping with a particular problem such as building security. This type of dialogue shows the tenants that management is doing its best to keep the property safe and clean, encouraging their cooperation in these efforts.

Rapport between tenants and management can be improved by hiring a person with social work skills or training to handle tenant relations. This individual can act as a conduit of information from the residents to the manager and can assist with programs involving tenant participation. In many cases, a qualified representative can solve minor problems before they become large enough to require management's attention. The person responsible for tenant relations should display an interest in residential activities and social functions as a show of good will. Psychologists or sociologists trained in tenant-management relations are sometimes employed as consultants.

A manager and staff who are familiar with local public service organizations such as free legal-aid societies, low-cost medical clinics, job placement centers, and religious or ethnic organizations can enhance landlord-tenant rapport and help the occupants solve their financial and domestic problems. Stronger ties between the community and the public housing residents will erode prejudice and hostility between them.

Occupant Responsibility

Tenants should be educated about management procedures and policies and their own responsibility in the maintenance of the building. Many of them will have to be shown how to care for the equipment in their apartments and how to report maintenance problems. They should be encouraged to take pride in their homes and to report disruptive or destructive behavior. As tenants become more responsible, they are less prone to vandalism.

On-site job programs are one way of motivating residents to care for their surroundings. Nonunion tenants, even unskilled ones, can clean hallways, paint apartments, and tend to minor repairs on a part-time basis under this type of program. Besides promoting resident responsibility, on-site job programs have the added benefit of reversing the trend from strictly profit-oriented management to a more humanistic model. In the past, when housing authority operating budgets were based on the income known to be available rather than on the actual expenses necessary to operate and keep up the property, tenant services were almost nonexistent. On-site job programs reduce maintenance costs while providing service to the residents and giving them a chance to earn extra income to meet rental payments.

Management Plan

The manager should outline specific problems in each housing project: disadvantages of the neighborhood (such as vandalism); the physical condition of the interior and exterior of the premises; the quality of present building operation, administration, and staff; and the current state of tenant relations. With this outline, the manager can decide which areas need his or her personal attention and which can be delegated to a subordinate. Operating, maintenance, and enforcement policies can then be geared to the particular property.

An economic study of the property's financing structure will give the manager the data necessary to draw up a realistic and comprehensive budget. Existing rental rates should be compared to the rental income needed to meet projected expenses; then plans (such as an on-site job program or a stricter rental collection policy) for meeting extra costs can be formulated. Once the budget is drawn up it must be implemented. Each month the manager should measure actual progress against the prognosis and make appropriate adjustments.

THE FUTURE OF SUBSIDIZED HOUSING MANAGEMENT

The supply of qualified management personnel is inadequate to meet the current needs of the field. Government and private nonprofit owners of subsidized housing must be sure that managers get the continued training they need to supervise on-site employees and perform other duties as needed.

On-site employees for subsidized housing projects typically require closer supervision than their residential counterparts. This means higher management fees. In fact, it has been said that twice the money and five times the effort is needed to manage public housing as compared to middle-class, multitenant properties. Moreover, the operating climate in public housing projects does not always attract good managers. It could be improved somewhat if city authorities would cooperate in assisting a manager's legitimate attempts to deal with delinquent tenants.

In many cases, funds are needed for operating expenses or rehabilitation of the property. The owner generally is unable to contribute any cash until it is operating at a profit and he or she is receiving a return cash flow on the investment. The federal or city government or the mortgage holder may supply the necessary funds.

If the only alternative is to let the building deteriorate until the loss is complete, the mortgage holder may ease the burden on the owner by foregoing mortgage payments for a period or recasting the loan. City and federal governments can help by contributing to the many programs that increase recreational facilities and educate tenants. A program for helping tenants budget their income and cope with their responsibilities might be helpful in solving the economic problems of a public housing development. Whatever path is chosen, though, the project will be long-range and will require extraordinary endurance, skill, and devotion on the part of the property manager.

SUMMARY

The three basic alternatives to urban blight are conservation, correction, and clearance. Conservation entails minor repairs and remodeling, while correction involves major structural alterations and repairs of entire systems. Clearance is the razing of entire areas to make way for new construction. The property manager must be able to decide which solution is indicated for any particular building.

Most subsidized housing is constructed with financial assistance from the Department of Housing and Urban Development (HUD). The Federal Housing Administration (FHA), a HUD agency, insures mortgages and grants government subsidies to non-profit groups who sponsor the construction of low-income housing. Local government housing authorities receive money from HUD for the acquisition and operation of existing buildings or privately built new housing for low-income tenants.

Managers who work directly for FHA have detailed procedural guidelines to follow and numerous records to keep, whereas managers of privately owned housing projects have to develop their own methods for handling the properties entrusted to their care. The actual physical operation of low-income housing is not substantially different from that of other residential properties except for the harder usage endured by the former. Maintenance costs, tenant turnover, rent loss, and collection costs are generally greater for such properties.

The key to success in the management of subsidized housing lies in the ability to be firm, equitable, and responsive to tenants while instilling in them a sense of responsibility for the condition of the property. Economic and social barriers between landlord and tenant make it difficult for them to communicate with each other. The great disparity of attitudes and expectations between recipients of government aid and the government agencies themselves add to the demands placed on managers of subsidized housing.

All in all, the management of subsidized housing presents a unique challenge for socially aware property managers.

QUESTIONS: CHAPTER 16

1. A building which is beginning to decay but still has substantial economic use would be a likely candidate for.

   a. correction.   c. rehabilitation.
   b. clearance.   d. conservation.

2. In urban renewal, if an apartment building is completely gutted and new plumbing, electrical, and heating systems are installed, the process is called:

   a. redevelopment.   c. clearance.
   b. correction.   d. conservation.

3. Government-subsidized urban renewal programs include:

   I.   financing new construction of public housing units.
   II. subsidizing rentals of existing buildings.

   a. I only   c. both I and II
   b. II only   d. neither I nor II

4. The Federal Housing Administration:

   I.   sponsors rental and mortgage insurance programs.
   II. encourages private participation in the development of low-income housing.

   a. I only   c. both I and II
   b. II only   d. neither I nor II

5. Urban renewal programs have been used:

   I.   only for residential rehabilitation.
   II. to correct all types of urban blight.

   a. I only   c. both I and II
   b. II only   d. neither I nor II

6. List five major problems encountered by managers of government subsidized housing.

   a. _____   d. _____
   b. _____   e. _____
   c. _____

7. Because of the nature of government subsidies, the manager of low-cost housing:

   I.   cannot screen tenants as he or she could for other residential properties.
   II. can afford to be lenient about late rental payments.

   a. I only   c. both I and II
   b. II only   d. neither I nor II

8. The manager of low-cost housing should consider employing a person to handle tenant relations because:

    a. tenants try to take advantage of management with their complaints.
    b. this person can save the manager time by screening tenant complaints.
    c. this person can provide extra service to the tenants and gain their cooperation.
    d. supervising maintenance is a full-time job for the manager.

9. List three benefits of an on-site job program in which residents are hired to help maintain and repair the building.

    a. _____
    b. _____
    c. _____

10. List three sources a manager may apply to for funds for operating expenses or rehabilitation of a low-cost housing project.

    a. _____
    b. _____
    c. _____

11. The HUD Section 8 Housing Assistance Payments contract:

    I. specifies the total rental rate for a housing unit, as well as the portion payable by the family.
    II. serves as a lease between the owner of the project and the tenant.

    a. I only   c. both I and II
    b. II only   d. neither I nor II

12. HUD contracts with property managers of subsidized housing are usually for a period of:

    a. 6 months.   c. 3 years.
    b. 1 year.   d. 5 years.

13. Which of the following personal attributes of a manager is *not* an important factor in tenant relations?

    a. firmness   c. responsiveness
    b. availability   d. ability to delegate authority

14. A manager who works for the Federal Housing Administration is called a(n):

    a. AMB.   c. CPM.
    b. ARM.   d. FHM.

15.   The standard HUD lease form shown in this chapter:

   I.   prohibits the tenant from assigning or subletting the premises without written consent of the landlord.
  II.   specifies that utilities are to be paid by the tenant.

      a.   I only   c.   both I and II
      b.   II only   d.   neither I nor II

17
Creative Management and the Future

As real estate ownership became more complex and the economic situation tightened, the property manager's role took on added dimensions. Real estate owners' needs for accurate property analysis, market research, and efficient property administration grew more acute. Keeping financial records was no longer an end in itself but a means of gathering valuable data for future operating decisions that would affect a property's profitability.

Analysis of statistics and performance data on a property to determine its highest and best use and to plan for the future is the most creative function of the property manager. This phase of management requires sound judgment; here the field of real estate management truly attains professional status.

Right now there are many opportunities for property managers to serve as consultants for lenders and investors in the real estate market. Developers often seek the advice of a professional property manager before committing themselves to a new project. With the guidance of a manager, owners of older properties can convert them into a more profitable real estate venture.

CONSULTING FOR FINANCIAL INSTITUTIONS

The high cost and low availability of mortgage financing during the recent inflationary period was evident in the marked decrease in new construction starts. The banking facilities that usually supplied mortgage funds were loaned out to capacity, so real estate buyers had to seek financing from less traditional sources such as investment trusts and pension funds. Not only have these institutions increased the amount of mortgages they hold in recent years, they have also turned to real estate as an equity investment for themselves. Since they are not familiar with the real estate market, institutional investors present the professional property manager with an unusual opportunity to serve as an investment counselor.

Institutional Investors

Financial institutions are seeking new avenues of investment other than the stock market to cushion the impact of inflation. Many are selecting real estate ownership as a higher yield investment opportunity.

Pension funds are one of the most noteworthy factors in the increase of institutionally owned real estate. Interest in real property as an investment medium for pension funds was sparked in 1971, with the establishment of a separate account by Prudential Insurance Company. This account, held by qualified pension plans, was a joint fund invested in real property. During the last several years, major banks, insurance companies, and other financial institutions have offered similar investment plans for pension funds.

The implications of this trend for the property management field are far-reaching. The decision to shift to real estate as an investment vehicle is made by financiers, *not* by skilled real estate licensees. Many of these institutions do not have a trained and experienced real estate investment staff. They also suffer from common misconceptions about the skill, time, and effort required to operate and manage a piece of property. Most institutional investors are unable to devote enough time and personnel to the management phase of their operations. The pressure to invest the flow of capital consumes most of an institution's corporate brainpower and interest. Diversification of a particular institution's holdings, both by property type and by geographical location, makes it impractical for a company to manage its own investments. Thus, management of institutionally owned real estate has become a vital new area of growth for professional property managers.

Managers not only contribute to the efficient operation of investment property, they also play a vital advisory role in the initial acquisition of such property. They provide corporate decision makers with an in-depth study of property under consideration for purchase. Their careful analysis of the physical characteristics of the building, the organizational structure of its operations, and the composition of the staff leads to recommendations on the soundness of the investment and the changes required for greater operating efficiency. Forms like Figure 57 codify these analyses.

Institutional Lenders

When the economic climate in an area shifts, real estate lenders change from loan administrators to asset managers. Billions of dollars worth of property currently held in mortgages by insurance companies, investment trusts, and pension funds could become involuntarily owned by these investors through foreclosure on defaulted loans. When this occurs, the first thing the investor needs is a goal-oriented management plan.

The results of an effective management plan should be rapid stabilization of the defaulting property and future disposition of the premises at a price that will be acceptable to the lender. A professional analysis of the property will disclose whether it is better to let it go at a distress-sale price (less the debt balance), and thus limit the loss, or to acquire ownership and bring the property up to the break-even point. Since the institutions involved are traditionally equity investors rather than mortgage lenders, they usually solicit the advice of a skilled property manager to design a plan of action that can minimize loss and eventually produce an operating profit.

Figure 57: CASH FLOW AND TAX BENEFITS OF INVESTMENT PROPERTY OWNERSHIP

CASH FLOW AND TAX BENEFITS OF INVESTMENT PROPERTY OWNERSHIP

Address of Property _____

Prepared by _____

A. Purchase Price
- a. Land allocation $ _____
- b. Building allocation
- c. Other allocation
- d. TOTAL PURCHASE PRICE
- e. Mortgage loan amount
- f. Cash equity

STABILIZED NET OPERATING INCOME $ _____

PURCHASER'S INCOME TAX BRACKET (inclusive of this property)   _____ %

B. Mortgage Terms
- a. Length of loan term   _____ years
- b. Interest rate   _____ %
- c. Annual payments (Princ. & Int.) $ _____

C. Depreciation
- a. Estimated Economic Life (Bldg.)   _____ years
- b. Estimated Economic Life (Others)   _____ years
- c. Depreciation Method (Bldg.)
- d. Depreciation Method (Others)
- e. Is purchaser "first user"?   Yes _____ No _____

Year	D Net Operating Income	E-1 Mortgage Loan Interest	E-2 Mortgage Loan Principal	F Cash Flow (D−E1-E2)	G Total Depreciation	H Deductions For Income Tax Purposes (E-1 + G)	I Taxable Income (D − H)	J Taxable Loss (D − H)	K Tax Payable (I×Tax%)	L Tax Savings (J×Tax%)	M* Cash Available After Mortgage Payment & Income Tax Effect	N Total Cash & Amortization Benefits After Taxes (M + E 2)
1												
2												
3												
4												
5												
6												
7												
8												
9												
10												
TOTALS												

Yield _____ % _____ % _____ %

NOTE:
All calculations assume the value of the property will remain constant and assumes no capital expenditures will be required to retain the Net Income stream (D) above. These projections are general in nature and subject to individual exceptions and should be reviewed and discussed with your certified public accountant and legal counsel.

Columns I & J: Only one column is applicable in any one year. If D is greater than H, use column I; if H is greater than D, use J.

*Column M: This figure will be column F minus K or column F plus L, as applicable.

SUMMARY OF CASH AND TAX BENEFITS OF OWNERSHIP

	10 yr. Total	10 yr. Avg.
1. Cash Flow (Before Income Tax Effect) (D − E1 − E2 = F)		
2. Tax Savings (Deductible from other taxable income)(Column L)	+ ____	
3. Tax Payable (Column K)		
4. Sub-Total of items 2 and 3 (This figure may be a + or −)	____	
5. Total cash benefits after taxes (Column M) (Item 1 + or − Item 4)	____	
6. Add: Principal paid on mortgage - "Tax Free" (E2)	____	
7. TOTAL CASH AND AMORTIZATION BENEFITS - - AFTER TAXES (Column N)	____	

Copyright 1968, The Institute of Real Estate Management

313-978

NEW OPPORTUNITIES IN EXISTING PROPERTIES

Creative management planning for existing properties is almost unlimited in scope, varying with the type, location, and physical condition of the property and with area demand. Possible programs include upgrading current use, changing the usage through remodeling and capital improvement, or razing the structure and replacing it. This area of property management holds the greatest potential for creativity and personal reward. Successful managers know how to analyze the existing problems of a particular property and generate innovative yet realistic answers. The solutions explored in this chapter are representative samples of the broad range of possibilities open to the dynamic manager.

The property manager should be aware of income tax incentives available for the preservation and rehabilitation of historic buildings. While the application process is involved and cumbersome, this specialized treatment may make a project financially feasible which otherwise would not be possible.

Loft Buildings

The loft building is the albatross of many management firms. In the first half of this century, light manufacturing and jobbing firms that had to locate close to railheads and central business districts to satisfy their transportation and labor needs were housed in multistory industrial buildings similar to the one shown here.

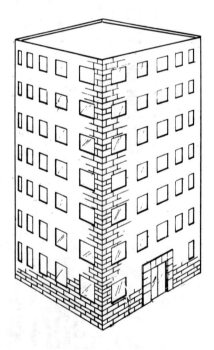

These are called *lofts,* a reference to the fact that their interior floor space is not specialized. One floor is a single open area, divided only by the support columns for the building. Loft buildings generally are designed with a minimum of tenant amenities, which at best include heat and janitorial service. The sacrifice in services is somewhat offset by the comparatively low rents for these structures.

When the exodus to the suburbs began during the 1950s, large lofts on the fringe of a central business district became much less desirable to potential industrial tenants, so the vacancy rate in these properties soared. Many existing loft structures are architectural nightmares and suffer from the dual woes of deferred maintenance and functional obsolesence. Although urban renewal projects have eliminated the problem to some degree, their main targets are residential properties. Untenanted lofts still remain in and around the heart of the central business district in many cities. The professional manager in charge of this type of property can put it to myriad imaginative uses.

Structures that are situated closest to the downtown business district are the easiest to adapt to other uses. Many of these loft buildings can provide low-cost office space to businesses that do not require prestigious quarters for client reception. Organizations that need inexpensive facilities for a large number of employees or for storage of materials that are continually in use can sometimes be accommodated by loft space. These include insurance companies, trade associations, manufacturers' sales representatives, and government agencies. Some loft buildings in prime locations have been successfully converted into condominium apartments, shopping malls, restaurants, and bars.

Lofts that are located further from the central business district are more problematic. Lack of demand makes conversion to office space economically unsound. Conversion to warehouse or storage facilities is more profitable, especially when the building is near a major thoroughfare. Merchandise can be transported to an outlying loft more expeditiously than through inner-city congestion. A vacant loft building can also be leased to a trade school or business that requires a multistory structure. They have also been leased for office uses that do not involve the public, such as an accounting or data processing center.

Regardless of the approach adopted, a substantial amount of capital will be needed to convert or adapt a neglected loft building for its new tenants. It is difficult for tenants to visualize how the space will look after renovation, so alteration should be completed before tenants are solicited and the space is shown.

From Budget Motel to Miniresort

The shorter work week adopted by many businesses has enabled Americans to travel more. The average family takes 2.8 extended vacations per year and 7.6 weekend trips, according to the *Journal of Property Management.* For the most part, motels are undifferentiated necessities, slept in one night and forgotten the next. Nonetheless, the enterprising motel manager can increase the income from such property by improving it so that it plays a memorable role in a family's vacation.

Budget motels have been one of the few beneficiaries of the recent economic recession. Because money and gasoline are more scarce, Americans are not traveling as far or staying away as long as they once did. Well-informed real estate developers have been constructing budget motels at major highway interchanges, closer to urban centers. In many instances, these serve not only as an overnight stop but as the traveler's final destination. The motel does not need additional guest amenities and recreational facilities to attract vacationers. It can make itself a local informational hub and a point of access to nearby recreational facilities. The entertainment features of the surrounding area can be used to attract guests.

The burgeoning interest in outdoor recreational activities gives the budget motel manager a chance to convert his or her property into a miniresort. The manager can supply guests with a list of bicycle paths, hiking trails, golf courses, ski runs, riding stables, fishing spots, restaurants, and other attractions. The motel can be used as a home base for short trips into the countryside.

From a management standpoint, successful conversion to a budget resort hinges on two factors: the economics of scale and the desirability of the location. A chain of budget motels appears to be the best choice for conversion to miniresorts because of the economic advantages inherent in the centralized operating, advertising, management, and purchasing operations. However, the savings that result from affiliation with a national chain do not guarantee success. Miniresorts also must be close to areas of recreational interest.

The miniresort concept adds to the importance and responsibility of the motel staff. Guests look upon the manager as their host and guide, so he or she must be familiar with the surrounding area. The staff is expanded beyond the standard maintenance and cleaning crews to include employees whose main function is to attend to the needs of vacationers. Because the motel itself does not provide recreational facilities, friendly and reliable guest counseling is the backbone of a miniresort.

Altering Older Apartment Buildings

Most communities have apartment buildings whose physical condition, unit size, facilities, layout, or location are unappealing. Rehabilitation might make them more rentable, but new equipment and decor are not always the answer. In areas where two-bedroom units dominate the market, two or more smaller units can be combined to create larger apartments for which there is a greater market demand. In a market area with a high demand for studio apartments, two-bedroom units could be subdivided.

Present tenants can suggest improvements that will enhance the building's rentability. If inadequate parking is a problem, the owner might consider purchasing adjacent vacant space or creating a parking area on the present lot.

Condominium Conversions

Today, apartment owners are finding it difficult to keep operating expenses at a level that matches the rental income from their buildings. Faced with the prospect of holding a no-profit or low-profit property, many owners elect to sell. Because total sales are greater when apartments are sold individually (at retail) rather than when the entire building is sold (wholesale), many owners are converting their marginal-profit properties to condominiums. In addition to the money from unit sales, condominiums offer the advantage of monthly rental income from unsold units.

Market Analysis. A market analysis should always be made in anticipation of conversion to condominium ownership. Conversion entails legal, operational, and physical changes to a property. Before initiating such changes, the owner must determine whether the building is actually suitable for conversion. The property manager can provide him or her with data on all of its physical and operational aspects, and an attorney can supply information about zoning ordinances, tax laws, and status of ownership.

Location is the first consideration when making a market analysis in anticipation of conversion. The better the location, the more marketable the condominium units will be. Since they have more freedom of movement, renters can be more tolerant about location than buyers can. The *unit mix* of the building should be evaluated in terms of location. Studio units sell well in areas near the central city, whereas large, six- to eight-room condominiums are most marketable in prestigious areas. Units with one, two, or three bedrooms are sold most easily.

A minimum of *construction change* is desirable for conversion purposes. When appraising the property, the manager should remember that buyers demand much more than renters in the way of solid construction. Competitive market conditions may require that garage facilities, a security system, or recreational facilities be provided. Renovation and construction costs will have to be reflected in the sale price of the unit. A thoughtful analysis of market demand and purchasing capabilities give the manager an estimate of how many facilities he or she can afford to offer.

The *reputation of the building* is another point to consider. The halo effect from a property that is well regarded by neighborhood residents should attract desirable tenants to the condominium units. When apartments are converted to condominiums, renters become permanent owner-residents. The community's acceptance of the plan can stabilize property values for the converted units, thus making them more marketable.

From a marketing viewpoint, the most important sector to assess is the captive sales market—the *present tenant population.* These people evidenced interest in the property when they first selected the building as their residence. If the units are reasonably priced, they should have no trouble meeting the mortgage payments.

The rate of tenant turnover, the median tenant age, and the economic status of tenants have a direct bearing on whether or not renters become buyers. High turnover predicts a lower rate of tenant purchase than that projected for a property whose tenants have been in the building for 3 years or longer. Tenants between ages 30 and 60 are prime candidates for ownership. Economic status refers not only to the tenant's ability to make monthly mortgage payments, as evidenced by rental history, but also to the tenant's capacity to make a down payment.

The manager should maintain a low profile when gathering information about present tenants. Advance rumors about the conversion may cause tenants to leave unnecessarily. The benefits of persuading present tenants to become buyers will repay the extra effort made to keep the analysis discreet. Not only are marketing costs kept down when present tenants buy, but a positive response from residents can present a solid image to other purchasers.

The market analysis for conversion should weigh *marketing costs.* Whatever is required for the opening presentation should be budgeted. Funds should be allocated to decorate one or more model units to suit the taste of the target market and to obtain the sales literature, professional advertising, promotional assistance, and on-site personnel needed to run the program.

Legal Advice. If the market analysis is favorable, the property manager should consult an attorney about zoning regulations and other legal restrictions before implementing conversion plans. Many restrictive statutes and ordinances regarding condominium conversion have been passed in recent years; they contain required notice periods to tenants and other limitations that must be researched and met. The attorney will also prepare the legal documents needed to sell the property. These include the master deed to the premises, the condominium bylaws, a sample unit deed and subscription agreement, closing certificates, and legal papers associated with a garage, health club, or similar facility.

The attorney can be of assistance in drawing up the financial arrangements for the sales. Prearranged financing, which usually is mandatory, can be an important marketing tool. If the units are priced slightly higher, so that the owner can absorb closing costs, buyers can obtain financial assistance for high-ratio mortgages. Another method of financial aid helps tenants meet down payments by accepting their security deposits as partial fulfillment of this requirement. Whatever financial package is used to sell a unit, legal advice ensures that the information transmitted to the buyers complies with full-disclosure lending laws and other regulations.

GROUND-LEVEL OPPORTUNITIES

Because of the high cost of real estate taxes and liability insurance, unused land is a capital drain on its owner. After determining the highest and best use for a piece of land, the owner and the property manager will develop a feasible plan for attaining their goal.

Working With Developers

Owners of unimproved real estate often hire a developer to implement their preconceived plans for its usage. In these cases, the property manager works as consultant to the project developer and contributes his or her operational expertise. To predict the profitability of a proposed project, the manager and developer should include four factors in their *feasibility* study.

They first must decide whether the land area is of *adequate* size to accommodate the suggested project. If additional land must be acquired, the long-range effects of this capital investment and the resources available for funding it must be calculated. If the area is large enough, the next consideration is its *topography, geology,* and *soil structure.* The physical features of the land must fit the requirements for site preparation. The third step is an assessment of the *requirements of the project.* The manager and developer must conduct a full-scale property analysis that takes in the architectural and engineering design, utility services, transportation networks, and zoning and building codes needed for the project. The final determinant in the feasibility study is the *completed cost* of the project. A comprehensive cost estimate should include the price of the land; charges for site preparation, utility installation, access roads, and landscaping; the contract price for building construction; carrying charges for interest, taxes, and insurance during construction; financing charges; and fees for advertising and real estate brokerage.

However, no development can expect to succeed without a standard property management survey and market analysis, as suggested in earlier chapters. Here again, the property manager's expertise can help the project developer assess area demand for the proposed development.

Urban Land Institute

The Urban Land Institute (ULI) is an independent, nonprofit educational and research organization dedicated to improving the quality of land use planning and development. It was founded in 1936 to provide unbiased land use information for both the practitioner and the public. The institute's work is mainly accomplished through nine councils, which focus their activities on the following major areas: commercial and retail development; industrial and office park development; new communities and large-scale development; recreational development; residential development; urban development/mixed use; federal policy; development policies and regulations; and development systems and services.

Property managers planning a development of any kind will find the ULI an excellent source for information.

Miniwarehouses

Ground-level opportunities do not relegate the manager to the role of consultant on new projects. The enterprising manager will find a new frontier for exploration in *miniwarehouses*. Originating in Texas, miniwarehouses are a rapidly growing trend in real estate. Having swept through the southwest and California, miniwarehouses are presently moving into the east to capture markets in every major city.

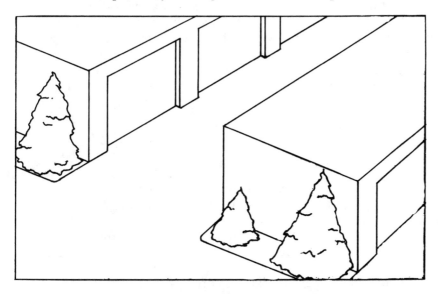

MINIWAREHOUSE

Miniwarehouses, otherwise known as self-storage units, fulfill a latent need within the real estate market by providing small, secure storage units for individuals and small businesses. Units range from 10 to 200 square feet in size and can usually be rented on either a monthly or an annual basis. This space gives homeowners convenient storage for surplus possessions and businesses a place for old records that would otherwise occupy more expensive office space.

A typical miniwarehouse complex consists of separate rows of concrete buildings with driveways between them, as shown above. Each building is

20 to 30 feet wide, with access doors on both sides. Behind each door is an individually locked and lighted storage unit. An apartment and office for a resident manager is usually part of the complex. Routine daily activities, such as leasing, grounds maintenance, tenant relations, monitoring the usage to which the space is put, and providing additional security can be taken care of by the resident manager. Since the owner usually does not have the skill to keep track of irregularly scheduled rental and mortgage payments, rental delinquencies, and other tasks created by the high tenant turnover in a miniwarehouse, this responsibility is often delegated to a professional property manager.

At present, the field is wide open for entrepreneurs who want to specialize in an area where no management guidelines are yet established. Market research and analysis will pave the way for a sound and profitable project. The property manager is well qualified to undertake these activities. The skilled and knowledgeable manager has a chance to guide the developer of the miniwarehouse throughout the construction phase and to perform the duties of a property manager after the project is operational.

Manufactured Homes

The appeal of manufactured homes has been heightened in recent years by the sky-rocketing cost of conventional housing. In many areas, manufactured homes can be purchased complete with furniture and appliances for less than one-fourth the cost of a conventional new single-family home of equivalent size. Since the popularity of the manufactured home continues to increase, a need has been created for new developments to accommodate them. This presents an opportunity not only in the development of new parks or subdivisions, but in the rehabilitation of older mobile home parks. Also, many older mobile home parks are being profitably modified to accept the temporary recreational vehicle owner on part of the property.

Investment Groups

Many opportunities exist for property managers to form or assist in organizing investment groups to purchase property. A property manager is in a unique position in many respects because he or she has direct contact with the owner, and is thus able to be the first to know of the owner's desire to sell a property. Also, accurate knowledge of the history of the property and its condition is extremely helpful in preparing information for prospective investors. There are many legal aspects to be considered, including security laws and tax regulations. Knowledge of the legal aspects and the ability to guide the selection of a legal entity, such as corporations, limited partnerships, and Sub-Chapter S corporations, for operation of the property is necessary.

The Future

The opportunities for a property manager to create projects are many. Farm and ranch management, leasing furniture and appliances, contracting with governmental agencies such as the General Services Administration and the U.S. Postal Service are only a few possibilities. As more money is channeled into real estate by passive investors, the need for professional property management will continue to expand.

The growing complexity of property management will require the property manager to be a well trained and skillful manager. Training through formal classes and programs sponsored by professional associations will be required if the manager is to keep up with his or her peers.

SUMMARY

Because the economics of real estate ownership have become more complex, professional managers are now needed to serve as investment, development, and renovation consultants and to perform traditional management and operational functions.

To cushion the impact of inflation, banks, insurance companies, investment trusts, and other financial institutions are turning to real estate ownership. They need a property manager's expertise in analyzing investment properties for acquisition, managing them for maximum profit, and disposing of unwanted parcels.

Management planning for existing properties that do not provide a high enough rate of return is another rewarding area of property management. The manager can upgrade the current use of a property by completely changing its usage through *alterations* and capital improvement or by *razing and replacing* existing structures. *Loft buildings* are a special challenge. Although this type of space often suffers from functional obsolescence and deferred maintenance, it can become profitable under imaginative management. Loft buildings near downtown business districts may be converted to low-cost office space. Buildings in outlying areas may be used as warehouse or storage facilities. With a certain capital expenditure, an innovative manager can turn a liability into an asset for the owner.

The recent recession and the growing popularity of the long weekend trip have strengthened the market for budget motels. An astute manager can improve a motel's chances in this competitive market by expending a little time and money to make it a *miniresort*. Additional guest amenities and facilities are unnecessary. The motel can capitalize on the recreational features of the surrounding area by simply offering information about and access to local points of interest. If the manager does not have time to act as a host and recreational counselor for guests, this role should be delegated to qualified staff people.

Older apartment buildings can be converted to fulfill market demand and improve their profit margin. They may be rehabilitated, redecorated, or altered so that unit size corresponds to tenant needs. Apartment buildings that are not profitable to the owner are sometimes converted to condominiums and sold. A professional property manager helps an owner decide whether or not to follow this course of action by preparing a market analysis, estimating costs and returns, and obtaining legal advice.

The owner of raw, unimproved land might hire a developer to implement some preconceived plan for its use. The manager must then work with the developer to complete a *feasibility study* on the profitability of the proposed project. Feasibility studies usually include considerations such as land area, physical features of the land, the requirements of the project, and estimated costs.

Miniwarehouses, also known as self-storage units, provide small, secure storage units for individuals and small businesses. A typical miniwarehouse complex consists of rows of concrete buildings containing individually locked storage units and an office for the resident manager, who carries out leasing, maintenance, and security duties. Miniwarehouses offer the professional property manager a challenge in market research and development and in supervision of operations.

The development of subdivisions and rehabilitation of mobile home parks present opportunities for a property manager to capitalize on the increasing demand for manufactured homes.

Organizing and managing investment groups and the properties they purchase will continue to be a growing field for property managers with expertise in the legal and technical aspects of syndicating investments.

The future of property management holds many opportunities for creative property managers. The growing complexity of management can be turned to advantage by the property manager who has prepared himself or herself by advanced formal training.

QUESTIONS: CHAPTER 17

1. Institutional investors:

    I.   have been turning to stocks instead of real estate as an investment opportunity.
    II. often invest pension funds in real property.

    a. I only   c. both I and II
    b. II only   d. neither I nor II

2. Banks, insurance companies, and other institutional investors in real estate need professional property managers because:

    I.   their holdings are often geographically diversified.
    II. their personnel are not skilled in real estate management.

    a. I only   c. both I and II
    b. II only   d. neither I nor II

3. Institutional lenders sometimes become owners of real estate involuntarily because of default on a mortgage. List the two goals of an effective management plan in such cases.

    a. _____
    b. _____

4. In general, loft buildings:

    a. have a low vacancy rate.
    b. have not suffered from obsolescence because their space is undifferentiated.
    c. provide few tenant amenities.
    d. command comparatively high rents.

5. List two possible uses for converted loft buildings.

    a. _____
    b. _____

6. When planning construction of a miniresort, the manager must consider:

    I.   travel trends toward shorter, more frequent vacations.
    II. existing recreational resources of a location.

    a. I only   c. both I and II
    b. II only   d. neither I nor II

7. The most distinctive and important feature a miniresort offers to its guests is:

    a. extra amenities and facilities.
    b. information on attractive features of the locality.
    c. easy access to highways.
    d. low prices.

8. List two alternatives a manager may suggest when the income from an apartment building is insufficient.

    a. _____
    b. _____

9. When converting an apartment to a condominium, important factors to consider in the market analysis include:

    I.   location.
    II. age of tenants.

    a. I only   c. both I and II
    b. II only   d. neither I nor II

10. List three functions an attorney should perform when converting an apartment to a condominium.

    a. _____
    b. _____
    c. _____

11. Miniwarehouses are often used for all but which of the following?

    a. storage of excess furniture by homeowners
    b. storage of old records by small businesses
    c. storage of seasonal items such as garden equipment
    d. storage of raw materials used in industrial operations

12. List the four factors that should be examined in a feasibility study for a new project.

    a. _____
    b. _____
    c. _____
    d. _____

13. Miniwarehouses:

    I.   require no on-site management.
    II. can be built with a minimal capital expenditure.

    a. I only   c. both I and II
    b. II only   d. neither I nor II

14. An apartment building contains 50 three-bedroom units that should rent at $300 per month, but suffers from a 40-percent vacancy rate. The property manager who is called in as a consultant on this problem determines that market demand in the area is predominantly for one-bedroom units. Conversion of 30 of the three-bedroom units into 60 one-bedroom units would cost about $100,000, and the one-bedroom units could then be rented at $200 per month. Assuming 100-percent occupancy from the date of conversion, how long would it take before the initial capital expenditure for converting the units is repaid by the additional rental income?

    a.   6 months   c.   2 years 6 months
    b.   1 year   d.   2 years 9 months

15. When considering converting an apartment building to condominiums, the property manager must remember that:

    I.   a building will command a higher price if sold as a whole than if apartments are sold individually.
    II. funds must be allocated for marketing costs such as brochures, advertising, and leasing personnel.

    a.   I only   c.   both I and II
    b.   II only   d.   neither I nor II

16. Tax treatment of preservation and rehabilitation of historic buildings:

    I.   is an involved process.
    II. may make a project financially feasible which would not otherwise be possible.

    a.   I only   c.   both I and II
    b.   II only   d.   neither I nor II

Glossary

Accelerated Cost Recovery System (ACRS). A mandatory method of calculating depreciation for tax purposes passed into law in 1981.

Accredited Management Organization (AMO). A professional designation awarded to qualified property management firms by the Institute of Real Estate Management.

Accredited Resident Manager (ARM). An individual who has completed IREM's educational program for resident managers.

actual eviction. Forcible removal of a tenant from a property by an officer of the court after a judgment decree for possession has been issued in favor of the owner.

advertising. Purchased space in a newspaper, magazine, or other medium used to attract public attention to a commodity for sale or lease.

agent. An individual who is legally empowered to act on behalf of another.

anchor store. *See* KEY TENANT.

Area Management Broker (AMB). A property manager who works directly for the Federal Housing Administration managing subsidized housing under a 3-year contract.

assessment. A monthly fee paid by cooperative and condominium members to cover maintenance costs for the property. 2. A special real estate tax levied by the government to finance improvements in the area.

assignment. Transfer of a tenant's remaining rental right in a property to a third party.

automatic extension clause. A lease covenant providing that a lease will be renewed indefinitely until one of the parties gives notice of the intent to terminate at the end of the lease term.

blight correction. Rehabilitation of residential properties that have deteriorated significantly.

blight prevention. Conservation of residential properties with substantial economic use.

BOMA Chart of Accounts. The standardized system of income and expense accounting for office properties developed by the Building Owners and Managers Association International.

bond coverage. Insurance protecting individuals or firms against default in the performance of their duties.

break-even point. Occupancy level at which gross income for a property equals the total fixed and variable operating costs.

Building Owners and Managers Association International (BOMA). An international organization of office building owners and managers. It fosters professionalism through its educational programs, forums, and publications.

Building Owners and Managers Institute International (BOMI). An independent educational organization supported by BOMA. Its courses lead to the designations Real Property Administrator (RPA), Systems Maintenance Technician (SMT), and Systems Maintenance Administrator (SMA).

building standard. The specific set of amenities and alterations a landlord is willing to make free of charge for an incoming commercial tenant.

bulk purchasing. A method of cutting operating costs for a property in which supplies are purchased in large quantities and stored for later use. Also called *volume buying.*

business cycle. A wavelike movement of increasing and decreasing economic prosperity consisting of four phases: expansion, recession, contraction, and revival.

cancellation option. A lease clause granting the tenant the option to cancel at the end of a predetermined term.

capitalization. A method of relating a property's value, its net annual income, and rate of return on the owner's investment, computed as follows:

$$\text{capitalization rate} = \frac{\text{income}}{\text{value}} \times 100\%$$

cash flow. An item in a property's financial operating reports that represents the net operating income minus the total of mortgage payments.

cash flow statement. A yearly financial report showing the bottom-line return after taxes.

Certified Apartment Manager (CAM); Certified Apartment Property Supervisor (CAPS); Certified Apartment Maintenance Technician (CAMT). Designations awarded by the National Apartment Association (NAA) for appropriate courses of study.

Certified Property Manager (CPM). A property manager who has fulfilled the Institute of Real Estate Management's requirements for this professional designation.

Certified Shopping Center Manager (CSM); Certified Marketing Director (CMD). Designations granted to qualified shopping center managers and marketing directors who have satisfied the requirements and educational programs of the International Council of Shopping Centers.

coinsurance clause. A common provision in insurance policies that limits the liability of the insurance company to that proportion of the loss which the amount of insurance bears to a percentage of the value of the property.

collectable income. Gross income from a property minus vacancy and other types of rent loss. Also called *gross adjusted income.*

Community Associations Institute (CAI). A professional organization offering educational programs for persons involved in homeowners, condominium, and cooperative associations.

community center. A shopping center of about 100,000 to 250,000 square feet (20 to 70 retail spaces) supported by more than 5,000 families.

comparative income and expense analysis. A financial study of the projected income from a property in as-is condition versus financial returns from that property if suggested capital improvements were implemented. Property managers use the analysis to demonstrate to owners the return on proposed capital expenditures.

competitive bids. Work estimates submitted to the property manager by service contractors, suppliers, tradespeople, or construction contractors.

concession. A negotiable point in a lease, decided in the prospective tenant's favor.

conditions, covenants, and restrictions declaration. A document that establishes condominium ownership, defines the property, and sets up an owners association.

condominium. Space in a multiunit building whose occupants hold title to an individual unit plus an undivided fee simple interest in the common elements.

conservation. Minor repair, renovation, and restoration of residential buildings that have substantial economic use remaining. Also called *blight prevention.*

constructive eviction. A situation in which a tenant must abandon the premises due to the landlord's negligence in providing essential services.

contract services. Maintenance tasks performed by outside laborers on a regular basis for a specified fee.

contraction. A phase of the business cycle characterized by decreasing production.

cooperative. A residential multifamily building owned by a trust or corporation for the benefit of the persons living therein, who are beneficial owners of the trust or stockholders in the corporation, each possessing a proprietary lease; all owners have joint liability for the mortgage on the property.

corporate cooperative. Cooperative in which legal ownership of a building is held by a corporation created for that purpose.

corrective maintenance. Actual repairs necessary to keep a property in good condition and operating smoothly.

cost-plus. A method of paying construction contractors in which the contractor furnishes a preliminary estimate for the proposed job and is paid the actual cost of the work plus a percentage for profit.

cyclical fluctuation. *See* BUSINESS CYCLE.

declining balance depreciation. A method of computing accelerated depreciation which adjusts the straight-line depreciation rate according to a percentage factor.

default. Nonperformance of a duty; failure to meet an obligation when due.

Department of Housing and Urban Development (HUD). A government agency authorized to construct and provide financial assistance to housing developments for low-income tenants.

depreciation. Loss of value due to physical deterioration, functional obsolescence, or economic obsolescence.

direct management costs. Expenses that can be attributed directly to the operation of a management firm or department.

dispossess proceedings. A suit brought by a landlord to evict a tenant for defaulting in the terms of the lease.

Dun & Bradstreet. A credit reporting agency that publishes credit ratings for many corporations and businesses.

economic oversupply. A market condition in which available rental space is priced beyond the financial capabilities of potential tenants.

electronic data processing. The use of a computer to compile information.

equity. An owner's interest in a property over and above any liens against it.

escalation clause. A lease clause providing that the rental rate will increase or decrease according to a selected index of economic conditions, such as the consumer price index.

estate for years. A leasehold estate that continues for a specified period of time.

estate from period to period. A leasehold estate that is automatically renewable for an indefinite period of time.

eviction notice. A landlord's legal notice to a tenant explaining the tenant's default under the terms of the lease and informing him or her of a pending eviction suit.

expansion. A phase of the business cycle characterized by increasing production.

expansion option. A lease clause granting a tenant the option to lease additional adjacent space after a specified period of time.

Experience Exchange Report. An annual BOMA publication containing income and expense statistics for office properties classified by type of building, area, etc.

feasibility study. A report on the potential profitability of a proposed real estate project. It includes considerations such as land area, physical features of the land, requirements of the project, and estimated cost.

Federal Housing Administration (FHA). An agency of the Department of Housing and Urban Development authorized to provide rental and mortgage insurance and subsidies to developers of low-income housing.

Federal Insurance Contributions Act (FICA). A federal regulation requiring employers to pay retirement fund taxes (social security) for employees.

Federal Unemployment Tax Act (FUTA). A regulation requiring employers to file federal unemployment tax returns for employees.

five-year forecast. A long-term projection of estimated income and expense for a property based on predictable changes.

fixed expense. An expense item in a property's operating budget that does not fluctuate with rental income.

flat fee. A property management fee expressed as a dollar amount per year or per month.

gross floor area. A method of measuring industrial space in which area is the total of all floor space within the exterior walls of the building, with no allowance made for structural projections and with a required minimum ceiling height of 7½ feet.

gross lease. A common residential lease under which the tenant pays a fixed rental and the landlord pays all operating expenses for the property.

gross sales. The total sales made by a retail tenant at a leased premises. A proportion of gross sales is charged as rental consideration under a percentage lease.

ground lease. A type of net lease, usually used with industrial real estate, under which the owner of a tract of land leases the property to a tenant who constructs his or her own building on the site. Also called a *land lease*.

income and expense report. A monthly financial report showing the income from the property, operating expenses, and the amount remitted to the owner.

incubator space. A building located in an industrial park. It is divided into small units of varying sizes to accommodate young, growing companies that want to combine office and industrial space at one location.

index lease. A lease containing an escalation clause.

indirect management costs. Expenses in the budget of a real estate agency or parent company that are partially attributable to the operation of the management department.

industrial park. A suburban industrial subdivision designed to offer comparatively small firms land in outlying areas with good accessibility to transportation.

Institute of Real Estate Management (IREM). A subsidiary group of the NATIONAL ASSOCIATION OF REALTORS®, founded in 1933 to encourage professionalism in the field of property management.

institutional property. Office buildings owned and occupied by the same corporation.

International Council of Shopping Centers (ICSC). An organization of shopping center owners, managers, and major tenants that functions as a medium for the interchange of information about shopping center operations.

IREM Code of Ethics. A set of guidelines on good business conduct for professional property managers.

key tenant. A major department store in a shopping center. Also called *anchor store*.

labor-extensive industry. A business with a low concentration of employees per acre.

labor-intensive industry. A business with a high concentration of employees per acre.

labor-oriented industry. A business that tends to locate near a low-cost labor pool.

lease assumption. A transaction whereby a property owner agrees to take over the balance of payments on a prospective tenant's current lease if he or she rents space in the owner's property.

leasehold estate. A tenant's right to occupy real estate for a specified period of time in exchange for some form of compensation.

liability insurance. Insurance protecting a property owner or manager in case of damage to the person or property of another due to the owner's or manager's negligence.

load factor. The ratio of rentable space to usable space on a multiple-tenancy floor of an office building.

loft. A low-rent multistory building located in the central business district, originally used for a combination of manufacturing, office, and storage space.

loss factor. The ratio of rentable space to usable space on a single-tenancy floor of an office building.

management plan. The financial and operational strategy for the ongoing management of a property. It is based on market analyses, a property analysis, and the owner's goals and it consists of an operating budget, 5-year forecast, and sometimes a comparative income and expense analysis.

management pricing worksheet. A method of computing management fees by itemizing management activities, calculating the direct cost to the firm, and adding a percentage for profit.

market analyses. Regional and neighborhood studies of economic, demographic, and other information made by the property manager in order to determine supply and demand, market trends, and other factors important in leasing and operating a specific property.

market-oriented industry. A business that tends to locate near industrial users and consumers of its products.

maximum percentage lease. A type of percentage lease that sets a ceiling on the amount of rent to be paid.

merchants association. An organization of shopping center tenants intended to facilitate joint advertising, promotion, and other activities beneficial to the center as a whole.

minimum-guaranteed percentage lease. A type of percentage lease that requires the tenant to pay either a fixed minimum rental or a percentage of gross sales, whichever is greater.

miniresort. A budget motel that has been transformed into a desirable weekend vacation spot by capitalizing on local recreational areas and points of interest.

miniwarehouse. Small, secure storage units rented to individuals and small businesses, usually located in industrial parks.

neighborhood. An area within which common characteristics of population and land use prevail.

neighborhood center. A shopping center of about 30,000 to 100,000 square feet (15 to 20 retail spaces) catering to 1,000 families or more.

net lease. A common industrial lease form requiring the tenant to pay rent plus certain costs incurred in the operation of the property. Generally, *straight net* leases require the tenant to pay rent, utilities, real estate taxes, and assessments. *Net-net* leases require the tenant to pay rent, utilities, real estate taxes, assessments, and insurance premiums. *Net-net-net* or *triple-net* leases may require the tenant to pay all of the above expenses plus agreed-upon items of maintenance and repair.

net operating income. Gross collectable income from a property minus all fixed and variable operating expenses.

noncompeting tenant restriction. A lease clause granting a retail tenant an exclusive right to operate without competition on the property.

nonrecurring variable expense. A type of variable property expense (e.g., capital improvements) that occurs only once.

on-site job program. Employment of tenants occupying low-cost residential buildings to perform maintenance work in these buildings.

operating budget. A projection of income and expense for the operation of a property over a one-year period.

option to renew. A lease provision giving the tenant the right to extend the lease for an additional period of time on specified terms.

overage. A percentage of gross sales over a certain amount paid to an owner in addition to a minimum base rent; often required in percentage leases.

partial eviction. A situation in which the landlord's negligence renders all or part of the premises unusable to the tenant for the purposes intended in the lease.

participation certificate. Proof of membership in a trust cooperative granted in a particular amount.

per-unit cost method. A method of computing management fees based on the management firm's capabilities and the direct cost of managing a specific number of units.

percentage fee. A property management fee expressed as a percentage of the gross collectable income from a property.

percentage lease. A common retail lease requiring the tenant to pay a percentage of its gross income as rental consideration.

periodic costs. A type of fixed property expense (e.g., property taxes) that occurs on a regular but infrequent basis.

preventative maintenance. A program of regularly scheduled maintenance activities and routine inspections of the interior and exterior of the buildings, equipment, and grounds. Its objective is to preserve the physical integrity of the property, eliminate corrective maintenance costs, and ensure uninterrupted service to the tenants.

prime contractor. A construction supervisor who contracts with the property manager to oversee a job and then sublets the work to various skilled tradespeople.

principal. An individual who designates another as his or her agent. 2. The original amount of a loan.

profit and loss statement. An annual financial report of a property's actual net profit before taxes.

property analysis. A study made to familiarize a property manager with the nature and condition of a building, its position relative to comparable properties, and its estimated income and operating expenses.

property management. A branch of the real estate profession that seeks to preserve or increase the value of an investment property while generating income for its owners.

proprietary lease. The right of a cooperative member to occupy a unit in the building subject to certain conditions.

publicity. Editorial space in a newspaper, magazine, or other medium that is not paid for but serves to attract public attention to an individual, firm, or commodity.

real estate cycle. A specific cycle that occurs in the real estate segment of the general business economy; phases of the cycle are influenced by but are not identical to those of the business cycle.

Real Estate Investment Trust (REIT). An unincorporated trust set up to invest in real property.

real property. The earth's surface extending downward to the center and upward into space, including all things permanently attached thereto, by nature or by human hands.

Real Property Administrator (RPA). A property manager who has successfully completed BOMI's educational program and fulfilled other requirements for this professional designation.

recapture clause. A provision in a percentage lease that grants the landlord the right to terminate the lease at the end of a certain period if gross sales have not reached the level anticipated during negotiations.

recapture provision. A clause within an assignment and subletting lease clause giving the landlord the right to recover any space that the tenant is unable to occupy or sublease.

recession. The peak of the business cycle; the point at which supply equals and begins to surpass demand.

recurring variable expense. A type of variable property expense (e.g., redecorating costs) that occurs repeatedly on an irregular basis.

regional center. A large shopping center containing from 70 to 225 stores and more than 400,000 square feet of leasable area.

regularly recurring costs. A type of fixed property expense (e.g., cleaning costs) that occurs consistently each month.

rentable space. According to BOMA, the floor area of an office building minus allowances for stairs, elevator shafts, duct work, and other areas not available to the tenant.

rental center. A special leasing area located in a real estate development. It includes a display area, furnished models, and a closing area.

rent factor. A multiplier used to establish the rental rate for industrial properties, based on the rate of return the owner desires on the investment.

Resident Apartment Manager (RAM); Executive RAM. Designations awarded by the Apartment Council of the National Association of Homebuilders for completion of courses of study in apartment management.

resource-oriented industry. A business that locates near suppliers or raw materials necessary for its operations.

return on investment. A measure of the profitability of a property, computed either before or after income taxes, as follows:

$$\text{return on investment} = \frac{\text{(before tax) (after tax) cash flow}}{\text{equity}} \times 100\%$$

revival. The nadir of the business cycle; the point at which demand equals and begins to surpass supply.

sale and leaseback. An arrangement whereby an investor purchases real estate owned and used by a business and then leases it back to that business.

seasonal variations. Changes in the economy that recur at least once a year.

slum clearance. The razing of substandard and unsalvageable residential buildings for redevelopment.

special-purpose property. Hotels, resorts, nursing homes, theaters, schools, churches, and other businesses or organizations whose specialized needs dictate the design and operation of the building.

specific cycle. A wavelike movement, similar to the business cycle, that occurs in certain sectors of the general economy.

stabilized budget. Part of a 5-year projected budget, arrived at by averaging income and expense items over a 5-year period.

standard fire insurance. A basic form of insurance protecting a property against direct loss or damage.

step-up clause. A lease clause providing for rental rate increases of a definite amount at specific times over the term of the lease.

straight-line depreciation. A method of computing depreciation which assumes that the wearing-out process proceeds at a stable rate over the useful life of a building.

$$\text{depreciation rate} = \frac{100\%}{\text{years of useful life}}$$

straight percentage lease. A type of percentage lease that bases rental rate solely on gross sales.

strip center. A small shopping center of about 10,000 to 30,000 square feet (4 to 10 retail spaces) located at the edge of an urban area or in a suburb.

structural density. The ratio of the total ground floor area of a building to the total land area of the site on which it is built.

subletting. Partial transfer of a tenant's right in a rental property to a third party.

subsidized housing. Residential developments for low-income families that are insured or (indirectly) financed in part by a government agency.

sum-of-the-years'-digits depreciation. A method of computing accelerated depreciation by multiplying the remaining years of a property's economic life by the property's remaining value, then dividing by the *sum* of all the years in the remaining economic life of the property.

syndicate. A group of individuals or corporations formed to achieve a common business purpose, usually investment.

Systems Maintenance Technician (SMT); Systems Maintenance Administrator (SMA). Designations awarded to building engineers and maintenance personnel for completion of courses in building systems operation and maintenance by the Building Owners and Managers Institute International (BOMI).

tax participation clause. A lease provision requiring the tenant to pay a pro rata share of any increase in real estate taxes or assessments in addition to the basic rental.

technical oversupply. A market condition in which available rental space exceeds tenant demand.

tenancy at sufferance. A rental situation in which a tenant who originally obtained possession of the premises legally continues to occupy the property after the expiration of the leasehold interest and without the consent of the owner.

tenancy at will. An estate that gives the tenant the right of possession for an indefinite period, until the estate is terminated by either party.

tenant alteration costs. Construction, remodeling, and alteration expenses for work needed to make the premises usable by the tenant. These costs may be assumed by the tenant, the owner, or both and are a major point of negotiation.

tenant mix. The combination of retail tenants occupying a shopping center; must be considered carefully to achieve maximum profit for each merchant and the center as a whole.

tenant union. A local organization of residential tenants working for their common interests and rights.

trust cooperative. A cooperative in which legal ownership of a building is held by a trust company.

Uniform Residential Landlord and Tenant Act. A model law drafted in 1972 by the National Conference of Commissioners on Uniform State Laws. It standardizes and regulates the residential landlord-tenant relationship.

urban renewal. Renovation, rehabilitation, and redevelopment of substandard urban residential properties.

usable space. Floor area of an office building that can be used for tenant office space.

variable costs ratio. A method of expressing variable costs for a property as a percentage of total rental income:

$$\text{variable costs ratio} = \frac{\text{actual annual variable costs}}{\text{gross collectable income}} \times 100\%$$

variable expense. An expense item in a property's operating budget that increases or decreases with the occupancy level of the building.

variable-scale percentage lease. A type of percentage lease in which the percentage rental rate increases or decreases according to the volume of business done by the tenant.

volume buying. *See* BULK PURCHASING.

Answer Key

Chapter 1

1. a
2. d
3. c
4. a
5. c
6. a
7. c
8. d
9. c
10. d
11. c
12. b
13. a. free standing, single-tenant building
    b. strip center
    c. neighborhood center
    d. community center
    e. regional center
14. d
15. b
16. c

Chapter 2

1. b
2. a. boundaries and land usage
   b. transportation and utilities
   c. economy
   d. supply and demand
   e. social and cultural facilities
3. a. local chamber of commerce
   b. financial institutions
   c. local newspapers
4. b
5. a
6. b

7. b
8. d
9. a
10. d
11. a
12. a
13. c
14. c
15. a
16. d
17. b
18. c

Chapter 3

1. b
2. d
3. a
4. c
5. c
6. b
7. a
8. c
9. b
10. c
11. a. identification of property and parties
    b. term for agreement
    c. responsibilities of management
    d. responsibilities of owner
    e. management fee
    f. signatures
12. a
13. d
14. d
15. c
16. b

Chapter 4

1. a. advertising
   b. promotion
   c. selling activities
2. a. type and size of property
   b. supply and demand levels
   c. financial resources
3. b
4. c
5. a
6. a. mail out brochures or news-letters
   b. make personal presentations to brokers
   c. sponsor an open house
7. a. less expensive
   b. greater credibility
8. d
9. a. preview the space
   b. qualify the prospect
10. a. property specifications and spatial requirements
    b. urgency
    c. motivation
11. a. amount of space to rent
    b. expected rent-up period
    c. turnover of tenants
    d. sophistication of tenants and competitors
12. a. display area
    b. model space
    c. closing area
13. c
14. c
15. b
16. a. expense may be prohibitive
    b. Lack of past experience may prevent valid projections of future results.

Chapter 5

1. a. estate for years
   b. estate from period to period
   c. tenancy at will
   d. tenancy at sufferance
2. b
3. d
4. a. legal capacity

b. mutual accord
   c. consideration
   d. legality of object
5. a
6. d
7. b
8. d
9. a
10. c
11. d
12. a
13. a
14. d
15. a
16. d
17. a. They may be incomplete and/or out of date.
    b. If from a national tenant, such as a large retail chain, the land-lord may not be able to nego-tiate.

Chapter 6

1. b
2. a. owner's financial and strategic position
   b. area market and competition
   c. motivation and urgency of the prospect
3. d
4. a
5. b
6. c
7. c
8. b
9. b
10. a. assumption of tenant's current lease
    b. stationery and sign allowance
11. a. identity
    b. rental history
    c. financial status
12. d
13. a. Dun & Bradstreet or other credit reporting service
    b. local chamber of commerce
    c. better business bureau
    d. suppliers for tenant's business

14. c
15. a
16. a. exactly what the tenant wants
       to do
    b. whether the tenant can and
       will improve the space
    c. Will the improvements be
       an asset to the property?   a.

Chapter 7

1. b
2. a. regular meetings
   b. written questionnaires
   c. building newsletter
3. c
4. c
5. b
6. a. amount of rent
   b. repairs, alterations, and
      redecorating
   c. length of lease term
7. a
8. c
9. a. tenant
   b. manager's attorney
   c. manager
10. c
11. c
12. a. reminder notice of past-due
       rent
    b. legal notice of eviction suit
13. b
14. b
15. c
16. b

Chapter 8

1. a. preventative maintenance
   b. corrective maintenance
   c. routine housekeeping
   d. new construction
2. c
3. c
4. b
5. d
6. a. competitive bids
   b. negotiated contract
7. b
8. d
9. b

10. volume buying (bulk purchasing)
11. a. scope   e. materials
    b. location   f. number of person-
    c. priority   nel
    d. method   g. hours of work
12. a. decreased expenses for repair
    b. improved service to tenants
13. a
14. c
15. d
16. c
17. c

Chapter 9

1. a
2. d
3.   gross rental income billed
   + income from other sources
   − losses incurred
   − operating expenses
   ────────────────────
     net operating income
4.   gross receipts
   − operating expenses
   − total mortgage payments
   + mortgage loan principal
   ────────────────────
     net profit
5. a
6. a
7. c
8. a. W-2
   b. W-3
   c. W-4
   d. Federal Unemployment Tax
      Return
9. b
10. d
11. a. declining balance method
    b. sum-of-the-years'-digits method
12. a
13. c
14. a. standard fire insurance
    b. extended coverage endorsement
    c. consequential loss, use, and
       occupancy coverage
    d. general liability and workmen's
       compensation insurance
15. c
16. a. avoid it
    b. retain it
    c. control it
    d. transfer it

17. a. loss caused to others
    b. loss of user value
    c. loss of property
18. b

Chapter 10
1. a. lease files
   b. general correspondence
   c. work estimates
   d. financial file
   e. permanent property file
2. b
3. c
4. a. mainframe
   b. mini
   c. micro
5. c
6. c
7. a
8. c
9. d
10. a. secretary-stenographers
    b. service request clerks
11. c
12. a. occupancy cost
    b. general overhead
    c. general accounting costs
13. b
14. a. small size of property
    b. need for repairs or deferred maintenance
    c. undesirable location of property
    d. owner's demand for detailed reporting
15. b

Chapter 11
1. b
2. a
3. a. comparable value
   b. scarcity
4. c
5. b
6. a
7. d
8. c
9. c
10. a. wages
    b. variable expenses

c. fixed expenses
d. capital expenditures
11. d
12. a
13. a. depreciation information
    b. the owner's tax bracket
14. a. sell the property
    b. make a major capital investment
15. a. classified ads
    b. community college referrals
    c. word-of-mouth referrals
    d. activity in professional organization
16. b
17. a. maintenance person for instructions
    b. tenant for information
    c. manager for follow-up

Chapter 12
1. trust cooperatives
2. b
3. a. stock
   b. proprietary lease
4. b
5. d
6. c
7. c
8. b
9. subleasing the unit
10. a
11. a. maintain physical integrity of the building
    b. ensure ongoing operation and service
    c. minimize and report on operating costs
12. c
13. c
14. a. underestimating utilities
    b. use of inadequate (although inexpensive) service contractors
    c. lack of long-range planning
15. a
16. a. cooperative
    b. condominium
    c. planned unit development (PUD)

Chapter 13
1. b
2. c
3. d

4. a. cost
    b. accessibility
    c. environment of the property
    d. labor market
5. a
6. $\dfrac{\text{rentable space}}{\text{usable space}}$ = loss factor
7. d
8. a. signs
    b. brochures
    c. display ads
    d. direct mail
9. a. public relations
    b. referrals
    c. canvassing
10. direct mail
11. a
12. a. price advantage
    b. increased efficiency
    c. prestige
    d. economy
13. b
14. d
15. a
16. a

Chapter 14

1. a. strip center
    b. neighborhood center
    c. community center
    d. regional center
2. d
3.
    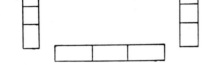
4. b
5. a
6. b
7. a. minimum-guaranteed
    b. straight percentage
    c. variable-scale
    d. maximum
8. c
9. d
10. d
11. b
12. c

13. a
14. Trade Winds
15. b
16. c

Chapter 15

1. a
2. a
3. a. market-oriented
    b. resource-oriented
    c. labor-oriented
4. c
5. b
6. b
7. d
8. d
9. a. taxes
    b. insurance
    c. utilities
    d. maintenance
    cost of building X percentage return
    desired = rent factor
11. b
12. a
13. a
14. a
15. a

Chapter 16

1. d
2. b
3. c
4. c
5. b
6. a. maintenance
    b. turnover
    c. vacancy
    d. rent loss
    e. high collection costs
7. d
8. c
9. a. increases resident responsibility
       for property
    b. helps reduce maintenance costs
    c. benefits residents financially
10. a. mortgage holder
    b. government agencies
    c. owner

11. a
12. c
13. d
14. a
15. c

Chapter 17
1. b
2. c
3. a. stabilization of the property
   b. profitable sale of the property
4. c
5. a. office space
   b. storage
6. c
7. b
8. a. alteration or rehabilitation
   b. conversion to condominiums

9. c
10. a. check zoning and other laws
    before conversion
    b. provide legal documents for
    the sale of units
    c. assist in developing financial
    arrangements for sales
11. d
12. a. land area available
    b. physical features of the land
    c. requirements of project
    d. cost of project
13. b
14. b
15. b
16. c

Index

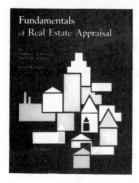
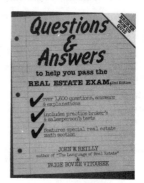
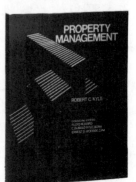